English G 21

B3

für Realschulen

Cornelsen

English G 21 • Band B 3

Im Auftrag des Verlages herausgegeben von
Prof. Hellmut Schwarz, Mannheim

Erarbeitet von
Barbara Derkow Disselbeck, Köln
Allen J. Woppert, Berlin
sowie Susan Abbey, Nenagh, Irland
Laurence Harger, Wellington, Neuseeland

unter Mitarbeit von
Wolfgang Biederstädt, Köln
Joachim Blombach, Herford
Helmut Dengler, Limbach
Jennifer Seidl, München
Andrea Ulrich, Berlin

in Zusammenarbeit mit der Englischredaktion
Dr. Christiane Kallenbach (Projektleitung);
Klaus G. Unger (verantwortlicher Redakteur);
Susanne Bennetreu (Bildredaktion); Britta Bensmann;
Dr. Philip Devlin; Bonnie S. Glänzer; Uwe Tröger

Beratende Mitwirkung
Anja Bersch, Waldstetten; Peer Brändel, Gütersloh; Uwe Chormann, Einselthum; Matthew George, Frankfurt (Main); Prof. Dr. Liesel Hermes, Karlsruhe; Bernhard Hunger, Dettingen; Gabriele Künstler, Altlußheim; Michael Semmler, Lünen; Karl Starkebaum, Diekholzen; Elke Storz, Freiburg i. Br.; Martina van de Velde, Toronto

Layoutkonzept
Aksinia Raphael; Korinna Wilkes

Technische Umsetzung
Aksinia Raphael; Korinna Wilkes;
Stephan Hilleckenbach; Rainer Bachmaier

Umschlaggestaltung
Klein & Halm Grafikdesign, Berlin

www.cornelsen.de
www.EnglishG.de

Druck: Mohn Media Mohndruck, Gütersloh

1. Auflage, 8. Druck 2016
broschiert
978-3-06-031312-9

1. Auflage, 7. Druck 2016
gebunden
978-3-06-031362-4

PEFC zertifiziert
Dieses Produkt stammt aus nachhaltig bewirtschafteten Wäldern und kontrollierten Quellen.
www.pefc.de
PEFC/04-31-1033

Dein Englischbuch enthält folgende Teile:

Introduction	Hier lernst du die jungen Leute von Band 3 kennen.
Units	die fünf Kapitel des Buches
EXTRA: Text File	viele interessante Texte zum Lesen (passend zu den Units)
Skills File (SF)	Beschreibung wichtiger Lern- und Arbeitstechniken
Grammar File (GF)	Zusammenfassung der Grammatik jeder Unit
Vocabulary	Wörterverzeichnis zum Lernen der neuen Wörter jeder Unit
Dictionary	alphabetische Wörterverzeichnisse zum Nachschlagen

Die Units bestehen aus diesen Teilen:

Lead-in	Einstieg in das neue Thema
A-Section	neuer Lernstoff mit vielen Aktivitäten und **Background File**
Practice	Übungen
Text	eine spannende oder lustige Geschichte
How am I doing?	Hier kannst du dein Wissen und Können überprüfen.

In den Units findest du diese Überschriften und Symbole:

Looking at language	Hier sammelst du Beispiele und entdeckst Regeln.
STUDY SKILLS	Einführung in Lern- und Arbeitstechniken
Dossier	Schöne und wichtige Arbeiten kannst du in einer Mappe sammeln.
All about ...	Hier übst du Wortschatz zum Thema der Unit.
WRITING COURSE	Schreibkurs in fünf Kapiteln mit Hilfen zum Schreiben von Texten
EVERYDAY ENGLISH	Übungen zum Bewältigen wichtiger Alltagssituationen
MEDIATION	Hier vermittelst du zwischen zwei Sprachen.
LISTENING	Aufgaben zu Hörtexten auf der CD
Now you	Hier sprichst und schreibst du über dich selbst.
PRONUNCIATION	Ausspracheübungen
REVISION	Übungen zur Wiederholung
WORDS	Übungen zu Wortfamilien, Wortfeldern und Wortverbindungen
Extra	Zusätzliche Aktivitäten und Übungen
	Partnerarbeit/Gruppenarbeit
	nur auf CD / auf CD und im Schülerbuch
>	Textaufgaben

Inhalt

Every year there is a 'Music for Youth Festival'. 10,000 young people come from all over the United Kingdom to play, sing, dance and listen to all kinds of music.

1 The festival

a) *Look at the poster. What kinds of music do you think you can play and listen to at the festival?*

b) *Find words and phrases to go with each photo – there are a few in the box.*

- listen to classical music/folk music/jazz/...
- go to a reggae/pop/punk concert
- learn to DJ/rap/do hip hop/...
- play the guitar/steel drum/...
- sing in a choir/rock band/...

A day at the festival

6
Hi. Are you in the girls' hostel too?
Aye, I am.
Do you know where it is?
No, I don't.

7
Well, let's go and find it together. I'm Latisha.
I'm Katrina. Er, Latisha, what's that?
Asian Fusion concert tonight!
Music for You

8
'That' is my instrument – it's a steel drum.
Great! I've always wanted to hear a steel drum band.
Well, you can: 9.30 tomorrow. Now, let's find our rooms.

9
Hey, Katrina!
Oh, hi Asif. Latisha, this is Asif. He's a roadie for his brother's band.
Asif!
Hi, Latisha. What have you got in there?
Hi, Asif!
Sorry, the boss is calling. Come to the gig tonight – 8 o'clock, OK?
Asian Fusion concert tonight!
Music for Youth

10
Asian Fusion concert tonight!
Want to be a DJ?
Come to the DJ
Workshop!
National Festival of Music for Youth
Asian Fusion concert tonight!

11
Want to be a DJ?
Come to the DJ
Workshop!
Saturday 10-12 - (Hall 3A)
hassan and the banglas
Asian Fusion concert
tonight!

12
Er, excuse me, I'm not in the festival, but I'd like to go to a concert. Is that OK?

Yes, I think so. You just have to buy a ticket. There's a good concert tonight.
13
Asian Fusion concert tonight!
Want to be a DJ?
Come to the DJ
Workshop!
Saturday 10-12 - (Hall 3A)
GIRLS' ACCOMMODATION
National Festival of Music for Yout
Asian Fusion concert tonight!
Yes, I saw that: Asian Fusion. What is that?
14
A mixture of Asian and western music. It's my brother's band. – I'm Asif. Hi.
Hi, Asif. I'm Robert. I'm in Birmingham with my parents – we're visiting family. It's really boring!

I know what you mean. You're from the US, aren't you?
No, from Canada – Toronto.
Hey, what about a snack?
Great idea: I'm hungry.
Asian Fusion concert
15

Do you play an instrument?
No, I don't. But I DJ.
Did you see – there's a workshop tomorrow?
16

Yes, I saw that. Maybe we can go together?
We'll probably have to pay.
17

That's OK.
Well, I hope it's not too much. Oh look, there are Katrina and Latisha.
Who?
18

19
Hi, come and sit down. This is Robert, from Toronto. This is Katrina, from the Orkney Islands ...
Hi!
... and Latisha from ...
... Manchester. Hi, Robert!
Hi, nice to meet you.

1 The four kids

a) *Start a file for Asif, Katrina, Latisha and Robert.*
Name: ... From: ... Music: ...
At the festival because: ...

b) *Look through the book. Where can you find the four kids from the photo story? Add information about them to your files.*

2 The music

Listen to four recordings from the festival. Which recording goes with which of the four kids? Why? You can use the phrases in the box.

I think the first recording goes with ... because she plays ...
... likes ..., so I think the second recording goes with him/her.

▸ *WB 1–3 (pp. 1–3)* • *WB Revision (pp. 4–7)* •
Text File 1 *(pp. 106–107)*

3 Now you

a) *Look at these questions. Make notes.*
- What kinds of music do you like?
- When and where do you listen to music?
- Do you sing? When? Where?
- Do you play an instrument? Which?

drums • electric guitar • flute • guitar • keyboard • piano • recorder • saxophone • trombone • trumpet

b) *Now stand (or sit) in a double circle. Ask three different partners the questions from a).*

c) **Extra** *Take notes. Report to the class on one of your partners.*

STUDY SKILLS **Learning words**

Collect words and phrases in a world field 'music'. This way it's easier to learn them.

▸ *SF Learning words (p. 125)* • *SF Taking notes (p. 132)*

My London

To: Katrina, Latisha, Robert

Subject: Meet on Messenger and visit London

Hi everybody!

Fantastic festival! It was great to meet you all. Let's all meet again on Messenger this Saturday at 6 pm, OK? But before that why don't you visit my website at www.asifspage.co.uk. You'll find five good reasons to visit me here in the capital. You're all welcome!

Asif

PS Robert, it's great that you and your parents are coming. CU soon!

1 The London Eye

This is the famous big wheel on the River Thames. It's 135 metres high. They say you get the best views of London from the Eye. I've always wanted to go on it – you can see all the sights from up there (not just Big Ben and the Houses of Parliament). But it's very expensive, so I have to have a good reason – like a visitor :-) So, join me! (No sound file yet.)

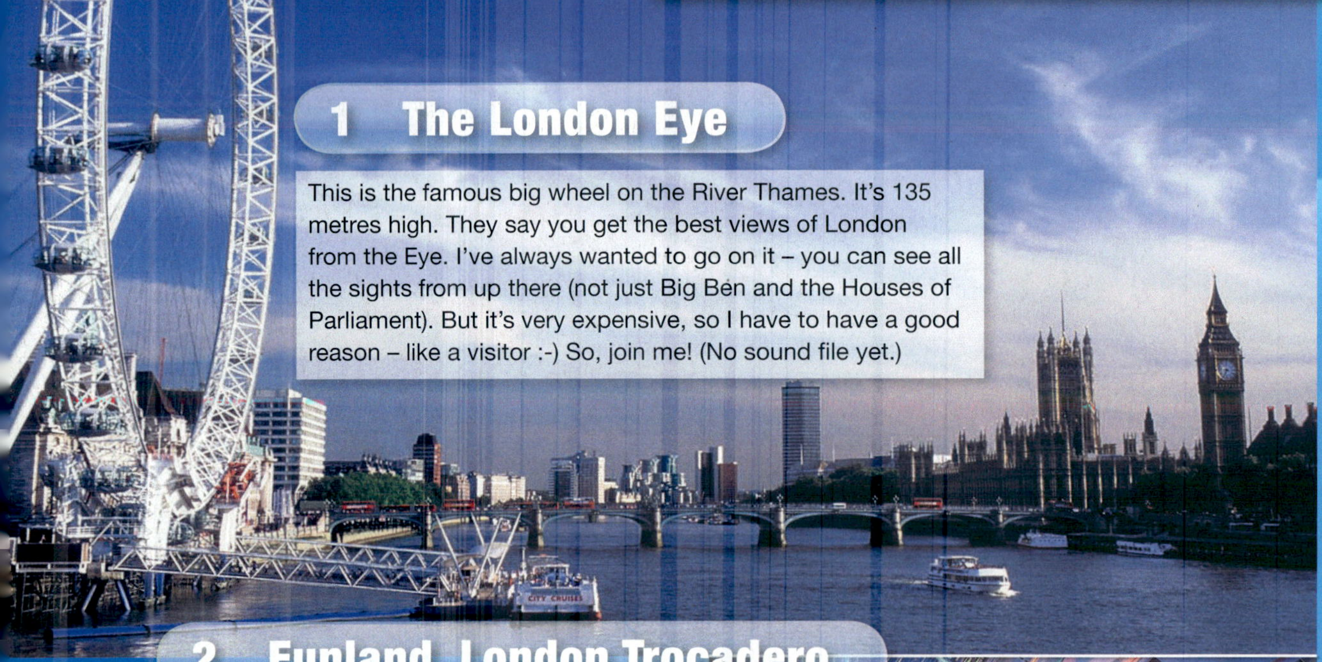

2 Funland, London Trocadero

This is one of my favourite places in London – although I've only been here three times! It's at Piccadilly Circus, right in the city centre and it's got hundreds of video and virtual reality games. Come and play with me!
Click here for my sound file.

3 Hyde Park

Hyde Park is one of the royal parks – yes, it belongs to the Queen! In the summer it's a great place for open-air concerts. Hassan hopes to play there one day – dream on, big brother!
Click here for my sound file.

Page

4 Natural History Museum

The world's greatest museum and it's free! Don't miss the dinosaurs and, best of all, the earthquake room. Join me inside a Japanese supermarket in the middle of an earthquake! Click here for my sound file.

5 Brick Lane

There are lots of great markets in London, but Brick Lane is 'my market'. It's quite near where I live in Tower Hamlets. Every Sunday lots of young people come here to look for trendy second-hand clothes. Brick Lane is full of interesting little shops and great Indian and Bangladeshi restaurants too. So it's a good place to try my favourite dish: lamb biryani (although my mum makes the best lamb biryani in London!). Click here for my sound file.

1 Asif's sound files

a) *Write down the letters A–D. Listen to Asif's sound files. Match them to the photos. Give reasons for your answers.*

b) **Extra** *Listen again and find out:*

- What is the man in the market selling?
- What band is playing in the park?
- What's the video game called? Who wins?
- What happens in the earthquake room?

2 Asif's tips

You've got one day in London. There isn't enough time for all of Asif's tips.

a) Think: *Choose two tips. Think of reasons.*

b) Pair: *Discuss your choices. Make one list with two things.*

\+ It's fun/cool/fantastic/cheap/...
You can only do/see/... this in London.
I like video games/shopping/...

– It's very expensive./
You probably have to wait a long time./
You can do that in other places.

c) Share: *Discuss your list with another pair. Agree on two things for your group.*

► P 1 (p. 20) • WB 1 (p. 8)

All about ... the London Underground

1 At Queensway underground station

Mr Smith Now, what kind of ticket do we need – single or return?
Robert Just like yesterday, Dad, Travelcards. We'll be on public transport all day.
Mr Smith Oh, right. But is it 9.30 yet? We can't use them till the rush hour is over.
Mrs Smith It's 9.25, dear. We'll wait.
Mr Smith What zones do we need?
Robert All the sights are in zones 1 and 2.
Mr Smith Right – just like yesterday. There, that was easy.
Mrs Smith Now let's try and find out where we are on this map ...

> *Find Queensway on the Tube map below.*

Robert Asif wants to meet us at the London Eye.
Mrs Smith That's near Waterloo Tube station.
Mr Smith So we have to find Waterloo and the best way to get there.
Robert That's easy, Dad. There's Waterloo. So we take the red line ...
Mrs Smith That's the Central Line.
Robert Thanks, Mom. We take the Central Line eastbound to Bond Street.
Mrs Smith Then we change to the Jubilee Line southbound and take it to Waterloo.
Mr Smith OK, now we only have to find the right platform.

> *Find Waterloo on the Tube map. Follow the Smiths' route from Queensway to Waterloo.*

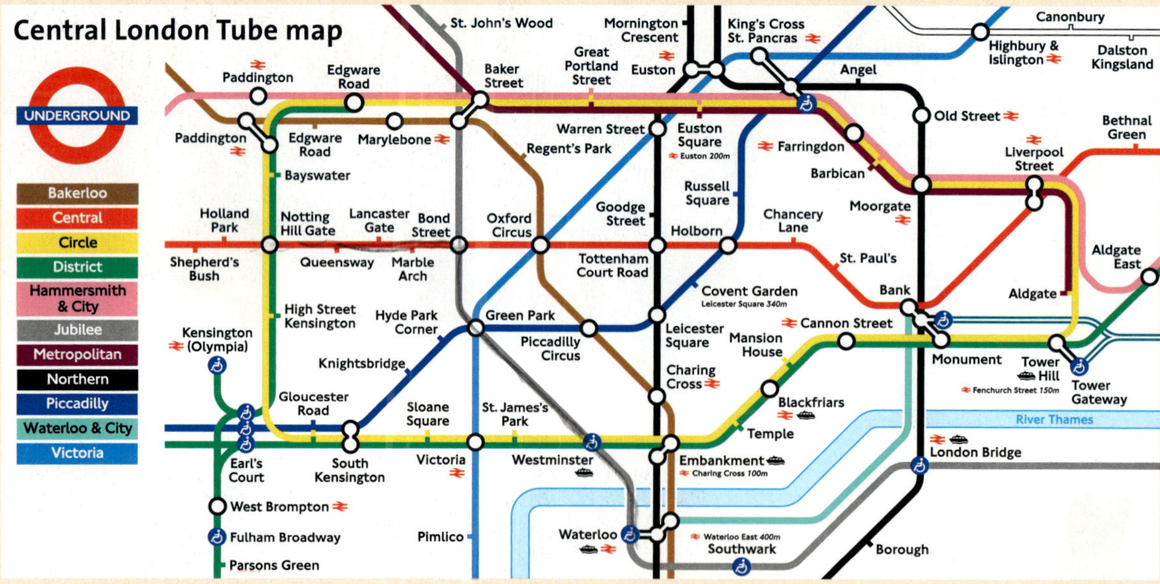

2 Excuse me please, how do I get to ...?

a) *Partner A: You're at Victoria Station. Ask your partner how you can get from there to the first three sights on the list.*

b) *Partner B: You're at Oxford Circus. Ask your partner how you can get from there to the last three sights on the list.*

London sights	Tube stations
Brick Lane	Aldgate East
British Museum	Russell Square
Trocadero	Piccadilly Circus
Hyde Park	Marble Arch
Natural History Museum	South Kensington
Houses of Parliament	Westminster

▸ P 2–3 (pp. 20–21) • WB 2–4 (pp. 9–10)

3 On the London Eye

a) *Look at the photos. Listen to the CD and find out:*

- *Who is on the London Eye?*
- *In what order do they take the photos?*

b) *Listen again. What do you learn about each building?*

STUDY SKILLS **Listening for detail**

Before you listen, think about what you want to find out. Listen for that only. Don't worry about other details.

▸ *SF Listening for detail (p. 129)*

A 'The Gherkin'

St Paul's Cathedral C

B Buckingham Palace

Hi, from the London Eye! D

▸ **Text File 2** *(p. 108)*

4 A postcard home

London Tower Bridge

Dear Grandma
We arrived in London yesterday morning. In the afternoon we went to the Tower and saw Tower Bridge. Did you know that a bus once had to jump across the bridge when it started to open – with the bus still on it?!
This morning we went on the London Eye – very cool!
See you soon!
Love, Robert

▸ *GF 1a: Simple past (p. 139)* • *P 4–6 (pp. 21–22)* • *WB 5–8 (pp. 10–12)*

5 In Brick Lane

After the Eye, Robert wanted to see where Asif lived.

Tower Hamlets was a surprise to Robert. 'There are more Bangladeshis than British people here,' he said.

'Actually, Robert,' Asif answered, 'most of us are British.'

'Right. Sorry.'

'That's OK,' Asif said. Then he pointed to a building. 'That's my mosque, by the way.'

'It doesn't look like a mosque,' Robert said.

'A mosque doesn't have to be in a special building,' Asif explained. 'This building was a church and a synagogue before it became a mosque.'

'Wow,' said Robert.

Asif went on. 'And can you see that building there? That's where I live. We can go there and have a sandwich.'

'Oh. Can't we have something Bangladeshi? I've never tried it. Maybe your mother's famous biryani?' Robert asked.

'Sorry,' said Asif. 'My mum's at work. But there are lots of places here in Brick Lane where you can get a cheap Bangladeshi meal.'

► *GF 1b: Present perfect (p. 139) • P 7–9 (p. 23) • WB 9 (p. 13)*

6 Time for lunch

Look at the dialogue. Scan the menu for the underlined words and suggest what Robert and Asif can eat.

Robert I'd like a mild or medium spicy dish.
He can try a … or a …

Robert I can't eat nuts.
He can't have a …

Robert Maybe something with chicken?
…

Asif I'd like something spicy or very spicy.
Maybe he'd like a … or a …

Asif I'd like vegetables – no, no, meat with a salad.
He can have a …

Asif I think I'll have lamb.
…

► *SF Scanning (p. 130) • P 10 (p. 24) • WB 10 (p. 13)*

Lunch menu (from 12 to 2.30 pm)

TIKKA DISHES (spicy)
We marinate meat in a yoghurt sauce, fry it with spices and herbs, then serve it dry with onion and a salad.

Chicken Tikka	£3.75
Lamb Tikka	£3.95

BIRYANI DISHES (mild)
Basmati rice with spices, nuts and sultanas.

Chicken Biryani	£4.25
Lamb Biryani	£4.25
Prawn Biryani	£4.75
Vegetable Biryani	£3.95

DANSAK DISHES (medium spicy)
We cook lentils in a sweet and sour sauce.

Chicken Dansak	£4.50
Lamb Dansak	£4.50
Prawn Dansak	£4.50
Vegetable Dansak	£4.25

JALFREZI DISHES (very spicy)
We cook meat with fresh green chillies and onion.

Chicken Jalfrezi	£4.50
Lamb Jalfrezi	£4.75
Prawn Jalfrezi	£5.00

7 Have you ever tried ...?

Asif So, how's your food?
Robert It's good.
Asif Have you ever eaten any other Asian food?
Robert Yes, I have. I ate Indian food at the festival in Birmingham.
Asif That's almost the same.
Robert Have you ever tried Japanese food? It's my favourite.
Asif Yes, I have. I tried it at school last year. We had an 'International Day'.
Robert Yeah, we have those too.
Asif And have you ever eaten anything really strange?
Robert I ate crocodile once. Does that count?

8 Now you

a) *Make a list with the words from the box. What do you think: Has your partner ever tried these foods? Write 'Y' or 'N'. Do you think he/she tried them before he/she was ten? Then write '<10'.*

Indian food • Italian food • Japanese food • Korean food • Russian food • Turkish food

b) *Talk to your partner. You get one point for each correct guess. Who gets more points?*
A: Have you ever tried Korean food?
B: Yes, I have.
A: One point for me. And when did you try it?
B: I tried it when I was eight.
A: That's another point for me. Your turn.

► *GF 1c: Present perfect or simple past (pp. 139–140) • P 11–14 (pp. 24–25) • WB 11–13 (p. 14)*

9 Extra Lost!

Asif Robert, I think we're lost.
Robert But you said you've been to this Trocadero place before.
Asif Yes, but I usually just take the Tube to Piccadilly Circus. But *you* wanted to take the red bus.
Robert Let's ask that man.
Asif OK. – Excuse me. Can you tell me the way to Piccadilly Circus?
Man Yes, of course. Go down this street till you come to a big street. That's the fourth one on your right. Turn right, then go straight on. Piccadilly Circus will be on your left.
Asif Thank you very much.

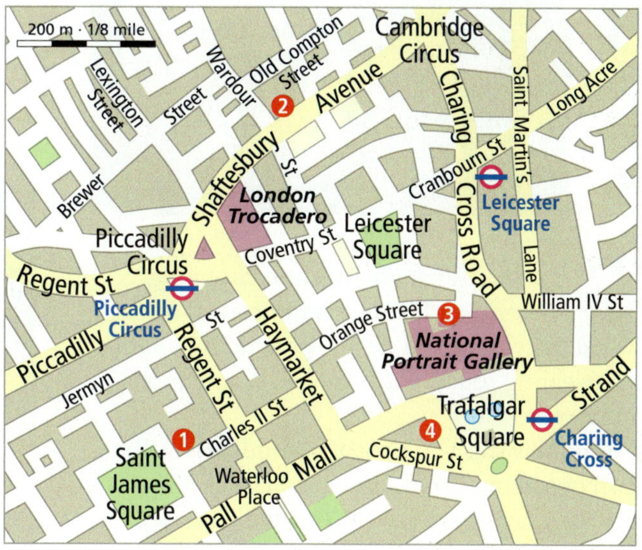

Where are the boys when Asif asks the way – at point 1, 2, 3 or 4?

10 Extra ROLE PLAY Asking the way

a) *Think of a place near your school. Ask your partner the way.*

Yes, of course. You ...

Excuse me. Can you tell me the way to ...?

go straight on/ past the ...

I'm looking for ... Can you help me?

I'm sorry, can you say that again, please?

turn right/left into ...

b) *Swap roles.*

Extra Background File **LONDON**

A day in London for kids on a budget

London is huge: 1572 **square kilometres. (That's almost twice as big as Berlin.) So, if you've only got one day, you have to plan carefully.** ▸ *SF Understanding new words (p. 124)*

Step 1 Buy a Travelcard. You can use all buses and the Tube all day. Just check that you buy it for the right zones. Oh, and wait till 9.30 before you start your day in the city – you can only use your Travelcard after the rush hour!

7.5 million people live in London (Berlin: 3.4 million) and another million come into the city to work every morning – so the rush hour is pretty busy.

Step 2 You want to go to one of London's famous musicals, but you're on a budget? No problem! Go to the half-price ticket place at Leicester Square and get your tickets for tonight. Then it's only five minutes' walk to Trafalgar Square and Nelson's Column.

Step 3 What about some shopping? Remember, London is the capital of cool! What the young and trendy people in London are wearing today, you'll find in your shops tomorrow.

But, how can you shop on a budget? Well, don't go along Bond Street or Regent Street. Try the markets at Covent Garden, Camden Lock or Brick Lane. You'll find young designers – maybe tomorrow's fashion stars – with interesting new ideas. And, of course, lots of great second-hand clothes!

Step 4 Londoners' favourite lunch is a sandwich. The English gave the sandwich its name, and today it comes in every size and flavour. If the weather's good, go and sit in one of the parks – sometimes there's even free music.

Step 5 Now it's time for a bit of culture. Don't worry, it won't hurt! Try the British Museum or the Tate Modern – both are FREE! You can see mummies at the one and exciting art at the other. And the museum shops are a great place to buy souvenirs or a present for the family.

Step 6 Do your feet need a break? How about a trip on the DLR (Docklands Light Railway)? It goes past the new buildings in the Docklands area. London is the richest city in Europe and one of the world's most important money centres. Just watch the skyscrapers fly past your window. (And by the way, you can use your Travelcard for this trip too.)

Step 7 How about an early dinner before the theatre? Try a noodle bar – they're cheap and good.

And then, on your way to the theatre, maybe you can spend your last two pounds on the magazine 'The Big Issue'. Homeless people sell it on the street. Every night, summer or winter, about 200 people – some of them young runaways – sleep on the streets. Buy the magazine and help the homeless.

1 A day in London

a) Make groups. Each person in the group has a number (A1, A2, ... / B1, B2, ...).

b) Each group chooses a different sight or activity in London. Each person in the group collects information (pp. 12–19, guide books, internet, tourist brochures etc.)

c) Discuss your information in your group. Then join students of other groups (A1, B1, C1, .../ A2, B2, C2, ...) to make a new group. Swap your information and plan a day in London. Report to the class.

▸ *SF Marking up a text (p. 132)* • *WB 14 (p. 15)*

1 WORDS City sights

a) Read the definitions and find the word.

1 If you go on one, you can see lots of sights from a river: boat tr – –
2 A building with old, interesting things in it: m – – – – –
3 A green place where people can walk, sit or play games: p – – –
4 People go on the London Eye for this: v – – –
5 Travel on an open-top one and you can see everything: b – –
6 Ships and boats come and go here: h – – – – – –
7 You go over one to cross a river: b – – – – –
8 A place in the open air where people buy and sell things: m – – – – –

b) **Extra** *Make a city sights mind map. Put the words from a) into it. Add more.*

2 WORDS A transport wheel

a) Choose words and phrases from the box and put them in a copy of the wheel. You can use some words more than once. The words with + are new. Only look them up if you have to.

+airport • bike • boat • bridge • bus • +bus pass • +bus stop • by car • driver • +ferry • +gate • harbour • line • northbound • +on foot • plane • platform • return ticket • river • road • rush hour • sea • single ticket • ship • southbound • station • street • +taxi • +ticket machine • train • +tram • Travelcard • Tube map • tunnel • underground

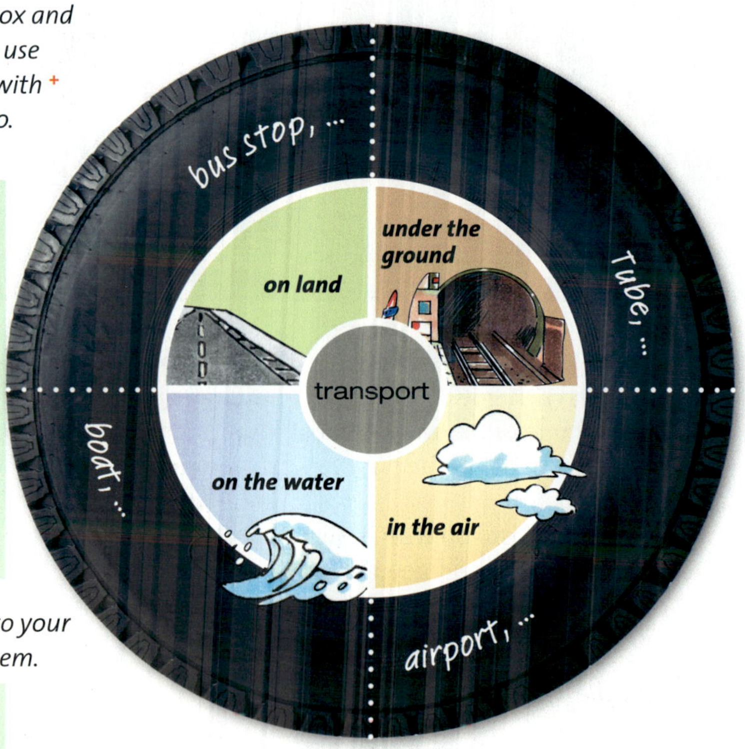

b) Write these verbs and prepositions into your exercise book. Match words from a) to them.

arrive at • ask for • drive over • drive through • get off • get on • go by • wait at

c) **Extra** *What town – in Germany or abroad – would you like to visit? Write a short text about the best way to get there.*

I'd like to visit ... The best way to get there is to fly. First you take the train to the airport. When you get off the train, ...

3 MEDIATION The ticket machine

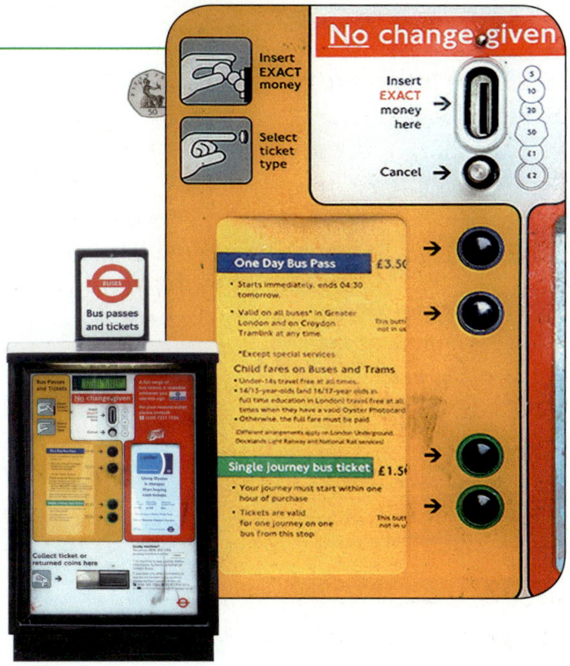

a) *Vanessa Beck and her parents know they have to buy a ticket from a machine before they get on the bus. But they need help.*

Herr Beck ___ Frag mal, ob uns jemand weiterhilft.
Vanessa ___ Excuse me. Can ...?
Woman ___ Yes, of course.
Frau Beck ___ Frag sie bitte, welches Ticket für uns drei am besten ist. Wir wollen ja den ganzen Tag viel herumfahren.
Vanessa ___ ...
Woman ___ I'd say a one-day bus pass for £3.50.
Frau Beck ___ Wohin können wir mit dem Ticket überall fahren?
Vanessa ___ ...
Woman ___ You can use it on all buses in London.
Vanessa ___ ...

b) *Listen and go on with the rest of the dialogue.*

4 REVISION A visit to the London Eye (Simple past)

Put the verbs in brackets in the simple past.

Asif and Robert *had* (have) a good time yesterday. In the morning the weather (be) great. Robert and his parents (walk) from their hotel to Queensway underground station. They (want to) meet Asif. They (take) the Central Line, (change) at Bond Street and (get off) the train at Waterloo. When they (come) out of the underground station, they (see) the London Eye. When they (arrive), there (be) lots and lots of tourists there, so they (cannot find) Asif. But then Asif (call) Robert. Because Asif (not have) much money, Mr Smith (buy) all the tickets. Then they (have to) wait for more than 45 minutes before they (can get) on the Eye. The two boys (find) the ride very exciting. After the ride, they (not want) to stay with Robert's parents so they (go) to Asif's part of London. Mrs Smith (not be) very happy about that, but Mr Smith (say), 'Have a good time!'

5 Extra REVISION When I was four ... (Simple past)

a) *Copy the card. Complete the sentences for yourself.*

When I was four I ... I didn't ...	**Last weekend** I ... I didn't ...
In my summer holidays I ... I didn't ...	**Two years ago** I ... I didn't ...

b) *Make a double circle. Tell your partner about yourself. Then listen to your partner and take notes about him/her.*

Elsa
4 – rode bike, didn't read
summer – went to Spain, didn't ...
...

Go to the next partner.
Tell him/her about yourself and your last partner.
Listen to him/her. Is anything the same?

6 WRITING A postcard (Writing better sentences)

In part 1 of the writing course, you'll learn to make your writing more interesting. At the end you'll write a postcard.

a) *Read the two postcards. Which one is more interesting? Can you say why?*

Dear Kim

I'm on Majorca.
I do lots of things here.
I go swimming in the pool.
I go to the beach.
I've met a few kids.
I like it.
I want to stay.

Love, Patricia

Dear Kim
Majorca is a great place. Every morning I go swimming in the pool here at the hotel, and in the afternoons I go to the beach. The beach is fantastic! But the best thing is: I've met really great kids from all over the world. I like it so much that I never want to leave.
Love, Patricia

How can you make your sentences more interesting?

- *Use **adjectives** (great, fantastic, ...), **time phrases** (every morning, in the afternoons, ...) and **adverbs** (really, very, quite, ...).*
- *Use **linking words** (and, but, so ... that, ...) to link sentences.*

b) *Make the sentences more interesting: add the words from the brackets to them.*

1 I'm having fun here. (really, lots of)
I'm really having lots of fun here.
2 We've got a pool. (fantastic)
3 I go there. (usually, in the mornings)
4 We have lunch in restaurants. (different, every day)
5 My parents take me to churches and museums. (in the afternoons, lots of)
6 I don't like the churches, but the museums are interesting. (very much, often)
7 We went to a show. (yesterday, really great)

c) *Use the words in brackets to link the sentences. Make changes if necessary.*

1 The weather is terrible. We can't go swimming. (so)
The weather is terrible, so we ...
2 The hotel isn't so good. The other guests are really nice. (but)
3 We have to stay another day. There's a problem with our plane tickets. (because)
4 I have a shower. The water is always cold after a minute. (when)
5 We get back home on Sunday. I'm going to send an angry letter to the hotel. (after)

d) *And now you can write your own postcard. You can put it in your DOSSIER.*

– *Start with a greeting.* → *Dear Laura / Hi Dan*
– *Say where you are.* → *I'm writing to you from ... / Everything here is ...*
– *Say what you usually do there.* → *Every day I go to ...*
– *Say what's special.* → *The weather / ... here is amazing. You can ...*
– *Say how long you'll be there.* → *I'll be here for another two weeks / ...*
– *Finish with a closing phrase.* → *Love, Sandra / Your friend, Lukas*

7 PRONUNCIATION now [aʊ] – no [əʊ]

a) *Listen to this dialogue. Then read it out loud.*

A: How old is your mouse?

B: Oh, I don't know. ... Well, now I know. It's about a thousand hours old. No, it's about two thousand hours old.

b) *Now say the words on the right. Which is the odd one out? Listen and check.*

1	shout	snow	phone
2	nose	down	photo
3	brown	slow	loud
4	open	cloudy	town
5	hope	window	trousers
6	about	cold	outside
7	pound	throat	smoke
8	clown	joke	suppose

8 REVISION A week in London (Present perfect)

Janina and Klara are in London. Look at their list of things to do.

a) *Say what Janina and Klara have (already) done and what they haven't done (yet).*

1 Janina and Klara have (already) visited the Tower of London.

2 Janina hasn't written a ... (yet).

b) *Write the sentences into your exercise book.*

Things to do in London

J + K	visit the Tower of London	✓
J	write a postcard	
K	buy a trendy T-shirt	✓
J	see a musical	
J + K	play video games at London Trocadero	
J + K	travel on the underground	✓
K	take photos of Buckingham Palace	✓
J	eat Indian food	

9 REVISION The Feely Family (Present perfect)

Partner B: Look at p.102. Partner A: Ask questions about pictures 1–4.

1 Why is Mrs Feely angry?

1 Mrs Feely – angry

2 Mo and Jo Feely – happy

3 Grandpa Feely – sad

4 Mr Feely – tired

Now answer your partner's questions about pictures 5–8.

5 She's scared because she's seen a ...

5 she – see big dog

6 she – write nice story

7 he – eat too many sweets

8 they – not close door

10 WORDS Food

a) *Which shop sells the different things from the box? Which things can't you find in them? Where can you find them?*

+bacon • +beef • biscuit • carrot • chicken • +egg • lamb • lettuce • milk • +mushrooms • +onion • +peas • +pork • potato • sausage • soup • +steak • sweets • toast • tomato • +turkey

b) *GAME What have you got in your shopping bag? Play a chain game.*
A: I've got onions in my shopping bag.
B: I've got onions and pork in my shopping bag.

11 What an interesting life! (Present perfect/Simple past)

a) *Write sentences about what Eddie has done. Leave an empty line under each sentence.*

1 Eddie has travelled to Canada.
...

2 Eddie has ...
...

1 travel / Canada

2 eat / crocodile

3 climb / Mount Everest

4 buy clothes / Brick Lane

5 sail / America

6 visit / Natural History Museum

b) *Listen to Eddie. Find out when he did these things. Write sentences on the empty lines.*

1 He travelled there in 2001.

12 I've done that – I did it last summer (Present perfect/Simple past)

a) *Write five sentence pairs – about what you have done and when you did it. Use these ideas.*

try Bangladeshi food/Indian food/...
travel to Greece/Canada/...
write an e-mail to somebody in another country
have a picnic in a park/forest
play a virtual reality game
buy second-hand clothes

1 I've tried Indian food. I tried it last summer.
2 ...

b) *Find somebody who has done the same things as you. Who did them first?*

A: I've tried English food. What about you?
B: I've never tried English food.
A: OK, thanks.
A: I've tried English food. What about you?
C: I've tried English food too.
A: When?
C: Two months ago – when I was in England.
A: I tried English food last year. So I did it first.

13 LISTENING Travel announcements

a) *Look at the pictures. Then write down the numbers 1–5. Listen to the announcements and match a picture to each number. The sounds can help you.*

b) *Now listen again and answer these questions. Remember: you needn't understand every word.*

1 Which platform do you need if you want the Bristol train?
2 Where do you have to change if you want to get to Waterloo?
3 You're travelling with Benjamin Müller. Where does he have to go now?
4 Where do you have to change if you want to go to Wimbledon?
5 What gate do you need if you want to fly to Berlin?

A

B

C

14 EVERYDAY ENGLISH Asking for and giving information

a) *When and where can you say these things? Match the questions and the situations.*

1 Excuse me, can you tell me the way to Tower Hill?
2 What's for lunch?
3 So, do you like Asian fusion?
4 Sorry, how much is it? Did you say two pounds fifty or two pounds fifteen?
5 Can you tell me, do you stop at Victoria Station?
6 How do you say 'umsteigen' in English?

a To your mum or dad in the late morning
b To a shop assistant
c To a bus driver in London
d To somebody on the street
e To your English teacher or another student
f To a new friend

b) *Listen for the phrases from a) on the CD. Were your answers correct?*

c) *Complete the dialogue.*

A: Excuse me, are you from here?
B: Yes, I am. ... can I ... you?
A: Well, I ... the leisure centre in Shaw Street. Can you ..., please?
B: Yes, of course. It's quite easy. Just ... a number 4 bus and ... at Shaw Street.
A: I'm ..., what ... you ...? Which bus do I need?
B: The number 4.
A: OK, ... very much.

d) **Extra** *Choose one of these situations and prepare a dialogue. Act it out in class.*

1 You are on holiday and have just met a girl from Sweden. Find out about her and tell her about yourself.
2 An American student is visiting your house. Explain to her what your mum has cooked.
3 A man from Italy is in your town. He wants to know how he can use public transport (how much it costs, where he can pay, ...).

Only a game

Do you play video games? And if you do, how often do you play them? Which ones do you find the most exciting? Or the most realistic?
Some of the new words in the text aren't in the Dictionary in this book. You can use your English–German dictionary if you need help.

▸ SF English–German dictionary (p. 126)

When they arrived at the Trocadero, Asif and Robert went to Funland.

'Wow!' Robert said.

'They've got over 250 video games,' Asif said. 'The virtual reality games are the best.'

'I've never played one,' Robert said. 'How do they work?'

'Well,' Asif explained, 'you wear this helmet. Then you can see places all around you. It's like you're really there.'

'Sounds cool,' Robert said. 'Let's try one.'

The two boys looked round. There were so many games! Then Asif saw something. 'Robert, over here!'

Robert was surprised to find his friend in a quiet corner. 'Are you sure we're allowed to go here, Asif?' he said. 'I think they're still building something here.'

'Oh come on,' Asif said. 'If they don't want us here, they'll come and tell us. Look at this.'

Robert looked at the table where his friend was. Next to the two VR helmets was a sign. Robert read it: 'Experimental game.'

'You didn't read the best part,' Asif said.

'What do you mean?' Robert asked. Then he saw it. Under the big black letters there were smaller ones: 'Play at your own risk.'

'This is a joke, right?' Robert asked.

'Of course it's a joke,' Asif laughed.

'But maybe it really is dangerous,' said Robert.

But Asif was already putting on one of the helmets. Robert didn't like the idea, but he took the other helmet and put it on.

'There's a menu,' Robert said. 'Can you see it too?'

'Yes, I can,' Asif answered. 'Look, we can choose a virtual world. They're all from the past here in London.'

'Elizabethan London?' Robert said. 'What's that?'

'The time of the first Queen Elizabeth ...' Asif said.

'No, I don't want that,' Robert said. 'What's the next one? Oh look, Roman London.'

'Everybody in togas?' Asif laughed. 'I don't think so.'

'The next one's Victorian London,' said Robert.

'That was part of my London project for school,' Asif told his friend. 'Let's do that.'

'OK,' said Robert. 'But how do we start it?'

'Push the button,' Asif told him.

Robert did what Asif told him. 'Hey, I can see my hand in the game!' he said excitedly.

'That's virtual reality,' Asif explained.

A few moments later, London in the year 1888 was all around them.

'Wow! Where are we?' Robert asked.

'This looks like Whitechapel,' said Asif.

'Whitechapel?' Robert asked.

'It's in the East End,' Asif said, 'not so far from my house. – Come on, let's look around.'

The two boys walked through the dirty streets. 'It's getting dark,' Asif said.

'Yeah, kind of scary,' said Robert.

'You know,' said Asif slowly, 'Whitechapel is where Jack the Ripper killed all those people.'

'Ooh,' laughed Robert, 'Jack the Ripper is coming to get you.'

'Don't make jokes about the murders,' a woman's voice said suddenly.

The boys turned to look. An old woman moved towards them. 'They found the last victim right there,' she said.

The boys looked where the woman was pointing. There was blood on the street and the walls. And there was a flower there.

'Lavender,' Robert whispered.

As they walked on, fog came down on the street. They heard a fog horn.

'We must be near the river,' Asif said.

Just then he felt something run over his foot. A rat! 'Did you see the rat too, Robert?' he asked.

'Yeah,' Robert said. 'You know what? This is getting too realistic for me.'

'Yeah, for me too,' Asif answered. 'Let's take these helmets off and try a different game.'

Both boys took off their helmets.

Asif looked around. 'Robert!' Asif called.

Robert already knew what his friend wanted to say. 'Nothing happened.'

'We're still here!' Now Asif was scared. 'How can that be?'

'I don't know! This was your idea,' Robert shouted. 'Do something!'

'I know,' Asif said. 'We can just pull the plug. Without electricity, the game will stop.'

'I don't see any plugs, Asif,' said Robert.

The boys could only see the fog, dirty brick walls, blood – and the lavender.

'There must be a plug somewhere,' Asif said. 'Check the walls!'

'There's blood on them!' Robert grumbled.

'So go over there and look,' said Asif. He was getting angry. 'It's only a game, Robert.'

Suddenly there was a flash.

'What was that?' Robert asked.

'What do you mean?'

'That flash.'

'I didn't see anything,' said Asif. 'Now just try and find a plug.'

The boys felt along the walls. No plugs – just cold bricks.

'You know what's strange?' Asif said. 'I can really feel these bricks. And I could feel that rat on my foot.'

'So?' asked Robert.

'The thing is: you can see and hear virtual reality. But you can't feel it.'

'Are you saying ...'

'Yeah,' said Asif. 'I think we're really here.'

'But how?'

Asif didn't answer. Out of the fog, they suddenly heard footsteps. They weren't far away, and they were getting closer.

'Asif, I'm scared,' said Robert.

Just then a lamp went on at the other end of the little street. A long shadow appeared on the street.

'It's him,' whispered Robert. 'It's Jack the Ripper.'

The shadow was moving closer, and it had something in its hand. A knife?

Then they heard a little voice. 'Flowers. Buy my flowers.'

'A flower girl,' Asif said.

'She's selling lavender, Asif,' Robert said. 'Like the flower where the last victim died.'

The girl came closer. 'Buy my flowers?' She looked into Asif's eyes. Her face was so sad. Suddenly Asif knew: the last victim was the girl's mother.

Asif put his arms around her. 'Everything will be fine.'

Suddenly there was light from an open door. 'What are you doing with that girl?' a man shouted angrily. 'We've seen enough murders here, you!'

Another light, another voice, 'It's him. It's the Ripper!'

'There's two of them!' a third voice shouted.

People started to come out of the houses. 'Get the police!' called one woman.

'We don't need the police,' said another.

'Yeah, we know what to do with murderers,' a man said.

'Stay away from the girl!' said the first man.

Asif took his arms from the little flower girl. 'We haven't done anything!' he shouted.

From far away the boys could hear police whistles. 'Quick, let's do it before the police get here!' said a woman.

'I think they're going to try and kill us,' Asif said.

'I don't want to die, Asif!' cried Robert.

Working with the text

1 What happened when ...

1 ... Asif and Robert arrived at the Trocadero?
They went to Funland.
2 ... they found an experimental game in a quiet corner?
3 ... Robert pushed the button for the virtual world of Victorian London?
4 ... Asif said, 'It's only a game, Robert'?
5 ... Asif put his arms around the girl?
6 ... the people thought that the boys were murderers?

2 Extra How Asif and Robert felt

Find at least one point in the story when Asif and/or Robert felt
a) excited b) scared c) strange d) surprised.
The boys felt ... when they saw the shadow (l. 136).

3 The ending

a) *What do you think will happen to Asif and Robert?*

b) *Listen and find out what really happens to them.*

4 Only a game?

How do Robert and Asif feel about the game in the end? Do you think they will play an experimental game again? What would you do?

5 Video games in your view

a) *What makes a video game a good game? Think of reasons.*

b) *What can be bad about video games? The ideas below can help you.*
– You sit in front of the computer all the time.
– Players haven't got enough time for other people.
– There's too much blood in lots of games.
– If you kill people in a game, maybe you'll hurt them in real life too.
– ...

c) *Are video games dangerous in your opinion?*

very dangerous • quite dangerous • not dangerous

▸ WB 15 (p. 16) • **Checkpoint 1** WB (p. 17)

How am I doing?

▸ *SF Multiple Choice (p. 129)*

a) *Fill in or choose the correct answers.*

London

1 London is on the River ...

2 Another word for the London Underground is 'the ...'

3 This bridge opens for ships: ...

4 The Trocadero is at a famous square in central London. Its name is ...

5 The Queen's home in London is ...

6 The British Parliament meets in the ...

Words

7 'Excuse me, how do I ... to Victoria Station?'
A come B go C get D move

8 'Does this line go to Leicester Square, or do I have to ...?'
A change B get off C get on D get around

9 The train to Manchester leaves from ... 9.
A station B line C platform D tram

10 Which word doesn't fit?
A ticket B bus C boat D underground

11 Which word is the group word?
A turkey B meat C pork D beef

12 Which word doesn't fit?
A peas B lettuce C bacon D carrots

Writing

13 It's been rainy, ... we've spent most of the holidays inside.
A because B so C when

14 Where can you add 'after' to this sentence?
A ... I spoke to the teacher, B ... I tried to work C ... harder.

15 Where can you add 'usually' to this sentence?
I don't A ... like trying food from B ... different countries, but I C ... liked the food at the Bangladeshi café.

16 Which is not the right way to finish a postcard?
A Love, Lisa B Your friend, Fritz C Dear Dora

Grammar

17 The boys ... to the Trocadero when Robert ... in London last week.
A go, be B went, was C are going, is

18 Robert ... lots of photos when he was in London.
A is taking B has taken C took

19 Katrina ... on the London Eye yet.
A have been B hasn't been C was

20 Have you ever tried Indian food?
A Yes, I did. B No, I didn't. C Yes, I have.

21 I'm sorry, Mrs Franks, but I ... my homework.
A have done B haven't done C didn't

b) *Check your answers on p. 226 and add up your points – one point for each correct answer.*

c) *If you had 17 or more points, well done! Maybe you can help students with fewer points. If you had 16 points or fewer, it's a good idea to do some more work before you go on to the next unit. Where did you make mistakes? The chart below will tell you what you can do to improve your English.*

No.	Area	Find out more	Exercise(s)
1– 6	London facts	Unit 1 (pp. 12–19), P 4 (p. 21)	WB 1, 3, 5, 14 (pp. 8, 9, 10, 15)
7–10	Word field: transport	Unit 1 (p. 14)	P 2, 3 (p. 20, 21), WB 2–3 (p. 9)
11–12	Word field: food	Unit 1 (p. 17)	P 10 (p. 24), WB 10 (p. 13)
13–16	Writing better sentences	Unit 1, P 6 (p. 22)	WB 8 (p. 12)
17–18	Simple past (Revision)	GF 1a (p. 139)	P 4, 5 (p. 21), WB 6 (p. 11)
19–21	Present perfect + simple past	GF 1b–c (pp. 139–140)	P 8, 9, 11, 12 (pp. 23–24), WB 11–13 (p. 14)

Island girl

1 Hoy

a) *Find the Orkney Islands on the map on the inside cover of this book. Look for Hoy, Mainland and Flotta on the map above.*

b) *Look at the photos and at the captions below. Which caption goes with which photo?*

3 **A** From Hoy you can see the sea cages of the salmon farms.

6 **B** There are lots of cows and sheep on Hoy.

4 **C** On the way to Hoy you can see the oil tanks at Flotta's oil terminal.

5 **D** The Old Man of Hoy is a huge rock – 137 metres high.

1 **E** The only way to get to Hoy is by boat.

2 **F** The salmon farmer's job is hard work.

2 A view from the air

a) *Look at the photos for a minute. Then close your eyes and try to remember as much as you can about them. Listen to the CD – keep your eyes closed – and go on an imaginary journey to the island of Hoy.*

b) *Did you enjoy the journey? What did you see, hear, smell and feel?*

► *P 1 (p. 38) • WB 1–2 (pp. 18–19)*

5

6

All about ... electronic media

1 Keeping in touch

Not only people in towns use electronic media. People in lonely places like the Orkney Islands probably need them even more!

Katrina McFadden lives with her family on Hoy. Her great-grandmother can remember when the boat brought the post to the island once a week. And her grandfather remembers when the first people on the island got a telephone. Today Katrina can't imagine life without chat, instant messages, social networking websites or text messages on her mobile.

2 Now you

a) *What media do you use? Fill in a copy of the chart for yourself.*

MEDIA	Use?	Every day	Often	Sometimes
Mobile phone				
– make phone calls	Y		✓	
– send text messages to my mates	Y	✓		
– take photos or make videos	N			
– download and listen to music	Y			✓
– download personal logos and ringtones	...			
Computer				
– do homework				
– play games				
– surf the internet				
– watch videos				
– download, listen to, make or mix music				
– chat or send instant messages				
– talk over the internet				
– visit social networking websites				

"I MET SOMEONE WONDERFUL IN A CHAT ROOM... AND THEN I FOUND OUT SHE'S A CAT!"

b) *Interview your partner and put his/her answers in your chart in a different colour. Answer your partner's questions.*

Have you got a mobile phone?
Do you use it to ...?
And how often do you ...?
What's your ringtone/favourite computer game/...?

c) **Extra** *GAME*

Write one or two interesting things about your partner on a piece of paper and put it in a box. Take a piece of paper from the box and try to guess who the person is.

This girl mixes her own music on her computer. She does that often. Who is she?

► P 2–4 (pp. 38–39) • Text File 3 (p. 109) • WB 3–6 (pp. 19–21)

3 To school by ferry

Every Monday morning, Katrina's mum drives her from their home in the north of the island to Lyness, in the south. Katrina is never ready, so every Monday her mum shouts: 'Come on, love! We must leave now or we'll be late for the ferry!'

The journey to Lyness takes about half an hour. From there Katrina takes the ferry to Houton, on the island of Mainland. A school bus picks her and the other kids up at the ferry and takes them to school in Kirkwall. That journey only takes half an hour.

Hoy – Winter Timetable
Arrivals and departures, 25 Sept until 5 May

Lyness	dep	0650	1405	1640
Flotta	dep	0710	1425	—
Houton	arr	0745	1500	1715
Houton	dep	0800	1520	1730
Flotta	dep	0845	—	—
Lyness	arr	0910	1605	1810

> *What time does Katrina have to leave her house on Monday mornings? When does she arrive at school?*

▸ *GF 2a: will-future (p. 140) • P 5 (p. 40) • WB 7–8 (p. 22)*

4 Now you

a) *How do you get to school? Do you do anything on the way? How long does your journey take? Make notes.*

I usually leave home at ...
I walk to ...
I go by bike/bus/tram/...
My mum/... drives me.
I usually pick up my friend ... /
stop at a shop / ...
The journey takes ...

b) *Ask three or more partners about their journey to school.*

c) **Extra** *Make groups of four. Who has the longest journey? Report to the class.*

5 An interview for TV

a) *A TV channel is making a documentary about Katrina's school. A film researcher has come to interview students.*
Look at these questions before you listen.

1. How old was Katrina when she had to leave the school on Hoy?
2. Where does Katrina stay from Mondays to Fridays?
3. Why does she miss Hoy?
4. What job does her father do?
5. What instrument does Katrina play? Where does she play it?
6. What's a ceilidh?

Listen and take notes. Listen again and check.

b) **Extra** *Katrina talks about the view from her bedroom window. What can she see?*
Would you like that view? Why/Why not?

▸ *SF Taking notes (p. 132)*

6 Trendy types

Linda So, did the interview go well?
Fiona Aye, it did.
Alison If they choose you, you'll be a star.
Linda Aye ... in a year or two you'll be able to buy us tea every afternoon ...
Fiona ... and you'll be able to ask for my autograph.
Linda Dream on!
Alison Oh don't start, you two! Let's go into town after school. I'd like to do some shopping.
Linda Aye. I want to go to the wee shop in Albert Street. If I don't get there soon, they won't have those new bags any more.
Alison Which new bags?
Linda You know, the bags from that magazine. I'll show you ... here, look – they're really trendy.
Fiona Not like Fishface with her awful old rucksack – so uncool.
Linda Well, what do you expect? She comes from Hoy! 'Trendy' isn't even a word on Hoy. I mean, look at her hair: that awful ponytail!
Fiona Oh oh, here comes Fishface!

Who is 'Fishface'? Why do you think the girls don't like her?

▸ *GF 2b: will-future (spontaneous decision) (p. 140)* • *GF 3a: Conditional sentences (1) (p. 141)* • *P 6–7 (pp. 40–41)* • **Text File 4** *(p. 110)* • *WB 9 (p. 23)*

7 Extra POEM Billy doesn't like school really

Billy doesn't like school really.
It's not because he can't do the work
but because some of the other kids
don't seem to like him that much.

They call him names
and make jokes about his mum.

Everyone laughs ... except Billy.
Everyone laughs ... except Billy.

by Paul Cookson

a) *What links the poem to* **6***? Explain.*
– In 6, the girls ... In the poem, the other kids ...
– In the poem, Billy feels ... Katrina probably ...

b) *What reasons do kids find to bully other kids? Collect ideas with a partner.*
clothes/face/glasses/...

c) *What can you do to stop bullying?*

8 A Friday night chat

Katrina was tired and upset when she got back home on Friday. She went to her room and turned on the computer. Great! Latisha was online. Katrina invited her to talk over the internet.

Katrina I'm so happy I found you online, Tish.
Latisha Me too. How was your week?
Katrina Oh, don't ask!
Latisha Why, what's wrong?
Katrina The 'Beauties' were horrible. They called me names again.
Latisha Hey, don't let them upset you.
Katrina If people called *you* 'Fishface', you would be upset too.
Latisha They're just stupid bullies, Katrina. If girls called me names, *I* wouldn't listen.
Katrina If I looked like you, *I* wouldn't listen!
Latisha Katrina, you look great. Hey, you *are* great. Are the 'Beauties' interesting? No! Did the school send *them* to the music festival in Birmingham? No! If I was you, I'd forget them.
Katrina I'd forget them if they didn't call me names all the time.
Latisha Just don't listen to them – you can do it!

▸ *GF 3b: Conditional sentences (2) (p. 141) • P 8–10 (p. 41) • WB 10–13 (pp. 23–25)*

Looking at language

a) *Write down the sentences with 'if' from 8. Underline the if-clause in blue and the main clause in red.*

If people called you 'Fishface', you would be upset too.
If girls ...

b) *Can you find the short form of 'would'?*

9 Feelings

a) *Think of a word to describe the 'Beauties'. Maybe you thought of 'gemein' – but what's that in English? Use a German–English dictionary to find out.*

gemein *boshaft* mean; *Witz* nasty; *gewöhnlich* common

STUDY SKILLS German-English dictionary

The entry above gives three translations for 'gemein'. How do you know which is right? The words in italics show the different meanings in German – the correct English translation follows it.

▸ *SF German–English dictionary (p. 127) • P 11–14 (pp. 42–43) • WB 14–16 (pp. 25–26)*

b) *Imagine your English friend Jamie has written to you about problems like Katrina's. Write Jamie an e-mail. Look up these words before you start.*

(nicht) beachten • damit fertig werden • um Rat fragen • aus dem Weg gehen • sich an einen Lehrer wenden

10 Extra SONG

If I had a million dollars

Listen to the song. The singer would buy a few things if he had a million dollars.
How many can you find in the song? What would you buy if you had a million dollars?

Extra | Background File | SCOTLAND

Traditional ...

Only 5 million people live in Scotland. (England is almost twice as big and has got 50 million people.) Oh, and by the way, don't call the Scots English – they don't like it!

Highland Games

Every summer, towns and villages in the Highlands and all over Scotland have 'Highland Games'. You can see bagpipe competitions and all kinds of Scottish sports, like 'tossing the caber'.

Tartans

Scots often wear their tartans. But they don't buy a tartan dress or trousers just because they like them. They wear the traditional tartan of their family, or 'clan'. The picture here shows tartans for the MacDonald, MacKay and MacPherson clans.

The kilt

For a special day or a traditional festival, the men in Scotland often get out their kilts. The kilt is like a skirt – but don't call it that. The material is a wool tartan – sometimes eight metres of it! You want to know what men wear under their kilts? Don't ask – they'll tell you: nothing!

Music

It isn't just bagpipes. The Scots always enjoy a song – in English or in Gaelic, the traditional language of parts of Scotland. There's a famous one about Scotland's 'Bonnie Prince Charlie'. Maybe you know it?

Food and drink

No special day in Scotland would feel quite right without haggis (a kind of large sausage), shortbread (not a bread, but a biscuit) and of course a glass of whisky.

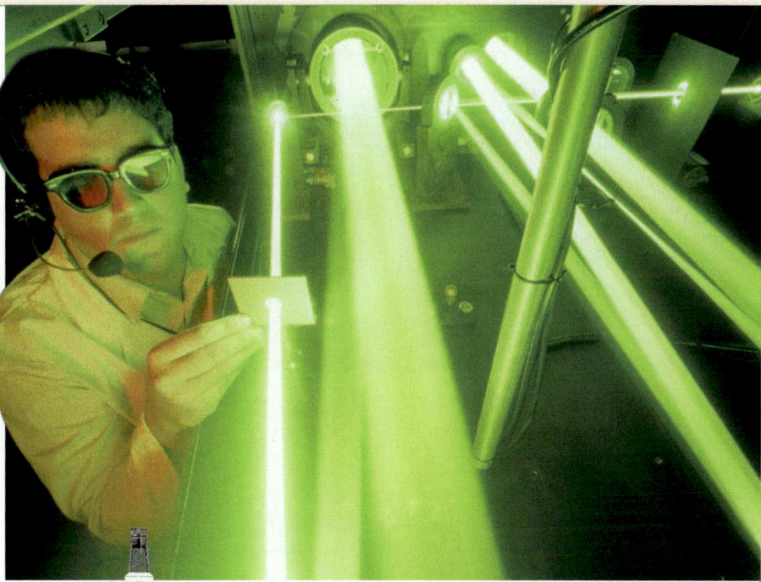

… AND MODERN!

From the Orkney Islands to Gretna Green, Scotland is a modern country. It has got exciting cities, big oil fields and a lot of high-tech companies.

Technology

Lots of high-tech companies have opened in Scotland. Scientists there were the first in the world to clone a sheep, and now they're doing exciting things with lasers.

Oil

In the 1970s the big oil companies found oil in the North Sea. Now there's lots of money in Aberdeen and other towns near the oil rigs.

Festival time

Every summer, Edinburgh, the capital of Scotland, invites the world to enjoy the Edinburgh International Festival, with music, theatre and dance. And there's the Edinburgh Festival Fringe with alternative theatre and street entertainment.

There's a lot to do in Edinburgh at other times of the year too. Around 31 December, for example, you can enjoy four days of concerts and fireworks together with thousands of people.

1 Great Scots

a) *Each group chooses a different person from the box. Find out when and where that person lived or lives and why he/she is famous. (Use an encyclopedia or the internet.)*

Alexander Graham Bell • Robert Burns • Sean Connery • Sir Alexander Fleming • Mary, Queen of Scots • James Watt

b) *Make a poster about your person and present it to the class.*

- Our poster is about …
- He/She was born in … (and died in …)
- The picture shows …
- He/She is famous for many things: First, …
- That's the end of our presentation. Have you got any questions?

► *SF Giving a presentation (p. 128) • WB 17 (p. 27)*

1 WORDS Town and country

a) *Which words go with 'town'? Which go with 'country'? Which go with both? The photos can help you.*

+bay • bookshop • +busy • +canal • +car park • cathedral • church • city • city centre • +coast • department store • dirty • farmhouse • forest • hill • +hilly • hotel • house • lake • mountain • noisy • park • post office • quiet • restaurant • river • school • shop • station • theatre • town • valley

b) *Finish these sentences.*

1 In most towns and cities you can find ...
2 Cities are often ...
3 In the country there are ...
4 People like walking along ...

c) **Extra** *Look at the photos again. Where would you like to live? Why?*

2 WORDS Electronic media

a) *Complete the text with the words below.*

chat • computer • download (2x) • logo • plays • ringtone • send • surf • text messages

Katrina has got her own ... in her room at home. She uses it to ... with friends and to ... the internet. It's cheaper for her to ... instant messages to her friends than to send ... on her mobile.

Katrina loves music, so she often uses her pocket money to ... her favourite songs. She hasn't got an MP3 player, but her mobile ... MP3s. Her ... on her mobile is a picture of a fiddle, and of course her ... is fiddle music. But it isn't a ... – it's her on her own fiddle!

b) *Choose five words from the box and make your own sentences.*

3 PRONUNCIATION Stress in words with three or more syllables

a) *Write the words from the box in a copy of the chart. Do you think the stress is on the first, second or third syllable?*
With a blue pen, make a tick for each word.

	1st	2nd	3rd
accident	✓		
amazing			
...			

accident • amazing • cathedral • disappear • discussion • electronic • expensive • helicopter • hospital • information • instrument • parliament • policeman • presentation • telephone

b) *Listen. Where do you hear the stress? Make red ticks in your chart. Were your ideas in a) correct?*

4 WRITING An e-mail to a friend (Using paragraphs)

a) *Read this e-mail about a trip to Edinburgh. What would make it easier to read?*

Dear Katie, It was my granny's birthday last Monday. She's always wanted to visit Scotland's capital – so she went to Edinburgh! I was happy to go with her. At 9.30 in the morning we arrived at Edinburgh station and went into town by bus. After that we got on a tour bus and saw the sights. The best thing was the tour of Edinburgh castle (photo). In the afternoon we did some shopping on the Royal Mile. I bought a Scottish hat for my dad. Later we had a delicious dinner. At 9.00 pm we were back at the station. I was really tired but it was a great day! It's amazing that we saw so much. Tom

All texts – not just e-mails – are easier to understand if you give them a structure. Look at this example.

At the beginning say what your text is about.

Start a new paragraph for each new idea.

Finish with a personal statement.

Hi Michael!

I promised to send you an e-mail about our trip to the Orkney Islands – well here it is at last!

We had a great time. :-) We were lucky with the weather – lots of sun and not much rain – so we saw a lot. Here are some photos.

We started on Mainland – yes, the biggest island is really called Mainland. There's lots to see there. The towns of Stromness and Kirkwall are nice, but very quiet!

On the third day we took a ferry from Kirkwall to the island of Hoy. There we did the famous walk to see the Old Man of Hoy. The big rock doesn't really look like an old man, but it is quite cool.

Mail me soon with your news.

Love, Jenny

b) *With the help of this example, rewrite the first e-mail in a).*

c) *Now write an e-mail to one of your friends about a day out. Remember:*

Start with an interesting opening sentence.	– *Guess what happened to me today!* – *Did I tell you that ...?*
Start a new paragraph for each new idea.	– *After that ...* – *At lunchtime ...* – *Before we ..., we ...*
Finish with something personal.	– *I hope I'll see you soon.* – *Must stop now. Please write back soon.*

5 REVISION I think Katrina will ... (will-future)

a) *How well do you know Katrina? How well do you know Hoy? Look at the pictures and write down what you think Katrina will and won't do next weekend. Give reasons.*

1 I think Katrina will sleep till 10.30 next Saturday morning because ... She won't ...
2 I think Katrina won't ... next Saturday afternoon because ... She will ...

1 next Saturday morning

sleep till 10.30

get up at 8.00

2 next Saturday afternoon

play her fiddle

go shopping

3 next Saturday evening

go to the disco

chat with her friends

4 next Sunday afternoon

go to a café

read a book

5 next Sunday evening

play games with her brother

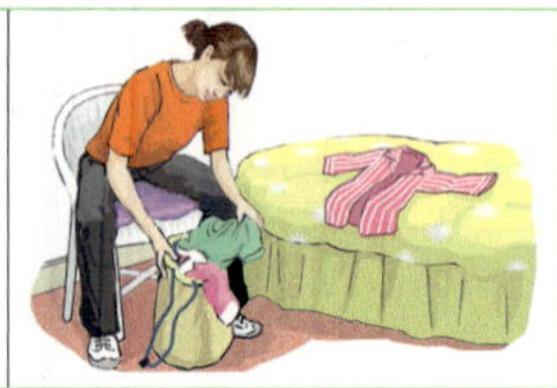
pack her things

6 next Sunday night

go to bed early

travel to Kirkwall

b) *Compare your sentences with a partner's.*

6 WORDS friendly/unfriendly (word building)

a) *Add 'un-' to these adjectives. How does that change their meaning?*

fair	*unfair*
friendly	
happy	
healthy	
safe	
tidy	

Unfair means not fair.
Unfriendly ...

b) *Complete the following sentences with the adjectives from a).*

1 Jane is ... because she has lost her favourite pen.
2 Don't eat so much fast food. It's really ...
3 Ben can never find anything. He's a very ... boy.
4 Jill never says 'hello' when you meet her. She's a really ... person.
5 Don't go over that bridge. A bus drove into it and now it's ...
6 Nobody likes our history teacher because he has favourites. He's very ...

7 REVISION If it's sunny, ... (Conditional sentences type I)

a) *Complete the sentences. Write a positive and a negative statement. You can use the ideas below.*

1 If it's sunny next Saturday, I'll go on a bike trip.
If it's sunny next Saturday, I won't practise the fiddle.
2 If I'm online next weekend, ...
3 If I'm at home alone on Saturday, ...
4 If I'm in town next weekend, ...
5 If I don't see my friends on Sunday, ...
6 If it's warm on Sunday, ...

chat with my friends | play ... | watch ... | have a party for ... | be ... | send text messages | tidy my room | go for a walk | go dancing/swimming/...

b) **Extra** *Make appointments with three students for 10, 11 and 12 o'clock. When your teacher says a time, go to your appointment. Tell your partner what you will and won't do and listen to his/her plans.*

8 Fiona's dreams (Conditional sentences type II)

Fiona often dreams about what it would be like if she lived in London. Match the sentences.

1 If I lived in London, — I would probably see the Queen.
2 If my parents visited me, — I would have a fantastic life.
3 If a film-maker saw me in a school play, — I would take them for a ride on the London Eye.
4 If I waited outside Buckingham Palace, — I would be so much happier.
5 If I didn't live in a small town, — I would probably become a film star.

9 If I became a film star (Conditional sentences type II)

a) *Fill in the correct forms of the verbs in brackets.*

1 If I (become) a film star, I'd be rich.
2 If I (have) parties, I'd invite lots of guests.
3 If my friends (come) to see me, I'd show them all the film studios.
4 I'd give them free tickets if they (want) to see my films.
5 My photo would be in the newspaper if I (meet) the Queen.
6 I'd be so excited if I (be) in a film.
7 If I (hate) a role, I (not take) it.
8 If I (not like) an actor, I (not work) with him.

b) *What would you do if you were a star? Write three sentences. Compare.*

10 If I lived on the island of Hoy (Conditional sentences type II)

If I Was An Apple

If I was an apple
And grew on a tree
I think I'd drop down
On a nice boy like me.

a) Think: *Complete the following sentences.*

1 If I lived on the island of Hoy, I'd chat on the internet every night/ I'd ...
2 If my parents had a million euros, ...
3 If somebody called me 'Fishface', ...
4 If I didn't live in Germany, ...
5 If I was 21 years old, ...
6 I wouldn't be fit if ...
7 My English teacher would be really angry if ...
8 People would be happier if ...

b) Pair: *Read out your sentences. Together choose your three favourite sentences.*

c) Share: *Join up with another pair. Choose your three favourite sentences. Read them to the class.*

11 STUDY SKILLS Using a German-English dictionary

a) *Find the correct English translations for the German words.*

1 faul • Don't take the apple. It's ...
• My friend is a really ... pupil.

2 Birne • I love apples but I don't like ...
• The lamp doesn't work. I think the ... is broken.

b) *Find the correct English words and phrases for the underlined German words in these sentences.*

1 Katrina hat eine schöne Sicht von ihrem Fenster.
2 Um 8.00 war die Fähre außer Sicht.
3 Aus meiner Sicht ist Katrina ein nettes Mädchen.

c) *Find the correct English translations for these German phrases.*

1 im Internet
2 ein Glas Apfelsaft
3 am Himmel
4 eine Brille
5 ihm aus dem Weg gehen
6 sie kämmte sich die Haare

12 Loch Ness and Edinburgh

a) *Partner B: Look at page 102.*
Partner A: A student has written this text about Loch Ness. Seven statements in it are wrong. Read it through quietly. Then read it out loud to your partner. He/She will correct the incorrect statements.

Loch Ness

Loch Ness is one of the most famous places in Wales. It's a lake in the North of Scotland. The word loch is Scottish and means water. Loch Ness is 73 kilometres long. It's the longest lake in Britain. The water is so dark at the bottom that people can't see when they go down into the lake.

Everybody in Scotland says that there is a big monster in the lake. They've given it a name: Nessie. Most people think that Nessie is real, and every year hundreds of tourists come to Loch Ness to try and see her. There are even photos of her.

If you want to find out more about Loch Ness, you'll have to go to Scotland.

b) *Now listen to your partner's text about Edinburgh. When you hear an incorrect statement, correct it with facts from the box below.*

Facts about Edinburgh

1 Edinburgh is on the east coast of Scotland.
2 Edinburgh is the second largest Scottish city.
3 More than 13 million tourists come to visit Edinburgh every year.
4 Visitors come to see famous places like Edinburgh Castle or Princes Street.
5 Thousands of people visit the Edinburgh International Festival every summer.
6 Edinburgh is the home of Alexander Graham Bell, the 'father' of the telephone.
7 J.K.Rowling wrote her first 'Harry Potter' book in a café in Edinburgh.

13 MEDIATION The Ba'Game

Read this article from a tourist brochure about the Ba'Game in Kirkwall. Write down the most important information in three or four German sentences for a family friend.

Every year at Christmas and on New Year's Day, there's a special game in the streets of Kirkwall, the capital of the Orkney Islands: the Ba'Game. There are two teams, the Uppies and the Doonies (Downies). The Uppies live in the hilly part of Kirkwall; the Doonies are from the flat part by the sea. And there are two games, one for boys and one for men.

To win the game, the Uppies have to take the ba' – a three pound leather ball – to a wall at the south end of the town. And the Doonies have to throw the ba' into the water of Kirkwall's harbour, in the north.

Each team usually has between 200 and 300 players. There are no rules: the players can kick and push people, punch, smash windows, run through houses or even over rooftops. The men's game can take five or six hours, sometimes even longer. And when the game is over? A player from the winning team gets the ba' and usually hangs it in the window of his living room.

14 EVERYDAY ENGLISH Talking about places

a) *Listen to the people on the CD. Each person talks about where he or she lives. While you listen, take notes about Glasgow, Stirling and Helmsdale in a copy of the chart on the right.*

	Glasgow	Stirling	Helmsdale
where?			
number of people?			
what's special?			

b) *Use your notes from a) and make lists of words and phrases for*
- where places are
- people in a village, town or city
- what's special about a place

Add to the lists. The ideas in the box will help you. Then compare your lists with a partner's.

- in the middle/north/... of Germany
- on the coast / on Lake ... / on the River ...
- in the ... Mountains / the ... Forest
- About ... people live in ...
- It's ... km from ... / not far from ...
- It's very green/hilly/quiet/exciting/...
- It's got ...

c) *Prepare and act out a dialogue about where you live.*

A: Where are you from?
B: I'm from a place called ..., in Germany.
A: Really? Where's that?
B: Well, it's on the ...
A: How many people live in ...?
B: Well, we've got about ...
A: Is it a nice place...?
B: Yes, I like it. It's got ..., and the people are ...

d) **Extra** *Prepare and give a short talk about where you live.*

Orkney Star

Before you read 'Orkney Star', look at the pictures. What do you think the story is about?

Another weekend was over. Katrina looked sadly out of her bedroom window. It was still dark, so she couldn't really see the sea. But in her head she could. The sea and the little boat in the bay, ready to go out and check the salmon cages. She liked to go out with her dad on the boat ...

'Katrina!' her mum called. Katrina took her little old teddy bear and pushed him down into the bottom of her bag. She closed the bag and took her fiddle. She looked round her room once more – then she turned off the light and went downstairs.

'Here you are, love. I've made some toast and a cup of tea.'

'I'm not hungry, Mum.'

'Och, you must eat something – it's a long time till lunch – and the boat will be cold.'

Her mum always drove her to the ferry at Lyness. The ferry left at 6.50, so they were usually in the car at ten past six. You had to drive slowly because sheep often ran across the road.

This Monday morning it was rainy and windy. As they came up over the hill, the wind whistled around the car and the rain hit the windscreen loudly.

'You'll have to go downstairs on the ferry today,' Katrina's mother said.

'Yes. I hate it down there,' Katrina said. 'I always like looking at the island one last time and down there you can't see anything.'

Her mum smiled. 'The island will still be here when you come back on Friday, love!'

When Katrina got to school there was just time to put her bag in the classroom and then she had to run to Assembly.

'And now some school announcements,' the head teacher said. 'As you all know, Scottish Television are going to make one of their "Going to school in Scotland" documentaries here at our school. And they've chosen a student from S3 to be "the star"...'

Fiona smiled and whispered to Alison: 'Hollywood here I come!' But Alison wasn't listening to Fiona. She was listening to the head teacher.

'... it's ... Katrina McFadden. So, good luck to Katrina. And now ...'

Katrina didn't hear the rest of the announcements. There had to be a mistake: Why her? She couldn't believe it.

When she got back to her classroom lots of kids came and talked to her.

'Great, Katrina!', 'Cool, Katrina: you'll be a star soon!' Now Katrina started to feel excited.

At break the 'Beauties' came over to her: 'Amazing, Katrina!' Fiona said. 'Were you surprised?'

'Er, yes,' said Katrina.

'We were too,' said Linda.

'Shh, Linda,' said Fiona. 'Katrina, we thought you might need some help.'

'Help?' Katrina asked, 'Er ... with what?'

'With shopping,' said Fiona. 'We know some nice wee shops in Kirkwall – we could help you to buy some trendy new clothes ...'

'And a new bag!' added Alison.

'But I don't need any new clothes, or a new bag,' said Katrina.

'Well what about your hair? I've got this friend: she's a great hairdresser,' said Fiona.

'Maybe the film crew would like to film you at the hairdresser's?' added Linda.

'But I don't want to go to the hairdresser's.

My mum always cuts my hair,' said Katrina.

'But Katrina, we only want to help. Ponytails just aren't trendy any more,' said Alison.

'That's OK!' said Katrina. 'When the wind blows I like having my hair out of my face. It's fine just as it is, thank you.'

The 'Beauties' walked away. 'Once a fishface, always a fishface!' said Alison.

'Yes, and now we won't be able to get into the film!' added Linda.

It was cold and windy when the film crew came to the school. Katrina walked across from the hostel in her wellies and anorak. She didn't know if she was more excited or more scared.

'Why did they choose me?' she thought. 'Film people are trendy, aren't they? They'll probably think I'm really boring!'

'Ah, here she is!' said the head teacher. 'This is Katrina McFadden. Katrina, this is the director's assistant, Sheena Burns.'

'Hi, Katrina. It's really nice to meet you. Call me Sheena.'

Katrina smiled: Sheena was about 23. She wore her jeans in green wellies and a green anorak. And she wore her hair in a ponytail.

'Hello, Sheena,' she said.

'Now, I'm going to take you to meet the director. Bill is really nice. We're going to film in the school today and tomorrow and on Hoy on Thursday and Friday. The head teacher has said you don't have to come to school on Friday, OK?'

'OK,' smiled Katrina.

'We're going to start with an interview,' Bill explained, 'Just like the interview with the researcher, but this time we'll film it!'

'Come and sit here,' said Sheena. Katrina sat down.

The electrician smiled at her. 'I'm Fred,' he said, as he moved one of the lights to the right.

'And I'm Emma: I'm the sound assistant and I'm going to put this little microphone on your sweatshirt.'

'And I'm Alistair: I'm the real boss here,' laughed the cameraman. 'If you're nice to *me*, you'll look *good* in the film. If you aren't nice to me, well ...'

'Don't worry!' said Sheena, 'They always have to make their little jokes. Is everybody ready?'

Katrina didn't feel ready, but Bill and Sheena smiled at her.

Bill began to ask questions. 'Katrina, you live on Hoy, but you have to come to school on Mainland. Do you like living away from home?'

'No, I don't,' answered Katrina, 'The hostel's not bad, but I'd really like to be at home with my family.

'Tell us about your journey to school on a Monday morning.'

'Well, it starts at about six o'clock ...'

The interview was going well but then suddenly there was a very loud noise. It was the bell for break.

'Oh dear!' said Emma, the sound assistant.

'Don't worry,' said Bill, 'Come on, let's go out and film the kids at break.'

So Katrina and the crew joined the rest of the school for break.

Later, when they went outside to film Katrina as she walked up the hill from the hostel, Sheena whispered: 'Who were those girls, the ones with the disco clothes and too much make-up?'

'Oh,' smiled Katrina, 'you mean the "Beauties".'

'Beauties? I don't think so!' said Sheena. 'Clones, maybe, but not beauties!'

'They call me "Fishface",' Katrina said.

'That's not very nice!' Sheena looked at Katrina. 'They must be really jealous.'

'Jealous? Of me?' Katrina asked.

'Sure,' Sheena smiled. 'You're a great person, you're a great fiddle player, and *you* are the star of our documentary. They *must* be jealous!'

The filming finished on Friday evening at Katrina's home on Hoy. The crew stayed for dinner – her mum made clapshot, a delicious Orkney stew with meat and potatoes and swedes in it. After dinner Mr McFadden said: 'And now you must join us at the community hall for a Friday night ceilidh!'

'Don't worry,' said Katrina, 'It's just a dance.'

Katrina and her father grabbed their fiddles and they all went to the community hall. Katrina's uncle and cousin were waiting: 'At last! Two fiddles don't make a band, but four do!' And the dancing began.

Working with the text

1 What's the story about?

a) *Was your answer to the question on p. 44 right?*

b) *Here are headings for the different parts of the story. Put them in the right order.*

1 Let's go to the ceilidh
2 Katrina meets Sheena
3 The film crew
4 An announcement at Assembly
5 Monday morning at home
6 'Clones, maybe, but not beauties'
7 On the way to the ferry
8 Katrina and the Beauties

c) *Write two sentences about each part.*

2 What did they mean?

Who made these statements? When? Why?

1 'The island will still be here when you come back on Friday, love!' (ll. 33–34)
2 'Once a fishface, always a fishface.' (ll. 82–83)
3 'Clones, maybe, but not beauties.' (ll. 180)

3 Katrina

a) *The film researcher chose Katrina: what do you think were her reasons?*

b) *Why were the 'Beauties' horrible to Katrina before (p. 34)? Why are they suddenly nice to her in the story? What do you think of them?*

c) *Katrina doesn't want help from the 'Beauties' (ll. 57–81). Do you agree with her? Why?*

4 Extra The interview

The director interviews Katrina. Make up the beginning of the interview. Start like this …

Director 'Katrina, where are you from?'
Katrina 'I'm from …'

5 Extra The film people

a) *Film people have a lot of different jobs. Find them in the story. Add more if you know more.*
director's assistant, interviewer, …

b) *Say what each has to do during the filming.*

► **Text File 5** (p. 111) • WB 18 (p. 28) • **Checkpoint 2** WB (p. 29) • **Selbsteinschätzung 1–2** WB (pp. 32–33)

How am I doing? ► SF Multiple Choice (p. 129)

a) *Fill in or choose the correct answers.*

Scotland

1 Hoy and Mainland are two of the ... Islands.
2 Edinburgh is the ... of Scotland.
3 Scotland is famous for a kind of fish. People keep them in special farms or cages in the sea: ...
4 Ceilidhs are a kind of party in Scotland where you can ...
5 The Old Man of Hoy is a huge ...
6 The Scottish word for lake is ...

Words

7 Where won't you find many trees?
A forest B city park C car park D country
8 Which word doesn't fit?
A coast B sea C lake D river
9 It's usually cheaper to send somebody a ... than to make a phone call.
A logo B text message C download D chat
10 Which verb doesn't go with 'video'?
A watch B play C turn D make
11 The film team had a ... time on Hoy.
A huge B big C large D great

German–English dictionary

12 Which word won't you find between 'Perücke' and 'Pflaster'?
A pflanzlich B Pfannengericht C petzen D Perspektive

13 You want to translate 'geht' in the sentence, 'Die Spülmaschine geht nicht.' You look up 'gehen' and find these German meanings. Where will you find the translation – under:
A laufen? B funktionieren? C dauern? D handeln?
14 Imagine you find three English translations for a German word. What do you do then?
A Look up all three in an English–German dictionary. B Use the first one – it's usually right. C Think of a different German word and look it up.

Grammar

15 If my brother ... to the party, I ... at home.
A will go, will stay B go, stayed C goes, will stay D would go, stay
16 If kids in my class ... horrible to me, I ... my teacher.
A were, would tell B would be, tell C would be, would tell D are, would tell
17 If I ... in his class, I ... happy.
A would be, was B was, would be C was, be D am, would be

b) *Check your answers on p. 226 and add up your points – one point for each correct answer.*

c) *If you had 14 or more points, well done! Maybe you can help students with fewer points. If you had 13 points or fewer, it's a good idea to do some more work before you go on to the next unit. Where did you make mistakes? The chart below will tell you what you can do to improve your English.*

No.	Area	Find out more	Exercise(s)
1– 6	Scotland facts	Unit 2, pp. 30–37, p. 42	WB 1, 17, (pp. 18, 27)
7– 8	Word field: town and country	Unit 2, pp. 30–31	P 1 (p. 38), WB 2 (p. 19)
9–10	Word field: electronic media	Unit 2, p. 32	P 2 (p. 38), WB 3 (p. 19)
11	The German word 'groß'	Blue box (p. 157)	—
12–14	German–English dictionary	Unit 2, A 9 (p. 35), SF (p. 127)	P 11 (p. 42), WB 15 (p. 26)
15	Conditional I	GF 3a (p. 141)	P 7 (p. 41), WB 9 (p. 23)
16–17	Conditional II	Unit 2, LaL (p. 35), GF 3b (p. 141)	P 8–9 (p. 41), WB 10–13 (p. 23–25)

1 WORDS In the country

Words about the country are important in the practice test on pages 50 and 51.

a) *Complete the mind map with country words and phrases.*

b) *Swap with a partner and compare. Can you add anything?*

2 STUDY SKILLS Describing pictures

▸ *SF Describing pictures (p. 128)*

In a test you might have to describe a picture. Where are these people/things in the picture? Use phrases from the box.

1 farmer	3 dog	5 boy	7 mountains
2 birds	4 horse	6 bike	8 house

1 farmer – in the foreground
2 birds – ...

at the top • in the background on the left • in the foreground • in front of the house • in the middle • next to the field • between two trees • behind the horse

3 The birds are flying (Present progressive)

You use the **present progressive** *to say what's happening in a picture.*

a) *Write the* **-ing** *form of the verbs in the box. Be careful with the spelling.*

arrive • chat • cycle • eat • fly • get • give • hide • meet • play • take • win • write

arrive	arriving
chat	...

b) *Complete the sentences with verbs from the box in a). Use the* **present progressive**.

1 I can see some birds. They*'re flying* through the air.
2 That must be the farmer next to the carrot field. He ... to somebody on his mobile.
3 The dog looks happy. It ... with a red ball.
4 The rabbits are happy too. They ... carrots.
5 I think the girl is the farmer's daughter. She ... the horse an apple.
6 That could be her brother. He ... behind the horse.

4 Katrina's day (Simple past)

*In the practice test you will have to write a short story or report. We usually do this in the **simple past**. Fill in the **simple past forms** of the verbs.*

1 Yesterday Katrina ... at twenty to six. (get up)
Yesterday Katrina got up at twenty to six.
2 Later she ... a hot breakfast. (have)
3 It ... windy and rainy when her mum ... her to the ferry at Lyness. (be, drive)
4 Two hours later she ... at school. (arrive)
5 At Assembly there ... announcements. (be)
6 Katrina ... very surprised when she ... her name. (be, hear)
7 She ... the other announcements. (not hear)
8 After school she ... her parents and ... them the news about the TV film. (call, tell)

5 Spelling (Plural of nouns)

Remember that nouns have different plural forms. Write the plural of the words from the box in a copy of the chart.

book • bookshelf • box • class • day • family • film • hobby • man • mouse • party • pen sheep • teacher • watch • wife • woman

-s	-es	-ies	-ves	irregular
books			*bookshelves*	

6 STUDY SKILLS Writing (Linking sentences)

Linking words and time phrases can make stories and reports clearer and more interesting. Read this story. Choose the right word or phrase for each gap.

An appointment in Victoria Road

... (Every day in August/One day in August) when Asif was having breakfast he found a note from his brother:

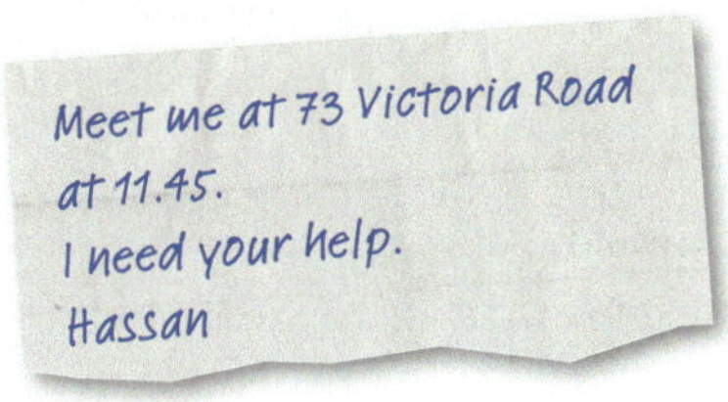
Meet me at 73 Victoria Road
at 11.45.
I need your help.
Hassan

Asif looked at his watch. Only 8.55. He had enough time to do a few other things before he met Hassan. ... (First/The next day) he checked his e-mails. ... (After that/First) he tidied his room. ... (At two o'clock/Then) he got his bag. It was very hot, ... (because/so) he packed two bottles of water.

73 Victoria Road was a pet shop. 'What can Hassan want here?' Asif wondered. 'And where is he?' He drank some water and waited, but Hassan didn't come. ... (Two hours later/Two hours earlier) Asif picked up his bag and went home again.

'Where were you?' Hassan asked when Asif got home.

'I waited at that pet shop for hours,' Asif said.

'But number 73 is a music shop,' Hassan answered. 'I had to get a big new drum for the band. And ... (although/that's why) I needed help.'

... (Suddenly/Because) Asif had an idea. 'There's more than one Victoria Road in London, isn't there?' he asked.

'And you went to the wrong one!' Hassan said.

Asif smiled, ... (and/but) he didn't really think that it was very funny.

'Listen, ' he said. '... (if/then) you want my help again, just give me the full address.'

► WB (pp. 30–31)

1 Reading

Robin Hood and Little John

Everybody knows that Robin Hood was a famous outlaw[1], and that he stole from the rich and gave the money to the poor. And everybody knows about 'Little' John, the big tall outlaw and Robin's number 2 man. But not so many people know the story of how the two men met.

One day Robin was fed up. He wanted something exciting to do, so he went out into the forest alone to see what he could find.

That same day, John Little, a shepherd[2], was fed up too. The terrible Sheriff of Nottingham had taken away all his land, and so he had no place where he could keep his sheep. He gave all his sheep away and left his little village to look for work in the nearest town. The road took him through Sherwood Forest, where there were many thieves and robbers.

And so it happened that John and Robin found themselves in the same place at the same time: a very narrow[3] bridge over a river. One man wanted to go one way; the other wanted to go the other way. And so they met in the middle.

Robin spoke first. 'Please go back, sir, so that I can cross the bridge. I was here before you.'

John was sure that that wasn't true, and he didn't want to go back. If he went back, he would have to turn round, and then he wouldn't be able to see the other man.

'What if he's a thief?' John thought. 'Maybe this is a trick, and he's going to steal my money.'

'No, sir,' John answered, 'I believe I was here first. You go back.'

Robin got his bow[4] ready. When John saw this he said, 'You seem like a fair man, sir. As you can see, I haven't got a bow. You don't want to kill a man who hasn't got a chance, do you?'

Robin agreed. 'You're carrying a staff,[5] I see. If you wait here, I will quickly make a staff. Then we can have a fair fight[6].'

John waited on the bridge as Robin cut a tree and made a staff. Some minutes later Robin went back on the bridge and the fight began.

It didn't take long till Robin was in the water. John ran down to pull him out of the river.

'You saved me!' said Robin, surprised. 'You are a good man. What's your name, sir?'

'John Little,' answered the big man.

Robin thought that was a very funny name for a man as big as that, and he laughed. 'From now on, I will call you Little John. If you like, Little John, you can join me and my men and wear our green clothes.'

And so it happened that Robin Hood and Little John became best friends and had many adventures in their fight against the Sheriff of Nottingham.

a) *Choose the right answers:*

1 Robin Hood was ...
A a sheep farmer. B a friend of the poor.
C Little John's number 2 man.

2 Robin met John Little
A in a river. B on a bridge over a river.
C under a big tree.

3 When Robin met John, he first wanted to
A push him into the water. B kill him.
C cross the bridge and move on.

4 John
A gave Robin his staff. B killed Robin.
C pulled Robin out of the water.

b) *Are these statements true or false? Why?*

1 Robin thinks it's boring to spend time in the forest.
This statement is true/false because ...

2 John thinks that Sherwood Forest is a dangerous place.

3 Both John and Robin are fair men.

---

[1] outlaw ['aʊtlɔː] *Geächteter* [2] shepherd ['ʃepəd] *Schafhirte*
[3] narrow ['nærəʊ] *schmal* [4] bow [bəʊ] *Bogen* [5] staff [stɑːf] *Stock*
[6] fight [faɪt] *Kampf*

2 Speaking

a) Describe the picture. Say:
- what kind of place you can see
- where the things/people are
- what's happening.

It's a picture of the country. In the background you see the coast. There's ...

b) Say more about the two people in the foreground:
- what kind of people you think they are
- how you think they feel at the moment

Give reasons for your ideas.

I think the woman is rich. She's checking her watch, so she's ...

3 Writing

a) Read the beginning of a story about the man and the woman in the picture above.

★ A meeting on a country road

One hot day in June a young woman was driving along a country road. She was in a hurry because she was late for an appointment. Suddenly she saw lots of sheep on the road, so she had to stop. She jumped out of the car and went over to the shepherd.
'Good afternoon, young lady,' he said. 'Lovely weather today, isn't it?'

b) Finish the story in about 80 words. Say if
- *the woman had an argument with the man*
- *she arrived at her appointment in time*
- *she ever saw the man again.*

Remember

When you finish your story:
- count the words
- check the spelling
- check the grammar
- check for other mistakes you often make.

World of sport

1 A teenager's room

a) *What can you see in the room? Make notes.*

b) *What does the room tell you: does a boy or a girl live there? What do you think he/she is interested in?*

I think it's a girl's/boy's room. He/She likes/plays ... His/Her favourite sport/... is ...

2 Extra The profile

a) *Look at the profile. Who is footie_girl?*

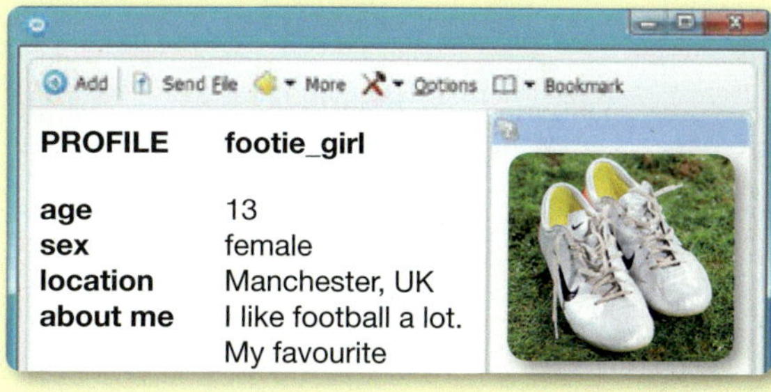

b) *Look at your notes from 1a) above. Complete footie_girl's profile.*

3 Now you

a) *How does your room show what you are interested in? (Remember: you can use a German-English dictionary if you don't know a word.)*

- I share a room with ... /I have my own room.
- I've got ... in my room. That's because ...
- I'm interested in ..., so my bedspread is ... / my curtains are ... /my furniture is ...
- On the walls I have ... /In the corner there's ...
- My room is very tidy/untidy. There are always ... on the floor/desk/...
- My family comes from ..., so I love ...
- My dream is to ... You can see that because ...

b) **Extra** *Now write your profile. You can add a picture and put it in your DOSSIER.*

► P 1 (p. 60) • WB 1–2 (p. 34)

All about ... sport

1 Latisha's sports

► P 2 (p. 60)

2 Now you

a) *What sports do you do at school or in your free time? Choose one. Then make a mind map. If you don't know a word, you can use a dictionary.*

b) *Talk about your mind maps.*

3 ACTIVITY

a) *On a piece of paper write two short texts like Latisha's for your sport from 2.*

I love basketball because it's fun to run around a lot after school. I'm an Alba Berlin fan and ...

b) **Extra** *Draw cartoons or add photos to your texts. (Later you can put them in your DOSSIER.)*

c) *Hang up your papers in the classroom. Walk round and read them. Choose your favourite. Guess who wrote it. Check.*

A: I think you wrote about ice hockey because I know you play ice hockey.

B: Right!/ No it wasn't me, I wrote about ...

► P 3 (p. 61) • WB 3–4 (p. 35)

4 A Friday evening chat with friends

scottie so how's your exchange student?
[banglaboy has entered the room]
footie_girl don't know really – arrived this aft. bad timing – big match on sat
banglaboy hi room. footie_girl: who ru talking about?
footie_girl hi banglaboy. the german girl who's staying with us
banglaboy a holiday friend?
footie_girl no, an exchange student who I'm going 2 visit next year
scottie cool
footie_girl oops, mum is calling me 2 dinner. hafta go! bye all
[footie_girl has left the room]

Footie_girl ran downstairs to the dining room.

Mrs Byrd There you are, Latisha. The food is getting cold.
Latisha Sorry, Mum.
Anna Have you finished your homework, Latisha?
Latisha Homework? Oh right. No. I still have to do some Maths.
Mrs Byrd Maybe you can do something with Anna first. She says she wants to go to a shop that sells cheap CDs.
Latisha I have to practise the drums then.
Mrs Byrd Latisha, we have a guest who has come a long way to be here. I'm sure you can find some time for her.
Latisha Yes, Mum.

> *Do you understand chat language? Match.*

ru	Saturday
hafta	chat room
room	afternoon
sat	to
2	have to
aft	are you

> *What are the real names of the people in the chatroom?*

Mrs Byrd Well, Anna, I've made stewed chicken. It's a dish that my grandma brought with her from Trinidad.
Anna That sounds very nice, Mrs Byrd.
Mrs Byrd Please start, Anna.
Anna Er, OK … Do you say 'Good appetite!' in English?
Mrs Byrd No, we don't. Is that what you say in German?
Anna Yes. What do you say in English?
Mrs Byrd I don't know really. Sometimes we say 'Enjoy!', but we usually just eat.

> *What does Latisha want to do after dinner? Do you think she likes Anna?*

Looking at language

a) *Complete these sentences from 4:*
- the German girl *who*'s staying with us
- an exchange student … I'm going to visit
- a shop … sells cheap CDs
- a guest … has come a long way
- a dish … my grandma brought

b) *What do* **who** *and* **that** *refer to?*
In the first sentence, 'who' refers to 'girl':
the German girl who's staying with us

In the second sentence, …

▸ *GF 4: Relative clauses (p. 142) • P 4–6 (pp. 61–62) • WB 5–7 (pp. 36–37) •* **Text File 6** *(p. 112)*

5 A Saturday in Manchester

'Well, here we are,' Latisha said.

As they got off the bus Anna saw a sign:

'What does that mean?' she asked.

'Well,' Latisha explained, 'it means the Lowry is a museum that everybody in the family will love.'

'Oh, OK,' Anna said. 'And what does Lowry mean?'

'Lowry? He was an artist from Manchester.'

'An artist? You mean he worked in a circus?'

'No!' Latisha laughed. 'An artist is somebody who paints pictures. – Now let's go to Old Trafford.'

'What's Old Trafford?'

'It's the stadium you can see over there. Manchester United play at Old Trafford.'

'Oh no,' Anna said. 'I'm not interested in football. Let's go to the Lowry.'

'OK, let's make a deal. I'll go with you to the Lowry if you come to my match this afternoon. That way we'll both do something we want to do and something we don't want to do.'

'I think that's fair. OK.'

Looking at language

a) *What's different?*
a museum the whole family will love –
a museum that the whole family will love

b) *There are three more relative clauses without **that** in **5**. Can you find them?*

▸ *GF 5: Contact clauses (p. 143) • P 7 (p. 62) • WB 8 (p. 38)*

STUDY SKILLS Paraphrasing

How does Latisha explain 'artist' to Anna?
To explain a word you can use a ***more general word*** and a ***relative clause***:

It's somebody/a person who ...
an animal/a place that ...
something that you use to ...

▸ *SF Paraphrasing (p. 134)*

6 GAME Paraphrasing

Make groups of five or six. Take turns to paraphrase words from the box. Can the others guess which word you're paraphrasing?

apple • camera • caretaker • choir • classmate • customer • department store • drum • frog • hairdresser • knife • murderer • museum • pet • rain • roll • school • tennis

▸ *P 8–9 (p. 63) • WB 9–10 (pp. 38–39)*

7 The match

Listen to the CD to find out about Latisha's match.

1 What's the name of Latisha's team?
2 What's the score two minutes before the end of the game?
3 Who scores the last goal for Manchester?
4 What does Anna think at the end of the match?

8 A match report

Manchester

JUNIOR FOOTBALL NEWS

Manchester United U14 beats Rochdale

Manchester United U14 will play in the cup final after their win against Rochdale in an exciting semi-final in Manchester on Saturday. Although both teams played a good game, Manchester was the stronger team in the end. The score was 1–1 at half-time. Rochdale came back with an early second-half goal by Charlene Gordon. Sandra O'Keefe quickly followed with a goal for Manchester. It looked like a draw till the 59th minute, when Manchester's Latisha Byrd scored the final goal of the match.

Rochdale goalkeeper Sue Waites couldn't stop Byrd's winning shot

TOP

What was the final score? Fill in a copy of the chart about the report.

Who played?	*Manchester United U14 girls and Rochdale*
What is the report about?	…
When was the match?	
Where was the match?	
Why did Manchester win?	

▸ *P 10 (p. 64) • WB 11–12 (pp. 39–40)*

9 You and sports

a) *Fill in a card like the one on the right for yourself. Write down reasons for your answers.*

b) *Make a double circle and talk to three different partners about their answers. Take notes.*

A: What's the sport that you like best?
B: I like ice hockey best.
A: Why do you like ice hockey?
B: Because it's fast and exciting.

c) **Extra** *Tell the class three interesting things you learned about your classmates.*

The sport that I like best: *ice hockey – fast, exciting*	A sport that I don't like: *golf – boring, nothing happens*
The sports star who I like best: *Podolski – funny, …*	A sports star who I don't like: …

▸ *P 11–13 (p. 65) • WB 13–17 (pp. 41–43) •* **Text File 7** *(p. 113)*

Extra | Background File | MANCHESTER – a great city for sport

1 On the radio

a) Look at the photos and write down the numbers 1–4. Then listen to the radio programme 'Great cities for sport!'. Match each section of the programme to a number.

b) Listen again and write down two facts about each section.

1 Manchester is probably most famous for its very successful football team, Manchester United.

2 If it gets too hot, take a dive into the Aquatic Centre.

③ And let's not forget the other Old Trafford – the famous cricket ground.

④ The strangest-looking sports venue in Manchester has to be the Velodrome! They have great cycle races there – for the disabled too.

2 Now you

a) *Choose a sportsman or sportswoman. Find out about him/her (internet, magazines, ...).*

b) *Prepare and give a short presentation about your sportsman or sportswoman.*

▸ *SF Giving a presentation (p. 128) • WB 18 (p. 43)*

1 WORDS Spot the difference

Partner B: Go to page 103.
Partner A: Look at the picture. Tell your partner what you see in the rooms. Use words and phrases like **next to**, **on the left**, **on the wall**.
Ask about his/her picture. Your partner has to spot the differences. Take turns: listen to your partner's description and spot the differences.

A: In my picture, there's a ... upstairs on the wall on the left. What about your picture?
B: Yes, in my picture it's there too. / No, in my picture it's on the wall on the right. – Now, in my picture, the ... is downstairs ...

▸ *SF Describing pictures (p. 128)*

2 WORDS Sports

a) *Look at the pictures 1–8. Which piece of equipment is missing from each? Choose from the box.*

Equipment:

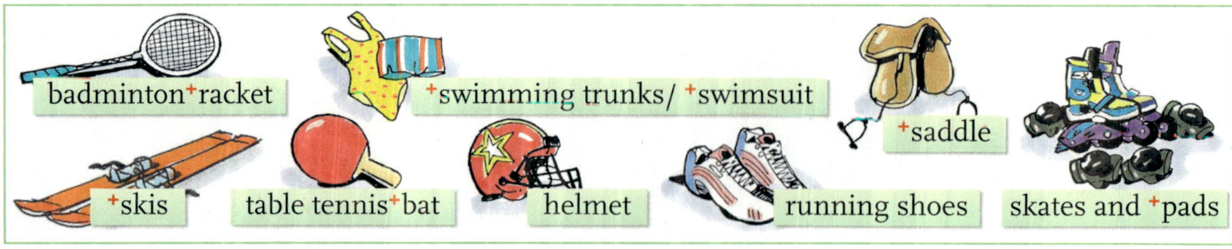

1 *In picture 1 the swimming trunks and swimsuit are missing.*

b) *Now match a location to each sport:*

+court • +bridle path • +half-pipe • field • pool • +ski slope • sports hall • +running track

c) **Extra** *Write one or two sentences about each sport: Where do you do it, what do you need?*

1 *You go swimming in a pool. You need swimming trunks or a swimsuit. ...*

3 REVISION Hobbies (Word order in subordinate clauses)

Remember

	S V O S V O
English:	Latisha wears a red shirt when she plays football.
German:	Latisha trägt ein rotes Hemd, wenn sie Fußball spielt.
	S V O S O V

a) *Complete these sentences.*

1 Latisha likes football because (lots of goals/scores/she).
2 She goes to the fan shop when (she/a new Manchester United poster/wants).
3 She would be excited if (met/one of the players/she).
4 Asif doesn't want to go back to the Trocadero after (had/he/so many problems there).
5 Asif would like to play in his brother's band because (their music/likes/he).
6 Robert is happy when (he/is watching/ice hockey matches).
7 Katrina and her dad go to lots of ceilidhs because (the fiddle well/they/play).

b) **Extra** *On a piece of paper, write three sentences like in a) about your free-time activities. Put your sentences in a box. Take a piece of paper and read it out. Can the group guess who wrote it?*

4 What would you like? (Relative clauses)

a) *Write sentences. Use* **who** *for people and* **that** *for things. Sometimes there's more than one right answer.*

I'd like	a teacher a car a computer a friend a brother a dog a camera an aunt	who that	comes and sits with me when I'm lonely. is fun to drive. doesn't tell our parents when I do something wrong. listens to my problems. gives me lots of nice presents. is really fast and easy to use. explains things well and is funny. takes good pictures.

b) **Extra** *What would you like? Make your own sentences.*

5 Who's the boy who ...? (Relative clauses)

Make the two sentences into one question. Use **who** *for people and* **that** *for things.*

1 Who's the boy? *The boy* is dancing with Sandra.
Who's the boy **who** *is dancing with Sandra?*
2 What's the name of the big wheel? You can see *the big wheel* on the river Thames.
What's the name of the big wheel **that** *you can see ...*
3 Where's the music shop? *The music shop* has got lots of cheap CDs.
4 What's the name of the video game? *The video game* shows you Roman Britain.
5 Do you know the player? *The player* has just scored the goal.
6 Who's the actor? You can see *the actor* in that new film.
7 Can I have a new mobile? I can use *the mobile* as a camera.
8 Do you know a museum? I could visit *a museum* with my English friend.

6 Famous people (Relative clauses)

Make sentences about the famous people in the photos.

- **Wayne Rooney**
- a footballer
- for Manchester United

- **Robbie Williams**
- a singer
- millions of fans love him

1 *Wayne Rooney is a footballer who plays for ...*

2 *Robbie Williams is a singer who millions ...*

- **Keira Knightley**
- the actor
- plays Elizabeth Swann in 'Pirates of the Caribbean'

- **Nathalie Portman**
- the actor
- you can see her in the Star Wars films

- **Arthur Conan Doyle**
- the writer
- wrote the Sherlock Holmes stories

- **J K Rowling**
- a British writer
- lots of kids read her

7 The Petersons and their pets (Relative clauses without relative pronouns)

a) *Find out the names of the people and pets in the picture. Copy and complete the chart.*

1 Pepper is a name you give a black animal.
2 Pepper is the dog Peter and Paul are touching.
3 Pat is the dog Peter is holding.
4 Pat is the dog Paula is touching.
5 Petunia is the dog Pamela is kissing.

father	
mother	
boy	
girl	
big black dog	
small brown dog	
small white dog	

b) **Extra** *You can leave out* **that** *or* **who** *in two of the cat's sentences. Find the sentences.*

1 I'm the pet that isn't in the family picture.
2 I'm the pet that the dogs hate!
3 Pamela is the person who feeds me.
4 She's the person who I like best.

8 STUDY SKILLS Paraphrasing

Partner B: Go to p. 103.

a) *Partner A: Explain the following words to your partner – but don't use the word. The phrases on the right will help you.*

A: It's a person who ...
B: Oh, do you mean a ...?

coach • cooker • lion • potato • waitress

It's somebody/a person who ...
It's something/a vegetable/a ... that ...
It's something that you use to ...
It's a thing/an animal ...

b) *Listen to your partner and guess his/her words.*

c) *Now try to explain the words from the box on the right in English. Your partner has to guess the German word.*

Eisbär • Fernseher • Krankenschwester • Säge • Tennisschläger • Verkäuferin

9 MEDIATION Where I'm from

Anna has brought a book about Chemnitz, her home town and Manchester's twin town, as a present for Latisha's parents. She has made some notes. Imagine you're Anna. How would you explain the page below to the Byrds? Remember: don't translate the texts – just give an idea of what they're about.

Chemnitz und das Erzgebirge

Chemnitz liegt am Rande des Erzgebirges und ist ein wichtiges Zentrum für die gesamte Region. Die drittgrößte Stadt Sachsens bietet eine aufregende Kombination aus Tradition und Moderne.

Wenn man ans Erzgebirge denkt, denkt man sofort an Weihnachten. Hier schnitzt man traditionell die wunderschönen Holzengel, die auf der ganzen Welt so beliebt sind. Einige Werkstätten, wie die hier abgebildete in **Seiffen**, kann man besichtigen und den Kunsthandwerkern beim Anfertigen der kunstvollen Figuren zusehen. Die Werkstätten sind nicht nur in der Weihnachtszeit in Betrieb!

Bergbau. Noch immer baut man im Erzgebirge das Erz ab, von dem es seinen Namen hat. Sowohl Zinn als auch Silber werden hier abgebaut. Besucherbergwerke geben einem einen tollen Einblick in die Welt unter Tage.

Werkstatt	workshop
Bergbau	mining
Zinn	tin
Silber	silver

10 WRITING A report (Structuring information)

a) *When you read a report on a match or other event, you want:*

- quick information on what happened
- the important information first, details later

Which of these texts is the better report? Why?

Remember

A report usually answers the '5 Ws': Who? What? When? Where? Why? – and sometimes How? – but not always in that order.

United beat Chelsea 2–1 in a fast and exciting game in London last Saturday. There were no goals until the last minute of the first half, when Manchester's Wayne Rooney scored a beautiful goal past Chelsea goalkeeper Petr Cech. Chelsea looked nervous after the

It was a fine and sunny day last Saturday when Manchester United and Chelsea met for their big match. 'A great day for football,' I thought. 'Not too warm and not too cold.' The game started a few minutes after 2 pm because the Chelsea players arrived

b) *Here are some notes for a report on a football match. Can you find the '5 Ws'?*

Bristol South against Redcliffe

first match of year

first half ended 0–0

slow start

boys U14 football

final score: Bristol South 1, Redcliffe 0

at Redcliffe's pitch

29th August

lots of mistakes by Redcliffe

second half very fast

South's Tim Hooley scored only goal

c) *How can you structure this information?*
You can use a mind map like this ...

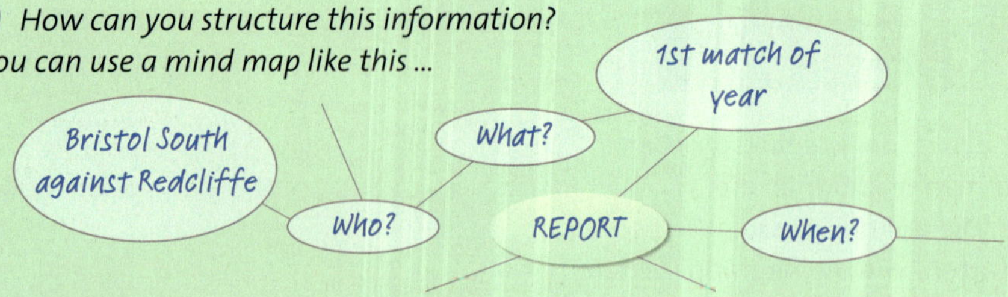

... or a chart like this:

Who?	What?	When?	Where?	Why?	How?
		29th Aug			

Choose the method that works best for you and structure the information.

d) *Use your mind map or chart from c) to write a short report (two or three paragraphs) on the match between Bristol South and Redcliffe.*

11 PRONUNCIATION (Different stress in English and German words)

a) *Copy the* ***German words*** *and the* ***English words*** *into your exercise book. Where is the stress in each word? Underline the stressed syllable.*

Appetit • April • Konzert • Instrument • Problem • Programm • Pullover • Thermometer
appetite • April • concert • instrument • problem • programme • pullover • thermometer

b) *Listen and check. Were you right?*

12 Extra LISTENING Keep fit in your English lesson

a) *Match the keep-fit instructions to the pictures. Try to guess any words that you don't know.*

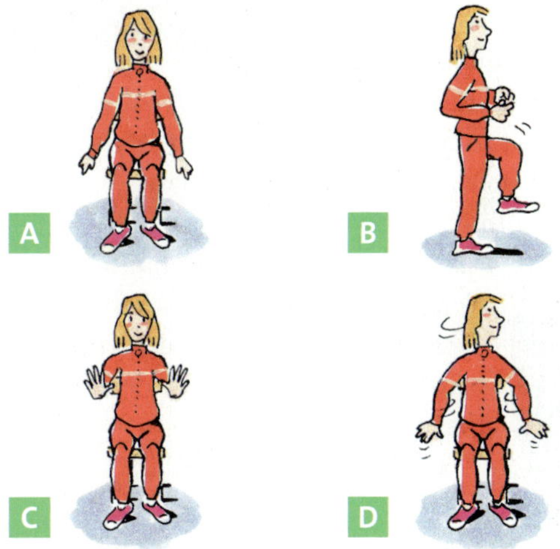

b) *Listen to the CD and do the exercises.*

13 EVERYDAY ENGLISH Talking to people at meals

a) *Remember how you can sound friendly when you talk to people:*

Remember
- Say 'please' and 'thank you'.
- Don't answer with just one word.
- Use the other person's name.
- Don't just talk about yourself – ask questions too.

Now listen to the conversation at the Byrds' dinner table on Saturday night. Put the phrases below in the right order. Listen again to check your answers.

A Well, please start!
B Yes please, Mrs Byrd.
C What did you do today, Anna?
D Would you like some more chicken, Anna?
E And what about you? What did you do today?
F Thank you. Enjoy!
G Well first we went to the Lowry ...
H Latisha, how do you say ...?
I Thank you, James.
J Mmm, that looks good.

b) *A foreign visitor is having dinner at Don's home. Use phrases from a) and write a dialogue. Then act it out.*

Don ___ I hope you like sausages, Michael.
Visitor ___ I love sausages, thank you.
Don ___ Well, please start.
Visitor ___ ...

Who needs legs?

Partner B: Go to p.104.
Partner A: Work with this text.

Nathan Stephens was born in a village in Wales on 11th April 1988. When he was a baby he learned to walk early. 'He took his first steps when he was only ten months old,' says his mother Helen. 'He just got up and walked.'

As a little boy Nathan loved sport. At school he played football and in his free time he learned to ride. He loved animals. 'When I grow up, Mum,' he said, 'I'm going to work with animals.'

For his ninth birthday Nathan asked his parents for a pair of riding boots and a new riding hat. And he was really excited when he came down to breakfast on 11th April 1997 and there they were.

'Thanks Mum and Dad! They're great!'

After school that day, some cousins and friends came to tea. It was a sunny spring day, so after tea the boys asked if they could go down to the old railway line to play. There were no trains there any more, so it was a favourite place for kids to play.

'Just remember to stay away from the new railway line,' called Nathan's mum as they ran into the woods.

Nathan remembers that afternoon. 'It was my ninth birthday. I went out to play with my friends. Our parents always said to us : "Don't go near the new railway line where the trains are" – but you know, boys often do things they aren't allowed to do! Well, I saw this slow freight train. "I'll jump onto it and take a ride," I thought. I jumped, but I fell ... under the train. It cut off both my legs.'

'A doctor and paramedics were already there when I arrived,' says Nathan's mum. 'I knew that he understood how bad it was because he asked "Will I have to be in a wheelchair now?"'

'All he said to me as they put him in the ambulance was, "Sorry, Mum".'

Working with the text

1 Who is Nathan Stephens?

a) *Read the text. Take notes on these questions:*
- Where and when was Nathan born?
- What sports did he do as a little boy?
- Where did he go to play on his ninth birthday?
- What happened there?

b) *Answer your partner's questions about Nathan. Then ask him/her what happened next.*
- When did he take his second 'first steps'?
- What sports did he do when he was ten?
- When did he win his first athletics medals?
- What are his hopes?

Take notes.

2 A timeline

a) *Copy and complete this timeline.*

Nathan born

1988 1997 1998 2002 2004 2006 2008 2010

b) *Swap timelines. Correct your partner's if necessary.*

DOSSIER *A sports star*

Find out about an interesting sports star (for example, the one you chose on p. 59). Draw a timeline for him/her and put it in your dossier.

► **Text File 8** *(pp. 114–116)* • *WB 19 (p. 44)* •
Checkpoint 3 *WB (p. 45)*

How am I doing?

***a)** Fill in or choose the correct answers.*

Reading – Facts from the unit

Scan the unit for the right answers.

1 What instrument does Latisha play?
2 Where did Mrs Byrd's grandma come from?
3 What's the name of the Manchester museum the whole family will love?
4 What's the football stadium in Manchester where Manchester United play?
5 What's the name of the young sports star who lost his legs when he was nine?

Paraphrasing

6 Which of these is not a general word?
A place B somebody C dinner D thing
7 Which is the best way to paraphrase helmet? It's ...
A black and hard. B a thing for skaters. C like a hat. D something skaters wear on their heads.

Talking to people

8 Which answer to the question 'Where are you from?' is a bit unfriendly?
A I'm from Germany. B Berlin. C I'm from Berlin, in Germany. D I'm from Berlin, the German capital.
9 Which of these is not a good idea when you talk to English people?
A Use the people's names often.
B Say something nice about England.
C Use complete sentences.
D Talk about yourself all the time.

Words

10 Which word doesn't fit?
A pitch B racket C field D court
11 Another word for 'supporter' is ...
A draw B score C fan D match
12 Which word doesn't fit?
A racket B helmet C bat D sports hall
13 Match the sports and the places:
1 skiing 2 ice hockey 3 football 4 badminton
A pitch B slope C ice rink D court
14 Match the rooms and the things in them:
1 living room 2 bathroom 3 kitchen
A sink B armchair C shower
15 Which of these things will you probably not find in a kitchen?
A sink B fridge C cooker D lift

Grammar

16 I've just met a girl ... likes football.
A who B where C which D how
17 Put the sentence parts in the right order to finish the sentence, 'Manchester is a city ...'
I / to visit / that / want
18 Read this sentence: 'Frau Marx is the teacher most students at our school like best.'
What information does it give you?
A Frau Marx likes the students. B Most students like Frau Marx. C Frau Marx likes the school. D Most students like the school.

***b)** Check your answers on p. 226 and add up your points – one point for each correct answer.*

***c)** If you had 15 or more points, well done! Maybe you can help students who had fewer points. If you had 14 points or fewer, it's a good idea to do some more work before you go on to the next unit. Where did you make mistakes? The chart below will tell you what you can do to improve your English.*

No.	Area	Find out more	Exercise(s)
1– 5	Facts from the unit	Unit 3, pp. 52–59, 66	WB 18–19 (pp. 43–44)
6– 7	Paraphrasing	Unit 3, p. 56, SF (p. 134)	P8 (p. 63), WB 9 (p. 38)
8– 9	Talking to people	Unit 3, P13 (p. 65)	P13 (p. 65)
10–13	Word field: sport	Unit 3, p. 54, P2 (p. 60)	P2 (p. 60), WB 3–4 (p. 35)
14–15	Word field: the house	Unit 3, P1 (p. 60)	WB 1 (p. 34)
16–18	Relative clauses	Unit 3, (pp. 55–56), GF 4–5 (pp. 142–143)	P4–7 (pp. 61–62), WB 5–8 (pp. 36–38)

Growing up in Canada

1 Canada

a) *What do you know about Canada?*

b) *What do the charts and the two big photos tell you about Canada?*
Canada is much bigger than Germany. But Germany has ...

	size	population
Canada	9,984,670 sq km	32,834,000
Germany	357,092 sq km	82,310,000

	snow	coldest month	hottest month
Toronto	Nov – Mar	Feb *(–4 °C)*	July *(22 °C)*
Inuvik	Sep – May	Feb *(–24 °C)*	July *(19 °C)*
Berlin	Dec – Feb	Jan *(2 °C)*	June *(23 °C)*

2 Growing up in Canada

a) *How do Canadian kids spend their free time? Fill in the chart below.*

b) *Tell the class about your chart.*

What Canadian kids do	same as German	different from German
they go on dates	✓	
they go to films		
...		

▸ P 1 (p. 76) • WB 1 (p. 46)

All about ... parents and teenagers

1 Different points of view

Which of these statements do you agree with? Which do you think are wrong? Why?

My mom always tells me to turn the music down – that's not fair! My friends all listen to loud music. Rap and hip hop have to be loud!

I like rap and hip hop too – the lyrics are exciting and rappers sing about what's important to me.

I'm lucky, my parents are easy-going – they even like my music. But they're strict about what I spend my pocket money on! My dad always says that I waste money on the latest fashions and the newest cellphones, just because my friends have them.

Adults just don't understand. You can't wear last year's clothes or use an old-fashioned cellphone. Your friends would laugh at you.

My parents don't let me colour my hair! And they always say that I waste so much time. But I'm not the only one who chats or plays computer games for hours. It's what kids do!

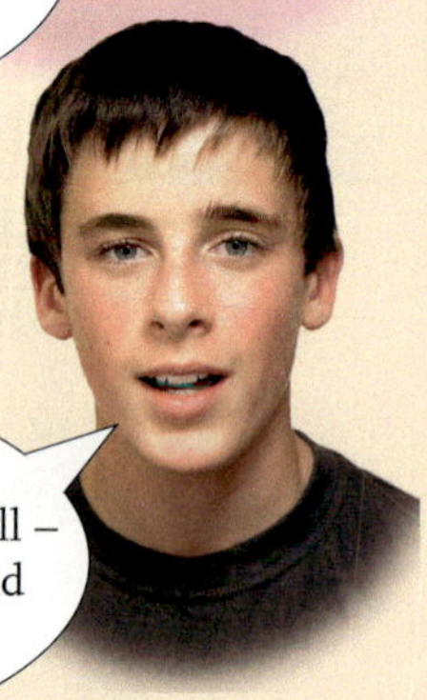

I agree. Sometimes I just want to hang out. My days are so full – school, then judo, hockey and my DJing. After that I just have to relax!

▸ *P 2 (p. 76)* • *WB 2–3 (p. 47)*

2 Now you

a) *What things do adults say to you and your friends that make you angry? Make notes.*

b) *Choose two of the ideas from a). Write two dialogues like the ones on the right between an adult and a teenager. In one dialogue they just argue. In the other dialogue the two find a compromise.*

c) *Act out your dialogues for the class.*

Adult	You always waste so much time!
You	What are you talking about?
Adult	Well, you just sit in front of your computer all day and do nothing.
You	...

Adult	Turn the music down!
You	But it's a really good song!
Adult	But it's too loud!
You	I'll close the door, OK?
Adult	Thank you.

▸ *P 3 (p. 76)*

3 My mom is so strict

Jessica My mom is so strict! I had to clean my room after school yesterday, so I didn't have time to go to the mall. Now I'll have to wait till tomorrow to get Ashley's birthday present.

Jordan What are you going to get her?

Jessica Don't know. Maybe a CD. – Hey, are you all going to be at Ashley's party on Saturday?

Emily I haven't asked my parents yet, but I'm sure I won't be allowed to go.

Robert You're never allowed to go anywhere, Emily!

Jessica Well, I'll be there, but I'll probably have to be home by ten.

Robert Ten? Your parents are even worse than mine. At least I'm allowed to stay out till 11 if there's no school the next day.

Jordan So you're going to be at the party?

Robert No, we're going to drive up to our cabin for the long weekend.

Jessica Right after school on Friday?

Robert No, I'm going to DJ at the centre on Friday, so we won't be able to go till Saturday morning.

Jordan Oh look, here comes Sam.

Sam Hi, guys. Hey Robert, I have to talk to you.

> *Who won't be at the party? Why not?*

4 Are you allowed to ...?

a) *Write down three things you're allowed to do and three things you aren't allowed to do.*

b) *Draw a window like the one below. Talk to your partner and fill in the window.*

A: I'm allowed to watch TV till 10 o'clock. What about you?

B: I'm not allowed to do that. But I'm allowed to sleep till 11 on Saturdays. What about you?

	My partner is allowed to ...	My partner isn't allowed to ...
I'm allowed to ...	My partner and I are allowed to ...	I'm allowed to ..., but my partner isn't.
I'm not allowed to ...	I'm not allowed to ..., but my partner is.	My partner and I aren't allowed to ...

c) *Report to the class.*

I'm allowed to watch TV till 10 o'clock, but Marcel isn't. He's allowed to ...

► *GF 6 Modal substitutes (pp. 144–145) • P 4–7 (pp. 77–78) • WB 4–7 (pp. 48–49)*

5 Extra Dragon boats

a) *Listen. What does Sam invite Robert to do?*

b) *Read the questions below. Then listen again and answer them.*

1. What is a dragon boat?
2. How many people are there in a dragon boat crew?
3. How many people race dragon boats in Toronto?
4. What does Robert's mum say?
5. What does Robert decide?

► *SF Listening for detail (p. 129)*

6 A school discussion – Part 1

In 1999 the Canadian province of Ontario stopped the traditional spring bear hunt. People wanted to protect the bears. Now a lot of people want to bring back the spring bear hunt.

Some students at Robert's school are having a discussion in one of their lessons.

Sam I think we need the bear hunt. There are too many bears and not enough land.

Jessica That's a good point. We have to protect ourselves.

Emily Sorry, I don't agree. You can protect yourself from a bear without the hunt!

Robert That's true. And another point: the bears were here first, not us.

Jessica Maybe, but there've been lots of bear attacks in the last few years. The bears aren't afraid of us any more.

Sam Exactly. And did you know – there's this town in the north where people can't go out because there are bears in the streets.

Robert Sure, but that's not a very good argument. They can only blame themselves! They built their dump in an area where there are lots of bears.

> *Who is for the bear hunt? Who is against it?*
Sam is ... because he says ...

7 A school discussion – Part 2

a) *Look at the discussion in 6. Copy the chart below and write down the phrases the students use to make a new point, to agree and to disagree.*

make a new point	agree	disagree
I think	That's a good point.	...

b) *Continue the dialogue with these arguments. Use phrases from a) to link the arguments.*

1 ... I don't want to find myself on a bear's menu just because it's hungry.

2 ... A bear just wants to feed itself and its babies.

3 ... And hunters often kill mother bears and then their young die.

4 ... It's better to kill the bears before they kill us!

c) *Read your dialogue to the class.*

d) **Extra** *Which arguments from 6 and 7 do you find the most convincing? Why?*

Looking at language

*Complete a copy of the chart below with words from **6** and **7**:*

	-self	-selves	
I	myself	we	
you		you	yourselves
he	himself	they	
she	herself		
it			

► GF 7: Reflexive pronouns (p. 145) • P 8–10 (pp. 78–79) • WB 8–11 (pp. 49–51) • **Text File 9** (p. 117)

8 Robert 'DJ Bobby' Smith

'How do you feel?' the leader of the youth group asked Robert. The hall at the community centre was full for the junior disco.

'A bit nervous,' Robert answered.

'It's time,' said the youth leader and went to the microphone.

'Welcome to our holiday weekend disco. We've got three young DJs tonight. All three have taught themselves to DJ. And maybe they'll learn a thing or two from each other tonight.

'Our first DJ is somebody you all know: it's Robert 'DJ Bobby' Smith.'

Robert jumped onto the little stage.

'Hi, everybody. I'd like to start with a mix of all your favourite Canadian pop stars. First, Avril Lavigne with one of her first big hits, ...'

▸ *GF 8: each other (p. 146) • P 11 (p. 79) • WB 12 (p. 51)*

9 SONG Sk8er boi

Sk8er boi *by Avril Lavigne*

He was a boy, she was a girl
Can I make it any more obvious?
He was a punk, she did ballet
What more can I say?
He wanted her, she'd never tell
secretly she wanted him as well.
But all of her friends stuck up their nose
they had a problem with his baggy clothes.

(Chorus)
He was a sk8er boi, she said see ya later boy
he wasn't good enough for her,
she had a pretty face but her head was up in space,
she needed to come back down to earth.

a) *What does the girl in the song think about Sk8er boi? What do you think about the girl/Sk8er boi?*

b) *Listen. What happens five years later?*

▸ *P 12–13 (pp. 79–80) • WB 13–17 (pp. 52–54)*

10 Extra Now you

a) *Prepare a DJ's introduction to your favourite song. What kind of music is it? What do you know about the singer/band? Why do you like the song? Make notes.*

b) *Bring your song to class and use your notes to introduce it. The phrases below can help you.*

This song is rap/hip hop/techno/pop/... •
a(n) nice/happy/angry/... sound •
I always think of ... when I hear this song. •
The group/singer is from Canada/... •
great lyrics

Extra Background File CANADA

	Canada	Germany
Head of state	British King or Queen	President
Capital	Ottawa	Berlin
Biggest city	Toronto (2,481,494)	Berlin (3,399,511)
Official language	English and French	German

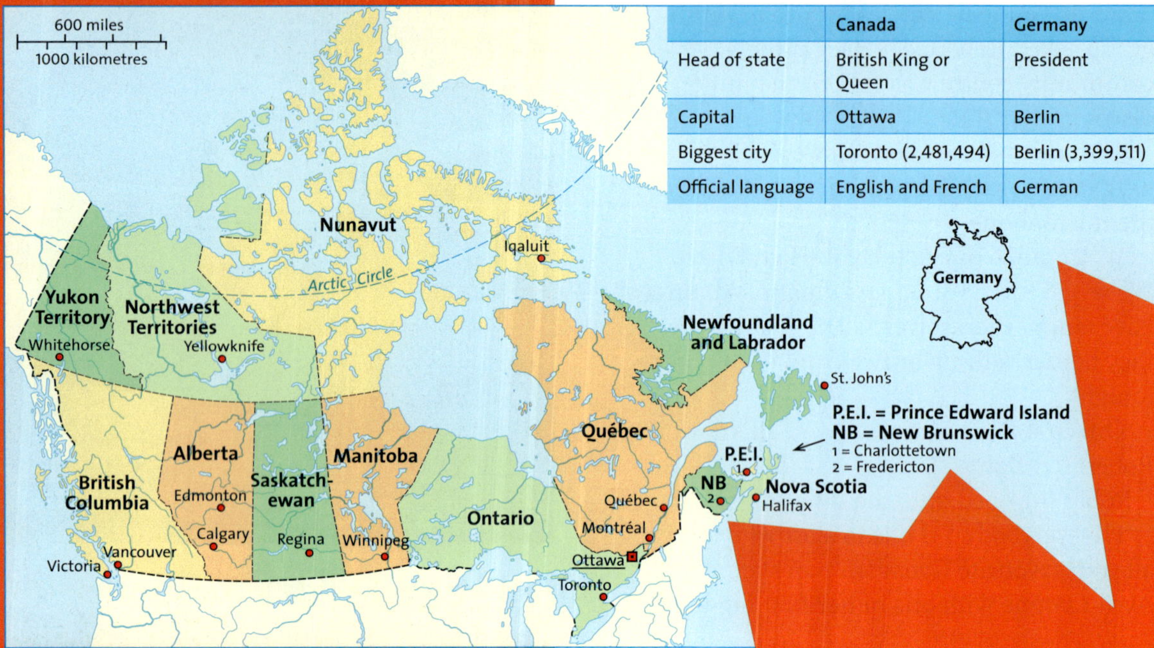

Canadian settlers

The Vikings were the first Europeans in what we now call Canada. They arrived around the year 1000.

In 1497 John Cabot left Bristol, crossed the Atlantic and landed in Newfoundland, part of north-east Canada.

In the 16th century the first French settlers in Canada lived near a mountain that they called *Mont Réal*. Canada became a French colony, New France. But in 1763 France lost Canada to the British.

Today people in the province of Quebec still speak French and *Mont Réal* has become Montreal, Canada's second biggest city.

Immigration to Canada

Today Canada is an independent country. Just over 50% of people there have British or French roots. But just under 50% have roots in other countries all over the world. So today Canada really is a multi-cultural place.

Aboriginals of Canada

Aboriginals like the Inuit and the 'First Nations' (Indians) have lived in Canada for thousands of years. Now only about 4.4 % of Canadians are Aboriginals.

The Aboriginals have tried to get their traditional lands back. In 1999 the Inuit finally got a large part of Northern Canada back: Nunavut – 'Our land' in their language. Today 30,000 people live in Nunavut – which is as big as Western Europe.

Many First Nations live on reserves all across Canada.

Canadian Sports

Canadian First Nations played the game of **lacrosse** first, hundreds of years ago. Today it's Canada's national summer sport.

The players have to get a small ball into a goal with the crosse – a stick with a net.

People all over North America and in England play this very fast team sport.

Ice hockey is Canada's national winter sport – the Canadians just call it 'hockey'. Toronto's team – the *Maple Leafs* – is one of the best teams in the country.

In the long winters, lots of people play hockey outside.

1 Now you

a) *What do you find most interesting on these two pages? Why?*

I thought it was interesting that ...

I thought Canada was ...

I didn't know Canada was ...

b) *Choose one section and write a text like it about Germany. You can add pictures. Put it in your DOSSIER.*

► WB 18 (p. 55)

1 WORDS Numbers

a) *Partner B: Go to p. 105.*
Partner A: Read out these numbers to your partner:

17 • 5 • 76 • 104 • 1,516 • 15,243 • 100,000

Then write down the numbers that your partner reads out to you. Swap papers and check.

b) *Fill in the gaps in the sentences on the right with words and phrases from the box.*

degrees • million • ten-kilometre walk • twenty +per cent (20 %) • +90-kilogram bear • six point seven (6.7) • +thirteen-year-olds • +200 km per hour (kph)

1 The population of Canada is almost 33 ...
2 A fast car can go ...
3 He was tired when he got home from his ...
4 I hope I don't meet a ... in the woods!
5 In the summer it can be almost 40 ... in Toronto.
6 Most ... are very untidy.
7 French is the first language for ... million Canadians. That's about ... of the population.

2 WORDS Parents and teenagers

a) *Find the opposites in the box on the right.*

cool • easy-going • fair • +intolerant • nervous • old-fashioned • +relaxed • strict • +tolerant • trendy • uncool • unfair

b) *What kind of things do parents say? What do teenagers say? Look at the speech bubbles and make two lists.*

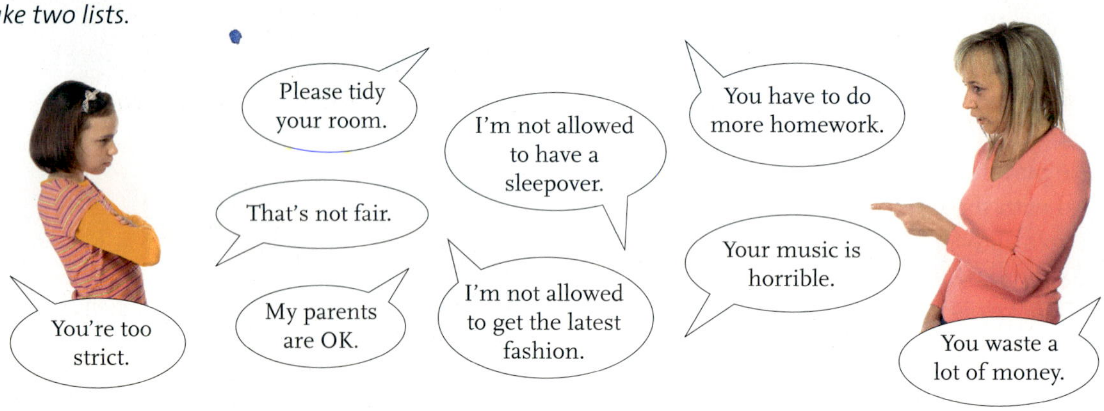

3 REVISION Canada (Relative clauses)

Make sentences with **who** *or* **that**.

1 Canada is a country	who / that	about 300,000 Germans visit every year.
2 Snowshoeing is something		lots of Canadians do in winter.
3 Avril Lavigne is a singer		was born in Canada.
4 Hockey is a sport		lots of Canadians play.
5 The black bear is one of the many wild animals		you can see in the Canadian woods.
6 French Canadians are people		live in Canada and speak French.
7 Rappers are artists		lots of Canadian teenagers like.

4 School rules (*have to* and *be allowed to*)

a) *Make sentences about some of the rules at Robert's school.*

– arrive in time for lessons
– turn off cellphones in the classroom
– look after their books
– do their homework every day

– wear caps or jackets in class
– cycle or skate in the school building
– smoke in the school yard or building
– bring guns or knives

Students have to arrive in time for lessons.

They aren't allowed to ...

b) **Extra** *Are the rules at Robert's school good rules?*

5 Robert wasn't able to ... (*be able to* and *be allowed to*)

a) *Make sentences about Robert. Use the information in the charts.*

be able to	*5 years ago*	*in 5 years*
– speak French	–	+
– ride a bike	+	+
– climb through small windows	+	–

be allowed to	*5 years ago*	*in 5 years*
– stay out late	–	+
– go to nightclubs	–	+
– go on holiday alone	–	+

Five years ago Robert wasn't able to speak French.
In five years he'll be able to speak French

Five years ago Robert wasn't allowed to ...

b) *Make sentences about yourself like the sentences in a). Compare them with a partner's.*

6 Crazy School 2050 (Modal substitutes)

a) *Some of Robert's friends have planned a crazy school for the year 2050. Complete the sentences on the right to describe their school.*

b) **Extra** *Plan your own crazy school of the future. Write at least three sentences to describe it: one with '(not) be allowed to', one with '(not) be able to' and one with '(not) have to'.*

(not) be allowed to

1. Students *will be allowed to skate* (skate) through the school.
2. Teachers *won't be* ... (not/start) lessons before the students say it's OK.
3. Students ... (eat) in class.
4. Teachers ... (not/give) students homework.

(not) be able to

5. Students ... (take) lessons in lots of things – riding, cars, how you can become a star, ...
6. Teachers ... (not/teach) before 10 o'clock because there won't be any students.

(not) have to

7. Teachers ... (wear) school uniforms.
8. Students ... (bring) their cellphones to school.
9. Students ... (not/listen) to their teachers.

7 MEDIATION At the cabin

a) Do you remember how you can paraphrase a word? Use phrases like the ones in the box on the right. Now write explanations for these words:

park • rucksack • salmon • tourist

It's somebody/a person who ...
an animal / a place that ...
something that you use to ...

b) Lisa and her mother are staying at a cabin. How can Lisa explain 'Gasflasche' in the situation below?

Frau Kraft Ich glaube, man braucht hier Gasflaschen zum Kochen. Frag mal, wo wir hier welche kriegen können.

Lisa Ich probier's. – Excuse me, we're looking for ... Sorry, I don't know the word in English ... it's ...

c) Listen and go on with the rest of the dialogue. Take Lisa's role.

STUDY SKILLS Mediation

If you don't know an important English word, try to paraphrase it.

► *SF Mediation (p. 133)*

8 Mum and Dad are on strike (Reflexive pronouns)

Complete the sentences with the reflexive pronouns **myself**, **yourself**, **himself**, **herself**, **ourselves**, **yourselves**, **themselves**.

1. Mr and Mrs Jones are on strike, so the children have to cook for *themselves*.
2. Mr Jones usually looks after Jill in the afternoon, but today she has to look after ...
3. Mrs Jones usually teaches Jack the guitar, but he knows: 'Today I'll have to teach ... .'
4. Jack usually talks to his mum and dad, but today he has to talk to ...
5. Jill's mum usually puts her to bed, but today she told her: 'You'll have to put ... to bed tonight.'
6. Mr and Mrs Jones usually shop for the children, but today Jack told Jill: 'Mum and Dad are on strike, so we have to shop for ...'
7. 'Why are you on strike?' the children ask them. But they only answer: 'Don't ask us. Ask ...!'

9 A not-so-lucky day (Reflexive pronouns)

Decide if you need a reflexive pronoun or not. You can look at the blue box on p. 168 for help.

Today has been an awful day. My friends and I wanted to meet ... after breakfast. But when I went to clean ... my teeth, there was no water. 'That's OK,' I said to ..., 'I can get water in the kitchen.' But then I remembered ... that there was a sign in the street about a water problem. So I got ... dressed and went to buy some water. I felt ... dirty and I was afraid that somebody would see me. So I walked quickly back home. But when I put the key in the door, it didn't open ...! 'What can I do?' I wondered ... . Then I remembered ... that my bedroom window doesn't close. I was able to pull ... up to it, but it was so small that I wasn't able to get in! I was just moving ... back out when a policeman came. Now I'm at the police station. Oh well, I can only blame ... for that!

10 LISTENING Kahasi and the loon (an Inuit hunting story)

a) *Before you listen, read the questions.*

1. Where did Kahasi live? What did he do every day?
2. What did the other boys do every day?
3. What did the loon say to Kahasi?
4. How did Kahasi find the walruses?
5. What happened then?

b) *Listen and take notes.*

c) *Listen again. Check your answers with a partner.*

d) **Extra** *Write/Tell the story in the simple past. Your notes will help you.*

Inuit blanket

loon

walrus

11 Are they looking at themselves or each other? (each other/themselves)

Partner B: Go to p. 105. Partner A: Look at the pictures. You and your partner have the same pictures, but in a different order. Talk to your partner about your pictures. Take turns.

1 look at

2 take photos of

3 think of

4 teach

5 think of

6 look at

7 take photos of

8 teach

A: In my picture 1 a boy and a girl are looking at themselves.
B: Oh, a boy and a girl are looking at themselves in my picture 6. In my picture 1 two girls are ...

12 EVERYDAY ENGLISH Talking about music

a) *Listen to the three songs by Canadian bands. What do you think of them? How do they sound? Who would like them?*

I think the first / ... song is ...
The music sounds ...
It's the kind of music that parents / ... like.

awful • boring • exciting • great • happy • fantastic • new • nice • old-fashioned • sad • strange • ...

b) *In groups of three, talk about the three songs. Take turns to start.*

I think ...
I don't agree.
You're right.
That's true.

c) *Report to the class. Which song does your group like best? Why?*

13 WRITING Telling a story (The steps of writing)

Read the beginning of a story.

It was a warm and sunny Sunday in June. Jessica and Emily were walking through High Park in the centre of Toronto.

'Wow!' said Jessica. 'Look at all those boats on the lake. What about a boat trip?'

'Actually,' Emily answered, 'I'd like to go to the swimming pool.'

Suddenly they heard a voice behind them. The two girls turned around and saw a boy, about 14 years old. He was wearing strange clothes and he looked a bit sad. 'Excuse me,' he said, 'but where is this place?'

'High Park,' Jessica answered.

It was clear that the boy didn't know where High Park was.

'High Park ... Toronto ... Ontario ... Canada,' Emily explained.

When he heard this, the boy looked very surprised.

What happens next? Who is the boy? Why is he in Toronto? Write the rest of the story in three steps:

1 Before you write: brainstorm ideas

You can ...
- write a list
- make a mind map

from another planet
looking for his parents
Jessica and Emily help him

STUDY SKILLS Brainstorming

You brainstorm a topic in two steps:
1 Write down all your ideas just as they come into your head – even the silly ones.
2 Look at your ideas. Choose the good ones and structure them.

► SF Brainstorming (p. 135)

2 Write

- Use adverbs and adjectives to make sentences interesting.
- Use relative clauses to make better sentences.
- Use time phrases and linking words to make things clearer.
- Start a new paragraph for each new idea.
- Find an interesting or funny way to finish your story. Give the story a title.

He looked at them shyly with his big, brown eyes.

We'll find somebody who can help you.

a bit later • after that • early in the morning • because • so • although

► Writing course 1: Writing better sentences (p. 22) • Writing course 2: Using paragraphs (p. 39)

3 Check and revise

Read your story and check it:
- Is your story clear?
- Do you need more details?
- Check the spelling, verb forms, ...

Then correct your text.

Two bear attacks

Read the articles and answer the questions.

Woman dies after bear attack

SEPTEMBER 12, 2007

An Ontario woman died and her husband was hurt after a bear attack at Missinaibi Lake on Saturday. Different groups are again asking parliament to bring back the spring bear hunt. Without the hunt, they say, bears are not afraid of people and see us as 'food'.

The attack happened late on Saturday afternoon. The victims were camping at the lake, about 80 km north of Chapleau, Ont. Police gave their names as Sarah Bennett, 31, and Marc Bennett, 30. Mrs. Bennett was a doctor.

"The bear attacked very suddenly," policewoman Sandra Farell said. "While it was attacking the woman, her husband fought it with a knife, but he wasn't able to save her. The bear escaped into the forest."

Dog saves man from bear

JULY 22, 2006

A man killed a black bear with a 15-cm hunting knife yesterday. The man said the bear saw him as 'lunch' and attacked him and his dog while he was canoeing in north Ontario.

Tom Tilley, a 55-year-old from Waterloo, Ont., said his dog Sam warned him, then ran to protect him when the bear came towards them in the woods north of Wawa. As Sam fought the 90-kg bear, Tilley jumped on it and killed it with his knife. Doctors say Tilley and his dog will be fine.

Hero dog Sam

Working with the text

1 Right or wrong?

Correct the wrong statements.

1. The attacks happened in Toronto.
2. A doctor and his wife died in a bear attack.
3. Tom Tilley and his dog saved each other.
4. Some people think the bears aren't afraid of people any more.
5. The bears died in both attacks.

2 The five Ws

Make a chart with the five Ws (who, what, when, where, why) for each of the articles.

3 Extra An interview

Imagine one of you is a reporter, the other Tom Tilley. The reporter interviews Tom about his canoe trip and the attack.

A fishing trip

Look at the pictures. Who are the people in them? Try and guess the right order of the pictures. Then listen and check.

A

B

C

D

E

F

Working with the text

1 Right or wrong?

Listen again and correct the wrong statements.

1 Robert saw a bear and told his father about it.
2 Mr Smith paddled through the rapids right after Robert.
3 Mr Smith hurt his foot badly.
4 Mr Smith had a plan to escape from the bear.
5 The bear ate the fish Mr Smith threw at it.
6 The bear ran away when it saw Robert's knife.

2 Extra A newspaper report

Agree on six or seven key facts about Robert and his dad's fishing trip. Then write a newspaper report (80–100 words) like the ones on p. 81. You can start like this:

A father and son from Toronto ...
over the holiday weekend. ...

► **Text File 10** *(pp. 118–119)* • *WB 19 (p. 56)* • **Checkpoint 4** *WB (p. 57)* • **Selbsteinschätzung 3–4** *WB (pp. 60–61)*

How am I doing?

a) *Fill in or choose the correct answers.*

Canada

1 Canada is much ... than Germany, but it doesn't have ... people.
2 Many Canadians enjoy outdoor activities like ..., ... or ...
3 Two important cities in Canada are ... and ...
4 Toronto is in the Canadian ... of Ontario.

Words

5 6.7 million Canadians speak French – that's about 20 ... of the population.
A million B point C per cent D kilograms
6 I can stay out late. My parents are very ...
A strict. B easy-going. C nervous. D uncool.
7 Why are you so nervous? Try to be more ...
A fair. B relaxed. C excited. D trendy.
8 I think you've got a good ... but I don't want to talk about it any more.
A bridge B line C point D result
9 My sister made a mistake, but I don't ... her for it.
A be angry with B have to C fight D blame
10 Do you know how you can protect yourself ... bears?
A from B about C for D over
11 I love that song. The music is good, but what I really like are the ...
A units. B lyrics. C books. D pages.

Writing

12 You can write a story in three steps: ... ideas, ... the text and finally check and ... it.
13 You can write down your ideas from brainstorming in a ... or in a ...
14 Your sentences often sound more interesting if you use ... and ...

Grammar

15 I ... go to the disco because my parents think I'm too young.
A have to B don't have to C am allowed to D am not allowed to
16 I can't swim, but I'm sure I'll ... swim after a few lessons.
A can B be allowed to C be able to D can't
17 If you want to travel, you'll ... work hard and make lots of money.
A must B have to C had to D needn't
18 I thought John was talking to ... but he was actually speaking on his mobile.
19 Which is the correct sentence:
A Robert felt proud when people liked his DJing.
20 B Robert felt himself proud when people liked his DJing.
21 A better way to say 'Robert took a photo of Sam and Sam took a photo of Robert' is 'Sam and Robert took photos of ...'

b) *Check your answers on p. 227 and add up your points – one point for each correct answer.*

c) *If you had 20 or more points, well done! Maybe you can help students who had fewer points. If you had 16 points or fewer, it's a good idea to do some more work before you go on to the next unit. Where did you make mistakes? The chart below will tell you what you can do to improve your English.*

No.	Area	Find out more	Exercise(s)
1– 4	Canada facts	Unit 4 (pp. 68–75)	WB 1, 16, 18 (pp. 46, 54, 55)
5–11	Words	Unit 4 (pp. 70+72), P1 (p. 76)	P1 (p. 76), WB 1b, 2, 14, 17 (pp. 46, 47, 52, 54)
12–14	Writing	Unit 4 P13 (p. 80)	P13 (p. 80), WB 15 (p. 53)
15–17	Modal substitutes	Unit 4 (p. 71), GF 6 (pp. 144–145)	P4–6 (p. 77), WB 4–5 (p. 48)
18–20	Reflexive pronouns	GF 7–8 (pp. 145–146)	P8–9 (p. 78), P11 (p. 79), WB 8–10 (p. 49–50)

1 STUDY SKILLS Understanding new words ▸ *SF Understanding new words (p. 124)*

If you read or hear a new word in a test, you can often guess the meaning.

What do the green words mean?

1. North Rhine-Westphalia and Saxony are two of Germany's 16 states.
2. Beer is a traditional German product. Almost every part of Germany produces beer.
3. It's important to pack glasses and other breakable goods carefully.
4. Coconuts grow on one kind of palm tree.
5. Greenpeace is an organization that tries to protect whales.
6. Recycling is easy: just take your old glass to the bottle bank.
7. It was a terrible storm. Almost everybody on the ship was seasick.
8. In this factory robots do all the work.

2 Spelling (Same sound, different words)

Different words sometimes sound the same. Be careful when you write them.

Fill in the missing words.

1. **hour, our** ['aʊə]
   The train was late. I waited for over an ...
   Is that ... train on platform 3?
2. **son, sun** [sʌn]
   The Browns have a ... and a daughter.
   They both wear hats when the ... shines.
3. **their, there** [ðeə]
   Who's ... ? – Oh, it's Malte and Hauke.
   They've got ... new bikes with them.
4. **know, no** [nəʊ]
   Do you ... our new teacher, Mrs Sprengel?
   ... , I haven't met her yet.
5. **hear, here** [hɪə]
   There are lots of birds ... in the forest.
   Can you ... the woodpecker?
6. **sea, see** [siː]
   We stayed in a caravan near the ...
   You could ... the beach from there.
7. **wear, where** [weə]
   ... is my new dress?
   I'd like to ... it to Matt's party.
8. **weak, week** [wiːk]
   Last ... the doctor told my grandma she had a ... heart.

3 Writing (The 5 Ws and how) ▸ *Writing Course 3: A report (p. 64)*

*In a test you might have to write a report. Remember to answer these questions: **who**, **what**, **when**, **where** and **why**. Often it's also important to say **how**.*

Put these phrases in the text. Which question does each phrase answer?

the whole family • we went by bus • on a Sunday • our visit to the zoo • it was my little sister's birthday • only three miles from our house •

A great day in the school holidays

The best thing about my school holidays was ... (1). We don't often go there, because it's so expensive. But ...(2), so Dad asked her where she wanted to go, and she chose the zoo. Dad said that ... (3) could go.
I couldn't wait, but at last the day came. We went ... (4) because Dad didn't have to go to work. I wanted to cycle because the zoo is ... (5), but Mum said it was too far, so ... (6).
It was great to see all the animals. We stayed all day and we enjoyed every minute.

1) our visit to the zoo = what
2) ...

4 Ashley's visit to Niagara Falls[1] (Word order)

Remember that English word order is often different from German word order. Choose the right place in the sentences for the words in brackets.

1 Ashley and her dad went ? to Niagara Falls ? . (last June)
Ashley and her dad went to Niagara Falls last June.
2 Their bus left Toronto at six am, so they had to ? get up ? . (very early)
3 And they almost missed the bus because Ashley ? her rucksack ? . (forgot)
4 She hurried back to the house ? the rucksack ? . (to get)
5 When they got to Niagara, ? they ? the amazing falling waters. (watched)
6 They had ? lunch at one of the many restaurants ? . (at 12.45)
7 Ashley's dad went ? after lunch ? . (to Victoria Park)
8 Everything was so interesting that Ashley wanted to stay ? there ? . (all weekend)

5 I've always dreamed of ... (Prepositions)

Complete the sentences with the correct prepositions.

1 I have always dreamed ... a holiday in Canada. (from/of) of
2 There's something special ... Toronto – it's a fantastic city. (about/on)
3 I was really interested ... the railway museum. (in/on)
4 All the information was ... English. (in/of)
5 I had to translate it ... German. (in/into)
6 We listened to the weather report ... the radio. (in/on)
7 There wasn't a cloud ... the sky. (in/on)
8 There were lots of cars ... the city centre. (in/on)
9 Our friends had warned us ... the traffic. (about/for)
10 It was quicker to go ... foot than to go ... car. (on/to, by/with)
11 I was tired, so I slept ... the train. (in/on)
12 We left early ... the morning and arrived late ... night. (in/on, at/in)

6 If we go to Toronto ... (Conditional sentences I and II)

a) *You're on holiday in Canada. You're planning a day trip to Toronto with a friend. Complete the conditional sentences (type I).*

1 If we go to Toronto, we ... lots of information. (need)
... we'll need ...
2 If we leave early, we ... more time in Toronto. (have)
3 We won't be able to explore the city if we ... a good map. (not have)
4 If we take sandwiches with us, we ... them in a park. (can eat)
5 If it rains while we're there, we ... something inside. (have to do)
6 If we check on the internet, we ... when the museums open. (know)

b) *Your mother thinks it would be better if you went to Ottawa. You don't agree. Complete the conditional sentences (type II).*

1 If we went to Ottawa, the journey ... much longer. (take)
... would take ...
2 If you left early enough, you ... lots of time. (have)
3 And if you ... at a youth hostel, you could have a second day in Ottawa. (stay)
4 If we spent the night in Ottawa, the trip ... more. (cost)
5 If you ... to Ottawa, you'd see the parliament building. (go)
6 I wouldn't be upset if we ... the Canadian parliament. (not see)

► WB (pp. 58–59)

[1] Niagara Falls [naɪˌægrə ˈfɔːlz]

1 Listening

A visit to Green Gables

Michael, a student, is working as a tour guide[1] on Prince Edward Island, Canada, during the summer. He's taking a tour group to the farmhouse Green Gables today.

Part 1:
The journey to Green Gables

Listen. Choose the correct answer for each question.

1 Lucy Maud Montgomery[2] ...
- A is a singer at a festival.
- B wrote books for children.
- C helped a young girl without parents.

2 Anne of Green Gables ...
- A is the hero of a successful children's book.
- B is a Canadian writer.
- C comes from Ottawa.

3 Linda ...
- A is a girl who has lost her parents.
- B works as a bus tour guide.
- C knows a lot about Anne of Green Gables.

4 Green Gables is ...
- A the house where Linda lives.
- B a place for children without parents.
- C a farmhouse with a link to a famous book.

[1] tour guide [gaɪd] *Reiseleiter*
[2] Maud Montgomery [ˌmɔːd mənt'gʌmari]

Part 2:
Lucy Maud Montgomery

a) *Read all the questions. Then listen and take notes about the dates and numbers you hear. Choose the correct answer for each question.*

1 Lucy Maud Montgomery was born in ...
- A 1847.
- B 1874.
- C 1908.

2 You can read Montgomery's books in ...
- A more than 50 languages.
- B more than 3 languages.
- C more than 12 languages.

3 Every year 'Green Gables' has ...
- A 200,000 visitors.
- B 2,200 visitors.
- C 6,000 visitors.

b) *Are these statements true or false? Give a reason for your answer.*

1 'Montgomery left Prince Edward Island because she hated it.'

2 'Montgomery's books are important for people who have never been to Canada.'

I think statement 1 is true/false because ...

2 Reading

Partner B: Go to page 105.
Partner A: Read about St. Jacobs, a village near Toronto. Then answer the questions below.

The Mennonite[1] Story
Mennonites are a religious group that came from Europe to America to be free. Since 1800 they have lived on farms around St. Jacobs. What do they believe? Why do many of them use horses, not cars? At the Visitor Centre you can learn about Mennonite history and culture. See the 13-minute DVD presentation, lots of photos and other documents. **$3 per person**

Discover St. Jacobs
Explore St. Jacobs on foot with our new walking-tour brochure. On sale at the Visitor Centre: **$2**

The Model Railway
See Waterloo County in miniature. Watch the old trains as they go past farms, a Mennonite Meeting House and the village of St. Jacobs.

1 You can buy a $2 brochure about ...
- A how to see St. Jacobs on foot.
- B Mennonite history.
- C railway history in Ontario.

2 Mennonites came to America because ...
- A there weren't enough horses in Europe.
- B they wanted to live in the St. Jacobs area.
- C they weren't free in Europe.

3 At the Visitor Centre you can learn about ...
- A how to drive a car.
- B the history of one of America's religious groups.
- C model trains.

3 Speaking

Partner A and Partner B: You're planning a day trip to St. Jacobs. Read the instructions below. You can make notes to help you with your dialogue. Then act out the dialogue.

Partner A	Partner B
Say you'd like to go to The Mennonite Story. →	Ask what that is.
Answer. Say when and why Mennonites came to America. →	Tell your partner about the Mennonites and the Farmers' Market.
Say why you'd like to visit the market. →	Describe the Mennonite Farm Tour.
Say you'd like to stay in the village. Tell your partner about the walking tour brochure. →	Ask what your partner wants to see in the village.
Tell your partner about the model railway. →	Say it's enough to do two or three things.
Agree. Say what you want to do and why. →	Agree or disagree with your partner's ideas.

4 Writing

Imagine you visited St. Jacobs yesterday. Write a report about your visit (about 90 words). Remember the 5 Ws.

[1] Mennonite ['mendnaɪt]

A teen magazine

Harbourfront centre

Harbourfront Community Centre · Toronto · Youth Group

The Harbourfront Community Centre Youth Group announces its latest project:

a **TEEN MAGAZINE**!

What will be in it?

THAT'S UP TO YOU!

So far our magazine has the following sections and editors:

sports
Editor:
Samantha Kowalski

music
Editor:
Robert Smith

movies
Editor:
Mitsu Nagora

fashion
Editor:
Nathalie L'Estane

Look at the poster. Describe the youth group's latest project.
Explain the difference between a magazine and an e-zine.

1 Now you

What teen magazines and e-zines do you know? What are they about? How often do you read them? Which sections (fashion, music, problem pages ...) do you like best?

Who will produce this magazine?

YOU WILL!

Everybody who's interested can send an article. If it's good, we'll publish it! Send your articles (with photos or drawings) to the editors. If you want to start a new section, contact Brandon at the centre offices.

What's next?

If the magazine is a success, we'd like to do an e-zine (an **e**lectronic maga**zine** that you can read on the centre's website). The e-zine will have more photos – plus sound files, videos and lots of links to other websites.

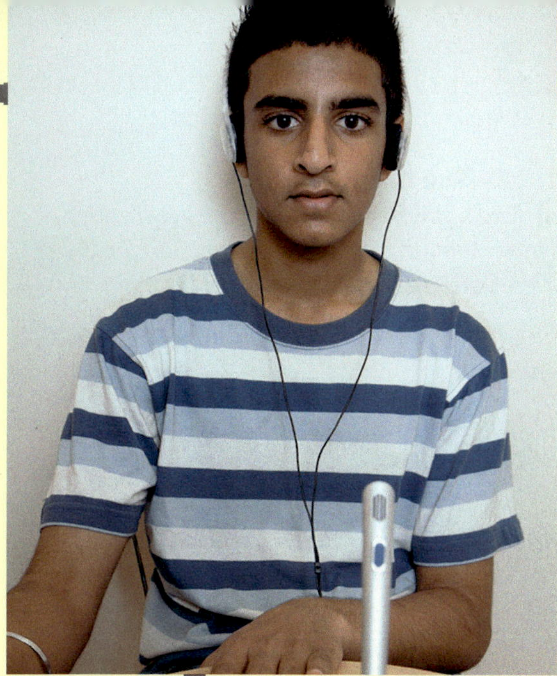

2 The photos

a) *Describe the photos. The words below will help you.*

headphones • microphone • monitor • webcam

– In the photo at the top of p. 88, Robert is ...

b) **Extra** *What do you remember about the people in the photos? Collect ideas in the chart.*

name	lives in	hobbies

► SF Describing pictures (p. 128)

3 A video chat

a) *Read the questions, then listen to the CD.*

1 Who asked for the video chat? Why?
2 Who comes later than the others? Why?
3 How do Robert's friends feel about his idea?
4 What kinds of articles does Robert want?

b) *Listen again. What ideas for articles do the four have? Take notes.*

c) *What do you think each of the four will do for the magazine? Write your ideas in your exercise book.*

► P 1–2 (p. 93) • WB 1–2 (p. 62)

1 The music section

a) *Find out what Robert and the others have written about. Skim the music section (pp. 90–92). Were your ideas on p. 89 right or wrong?*

b) **Extra** *Does anything surprise you? What and why?*

STUDY SKILLS | Skimming

Skimming is useful when you want to find the main ideas of a long text quickly.
- Don't read the text word for word.
- Look first at the title, the words in bold print, pictures and their captions.

▸ *SF Skimming (p. 131) • P 3 (p. 94) • WB 3 (p. 63)*

MUSIC Editor: Robert Smith

A day without music

by Latisha Byrd

My day usually starts and ends with music. I think a day without music would be very strange.

When I wake up in the morning the first thing I do is turn on my radio – a pop station, of course. Then I take the radio with me to the bathroom. And I bring it back with me so that I can listen to music while I get dressed.

When I go down to breakfast Mum has already got the radio on – her kind of music, not mine, but that's OK. It's music!

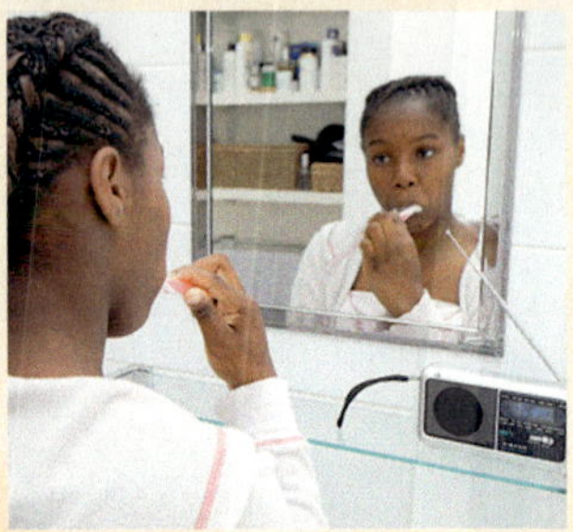

After breakfast I clean my teeth, get my school bag and put on my MP3 player. Then it's my music all the way to school.

If there was a day without music I would have to have a shower and get dressed in silence. Breakfast would be very quiet. And the journey to school would be quiet – and really boring.

In the afternoon I would have to do my homework in silence – terrible! Jazz dance lessons without music – impossible! Oh, and no steel drums. And in the evening – how would I relax without music?

So a day without music would be terrible!

> *When does Latisha listen to music?*

2 Now you

a) *Look at Latisha's text again. Collect words and phrases she uses to describe her day.*

When I wake up ...

b) *When do you listen to music? Write two or three sentences.*

A riddle

by Katrina McFadden

I'm a musical instrument.

I was born far, far away in Iran, over two thousand years ago. From there I travelled all over Europe, but you probably know me best as an instrument from one part of Great Britain.

I look very interesting: my body is leather and lots of pipes stick out of me! You blow into one. The other ones let the air out.

How do you play me? Well, you have to be very clever to play me. First you have to blow air into me. I keep it in my body. Then you have to squeeze it out again – very carefully – through the pipes. That's what makes the music.

Can you guess what I am?

Mika – the story of a singer

by Asif Azad

Mika was born in Beirut, the capital of Lebanon, in 1983.

His dad was American, his mum Lebanese. When he was one, the family moved to Paris. Just nine years later they moved again – this time to London.

He had liked life in Paris. Now he found it hard to settle down in a new country. The only thing he really enjoyed was music. So his mum sent him to a Russian music teacher. She taught him to sing – everybody thought he was very good at it. By his twelfth birthday he had already sung in an opera at Covent Garden.

But he decided that classical music wasn't really his thing. When he was younger he had written his own songs, but until the age of 12 he hadn't planned to become a pop singer. After Covent Garden he began to write more songs and to record them too.

When he was 23, his first single – 'Relax, take it easy' – was sold out in two days. His next song went to number one in the UK in one week! **A real success story!**

3 Musical instruments

a) *What is the answer to Katrina's riddle?*

A recorder B bagpipes
C trumpet D flute

b) *What words does Katrina use to describe how you play the instrument?*

blow, ...

► GF 9: Past perfect (p. 147) • P 4–5 (p. 95) • WB 4–6 (pp. 63–64)

4 Mika's life

a) *Answer these questions:*

- In which country was Mika born?
- Where does he live now?

b) *Make a timeline for Mika.*

5 SONG Relax, take it easy

Do you think the singer is happy or sad? Why?

My 'School's out for summer' playlist

by Robert 'DJ Bobby' Smith

5 'School's out'

by Alice Cooper

This had to be on the list because it's the song you'll always hear on the radio just before summer vacation – and I think it's great. (Of course if we get an e-zine off the ground, this is where the sound link would be!)

4 'This love'

by Maroon 5

Do you have a crush on somebody? Then this is the song for you. And summer is the time!

3 'The sound of San Francisco'

by Global Deejays

Summer is the time to travel. This great mix takes you to London, Paris … and San Francisco. And if you can't go that far, at least you'll want to get up and dance!

2 'Summer in the city'

by The Lovin' Spoonful

Everybody thinks you have to be by a lake or the sea in the summer, but I don't agree. This is a great song for city people in the summer.

1 'Come on over'

by Shania Twain

Vacation is a time to hang out with friends – it's what I like best. And that's what this song is about. Plus Shania Twain is my number 1 Canadian singer.

6 Now you

Which of the four articles do you like best/least? Why? Make notes, then talk to your partner.

I like Katrina's article best because it's funny.
– Oh, I like hers least. My favourite article is Asif's, because I really like Mika.

► P 6 (p. 96) • WB 7–8 (pp. 65–66) • Text File 11 (pp. 120–123) • Checkpoint 5 WB (p. 67)

1 WORDS All about music

a) *Read the definitions and find the music words.*

1 group of people who sing together
2 a round instrument you hit to make music
3 a part of a song that you sing more than once
4 you can download music onto this machine
5 the words of a song
6 you can listen to CDs on this machine
7 a place where people dance to music
8 the people who listen to music at a concert

b) *Copy the music network below. Put in the words from a) and the words from the box. (If you know more music words, you can add them too.)*

+album • +bagpipes • +career • +musician • +opera • +record • +(to) record • +(to) release • +single • +track • +tune

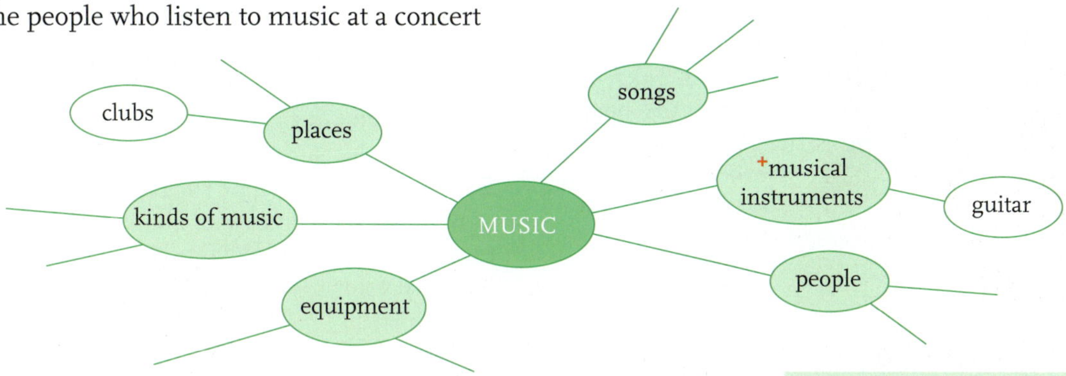

c) *Match the words and phrases in the blue box to one or more nouns in the green box. Write six sentences.*

1 Hassan has to rehearse for a gig next week.

buy tickets for • do • listen to • play a recording of • rehearse for • release • whistle

an album • a club • a disco • a festival • a gig • a musical • an open-air concert • a rehearsal • a show • a tune • my favourite track

2 LISTENING Numbers and spelling

a) *Listen to **part 1** on the CD. Write down the numbers. Compare with a partner. Listen again and check.*

b) *Listen to **part 2** on the CD. Write down the names. Compare with a partner. Listen again and check.*

c) **Extra** *Choose four names from this book. Write them down and dictate them to your partner. Check his/her results. Take turns.*

3 STUDY SKILLS Skimming

a) *Imagine you want to do a project on 'Robbie Williams – the singer'. Skim the two articles below to decide which will be more useful.*

Robbie Williams

Robbie Williams was born on 13 February, 1974, in Newcastle-under-Lyme in North Staffordshire, UK. He began his career with the band Take That, then left the band in 1995 for a solo career. He has sold more than 50 million albums and 15 million singles around the world.

Family

Williams grew up in Burslem, Stoke-on-Trent, Staffordshire. His parents are Catholic, but he does not see himself as a religious person.

He still sees his mother quite often and she has even been on stage with him at some of his concerts.
Williams isn't married, but he has had a few girlfriends, some of them famous.

Charity work

Robbie Williams loves giving, so in June 2000 he started the charity 'Give it sum' because he wanted to give something back to his hometown. 'Give it sum' has given over 2 million pounds to projects there. He said: 'I'm glad that the little help that I give can do great things.'
With the help of his friend Jonathan Wilkes he also organized a charity football match to collect money for Africa.

Robbie Williams

The English singer Robbie Williams (born **Robert Peter Williams** on 13 February, 1974, in Newcastle-under-Lyme, UK) has sold more than 50 million albums and 15 million singles around the world. In the UK he has sold more albums than any other solo singer in history. His success has made him very rich: he has probably got more than £100 million.

Take That (1990–1995)

Williams' early pop career started with the boy band **Take That**. (Of the band's nine UK number 1 singles, seven were with Robbie Williams.) His relationship with the others in the band was difficult. They said he was not interested enough in the work of the group. Williams left 'Take That' in 1995.

Solo success

In 1996 Williams sang his own version of the George Michael song 'Freedom' – it was more successful than Michael's original. His first solo album followed in late 1997. His name appears in the list of the Top 100 best-selling albums in UK history six times.
Although Williams has been very popular all over the world, he hasn't been as successful in **North America**. His best record in the US – 'Angels'– was only number 41 in the charts.

b) *Skim the article you've chosen. What are the three main ideas?*

4 A school band gig that went wrong (Past perfect)

Complete the sentences. Use the past perfect.

1. Tim couldn't play the guitar because he *had left* (leave) it on the bus.
2. Mike couldn't play the drums because he ... (hurt) his arm.
3. Julie couldn't sing because she ... (lose) her voice.
4. Chris couldn't play the piano because she ... (eat) too much.
5. Max couldn't play the trumpet because he ... (have) an accident on his bike.
6. Yvonne couldn't play the keyboard because she ... (cut) herself.
7. Fiona couldn't play the recorder because she ... (not sleep) the night before.

5 When it started to rain ... (Past perfect)

Complete the sentences for each picture. Use the simple past or the past perfect.

1a

The girl ... (go) inside when it started to rain.

1b

The girl ... (go) inside when it started to rain.

2a

The mice ... (run) away when the cat turned around.

2b

The mice ... (run) away when the cat turned around.

3a

The bank robber ... (leave) the bank when the police arrived.

3b

The bank robber ... (leave) the bank when the police arrived.

6 WRITING A short biography (Correcting your text)

a) *A student has written the beginning of a short biography of Shakira. Be careful: there are lots of mistakes in it! How many can you find?*

Shakira

Shakira was born in 1977. She was born in Colombia in South america. She have six brothers and sisters. One off them is her road manager. Shakira begun to rite songs at eight. The songs were in spanish. Soon was she on television, in a show for childs. When she is thirteen she sang some songs for the managers of a big music company. They sayed she could make three albums. That was the main reason why her career realy started. Shakira released her first album 'Magia' ('Magic'). She was 15. It wasn't a success – the shops only selled about 1,000 copies.

b) *There are 12 mistakes in the text. Did you find them all? If not, use this checklist:*

- Spelling – for example capital letters (*spanish*), missing letters (*rite*)
- Grammar – for example verb forms (*she have, begun*), tenses (*when she is thirteen*), word order (*Soon was she*), plural forms (*childs*)

c) **Extra** *Write the text again. Correct the mistakes and make these changes.*

- Start a paragraph for each new idea. (Make three paragraphs.)
- The text doesn't use linking words. (You can make one sentence from the first two. You can make one sentence from the last three – use 'when' and 'but'.)
- Write a new, more helpful first sentence. (Maybe some readers don't know that Shakira is a singer.)

d) *Now write your own short biography of a star. In your biography you should write about:*

- *when and where your star was born*
- *his/her family*
- *his/her school days*
- *how his/her career began*
- *his/her first CD/video/film ...*
- *...*

Correct your biography and write it out again.

Tip

Make a list of the kinds of mistakes you often make. Use the list as your own personal checklist.

Extra Project: Our music section

In this project, each of you will write an article for a section of a teen magazine (or e-zine). Then you will put the section together in a group of four or five.

Of course you can make your magazine section about another topic (sport, fashion, ...). This book will help you to produce a music section.

1 Step 1: Choose your topic

a) *What would you like to write about? First brainstorm ideas. Then mark your two favourite ideas.*

▸ SF Brainstorming (p. 135)

Why I love to play the drums
Music is my favourite subject
Why do they have to play terrible music in shopping centres?
Make your own ringtones
Madonna: the story of a singer
Why don't boys like to dance?
My top five songs about football
Musical instruments: the piano
Hip hop is the greatest!
Things that are better with music

b) *Talk about all your ideas. Agree with your group on who will write what.*

I'd like to write about ...

We can't have two articles about ... What's your second favourite?

2 Step 2: Collect information

Sometimes you have to collect information for your articles. Look at the list of sources below and what you can use them for.

Sources of information	Use for
internet	latest information, song lyrics, groups that are popular now
library, encyclopaedia	facts about people, places, instruments, ...
music magazines	interviews, photos
survey	latest trends, what your classmates like/don't like ...

Tip

- If you can, use English sources. (An English–German dictionary will help.) That way you won't make as many mistakes.
- If you find too much, skim. That helps you to decide which texts will be useful to you.

▸ SF English–German dictionary (p. 126) • P 1 (p. 100) • SF Skimming (p. 131) • SF Scanning (p. 130)

3 Step 3: Decide how to write up your information

a) Look again at the articles by Robert and his friends. How did they write up their ideas? Match the topics to the forms:

- music in my life
- a favourite instrument
- a famous singer
- favourite songs

- the story of his life
- a playlist
- a riddle
- the opposite: a day without music

b) Try to think of an interesting way to write your article.

a 'How to'-page with pictures

new lyrics to a famous song

a funny story about a man who goes crazy in a department store

a report on a concert video

Which ideas go with which topics in the list on p. 97? (There is more than one right answer.)

4 Step 4: Write and correct your article

a) Collect words you'll need before you start to write. You can find some words in the articles by Robert and his friends (pp. 90–92), others in your German–English dictionary.

► SF German–English dictionary (p. 127)

b) Write your article and get it ready to show your group.

► Writing course 4: The steps of writing (p. 80)

Tip

Use your own words. Don't just copy texts you have found in books or magazines or on the internet.

► P 2 (p. 100)

c) Correct each other's work in your group.

Tip

Try a 'correcting circle'! It works like this:

1 Each student in your group will watch for one kind of mistake, e.g.:
  - spelling (missing letters, plural forms, ...)
  - grammar („he, she, it, das 's' muss mit!", irregular verbs, ...)
  - ...

  Decide who is responsible for what.

2 Sit in a circle. Give your article to the student on your right.

3 Read the article that the student on your left has given you. Watch only for the kind of mistake that you are responsible for. If you find one, correct it.

4 When you have finished, give the article to the student on your right. Now correct the new article. Go on until you have your own article back.

5 Correct your article if necessary.

► Writing course 5: Correcting your text (p. 96)

5 Step 5: Publish your music section

a) *Agree on how you will publish your music section.*

Tip

If you're making an e-zine, add sound files, videos and links to other interesting websites.

You can ...
... write the articles by hand/on the computer
... make a poster and hang it on the wall
... make an e-zine and put it on the school website.

b) *Decide who will do the different jobs.*

Scan pictures – Marcel
Layout – Aischa & Elias
Design front page for section – Laura
Make photocopies – Oleg

c) *Put your music section together and publish it. Maybe you want to give it to other classes, parents at parents' evening, ...*

Tip

Put a copy of your article in your DOSSIER.

1 Extra STUDY SKILLS Research on the internet (using key words and phrases)

a) *To find information on the internet, you will have to use a search engine.*

Tips for internet research

- Think carefully: what are you looking for?
- Use a key word or phrase and enter it in your search engine.
- Check your spelling.
- If your results are not good enough or if there are too many websites:
  - add more key words or phrases.
  - use different key words.
- To look for a phrase, use quotation marks (" "), e. g. "interview with Shakira".

Remember: Don't print complete articles from the internet. Always use your own words!

b) *What key words would you use to find the answers to these questions? Write them down.*

1. When and where was Elvis Presley born?
   "Elvis Presley" born
2. Who sang the 2001 hit 'Can't get you out of my head' and where is he/she from?
3. What was the name of the Beatles' own record company?
4. What name did Madonna give her first child?
5. What musical instruments did the Bechstein family make?
6. What group did Phil Collins and Peter Gabriel belong to?

c) *Now try your key words from b) in an online search engine. Can you find the answers?*

2 Extra STUDY SKILLS Adapting a text

Imagine you have found this information on the singer Katie Melua. This is how you can use it to write about her life.

a) *Find the important facts and mark them up in a copy of the text.* ► SF Marking up a text (p. 132)

Ketevan 'Katie' Melua is a British singer and musician.

She was born in Kutaisi, Georgia, in 1984 and spent her first years in the capital Tbilisi and the town of Batumi. During this time the family was so poor that they lived in a flat without running water.

In 1993 the family moved to Belfast, Northern Ireland, where her father took up a position at the Royal Victoria Hospital. When Melua was fourteen, the family relocated to Redhill in England. Because she lived in so many different places at an early age, Melua can speak three languages: Georgian, Russian and English.

In November 2003, at the age of just 19, Melua released her first album *Call Off the Search*. It reached the top of the United Kingdom album charts and sold 1.2 million copies within five months. Her second album, *Piece by Piece*, was released in September 2005 and has gone platinum four times.

b) *Take notes:* Katie Melua – British singer; born Georgia 1984 …

c) *Use your notes and write your own text.*
Katie Melua is one of the most successful British singers. She was born in … She can speak …

How am I doing? – Units 1–5

This page will help you to check what you have learned in the whole book, not just in the last unit.

a) *Fill in or choose the correct answers.*

Facts about Britain

1 The three countries on the main island of the United Kingdom are England, ... and ...
2 The capital of the UK is ... It's on the River ...
3 The quickest way to get round London is on the ...
4 The ... are a group of islands north of Scotland.
5 Old Trafford is the name of the football stadium in ... in the north of England.

Words

Add at least three words to each of the word fields below. Name the word fields for extra points.

6 ticket, train, ferry, ride, ...
7 mobile phone, download, website, ...
8 car park, theatre, traffic, ...
9 train, supporter, draw, stadium, ...
10 gig, DJ, hip hop, ...
11 forest, river, mountain, bear, ...

Skills

12 If you want to find a word in a long text, you can ... the text for the word.
13 If you want to find the main ideas of a long text quickly, you can ... it.
14 If you don't know a word that you need, you can use different words to explain it. This is called ...
15 If you want to collect lots of ideas, you can try ... – alone or in a group.

Writing

16 The main idea of a paragraph is usually in the ...
17 Your writing will be clearer if you use time phrases and ...
18 What are the 5 Ws and what can you use them for?
19 Explain one 'trick' you can use to find mistakes in something you have written.

Grammar

20 Robert ... (not be) to New York yet, but he ... (go) to London last summer.
21 If you ... (be) in London now, what ... (want) to do?
22 *Use a relative clause to make one sentence:*
– Do you know the girl? The girl has just fallen off her bike.
– Mum likes the book. I gave her the book as a birthday present.
23 I wasn't hungry because I ... (already eat).
24 *Correct the mistakes:*
– The film was very exciting. It was about two spies who were trying to kill the other.
– My sister and I aren't allowed to ride our bikes when it's raining – my mum is afraid we'll hurt us.
– In three years I can speak English better. I felt myself ill and stayed at home.

b) *Check your answers and the number of points for each correct answer on p. 227. Add up your points.*

c) *If you had 30 or more points, well done! Maybe you can help students who had fewer points. If you had 29 points or fewer, it's a good idea to do some more work. Where did you make mistakes? The chart below will tell you what you can do to improve your English.*

No.	Area	Find out more	Exercise(s)
1– 5	Britain facts	Units 1–3	–
6–11	Word fields	All about ..., pp. 14, 32, 54, 70	WB pp. 3, 4, 7, 9, 13, 19, 35, 47, 62, 64
12–15	Skills	Skills File, pp. 124–137	WB pp. 11, 26, 49, 63
16–19	Writing	Writing course, pp. 22, 39, 64, 80, 96	WB pp. 12, 21, 40, 53, 65
20–24	Grammar	GF 1–9, pp. 139–147	WB pp. 11, 13, 14, 20, 22–25, 36–38, 39, 42–43, 48, 49–52, 63–64

Unit 1

9 REVISION The Feely Family (Present perfect)

Partner B: Answer your partner's questions about pictures 1–4 .

1 Mrs Feely is angry because her kids haven't ....
2 Mo and Jo ...

1 kids – not tidy room

2 they – have bath

3 parrot – die

4 he – not sleep enough

Then ask your partner questions about pictures 5–8. Why is Kitty Feely scared?

5 KittyFeely – scared

6 Julie Feely – proud

7 Tommy Feely – ill

8 Jill and Jenny Feely – cold

Unit 2

12 Loch Ness and Edinburgh

a) *Listen to your partner's text about Loch Ness. When you hear an incorrect statement, correct it with facts from the box below.*

Facts about Loch Ness

1) It is one of the most famous places in Scotland. **2)** The word loch means lake. **3)** Loch Ness is 37 kilometres long. **4)** Some people say there's a monster. **5)** Most people think that Nessie is only a story. **6)** Every year thousands of tourists come to Loch Ness. **7)** You don't have to go to Scotland to see Loch Ness: There are lots of websites with webcams from around the lake.

b) *A student has written this text about Edinburgh. Seven statements in it are wrong. Read it through quietly. Then read it out loud to your partner. He/ She will correct the incorrect statements.*

Edinburgh

Edinburgh is on the west coast of Scotland. With about 500,000 people it's the largest city in Scotland. It's also the Scottish capital.

Edinburgh is a very old town and it was the home of the Scottish queens and kings. Today more than 40 million tourists come to visit Edinburgh every year. Visitors come to see the famous old buildings and places like Buckingham Palace or Princes Street. And thousands come for the Edinburgh International Festival in the autumn.

Edinburgh is also the home of some famous people, like Alexander Graham Bell – the 'father' of the computer. And only a few people know that J.K. Rowling wrote her first Harry Potter book in her house in Edinburgh.

Unit 3

1 WORDS Spot the difference

a) *Look at the picture. Your partner will tell you what he/she can see in the rooms. Spot the differences in your picture.*
Take turns: tell your partner about your picture. Use words and phrases like ***next to****,* ***on the left****,* ***on the wall****. Ask about his/her picture.*

A: In my picture, there's a ... upstairs on the wall on the left. What about your picture?
B: Yes, in my picture it's there too. / No, in my picture it's on the wall on the right. – Now, in my picture, the ... is downstairs ...

8 STUDY SKILLS Paraphrasing

a) *Listen to your partner and guess his/her words.*

b) *Explain the following words to your partner – but don't use the word. The phrases on the right will help you.*

apple • breakfast • crocodile • doctor • teacher

It's somebody/a person who ...
It's something/a fruit/a ... that ...
It's something that you use to ...
It's a thing/an animal ...

B: It's a person who ...
A: Oh, do you mean a ...?

c) *Now try to explain the words from the box in English. Your partner has to guess the German word.*

Elefant • Flaschenöffner • Hausfrau • Thermoskanne • Torwart • Zeitung

Who needs legs?

> Birthday boy Nathan was fighting for his life yesterday after a two-hour operation. His mother Helen is by his bed where last night he was very very ill.

That was the report in the Sunday Mirror, a national newspaper, on 13th April 1997.

Three months later Nathan took his second 'first steps', this time with artificial legs. And soon after that he was back at school!

'Yes, Nathan has lost his legs, but he's as mad about sport as he was before,' his mum said a few months later. 'He still goes riding. And he plays football at school, as a goalkeeper. He sits in the goal and stops the ball.'

When he was ten years old Nathan started to play sledge hockey – ice hockey for the disabled. Trainers quickly spotted his talent.

Then when he was 14, Nathan also started to do athletics in the summer. A year later he won gold medals for javelin, discus and shot put at the Junior British Championships.

When Nathan was sixteen, in April 2004, he played for Great Britain at the World Sledge Hockey Championships – he was the youngest player. In 2006 he represented Wales at the Melbourne Commonwealth Games and Great Britain at the Winter Paralympics in Turin.

The BBC asked Nathan Stephens what his hopes were. Nathan answered: 'I hope I'll be able to be in the 2008 Summer and the 2010 Winter Paralympics. I hope we win more medals than before and that there's a lot about us on TV. That way people will understand better what we do.

Working with the text

1 Who is Nathan Stephens?

a) *Read the text. Take notes on these questions:*
- When did Nathan take his second 'first steps'?
- What sports did he do when he was ten?
- When did he win his first athletics medals?
- What are his hopes?

b) *Ask your partner about Nathan's earlier life. Take notes.*
- Where and when was Nathan born?
- What sports did he do as a little boy?
- Where did he go to play on his 9th birthday?
- What happened?

Then answer your partner's questions.

2 A timeline

a) *Copy and complete this timeline.*

Nathan born

1988 – 1997 – 1998 – 2002 – 2004 – 2006 – 2008 – 2010

b) *Swap timelines. Correct your partner's if necessary.*

DOSSIER ***A sports star***

Find out about an interesting sports star (for example, the one you chose on p. 59). Draw a timeline for him/her and put it in your dossier.

► **Text File 8** *(pp. 114–116)* • *WB 19 (p. 44)* •
Checkpoint 3 *WB (p. 45)*

Unit 4

1 WORDS Numbers

a) *Write down the numbers that your partner reads out to you. Then read out these numbers to your partner: Swap papers and check.*

15 • 7 • 93 • 303 • 2,684 • 13,155 • 300,000

11 Are they looking at themselves or each other? (each other/themselves)

Look at the pictures. You and your partner have the same pictures, but in a different order. Talk to your partner about your pictures. Take turns.

1 teach

2 think of

3 look at

4 take photos of

5 teach

6 look at

7 take photos of

8 think of

A: In my picture 1 a boy and a girl are looking at themselves.
B: Oh, a boy and a girl are looking at themselves in my picture 6. In my picture 1 two girls are ...

Getting ready for a test 2

2 Reading

Partner B: Read about St. Jacobs, a village near Toronto. Then answer the questions on the right.

The Mennonite Farm Tour
On market days only. The 1 hour 15 min. tour starts and ends at the Farmers' Market. Travel in a 'horse-drawn trolley', see the farms at work and enjoy the country. ☛ *Adults* $15. *Children* $7.50

St. Jacobs Farmers' Market
Thurs. and Sat. 7 am to 3.30 pm. Fresh, healthy food. Great atmosphere. Mennonite farmers travel to market by horse and buggy to sell their vegetables, sausage and maple syrup.

The Maple Syrup Museum
Learn how syrup is produced. You can buy maple syrup products at the 'Farm Pantry' near the Museum.

1 The Mennonite Farm Tour ...
- A is every day.
- B is on Thursdays and Saturdays.
- C starts at the Maple Syrup Museum.

2 You do the tour at 12.15. How much time will you have at the market after the tour?
- A under 1 hour
- B between 1 and 2 hours
- C over 2 hours

3 You can buy maple syrup ...
- A only at the 'Farm Pantry'
- B at the 'Farm Pantry' or Farmers' Market.
- C on the Mennonite Farm Tour.

Tip

The texts in this Text File are extra reading material. The footnotes at the bottom of the page explain the most important new words. Have fun with the texts!

► *SF Understanding new words (p. 124)*

TF 1 Pull in Emergency[1] adapted from 'Children's London', The Times

Too young to rock? Never! Band Pull in Emergency (13- and 14-year-olds) tell you how.

☆ Faith Bale

13, lead singer of the band **Pull in Emergency** from North London

'As most of us are only in Year 8, our friends have a problem: they can't get into our gigs. I went to an under-18s night a few days ago and it was great because everybody there was a teenager.

We haven't got the money for a rehearsal studio, so we practise at our drummer's house, in the laundry room. I sit on the washing machine and the others all squash in around it. We're getting a new player soon and I don't know how he is going to fit.

We want to attract people's attention[2] so we try to wear cool clothes *and* sound good.

Old, second-hand clothes are best, but you sometimes have to look at a lot of rubbish in some of the shops. I don't buy whole new outfits: I just add one new thing to an outfit that I already have – that way I save money.'

☆ Alice Costelloe

13, guitarist in P.I.E.

'I think it's good to try to go to as many gigs as you can. Some places let you in when you're over 14 – for example the Wireless Festival in Hyde Park (but the tickets are quite expensive). Or there's the Tin Pan Alley festival in Denmark Street (www.tinpanalleyfestival.co.uk). It's free – and for people of all ages. The Underage Festival[3] in Victoria Park is great because it's for teenagers between 14 and 17 only. We also went to the Love Music Hate Racism Festival in Trafalgar Square.

I buy all my instruments in Denmark Street. They sell guitars for £3000, but if you're in a teenage band you only need a £70 guitar.'

[1] (to) pull in emergency [i'mɜːdʒənsi] *im Notfall ziehen* [2] (to) attract sb.'s attention [ə'trækt, ə'tenʃn] *jn. auf sich aufmerksam machen*
[3] Underage Festival ['ʌndəreɪdʒ] *Festival für Minderjährige*

☆ Dylan Holmes

13, bass guitarist in P.I.E.

'We have some recording time in a studio with a sound engineer. It's all free because one of our parents knows the owner of the studio.
Young bands have to get help from parents and friends, but even if you can't get a studio, you can still make quite good recordings – on a computer or with a cheap microphone. And if you haven't got enough money for a good guitar, just buy a good effects pedal because it can change your whole sound.'

1 The article

True or false? Correct the wrong statements.

1. P.I.E.'s friends always go to their gigs.
2. P.I.E. practise in a rehearsal studio.
3. Alice tries to go to as many concerts as possible.
4. There aren't any concerts for people under 18.
5. P.I.E. play on cheap instruments.
6. Dylan thinks young bands need a recording studio.

2 Bands

a) *Collect words and phrases about bands.*

b) *Finish this sentence. Can you find more than one ending?*
As a young band you have to / you need ...

c) *What young bands do you know in Germany? Tell your class about them.*

3 The song 'Backfoot'

Listen to the song. How do you like it?
– I think the song is ...
– The music sounds ...

awful • boring • exciting • great • happy • fantastic • new • nice • sad • ...

Backfoot *by Pull in Emergency*
You say you love me so hold me,
You're running away, why won't you hold me?
Now you seem[1] to say you want me,
Oh running away has never been so easy ... as now.
(...)
You're running off,
You're running off,
Caught on the backfoot[2],
Palm on the handle.
(...)

[1] (to) seem (to be/do) [siːm] *(zu sein/tun) scheinen* [2] (to) be caught on the backfoot [kɔːt] *kalt erwischt werden*

TF 2 Two Elizabeths

England has had two Queen Elizabeths.

Elizabeth I became Queen in 1558, when she was 25 years old. There was always a lot of gossip[1] about her. The big question was: Who will the Queen marry?

Well, she never married anybody, but she had a number of 'favourites'. One of them was Walter Raleigh.

They met, so people say, one rainy evening at Shakespeare's Globe Theatre in London. The Queen wanted to get out of her carriage when she saw a large puddle.

'Why isn't she getting out?' people whispered. Walter Raleigh, a new face at court[2] – young and good-looking – saw why: the puddle. He quickly took off his very expensive new cloak and threw it onto the puddle.

The Queen smiled and allowed Mr Raleigh to help her down. She went into the theatre with dry feet and Raleigh became her new 'favourite'.

Just a few years later the Queen made Walter into 'Sir Walter' and allowed him to start a colony in America.

And what did Sir Walter bring back from America? Gold or jewels? No: a dirty vegetable called the 'potato' and a dry leaf called 'tobacco'.

Which brings us to the second Queen Elizabeth.

She was also very young when she became Queen in 1952 – just 26 years old. But she married and had four children.

One night in 1982, a man called Michael Fagan climbed first into the garden of Buckingham Palace and then into the Palace. There he went into the Queen's bedroom. And when she woke up in the middle of the night she found a strange[3] man by her bed.

Queen Elizabeth II is famous for being very calm[4]. And that night was an example. She asked the man to sit down and started to talk to him. After a few minutes she asked him, 'Would you like a drink?' He said, 'Yes, please.' So she picked up the phone.

'I'd like two gin and tonics, please. Oh, and my cigarettes,' she said.

The person on the other end of the phone knew that there was something very wrong. Why? Because the Queen has never smoked!

In a few minutes the police were there and took Mr Fagan away.

> *How does tobacco link the two stories?*

[1] gossip ['gɒsɪp] *Klatsch* [2] (at) court [kɔːt] *(am) Hof (der Königin)* [3] strange [streɪndʒ] *fremd* [4] calm [kɑːm] *ruhig*

TF 3 r u alone...?

1 The poster

Write down the question on the poster in correct English. Compare with a partner.

2 The people

a) *Who are the people in the poster? What do you think they're planning to do?*

b) *Why can't we see the man's face?*

3 The message

a) *What is the poster trying to say?*

I think the poster is trying to say: You have to be careful because ...

b) *Do you think this is a good poster? Why (not)?*

I think it's good because ...

I don't think it will help because ...

TF 4 Help beat[1] bullying

Help beat bullying

Stand up and speak out against bullying!
This anti-bullying poster won a poster design competition[2].

Natasha, 14, from London, designed it.

1 Anti-bullying poster

a) *Look at this page from a British teen magazine. What can you see?*
At the top on the left there's a photo of ...

b) *Take a closer look at Natasha's poster. Do you think it's good or not? Why?*
– I think it's good/not good because ...
– It shows/says ...
– The message of the poster is that ...

c) *Design an anti-bullying poster for your classroom. Put all the posters on the wall. Which is the best one?*

[1] (to) beat [biːt], beat, beaten ['biːtn] *besiegen* [2] competition [ˌkɒmpəˈtɪʃn] *Wettbewerb* [3] fat [fæt] *dick, fett*

TF 5 The lost girl (A folk story from the Orkney Islands)

A long, long time ago, there was a family on one of the islands in the north of the Orkney Islands. One day the daughter went out to catch some little fish. The father wanted to use them to catch big fish. The girl went out ... but she never came back. Her family looked everywhere, but they couldn't find her.

Years later the father and his two sons went fishing. The weather was fine when they left, but then a thick fog came. They didn't know how to get home. After a time, they came to an island. The three men got off the boat and walked until they came to a big, beautiful house. They knocked on the door, and a good-looking man opened it. He invited them in and said they could stay until the fog was gone.

The three men went inside. They could not believe how beautiful everything was. Then the man introduced[1] them to his wife. It was the lost girl! She welcomed her father and brothers warmly, asked how they were and about her mother and everybody else back home.

As they were talking, the man asked the father if he had any cows to sell. The father answered yes, he had one fine cow, and the man gave him a very good price for the cow. He paid in gold.

Now the father thought that he could find out the name of the island. 'Well,' he said, 'now you'll have to tell me how to get here, or I won't be able to bring the cow to you.'

'Och!' said the man. 'Don't worry about that. I'll come and get the cow.'

Then one of the brothers said, 'Father, the fog is going away.'

'Then we should[2] go,' the father said.

The girl asked, 'Is there anything here that you would like to take home with you?'

'Yes,' her husband said, 'you can take anything[3] in the house. Just say what you would like and take it with you.'

The girl looked at them hopefully. She thought her father would choose her. But he chose a large gold plate.

When they got to the boat, the good-looking man said, 'Just go that way, and you will soon be home.'

The father and his two sons did what he said and took their boat into the fog. As they came out the other side, they found that they were near their own island.

When they got home, the wife was very upset. 'An awful thing has happened,' she said. 'Our cow is dead.'

But the old man smiled. 'Och,' he said, 'that's all right. I got a good price for her.'

Nobody ever saw the island, the man or the girl again.

1 Understanding the story

Right or wrong? Say why.

1. When the father and brothers came to the island, they knew where they were.
2. The girl wanted to go home with her father and brothers.
3. The girl's father loved his daughter more than he loved gold.

[1] (to) introduce sb. [ˌɪntrəˈdjuːs] *jn. vorstellen* [2] Then we should ... [ʃʊd] *Dann sollten wir ...* [3] you can take anything: *du kannst nehmen, was (immer) du willst*

TF 6 Steel drums

Listen to the CD. What tune is the steel band playing? Then read the text and find out about the history of steel drums.

Elijah worked as a slave on a sugar plantation on the Caribbean island of Trinidad. His wife worked on the plantation too. And when his son was born, he was a slave too. It was the year 1830.

The life of a slave was hard. But on Saturday nights – just like today – there was time to relax. Then the slaves played the music and sang and danced to the tunes[1] that their parents and grandparents knew from Africa.

Elijah played the drum – a traditional African drum. He could beat[2] rhythms on it that were so exciting that his friends always got up and danced all night.

In 1838 the plantation owners had to free all the slaves on Trinidad. Elijah took his family to Port of Spain, the capital. He hoped to find work there.

Port of Spain today

He and many other freed slaves lived in a part of the city called Laventille. And there, on Saturday nights, he played his drums and his friends and neighbours danced.

But the people of Port of Spain thought the drums were too loud. They banned[3] them. The freed slaves had to make drums from bamboo. These drums were quieter, and they broke[4] easily.

Many, many years later, Elijah's great-great-grandson Winston Simon was playing a bamboo drum ... and it broke.

'This is a stupid drum,' thought Winston. 'I need a drum that won't break – and that makes more noise!' He looked round. There, at the side of the road, stood an old, empty oil drum[5].

'An oil drum,' thought Winston. 'Why not use it as a real drum?' He banged the top of the old oil drum. A dent appeared – and a bump. He banged first the dent, then the bump. A great sound came out – well, actually, two great sounds.

For weeks Winston banged and tested till there were lots of dents and bumps[6] on top of the drum. And when he played on the dents and bumps, 14 different sounds came out: the steel drum was born!

And from that day in 1946, the drums of the Caribbean played tunes, not just rhythms.

[1] tune [tju:n] *Melodie* [2] (to) beat [bi:t], beat, beaten ['bi:tn] *schlagen, spielen* [3] (to) ban [bæn] *verbieten* [4] (to) break [breɪk], broke [brəʊk], broken ['brəʊkən] *(zer)brechen* [5] drum *hier: Fass* [6] dents and bumps [dents], [bʌmps] *Dellen und Beulen*

TF 7 Football songs

You'll never walk alone

When you walk through a storm
Hold your head up high
And don't be afraid of the dark.
At the end of the storm
Is a golden sky
And the sweet, silver song of a lark[1].

Walk on through the wind,
Walk on through the rain,
Though your dreams be tossed and blown[2].
Walk on, walk on with hope in your heart,
And you'll never walk alone,
You'll never walk alone.

by Oscar Hammerstein

We are the champions

We are the champions, my friends
And we'll keep on fighting[3] till the end
We are the champions
We are the champions
No time for losers
'Cause we are the champions
Of the world

by Freddie Mercury

1 The songs

a) *Listen to the songs and read the words. Which song do you like better? Why?*

> the music is slower/faster/more beautiful/... •
> the singers sound more excited/happier/... •
> the song is about support for others

b) *Which song would you sing if your team is winning? Why?*

2 Now you

Which football songs (German or English) do you know?
Have you ever been to a football stadium for a football match/a pop concert/...? How did you like it?

---

[1] lark [lɑːk] *Lerche* [2] though your dreams be tossed and blown [tɒst] *etwa: auch wenn deine Träume in Gefahr geraten*
[3] (to) keep on fighting ['faɪtɪŋ] *weiterkämpfen*

TF 8 Tim, a rock and a rope[1] (adapted from Jacqueline Wilson's novel *Cliffhanger*)

Tim's father has sent him on an adventure[2] holiday for children. There's just one problem: Tim hates sports – all sports. Here's what Tim wrote in one of his postcards:

Do you think Tim is enjoying his holiday? Do you think he wants to go abseiling? Why/ Why not? Look at the other pictures. What do you think happens? Now read on.

'OK, Tim. You next.'

'No!'

'Yes,' said Jake, our team leader.

'No,' I said.

'You all have to go sooner or later,' said Jake.

'Later,' I said.

'No. Sooner,' said Jake.

'I can't,' I said.

'Yes you can, Tim,' said Jake and held my hand.

'He's scared,' said Giles.

'We're all scared,' said Jake. 'Especially the first time.' He looked me straight in the eye. 'But you'll see it's easy, Tim. Believe me. Now. Into the harness[4].'

Jake put me into the harness before I could get away. He was telling me things about this rope in this hand, that rope in that hand, but I couldn't listen. All I could hear was this terrible noise inside my head.

'Don't let go of[5] the rope, OK?' said Jake.

The noise in my head got louder and louder.

This couldn't be real. If I closed my eyes maybe it would all be a bad dream and then I'd wake up in bed at home with my teddy bear.

'Tim?' said Jake. 'Open your eyes! Now, your friend Biscuits is waiting for you down there. Come on. Start to walk backwards towards the edge[6].'

I walked backwards one step. Then another. Then I stopped.

'I can't!'

'Yes you can,' said Jake. 'You'll see. Over the edge. Don't worry. You can't fall. You just have to remember, you *don't* let go of the rope.'

I looked at him and started to go back some more. Then my feet suddenly lost contact with

[1] rope [rəʊp] *Seil* [2] adventure [əd'ventʃə] *Abenteuer* [3] (to) abseil ['æbseɪl] *(sich) abseilen* [4] harness ['hɑːnɪs] *(Kletter-)Gurt* [5] (to) let go of sth. *etwas loslassen* [6] edge [edʒ] *Rand, Kante*

the ground. I slipped[1] backwards and suddenly ... there I was! I was hanging.

'Help!'

I was desperate[2].

I had to hold on to something.

I grabbed at the rock.

I let go of the rope!

Suddenly I was sliding[3] backwards, backwards, backwards.

I screamed[4].

I grabbed the rock. I held on to it. I was crying[5].

I heard them up above me. They were shouting.

'He's fallen!'

'He's let go of the rope.'

'I knew he would.'

'Of course Tim had to do it wrong!'

'He's *stuck*[6].'

'Don't stop, Tim!' Biscuits called from below.

I turned my head and tried to look at him. The whole world started to move this way and that. Biscuits looked like he was millions and millions of miles below me.

'Help!'

'It's OK, Tim. Don't panic,' Jake called down.

'Don't panic, Tim, don't panic!' Kelly shouted. 'He's panicking, isn't he, Jake?'

'Shhh, Kelly. All of you. Go back, eh?' Jake said. 'Now. Tim. Listen. You've let go of the rope.'

'I know!'

'But it's OK. You can't fall. You're safe. Believe me.'

'I don't feel safe. I feel *sick*.[7]'

'Well, you can get down in a few seconds. All you have to do is grab the rope.'

'How???'

'Just let go of the rock and –'

'I can't!' Was Jake mad? I couldn't let go.

'You're safe in your harness,' Jake called. 'You needn't hold on to the rock. You just have to grab the rope. See the rope? Tim! Open your eyes!'

'I can't look down.'

'Look up. At me,' said Jake.

I turned my head up and opened my eyes a little. Jake was leaning right over the edge, not too terribly far away. He gave me a thumbs-up sign.

---

[1] (to) slip [slɪp] *(aus)rutschen* [2] desperate ['despərət] *verzweifelt* [3] (to) slide, slid, slid [slaɪd], [slɪd] *rutschen, gleiten*
[4] (to) scream [skriːm] *(auf)schreien* [5] (to) cry [kraɪ] *weinen* [6] (to) be stuck [stʌk] *festsitzen, feststecken* [7] I feel sick. [sɪk] *Mir ist schlecht.*

'That's good. Now. It's OK. Have a break if you like. It's not so bad now, is it?'

'Yes!'

'You can hang there all day if you really want,' said Jake.

'No!'

'Or you can grab that rope and walk down, one foot at a time, easy-peasy[1]. Mmm?'

I looked up at him.

'Can't you pull me up? Please?' I asked.

'We're trying to get you down, Tim, not up!' said Jake. 'You can do it. You're a brave[2] boy, Tim.'

He had to be joking!

'So just reach out[3],' Jake said.

I thought about it. My fingers were hurting terribly. I couldn't hang there forever. Maybe if I let go and grabbed the rope I could get down. So I let go of the rock, I reached out suddenly, I tried to grab ...

I swung round and it was so scary that I closed my eyes and grabbed the rock again.

The others were grumbling. But Jake didn't give up.

'Almost. Try again. Go on.'

So I tried again. I reached out. My hand was wet[4] with sweat[5] but I got the rope – I held on to it – I had it safe!

'Well done!' Jake called. 'There! I knew you could. Just hold on to it this time, eh? Now walk down. One step.'

I tried to move my feet. I couldn't feel them inside my boots. I made a little mouse's step downwards.

'Great!' said Jake. 'Now another step.'

My other leg moved. And I moved too. I was going down.

'There we go,' said Jake. 'That's it. You're getting it now.'

'I'm doing it!' I said and I walked down as carefully as I could.

'That's right. You're doing it, Tim,' Jake called. 'You're almost halfway down. Doing just great. Go on. Nice and easy. Good boy. Well done.'

'I'm doing it,' I whispered, 'I'm doing it. I'm doing it. It's awful. But I'm doing it.'

I went down quicker and quicker – and then suddenly I was at the bottom and Biscuits hit me on the back and congratulated me.

'You did it, you did it, you did it!' Biscuits sang.

Jake was cheering me from right up at the top of the rock.

'Well done, Tim! It wasn't so bad, was it? Do you want to do it again, eh?'

I shook[6] my head so hard that my helmet moved.

'Never ever ever again!'

1 Scary

a) *In a copy of the card, write Tim's next postcard back to his parents.*

b) *What's the scariest thing that you've ever done? Make notes (what? where? when? who? why? how?) and tell the class about it.*

[1] easy-peasy [ˌiːzi ˈpiːzi] *kinderleicht* [2] brave [breɪv] *mutig* [3] (to) reach out [riːtʃ] *die Hand ausstrecken* [4] wet [wet] *feucht, nass* [5] sweat [swet] *Schweiß* [6] (to) shake, shook, shaken [ʃeɪk], [ʃʊk], [ˈʃeɪkən] *schütteln*

TF 9 If you meet a bear ...

Safety in bear country

If you are in the mountain parks, you are in bear country. It's part of **Parks Canada**'s job to protect the grizzly and black bears that live here.

Here are the latest bear safety tips.

The best thing to do is to AVOID[1] a bear encounter[2]

Here's how ...

- Walk in a group of four or more.
- Make noise. This lets the bears know you are coming and gives them time to move away. Shout loudly every few minutes.
- Have bear spray ready and know how you can use it.
- Watch for fresh bear signs: paw prints, droppings[3], diggings[4].
- Never go near a bear. Stay at least 100 metres away.
- Be extra careful during berry[5] time, from late July to mid-September. Berries are a favourite food of bears.

If you meet a bear ...

- If the bear is close to you, go away slowly. Never run.
- Stay calm and move carefully. This will help to calm the bear and let it know that you are not dangerous.
- If you are in a group, stay together or join other people who are near you.
- If you have bear spray, get it ready.
- Talk to the bear.
- Leave the area. If this is impossible, wait until the bear moves away. Always leave the bear an escape route[6].

To survive, bears need a lot of space[7] and not many human[8] surprises.

1 What to do in bear country

Right or wrong? Say why.

1 The best way to avoid bears is not to make any noise.
2 In August bears aren't dangerous.
3 If you meet a bear, run as fast as you can.
4 Never talk to a bear.
5 Always wait until the bear moves away.

[1] (to) avoid [ə'vɔɪd] *vermeiden; ausweichen* [2] encounter [ɪn'kaʊntə] *Begegnung* [3] droppings (pl) *Kot* [4] diggings (pl) *Stellen, an denen Bären gegraben haben* [5] berry ['beri] *Beere* [6] escape route [ɪ'skeɪp ru:t] *Fluchtweg* [7] space *Platz* [8] human ['hju:mən] *menschlich*

TF 10 Poems – the four seasons[1]

1 Before you read

a) *Write down the names of the four seasons of the year. Add five words that go with each season.*

b) *Swap and compare with a partner.*

c) *Now read the poems.*

Who has seen the wind?

Who has seen the wind?
  Neither I nor you[2] ;
But when the leaves hang trembling[3]
  The wind is passing through.

Who has seen the wind?
  Neither you nor I;
But when the trees bow down[4] their heads
  The wind is passing by.

by Christina Rossetti

August heat

In August when the days are hot,
I like to find a shady spot[5],
And hardly[6] move a single bit

And sit –

And sit –

And sit!

anonymous

[1] season ['si:zn] *Jahreszeit* [2] neither I nor you ['naɪðə ... nɔ:, 'ni:ðə ... nɔ:] *weder ich noch du* [3] when the leaves hang trembling ['tremblɪŋ] *wenn die Blätter zitternd herunterhängen* [4] (to) bow down [ˌbaʊ 'daʊn] *senken* [5] a shady spot [ˌʃeɪdi 'spɒt] *einen schattigen Platz* [6] hardly ['hɑ:dli] *kaum*

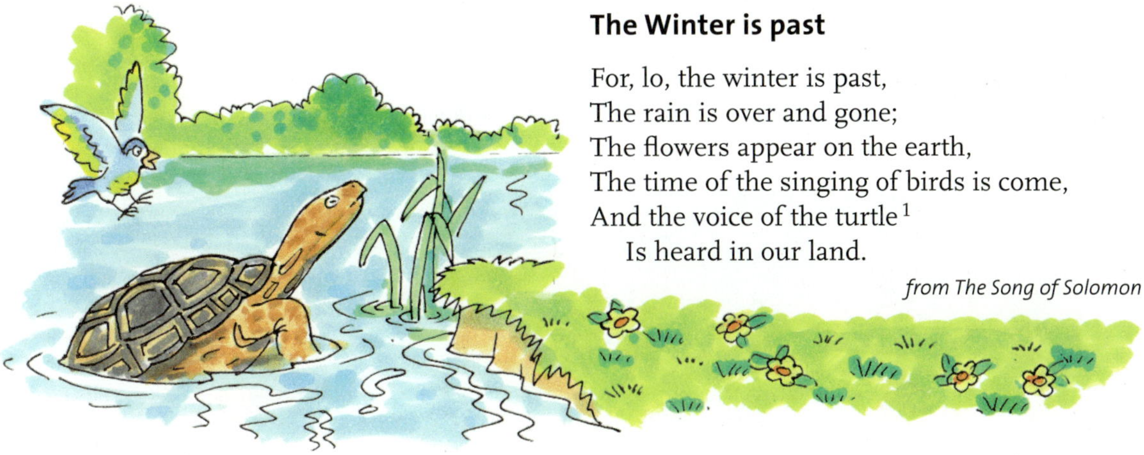

The Winter is past

For, lo, the winter is past,
The rain is over and gone;
The flowers appear on the earth,
The time of the singing of birds is come,
And the voice of the turtle[1]
Is heard in our land.

from The Song of Solomon

Snow storm

Oh, I am the King of Snowmen,
I've lived here for years and for years.
I've never been slushy[2]
Or melted, or mushy[3],
Or changed to a puddle of tears[4].

Oh, I am the King of Snowmen,
I'm jolly[5] and shiny and fat.
My home, small yet classy,
Has skies blue and glassy
And snowstorms that swirl[6] round my hat.

Oh, I am the King of Snowmen,
I've never been known to complain[7],
But sometimes my world shakes
With TERRIBLE earthquakes –
Take cover![8] They've started again!

by Clare Bevan

2 Your favourite

a) *Which poem did you like best? Why? Make a few notes.*

I liked ... best, because I like the winter/it rhymes/it's funny/easy/...

b) *Make appointments with three partners and compare your notes.*

c) *Learn your favourite poem. Recite it to the class and explain why you like it.*

3 Write your own poem

a) *Write a poem like the one below about one of the seasons.*

When it's cold and windy outside
I like it inside:
No wind, no snow
Tea and toast and
English songs on the
Radio.

b) *Read your poem to the class. You can add a picture and put it in your DOSSIER.*

[1] turtle ['tɜ:tl] *(Wasser-)Schildkröte* [2] slushy ['slʌʃi] *matschig* [3] mushy ['mʌʃi] *breiig* [4] a puddle of tears ['pʌdl], [tɪəz] *eine Tränenpfütze* [5] jolly ['dʒɒli] *fröhlich* [6] (to) swirl [swɜ:l] *wirbeln* [7] I've never been known to complain [kəm'pleɪn] *es ist noch nie vorgekommen, dass ich mich beschwert habe* [8] Take cover! ['kʌvə] *Geh(t) in Deckung!*

TF 11 'FANS'– a play by Ann Cartwright

1 Before you read

Look at the photo. What does it tell you about the four teenagers?
What do you think the play could be about?

Now read the play.

Scene:
Four friends sitting in their form room.
The girls are looking at teen magazines.
Tim is reading a computer magazine.

Kaz — He's lovely.
Shaz — He's got lovely hair.
Jaz — Lovely eyes.
Kaz, *Shaz*, *Jaz* — Ah!
Tim — Are you talking about me again?
Kaz, *Shaz*, *Jaz* — No!
Tim — Now you know you are really.
Kaz, *Shaz*, *Jaz* — We're not!
Tim — Well, who ARE you on about[1], then?
Shaz — Dermot Devlin!
Jaz — From the band Celtic Nomads.
Tim — Oh. Him. He's rubbish.
Kaz — He is not!
Tim — He looks like a girl.
Shaz — He does not!
Tim — He wears a dress!
Jaz — It's a kaftan, actually. It's ethnic.
Tim — You mean hippy. He's stupid. AND he can't sing.

Kaz — I wish he'd walk into the room.
Shaz — I wish he'd walk into the room right now.
Jaz — I wish he'd walk into the room right now – and I'd – and I'd scream[2].
Kaz, *Shaz* — Oo, and I would.
Tim — What for?
Kaz — Because he's lovely.
Shaz — You just don't understand, Tim. Read your computer magazine.

[1] (to) be on about ... *reden von/über ...* [2] (to) scream [skriːm] *schreien, kreischen*

Jaz — Yeah. All those hard-drives and mega-nothings.

Tim — There's more point to this than what you do.

Jaz — There isn't!

Tim — There is. At least I can look at these pictures and buy something. You can't look at a picture of Dermot Drill-Head and buy him, can you?

Kaz — Oo!

Shaz — Buy Dermot Devlin!

Jaz — Oo! You've started me off again[1] now!

Kaz — I'd pay anything.

Tim — But you can't! That's the point. You can't buy him.

Jaz — We can buy his music.

Shaz — And videos.

Kaz — Did you see his latest one?

Shaz — With him in the boat?

Jaz — Sailing towards that woman with the flowers in her hair?

Kaz — And the stars above their heads.

Shaz — And the breeze flowing softly across the canal.

Jaz — And he moves that oil-drum out of the way and that big bag of rubbish so that he can get to her.

Kaz — He's so strong!

Shaz — He's so romantic!

Jaz — And singing to her at the same time!

Kaz / *Shaz* / *Jaz* — Wow!

Tim — I feel ill.

Kaz — Oh, shut up.

Shaz — Have you heard his latest song?

Jaz — Oh, you mean 'Siren Dream'?

Shaz — No, no, that was his last one.

Kaz — Oh, I know the one! 'Tidal Wave Sensation'?

Shaz — No! That's the CD album. I mean his very latest, 'Flowing From The Heart'.

Kaz — Oh, yeah! I've heard that one! It's ever so romantic.

Tim — Got a water fixation, hasn't he? Is that because he's a big drip[2]? You do waste your money on that sad singer.

Jaz — He's not a sad singer! He's THE BUSINESS[3]!

Tim — It's such a shame[4].

Kaz — What is?

Tim — You're just pitiful[5] and totally obsessed[6].

Shaz — Let's have a look at YOUR magazine, then.

Tim — Give us that back!

[1] you've started me off again *etwa: jetzt bringst du mich wieder auf dieses Thema* [2] a drip [drɪp] *ein Waschlappen, eine Flasche (wörtlich: ein Tropfen)* [3] the business ['bɪznəs] *etwa: er ist DER HIT* [4] such a shame [ˌsʌtʃ‿ə 'ʃeɪm] *so ein Jammer, so eine Schande* [5] pitiful ['pɪtɪfl] *jämmerlich* [6] obsessed [əb'sest] *besessen*

Kaz — Yeah. Let's see how wonderful it is. Two pounds fifty?! Oh, you do waste your money on this sad computer stuff!

Tim — It's not sad! A madman singer in a dress singing a song about jump-leads to his girlfriend whilst[1] sitting on an oil-drum! Now THAT'S sad!

Jaz — Look at this! Page 14! Wow! New games!

Kaz — 'Deadliest Mortality Blood-Spurt Revenge'[2]? What kind of game's that?

Tim — A really good one.

Shaz — About what?

Tim — Gardening! What do you think?

Jaz — What do you have to do?

Tim — I'm not telling you.

Jaz — Why not?

Tim — 'Cause you'll make fun of me, that's why not.

Kaz — Now why should we make fun of your very serious computer magazine just because you've ripped our beloved Dermot to pieces[3]?

Shaz — We wouldn't do that, would we?

Jaz — Certainly not. We're mature[4].

Kaz — So go on, Tim.

Tim — All right, but you'd better not make fun of it 'cause it's really serious.

Jaz — We won't.

Tim — Well – there's two gangs – the Bloods and the Spurts – and you get to be in one of the gangs and fight the other one.

Kaz / *Shaz* / *Jaz* — What a load of rubbish!

Tim — I knew it! Shut up!

Kaz — Sounds really boring.

Tim — Boring?! It's brilliant! I've got the whole series.

Shaz — Series? There's more of them?

Tim — Yeah! There's 'Deadliest Mortality Blood-Spurt Revenge: The Beginning' followed by 'Deadliest Mortality Blood-Spurt Revenge: The Battle' followed by 'D.M.B-S.R.: The Hospitalization' followed by –

Jaz — Oh, don't tell me any more!

Kaz — How dreary!

Tim — I'm getting the next one for my birthday! You should see all the stuff I've got. And the posters! And what I really want is a virtual-reality set-up where I can really INTERACT with the gangs!

Pause.

Kaz — Shame, isn't it?

Shaz — Yeah. Pitiful.

Kaz — He's just totally obsessed.

Tim — Look who's talking![5]

Kaz — Look out. Teacher's coming.

---

[1] whilst [waɪlst] *während* [2] deadliest mortality blood-spurt revenge *Name eines Computerspiels, in dem viel Blut vergossen wird* [3] (to) rip sth. to pieces [rɪp] *etwas in Stücke reißen* [4] mature [mə'tʃʊə] *reif, vernünftig* [5] Look who's talking! *Das musst du/müsst ihr gerade sagen!*

Shaz — She'll be in here with her X-Files magazine again.

Jaz — She's on about that stuff all the time.

Tim — Was Shakespeare an alien?

Kaz — Did Wordsworth have a Close Encounter whilst looking at those daffodils?

Shaz — Now she IS obsessed.

Kaz / *Shaz* / *Jaz* / *Tim* — She's such a fanatic!

2 What's the play about?

*Describe in three or four sentences what the play is about. Were your ideas in **1** right?*

3 True or false?

a) *Are the statements true or false? Correct the wrong statements.*

1. Kaz, Shaz and Jaz are talking about Tim at the beginning of the scene.
2. Dermot Devlin dresses like a girl.
3. Dermot Devlin is a film star.
4. Kaz, Shaz and Jaz think computer magazines are hard to read.
5. Tim thinks the girls are obsessed with Dermot Devlin.
6. Tim likes video games about gardening.
7. The girls don't want to make fun of Tim.
8. All four make fun of the teacher.

b) *Are the statements true or false? Why?*

1 'Tim is tolerant.'
- A true, because the text says ...
- B false, because the text says ...

2 'The girls are tolerant.'
- A true, because the text says ...
- B false, because the text says ...

3 'Tim is arrogant.'
- A true, because the text says ...
- B false, because the text says ...

4 Do you agree?

a) 'It's such a shame (...) You're just pitiful and totally obsessed.' (ll. 95–98)
Do you agree with what Tim says about the three girls? Why (not)?

b) 'Oh, you do waste your money on this sad computer stuff.' (ll. 103–104)
'What a load of rubbish!' (l. 136)
Do you agree with what the three girls say about Tim? Why (not)?

5 Act out the play

a) *Each student learns a part from pp. 120–121 or pp. 122–123.*

b) *Make groups of eight – four students who learned the first half of the play, four who learned the second half. Perform the play for your class. Vote for the best group.*

Skills File – Inhalt

Im **Skills File** findest du Hinweise zu Arbeits- und Lerntechniken. Was du in den Skills-Kästen der Units gelernt hast, wird hier näher erläutert.

Was du bereits aus Band 2 von English G 21 kennst, ist mit **REVISION** gekennzeichnet,
z. B.
– **REVISION Understanding new words**, Seite 124
– **REVISION Describing pictures**, Seite 128.

Viele neue Hinweise helfen dir bei der Arbeit mit Hör- und Lesetexten, beim Sprechen, beim Schreiben von eigenen Texten, bei der Sprachmittlung und beim Lernen von Methoden.

Manchmal gibt es auch Aufgaben dazu.

STUDY AND LANGUAGE SKILLS

SF REVISION Understanding new words

Immer gleich im Wörterbuch nachschlagen?

Das Nachschlagen unbekannter Wörter im Wörterbuch kostet Zeit und nimmt auf Dauer den Spaß am Lesen. Oft geht es auch ohne Wörterbuch!

Was hilft mir, unbekannte Wörter zu verstehen?

1. Bilder zeigen oft die Dinge, die du im Text nicht verstehst. Schau sie dir deshalb vor dem Lesen genau an.
2. Oft hilft dir der Textzusammenhang, also die Wörter, die vor oder nach dem unbekannten Wort stehen,
   z. B. *We must hurry. Our train* **departs** *in ten minutes.*
3. Viele englische Wörter werden ähnlich wie im Deutschen geschrieben
   z. B. **brochure**, **electrician**, **president**.
4. Manchmal stecken in neuen Wörtern bekannte Teile,
   z. B. **arrival**, **a westbound train**, **snowshoes**.

- Alles klar? Dann überlege, was diese Wörter bedeuten:
  hilly • imaginary • head of state • a winning shot • useful • canal • material • realistic • colony • official

SF Learning words

REVISION Worauf solltest du beim Lernen und Wiederholen von Vokabeln achten?

- Führe dein Vokabelverzeichnis, dein Vokabelheft oder deinen Karteikasten aus Klasse 6 weiter.
- Lerne immer 7–10 Vokabeln auf einmal.
- Lerne neue und wiederhole alte Vokabeln regelmäßig – am besten jeden Tag 5–10 Minuten.
- Lerne mit jemandem zusammen. Fragt euch gegenseitig ab oder übt die Wörter mit Lernspielen (z. B. Vokabel-Domino, Schiffe versenken, Quartett, *Vocabulary Action Sheets*).

Finde die für dich beste Methode

- Du weißt nach zwei Jahren Englischlernen wahrscheinlich, mit welchen Methoden du am besten Vokabeln lernst: durch Hören und Nachsprechen, durch Bilder, am Computer (z. B. mit deinem *e-Workbook* oder dem *English Coach*) – oder indem du dir eigene Geschichten um die neuen Vokabeln ausdenkst, sie in Texte bzw. Lieder einbaust oder dich beim Vokabellernen in deinem Zimmer oder der Wohnung bewegst.
- Schreib die neuen Wörter auch immer auf und überprüfe die Schreibweise mithilfe des *Dictionary* oder *Vocabulary*.

Wie kannst du Wörter besser behalten?

Wörter kannst du besser behalten, wenn du sie in Wortgruppen sammelst und ordnest. Dazu gibt es verschiedene Möglichkeiten.

Du kannst ...

- **Gegensatzpaare** sammeln, z. B.
  old-fashioned – modern
  spicy – mild
  forget – remember
  sad – happy
  happy – unhappy

- Wörter mit **gleicher Bedeutung** sammeln, z. B.
  (to) train – (to) practise, film – movie
- Wörter in **Wortfamilien** sammeln, z. B.
  – **(to) dance, dance, dancer, dancing lessons**
  – **shop, shopper, shopping, shopping list, shop assistant** ...
  – **(to) ride (a horse/bike), (to) go riding, a bike ride, (to) take a ride, riding boots, riding hat**
- **Wortfelder** sammeln und ordnen, z. B. in Wortnetzen (*networks*) oder Wortlisten

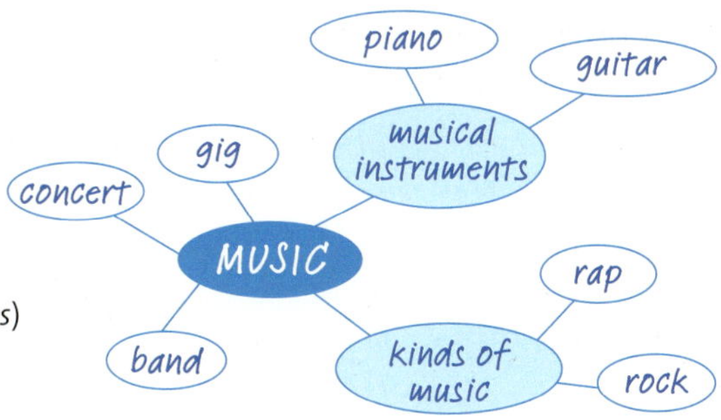

SF Using an English-German dictionary

▸ Unit 1 (p. 26)

Wann brauche ich ein englisch-deutsches Wörterbuch?

Du verstehst einen Text nicht, weil er zu viele Wörter enthält, die dir unbekannt sind? Dann kann dir ein englisch-deutsches Wörterbuch weiterhelfen.
Im Text „Only a game" auf S. 26 kommen eine Reihe von Wörtern vor, die du nicht kennst und die auch nicht in den EG 21-Wörterverzeichnissen aufgeführt sind, z. B. *experimental, at your own risk, lavender, Elizabethan, fog horn, rat, brick, footstep*.
Einige dieser Wörter kannst du sicherlich ableiten oder aus dem Zusammenhang erschließen. Wenn das nicht geht, hilft dir ein englisch-deutsches Wörterbuch.

Play at your own risk.

Something ran over his foot. A rat!

The boys could only see the fog, dirty brick walls, blood – and the lavender.

Wie benutze ich ein englisch-deutsches Wörterbuch?

- Die **Leitwörter** (*running heads*) oben auf der Seite helfen dir, schneller zu finden, was du suchst. Auf der linken Seite steht das erste Stichwort, auf der rechten Seite das letzte Stichwort der Doppelseite.
- rise ist das **Stichwort** (*headword*). Stichwörter sind alphabetisch geordnet: r vor s, ra vor re, rhe vor rhi usw.
- Die ***kursiv* gedruckten** Hinweise helfen dir, die für deinen Text passende Bedeutung zu finden.
- Die **Ziffern 1., 2.** usw. zeigen, dass ein Stichwort mehrere ganz verschiedene Bedeutungen hat.
- **Beispielsätze** und **Redewendungen** sind dem Stichwort zugeordnet. In den Beispielsätzen und Redewendungen ersetzt eine **Tilde** (~) das Stichwort.
- Die **Lautschrift** gibt Auskunft darüber, wie das Wort ausgesprochen und betont wird. ▸ English Sounds, p. 220
- **Unregelmäßige Verbformen**, die **Steigerungsformen der Adjektive** und ähnliche Hinweise stehen in Klammern.

riveting

rink [rɪŋk] Eisbahn
rinse [rɪns] **1** *Nomen; für Haare* Tönung **2** *Verb mit Obj; Kleidung, Haare* ausspülen; *Geschirr* (ab)spülen

rise [raɪz] **1** *Verb ohne Obj* (***rose, risen***) *aus Stuhl o. Ä.* aufstehen, sich erheben; *von Sonne* aufgehen; *von Rakete* aufsteigen; *von Preis, Temperatur* ansteigen; *von Wasseroberfläche* (an)steigen **2** *Nomen; von Preis, Temperatur* Anstieg; *von Wasseroberfläche* (An)Steigen; *von Sozialismus* Aufstieg; *von Gehalt* Gehaltserhöhung; ***give ~ to*** verursachen
risen ['rɪzn] *Part. Perf.* ☞ ***rise***
riser ['raɪzə]: ***be an early / late ~*** ein Frühaufsteher / Langschläfer sein
risk [rɪsk] **1** *Nomen* Risiko; ***take a ~*** ein Risiko eingehen; ***at one's own ~*** auf eigene Gefahr **2** *Verb mit Obj* riskieren; ***let's ~ it*** das Risiko gehen wir ein!
risky ['rɪski] (***-ier, -iest***) riskant
ritual ['rɪtjʊəl] **1** *Nomen* Ritual **2** *Adj* rituell
rival ['raɪvl] **1** *Nomen* Rivale, Rivalin; *von Firma, Mannschaft* Konkurrent(in) **2** *Verb mit Obj* (**-ll-**, *AE* **-l-**) *Person* rivalisieren mit; *Firma, Mannschaft* konkurrieren mit; ***I can't ~ that*** da kann ich nicht mithalten
rivalry ['raɪvlri] (*Pl* ***-ies***) Rivalität; *zwi-*

- Finde nun heraus, was die folgenden Wörter und Wendungen bedeuten:
  1. *at your own risk*
  2. '*rose*' in '*The rocket rose in the early morning.*'
  3. '*rises*' in '*The sun rises in the east.*'
  4. *brick*
  5. *lavender*
  6. *footstep*
- In deinem Wörterbuch werden vermutlich viele Abkürzungen und Symbole verwendet, wie z. B.
  jn.
  Obj
  Pl
  USA
  Finde heraus, was sie bedeuten.

SF Using a German-English dictionary ▸ *Unit 2 (p. 35)*

Wann brauche ich ein deutsch-englisches Wörterbuch?

Stell dir vor, du sollst einen Text über Katrina schreiben. Du findest, dass die Situation in der Schulherberge schwer für sie ist. Aber wie drückt man das auf Englisch aus? Was heißt „schwer" in diesem Fall?
In solchen Fällen hilft dir ein deutsch-englisches Wörterbuch.

Wie benutze ich ein deutsch-englisches Wörterbuch?

Viele Dinge sind dir wahrscheinlich vom *English-German dictionary* vertraut:

- **Leitwörter** (*running heads*) oben auf den Seiten helfen dir, das gesuchte Wort zu finden.
- Die **Stichwörter** (*headwords*) sind alphabetisch geordnet. **Beispielsätze** und **Redewendungen** sind den Stichwörtern zugeordnet. Die **Tilde** (~) ersetzt das Stichwort.
- Die ***kursiv* gedruckten** Hinweise helfen dir, die für deinen Text passende Bedeutung zu finden.
- Die **Ziffern 1., 2.** usw. zeigen, dass ein Stichwort mehrere ganz verschiedene Bedeutungen hat.
- Bei schwierig auszusprechenden Wörtern stehen auch Hinweise zu Aussprache und Betonung.
- Bei kniffligen Wörtern gibt es in vielen Wörterbüchern weitere Hilfen und Hinweise.

Schwester

schwer **1** *Adj; gewichtsmäßig* heavy ['hevi] (*auch Musik, Parfüm*); *schwierig* difficult, hard (*auch Arbeit*); *Wein, Zigarre* strong; *Essen* rich; *Krankheit, Fehler, Unfall, Schaden* serious ['sɪəriəs]; *Strafe* severe; *Gewitter, Kämpfe, Ausschreitungen* heavy, violent; ***schwere Zeiten*** hard times; ***100 Pfund ~ sein*** weigh [weɪ] 100 pounds; ***es ~ haben*** have a hard time; ***das ist ~ zu sagen*** it's hard to say **2** *Adv*: ***~ arbeiten*** work hard; ***~ beschädigt*** *Haus o.Ä.* severely damaged; ***ich bin ~ erkältet*** I've got a bad cold; ***er ist ~ zu verstehen*** it's hard to understand what he's saying; ***~ enttäuscht sein*** be* bitterly disappointed; ***das will ich ~ hoffen*** I really hope so; ☞ **schwerfallen, schwertun**

Schwerkraft … **Schwerpunkt** … **Schwert** sword … **schwertun**: … **Schwerverbrec…** offender … **schwerverwun…** **schwerwiegen…** ['sɪəriəs] **Schwester** … *als Anrede*

schwer krank

schwer

Das deutsche **schwer** hat drei Hauptbedeutungen:
1) *schwer von Gewicht*: **heavy**;
2) *schwerwiegend, ernst*: **serious**, **bad**;
3) *schwierig*: **difficult**, **hard**, **tough**.

Welche Entsprechung von **schwer** brauchst du in diesen Sätzen?
1. Das Leben im Internat ist schwer für Katrina.
2. Schultaschen sind für jüngere Schüler häufig zu schwer.
3. Heute Morgen war ein schwerer Unfall auf der Autobahn.
4. Die Matheaufgabe ist sehr schwer.
5. Nach einer schweren Krankheit kann er wieder zur Schule gehen.
6. Letzte Nacht gab es ein schweres Gewitter.

Tipp

Lies immer erst den **gesamten Wörterbucheintrag**, bevor du dich für eine bestimmte Übersetzung entscheidest. Nimm nicht einfach die erste Übersetzung, die dir angeboten wird!

SF REVISION Describing pictures

Wie kann ich Bilder beschreiben?

Wo?

- Um zu sagen, wo etwas abgebildet ist, benutze:
  at the top/bottom • in the foreground/background • in the middle • on the left/right
- Du kannst diese *phrases* auch kombinieren:
  at the bottom on the left • at the top on the right
- Diese Präpositionen sind auch hilfreich:
  behind • between • in front of • next to • under

Wie?

Geh bei der Beschreibung in einer bestimmten Reihenfolge vor, z. B. von links nach rechts, von oben nach unten oder vom Vordergrund zum Hintergrund.

Wie kann ich beschreiben, was die Personen auf dem Bild tun?

Um zu sagen, was die Personen auf dem Bild tun, benutze das **present progressive**.

Robert and Asif are standing inside the London Eye. They are looking into the camera.

SF REVISION Giving a presentation

Wie mache ich eine gute Präsentation?

Vorbereitung

- Schreib die wichtigsten Gedanken als Notizen auf, z. B. auf nummerierte Karteikarten oder als Mindmap.
- Bereite ein Poster oder eine Folie vor. Schreib groß und für alle gut lesbar.
- Übe deine Präsentation zu Hause vor einem Spiegel. Sprich laut, deutlich und langsam, mach Pausen.

Durchführung

- Bevor du beginnst, häng das Poster auf bzw. leg deine Folie auf den ausgeschalteten Projektor und sortiere deine Vortragskarten.
- Warte, bis es ruhig ist. Schau die Zuhörer an.
- Erkläre zu Anfang, worüber du sprechen wirst. Lies nicht von deinen Karten ab, sondern sprich frei.

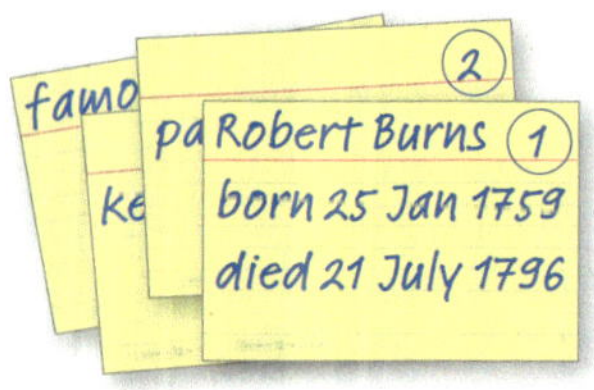

My presentation is about ...
First, I'd like to talk about ...
Second, ...

This picture/photo/... shows ...

Schluss

- Sag, dass du fertig bist.
- Frag die Zuhörenden, ob sie Fragen haben.
- Bedanke dich fürs Zuhören.

That's the end of my presentation. Have you got any questions?

LISTENING AND READING SKILLS

SF Listening for detail

REVISION Was muss ich beim *Listening* beachten?

Vor dem Hören
- Frag dich, was du schon über das Thema weißt.
- Nutze Überschriften oder Bilder, um zu erahnen, was dich z. B. bei einer Geschichte erwarten könnte.
- Bereite dich darauf vor, Notizen zu machen. Leg z. B. eine Tabelle oder Liste an.

Beim Hören
- Achte auf Geräusche, unterschiedliche Stimmen und wie Leute sprechen.
- Mach nur kurze Notizen, z. B. Anfangsbuchstaben, Symbole oder Stichworte, keine ganzen Sätze.
- Lass dich nicht verunsichern, wenn du mal einen Satz nicht verstehst.

Nach dem Hören
- Vervollständige deine Notizen sofort.
- Wenn du den Text ein zweites Mal hören kannst, konzentriere dich auf das, was du nicht sicher verstanden hast.

Wie kann ich Einzelheiten (*details*) heraushören?

1. Mach dir bewusst, welche Einzelheiten du heraushören sollst bzw. willst. Lass dich nicht von anderen Einzelheiten ablenken.
2. Manche Signalwörter machen es dir leichter, den Hörtext zu verstehen.
   Aufzählung: **and**, **another**, **too**
   Gegensatz: **although**, **but**
   Grund, Folge: **because**, **so**, **so that**
   Vergleich: **larger/older/... than**, **more**, **most**
   Reihenfolge: **before**, **after**, **then**, **next**, **later**, **when**, **at last**, **at the same time**
3. Wenn du Details wie Zahlen (z. B. Telefonnummern) oder Namen heraushören sollst, hilft es, sie beim Aufschreiben zu unterteilen, also z. B. statt 01715724589 lieber 0171 572 45 89.

SF REVISION Multiple-choice exercises

Worauf sollte ich bei Multiple-Choice-Aufgaben achten?

- Lies die Frage sehr genau durch.
- Bevor du dir die Lösungsangebote anschaust, deck sie mit Papier ab. Überlege dir, was die richtige Antwort sein könnte. Wenn das dann auch als eine Lösungsmöglichkeit angeboten wird, ist es meistens richtig.
- Lies immer alle vorgegebenen Lösungen, bevor du dich entscheidest.
- Sprich die Sätze mit den verschiedenen Lösungsmöglichkeiten leise nach. Oft hört man heraus, was richtig ist.
- Achte darauf, dass du nur **eine** der Antworten ankreuzt.
- Mach erst alle Aufgaben und geh zum Schluss zu den Fragen zurück, bei denen du unsicher bist.

1 Which is a famous London sight?
A Brandenburg Gate
B Eiffel Tower
C Buckingham Palace
D the Orkney Islands

2 What did Robert and Asif do at the Trocadero?
A play football
B eat Indian food
C visit Asif's family
D play a new game

SF REVISION Scanning

Lesen, um nach Informationen zu suchen

Du musst einen Text manchmal gar nicht genau lesen, wenn du nur bestimmte Informationen (für eine spezielle Aufgabe) brauchst. Suche den Text nach Schlüsselwörtern (**key words**) ab und lies nur dort genauer, wo du sie findest. Manchmal sind in Aufgaben bereits Schlüsselwörter vorgegeben, nach denen du in einem Text suchen sollst. So möchte Asif z. B. in A6 auf S. 16 *something spicy or very spicy*. Auf der Speisekarte findest du dazu solche Speisen unter TIKKA und JALFREZI DISHES, d. h. du brauchst nur dort weiterzusuchen.

Wie gehe ich vor?

Schritt 1: Bevor du auf den Text schaust
Denk an das Schlüsselwort, nach dem du suchst. Es hilft dir, wenn du es aufschreibst.

Schritt 2: Das Schlüsselwort finden
Geh mit deinen Augen sehr schnell durch den Text. Dabei hast du das Schriftbild oder das Bild des Wortes, nach dem du suchst, vor Augen. Das gesuchte Wort wird dir sofort „ins Auge springen".
Du kannst auch mit dem Finger durch den Text gehen: in breiten Schlingen oder Bewegungen wie bei einem „S" oder „Z" oder von oben nach unten und wieder herauf wie bei einem „U".
Wenn du das Schlüsselwort gefunden hast, lies nur dort weiter, um Näheres zu erfahren.

Schritt 3: Gegebenenfalls neue Schlüsselwörter finden
Es kann dir passieren, dass das Schlüsselwort, nach dem du suchst, im Text nicht vorkommt. Dann musst du überlegen, welche anderen Wörter mit den benötigten Informationen zu tun haben, und nach diesen suchen. Stell dir z. B. vor, du suchst auf einer Speisekarte ein Gericht mit Fleisch. Das Wort *meat* steht aber nirgends. Dann versuch es z. B. mit *lamb*, *chicken* oder *pork*.

Tipp

Wenn du wie bei Aufgabe 6 auf S. 16 nach mehreren Schlüsselwörtern suchen musst, scanne den Text nach jedem Schlüsselwort einzeln.

SF Skimming

▸ Unit 5 (p. 90)

Lesen, um sich einen Überblick zu verschaffen

Skimming bedeutet, dass du in kurzer Zeit einen Text flüchtig überfliegst, um dir einen Überblick zu verschaffen, worum es geht. Das ist z. B. sehr nützlich, wenn du herausfinden willst, ob ein Text, den du im Internet oder in einem Buch gefunden hast, die Informationen enthält, nach denen du (z. B. für ein Referat) suchst.

Wie gehe ich vor?

Wichtige Informationen über den Text geben dir

- die **Überschrift**
- **hervorgehobene** Wörter oder Sätze
- die **Bilder** und **Bildunterschriften**
- die **Zwischenüberschriften**
- der **erste Satz** jedes Absatzes
- der **letzte Satz** des Textes
- **Grafiken** und **Statistiken**
- die **Quelle** des Textes

'Hello Glasgow! It's good to be home!'

Franz Ferdinand play fantastic gig in their home town

Review by J. Colthorpe

Franz Ferdinand get Glasgow dancing

They have come a long way since they started out playing gigs in Glasgow's local indie clubs back in 2001. Two successful albums and a world tour later, Franz Ferdinand are one of the most popular bands in the world today. But last night they were back playing in their hometown, Glasgow, and this time to a much larger audience than they did six years ago.

Electric atmosphere

The atmosphere outside the concert hall was electric. The crowd were excited and many fans were already singing their favourite Franz Ferdinand songs. Inside the place was full and noisy; people were pushing through the crowds, hoping to get down near the stage. Soon the support band had finished and it was time for Franz Ferdinand to take to the stage.

All the favourite hits

'Hello Glasgow! It's good to be home!' shouted singer Alex Kapranos as he ran onto the stage. The crowd cheered as Alex started with "Jacqueline", the first song off their first album. He was soon joined by Bob Hardy on bass guitar as the song kicked in followed by Paul Thomsen on the drums. All of their popular songs followed to make up a 16-song, 90 minute set. They finished with their classic "Take Me Out" – the perfect song to end an excellent show.

Not only girls

Franz Ferdinand once said that they want to make music that girls can dance to. Well, they have certainly done that. Last night everybody was dancing, girls and boys.

New Amsterdam Music Review 18th December 2007

- Überflieg den Artikel, um herauszufinden, worum es darin geht.
- Dann mach die Aufgabe 1 auf Seite 90.

SF REVISION Taking notes

Worum geht es beim Notizen machen?

Wenn du beim Lesen oder Zuhören Notizen machst, kannst du dich später besser daran erinnern, wenn du etwas vortragen, nacherzählen oder einen Bericht schreiben sollst.

Wie mache ich Notizen?

In Texten oder Gesprächen gibt es immer wichtige und unwichtige Wörter. Die wichtigen Wörter werden Schlüsselwörter (**key words**) genannt und nur die solltest du notieren. Meist sind das Substantive und Verben, manchmal auch Adjektive oder Zahlen.

Tipp

- Verwende Ziffern (z. B. „7" statt „seven").
- Verwende Symbole und Abkürzungen, z. B. ✔ (für Ja) und + (für und) oder GB für Great Britain, K. für Katrina.
  Du kannst auch eigene Symbole erfinden.
- Verwende **not** oder ✕ statt „doesn't" oder „don't".

SF REVISION Marking up a text

Wann sollte ich einen Text markieren?

Du hast einen Text mit vielen Fakten vor dir liegen und sollst später über bestimmte Dinge berichten. Dann wird es dir helfen, die für dich wichtigen Informationen im Text zu markieren.

Wie gehe ich am besten vor?

Lies den Text und markiere nur die für dein Thema wichtigen Informationen. Nicht jeder Satz enthält für deine Aufgabe wichtige Wörter und oft reicht es aus, nur ein oder zwei Wörter in einem Satz zu markieren.

- Du kannst wichtige Wörter einkreisen.
- Du kannst sie unterstreichen.
- Du kannst sie mit einem Textmarker hervorheben.

The British Museum has one of the largest and most fascinating collections of mummies in the world outside of Cairo. The collection of mummies shows the visitor the unusual way the Egyptian people prepared the dead Pharaohs before they

The British Museum has one of the largest and most fascinating collections of mummies in the world outside of Cairo. The collection of mummies shows the visitor the unusual way the Egyptian people prepared the dead Pharaohs before they

The British Museum has one of the largest and most fascinating collections of mummies in the world outside of Cairo. The collection of mummies shows the visitor the unusual way the Egyptian people prepared the dead Pharaohs before they

ABER:
Markiere nur auf Fotokopien von Texten oder in deinen eigenen Büchern.

MEDIATION SKILLS

SF Mediation ▸ *Unit 4 (p. 78)*

REVISION Wann muss ich zwischen zwei Sprachen vermitteln?

Manchmal musst du zwischen zwei Sprachen vermitteln. Das nennt man **mediation**.

1. Du gibst englische Informationen auf Deutsch weiter:
   Du fährst z. B. mit deiner Familie nach Großbritannien und deine Eltern oder Geschwister wollen wissen, was jemand in einem Café gesagt hat oder was an einer Informationstafel steht.
2. Du gibst deutsche Informationen auf Englisch weiter:
   Vielleicht ist bei dir zu Hause eine Austauschschülerin aus England oder Dänemark zu Gast, die kein Deutsch spricht und Hilfe braucht.
3. In schriftlichen Prüfungen musst du manchmal in einem englischen Text gezielt nach Informationen suchen und diese auf Deutsch wiedergeben.

REVISION Worauf muss ich bei *mediation* achten?

- Übersetze nicht alles wörtlich.
- Gib nur das Wesentliche weiter, lass Unwichtiges weg.
- Verwende kurze und einfache Sätze.
- Wenn du ein Wort nicht kennst, umschreibe es oder ersetze es durch ein anderes Wort.

Was kann ich tun, wenn ich ein wichtiges Wort nicht kenne?

Vielleicht findest du es manchmal schwer, mündliche Aussagen oder schriftliche Textvorlagen in die andere Sprache zu übertragen, z. B. weil:
- dein Wortschatz nicht ausreicht
- dir bekannte Wörter „im Stress“ nicht einfallen
- spezielle Fachbegriffe auftauchen.

Manche Wörter kannst du umschreiben, z. B. mithilfe von Relativsätzen wie:
It's somebody/a person who ...
It's something that you use to ... ▸ *Paraphrasing (p. 134)*
It's an animal that ...
It's a place that ...

SPEAKING AND WRITING SKILLS

SF Paraphrasing ▸ *Unit 3 (p. 56)*

Worum geht es beim Paraphrasing?

Paraphrasing bedeutet, etwas mit anderen Worten zu erklären. Man kann vieles umschreiben, z. B. einen Gegenstand, eine Tätigkeit oder eine Person.

Paraphrasing ist auch besonders nützlich für **mediation.** ▸ *Mediation (p. 133)*

Wie gehe ich beim Paraphrasing vor?

- Man kann mit einem Wort umschreiben, das dieselbe Bedeutung hat:
  To begin is the same as to start.
  Oder man sagt das Gegenteil:
  To win is the opposite of to lose.
- Manchmal braucht man mehrere Wörter, z. B. wenn man etwas beschreibt oder erklären will, wie man es verwendet. Dabei benutzt man ein allgemeines Wort (**general word**) und nennt weitere Eigenschaften.
  A half-pipe is a location for skateboarders.
- Oder du beginnst mit **It's like ...**
  It's like a path through the woods or the fields and you can ride your horse on it. (*a bridle path*)
- Du kannst zum Umschreiben auch einen Relativsatz (**relative clause**) verwenden:
  A coach is a person who trains sports teams.
  A swimsuit is something that girls wear when they go swimming.

1. Umschreibe ein Wort aus der linken Spalte mit einem Wort aus der rechten Spalte. Benutze **the same as** oder **the opposite of**.

sad	parents
white	happy
clean	black
wonderful	dirty
mother/father	great

2. Schau dir diese Umschreibungen an. Findest du ein passendes Wort dafür?
- **It's a man or woman who looks funny and works in a circus.**
- **It's something you put food on.**
- **It's a place where you watch films.**
- **It's something that you use to play table tennis.**

3. What's wrong here? Correct the sentences.
- **A horse is a place where lots of supporters go to watch a match.**
- **A stadium is a meal that you eat in the evening.**
- **Dinner is an animal you can ride on.**

SF Brainstorming

▸ Unit 4 (p. 80)

Wofür ist Brainstorming gut?

Write a text about a great weekend oder *Prepare a presentation on …* – so oder so ähnlich lauten viele Aufgaben, die dir im Unterricht gestellt werden. Ob mündliche Präsentation oder das Schreiben eines Textes – bei beiden Formen ist es nützlich, wenn du im ersten Schritt möglichst viele Ideen zum Thema sammelst. Dabei hilft dir das Brainstorming. Schau dir die folgenden drei Brainstorming-Techniken an – sie kommen dir wahrscheinlich vertraut vor.

Drei verschiedene Brainstorming-Techniken

Technik 1: Making a list

Schreib die Ideen so auf, wie sie dir einfallen, und zwar für jede Idee eine neue Zeile.

Lies alle deine Ideen durch. Überlege, was davon für das Thema sinnvoll ist und wie du diese Ideen zusammenfassen kannst.

no homework
sleep late – every morning
watch DVDs
disco/party with friends
swimming pool
parents not at home
hang out

Technik 2: Making a mind map

1. Schreib das Thema in die Mitte eines leeren, unlinierten Blattes Papier. Male einen Kreis oder eine Wolke drum herum.
2. Überlege dir, welche Oberbegriffe zu deiner Sammlung von Ideen passen. Verwende unterschiedliche Farben.
3. Ergänze jede Idee, die zu einem Oberbegriff passt, auf einem Nebenast. Nimm dafür nur wichtige Schlüsselwörter. Du kannst statt Wörtern auch Symbole verwenden und Bilder ergänzen.

Technik 3: The 5 Ws

Schreib die 5 W-Fragen **Who? What? When? Where? Why?** in eine Tabelle. Die Ideen, die dir zu der jeweiligen Frage kommen, werden daruntergeschrieben.

who	*what*	*when*	*where*	*why*
I + friends	*do sports*	*Friday*	*at home*	*no homework*
no parents	*go to disco*	*Saturday*	*at friends'*	*no jobs to do*
	chat		*swimming pool*	*have fun*
	sleep late			

WRITING COURSE – ZUSAMMENFASSUNG

The steps of writing

1. Brainstorming – Ideen sammeln und ordnen (s. S. 135).
2. Schreiben. Dabei achte darauf,
   - deine Sätze zu verbinden und auszubauen (*Writing better sentences*)
   - deinen Text gut zu strukturieren (*Using paragraphs*)
   - bei einem Bericht die 5 Ws abzudecken (*Writing a report*).
3. Deinen Text inhaltlich und sprachlich überprüfen (*Correcting your text*).

Writing better sentences

▸ *Unit 1 (p. 22)*

REVISION Linking words

Eine Geschichte klingt interessanter, wenn man die Sätze mit **linking words** miteinander verbindet. Dabei gibt es mehrere Möglichkeiten:

- **Time phrases** wie **at 7 o'clock, every morning, in the afternoons, a few minutes later, suddenly, then, next ...**
- **Konjunktionen** wie **although, and, because, but, so ... that, that, when, while**
- **Relativpronomen** wie **that** und **who**. ▸ *Unit 3 (p. 55)*

Adjektive und Adverbien

- Mit Adjektiven kannst du eine Person, einen Ort, einen Gegenstand oder ein Erlebnis genauer beschreiben und interessanter gestalten. Vergleiche:
  The man looked into the room. ▸ **The young man looked into the empty room.**
- Mit Adverbien kannst du beschreiben, **wie** jemand etwas macht:
  The young man looked into the empty room nervously.

Using paragraphs

▸ *Unit 2 (p. 39)*

REVISION Structuring a text

Ein Text ist viel besser zu verstehen, wenn er mehrere Absätze enthält:

- eine Einleitung (**beginning**) – hier schreibst du, worum es geht
- einen Mittelteil (**middle**) – hier schreibst du mehr über dein Thema
- einen Schluss (**end**) – hier bringst du den Text zu einem interessanten Ende.

REVISION Topic Sentences

Am Anfang eines Absatzes sind kurze, einleitende Sätze (**topic sentences**) gut, z. B.

1. Orte: **My trip to ... was fantastic./... is famous for .../... is a great place.**
2. Personen: ... **is great/funny/interesting/clever ...**
3. Aktivitäten: ... **is great fun./Lots of people ... every day.**

Wie kann ich meine Absätze interessant gestalten?

- Beginne mit einem interessanten Einstiegssatz:
  Guess what happened to me today!/Did I tell you that ...?
- Fang für jeden neuen Aspekt einen neuen Absatz an.
- Beende deinen Text mit einer Zusammenfassung oder etwas Persönlichem.

Writing a report – structuring information ▸ Unit 3 (p. 64)

Worauf kommt es bei einem Bericht an?

Wenn du einen Bericht von einem Spiel oder Ereignis schreibst, beachte:
- Gib dem Leser **eine schnelle Orientierung**, was passiert ist.
- Beginne mit **wichtigen Informationen** und gib erst dann Detailinformationen.
- Achte darauf, dass du die 5 Ws immer abdeckst:
  Who? What? When? Where? Why? und manchmal auch **How?**

Correcting your text ▸ Unit 5 (p. 96)

Ein Text ist noch nicht „fertig“, wenn du ihn zu Ende geschrieben hast. Du solltest ihn immer mehrmals durchlesen:
- einmal, um zu sehen, ob er vollständig und gut verständlich ist
- noch einmal, um ihn auf Fehler zu überprüfen, z. B. **Rechtschreibfehler (*spelling mistakes*)** oder **Grammatikfehler (*grammar mistakes*)**.

REVISION Spelling mistakes

Lies deinen Text langsam, Wort für Wort, Buchstabe für Buchstabe. Wenn du unsicher bist, hilft dir ein Wörterbuch. Beachte folgende Regeln:

Tipp
- Manche Wörter haben Buchstaben, die man nicht spricht, aber schreibt, z. B. **walk**, **know**.
- Manchmal ändert sich die Schreibweise, wenn ein Wort eine Endung erhält, z. B. **take** → **taking**, **grumble** → **grumbled**, **happy** → **happily**, **fly** → **flies** (**aber** **stay** → **stays**), **run** → **running**, **plan** → **planned**.
- Beim Plural muss manchmal noch ein *-e* zum *-s*, z. B. **box** → **boxes**.

Grammar mistakes

Diese Tipps helfen dir, typische Fehler zu vermeiden:

Tipp
- Im **simple present** wird in der 3. Person Singular **-s** angehängt: **she knows**.
- **Unregelmäßige Verben**: Manche Verben bilden die Formen des *simple past* und des Partizip Perfekt (*past participle*) unregelmäßig. Die unregelmäßigen Formen musst du lernen. Die Liste steht auf S. 224–225.
  go – went – gone; buy – bought – bought
- **Verneinung**: Im *simple present* werden Vollverben mit **don't/doesn't** verneint, im *simple past* mit **didn't**, z. B. **My grandpa doesn't speak English. / He didn't learn English at school**.
- **Satzstellung**: Im Englischen gilt immer (auch im Nebensatz):
  a) subject – verb – object (SVO) ... when **I saw my brother**.
  als **ich meinen Bruder sah**.
  b) Orts- vor Zeitangabe **I bought a nice book <u>in the city yesterday</u>**.

tomato [tə'mɑːtəʊ], *pl* tomatoes Tomate II

wife [waɪf], *pl* wives [waɪvz] Ehefrau II

drop (-pp-) [drɒp] fallen lassen I

forget (-tt-) [fə'get] vergessen I

Grammar File – Inhalt

Im **Grammar File** (S. 138–149) wird zusammengefasst, was du in den fünf Units **über die englische Sprache** lernst.

In der **linken Spalte** findest du **Beispielsätze** und **Übersichten**, z.B.

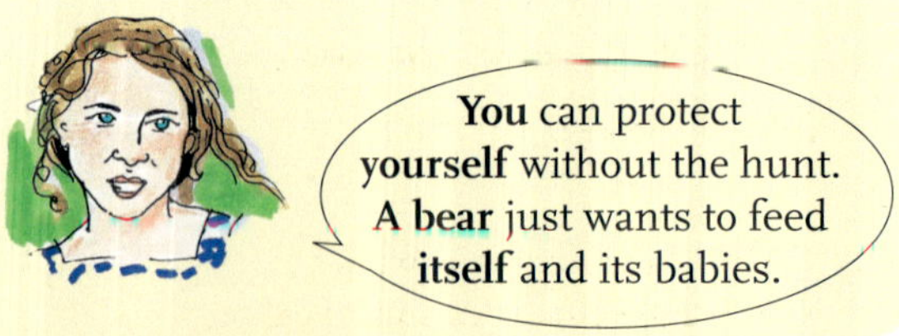

Reflexive pronouns

Singular

myself	(ich) mir/mich
yourself	(du) dir/dich
himself	(er`

In der **rechten Spalte** stehen **Erklärungen** und nützliche **Hinweise**. Das **rote Ausrufezeichen** (**!**) macht dich auf besondere Fehlerquellen aufmerksam.

Hinweise wie ► *Unit 1 (p. 15)* • *P 4–5 (p. 21)* zeigen dir, zu welcher Unit und welcher Seite ein **Grammar-File-**Abschnitt gehört und welche Übungen du dazu im Practice-Teil findest.

Die **grammatischen Fachbegriffe** (*grammatical terms*) kannst du auf den Seiten 148–149 nachschlagen.

Am Ende der Abschnitte stehen wieder kleine Aufgaben zur Selbstkontrolle. Schreib die Lösungen in dein Heft. Überprüfe sie dann auf Seite 149.

Unit 1

GF 1 The present perfect and the simple past in contrast

Das *present perfect* und das *simple past* im Vergleich

a) REVISION The simple past

Last weekend Robert **went** to London with his parents.

In the afternoon they **visited** the Tower, and then they **took** the Tube to Waterloo.

Asif **met** them at the London Eye and they all **had** a great time.

▸ *Unit 1 (p. 15) • P 4–5 (p. 21)*

Die einfache Form der Vergangenheit

Mit dem ***simple past*** berichtest du über Vergangenes – z. B., wenn du eine Geschichte erzählst.
Das *simple past* drückt aus, dass etwas zu einem **bestimmten Zeitpunkt** oder **in einem bestimmten abgeschlossenen Zeitraum** in der Vergangenheit geschah. (Frage: **Wann?**)
Daher findest du in *simple past*-Sätzen oft **genaue Zeitangaben** wie *last weekend, yesterday, a week ago, in 2005*.

b) REVISION The present perfect

Asif **has** already **visited** the London Trocadero.
... hat schon mal ... besucht

He **has** always **wanted** to go on the London Eye, but he **hasn't done** that yet.
... hat schon immer ... gehen wollen
... hat ... noch nicht getan

He and his friends **have** often **been** to Brick Lane Market.
... sind schon oft ... gewesen

▸ *Unit 1 (p. 16) • P 8–9 (p. 23)*

Das *present perfect*

Mit dem ***present perfect*** drückst du aus, dass etwas **irgendwann in der Vergangenheit** geschehen ist.
Daher findest du oft **Adverbien der unbestimmten Zeit** in *present perfect*-Sätzen, z. B.

already	schon (mal)	*always*	(schon) immer
just	gerade (eben)	*never*	(noch) nie
not ... yet	noch nicht	*often*	(schon) oft
ever?	jemals?	*yet?*	schon?

! Beim ***present perfect*** ist der genaue Zeitpunkt des Geschehens nicht wichtig oder nicht bekannt.

c) Present perfect or simple past?

▸ *Unit 1 (p. 17) • P 11–12 (p. 24)*

Present perfect oder *simple past*?

◂ 1 Asif fragt, ob Robert **überhaupt schon mal** türkisch gegessen hat – also ***present perfect***:

***Have** you ever **tried** Turkish food?*

◂ 2 Dann möchte er wissen, **wann** das war, und er fragt daher im ***simple past***:

*And when **did** you **try** it?*

◂ 3 Robert antwortet im ***simple past***, weil er den **genauen Zeitpunkt** nennt:

*We **went** to a Turkish restaurant last Saturday.*

Present perfect *oder* simple past? *Schreib den vollständigen Dialog in dein Heft.*

Robert ... you ever (visit) the Natural History Museum?
Asif Yes, I ...
Robert When ... you (go) there?
Asif We ... (go) in the summer holidays last year.
But I ... (not see) the British Museum yet.
Robert Oh, I ... (visit) that with my aunt und uncle a few months ago.

Unit 2

GF 2 The *will*-future for spontaneous decisions

Das Futur mit *will* für spontane Entschlüsse

a) REVISION The *will*-future

Katrina's mum **(Vorhersage)** Hurry up, Katrina! We'**ll be** late for the ferry.

Katrina **(Vermutung)** No, we **won't**. I'm ready now. And I suppose the ferry **will be** a few minutes late anyway.

▸ *Unit 2 (p. 33)* • *P 5 (p. 40)*

Das Futur mit *will*

Mit *will* + Infinitiv kannst du über die Zukunft sprechen. Du verwendest es für Vorhersagen und Vermutungen.

Die Kurzform von *will not* heißt *won't*.

b) Spontaneous decisions

Die Taschen aus der Zeitschrift. Ich zeig sie dir ... hier, schau.

▸ *Unit 2 (p. 34)*

Spontane Entschlüsse

Du verwendest das *will-future* auch, wenn du einen spontanen (nicht geplanten) Entschluss fasst. Oft handelt es sich dabei um Hilfsangebote oder Versprechen.

! Im Deutschen steht bei einem spontanen Entschluss meist die Gegenwart. Im Englischen muss das *will-future* stehen:
I'll show you ...
Ich zeig sie dir ...

GF 3 Conditional sentences Bedingungssätze

a) REVISION Conditional sentences (type 1)

Alison If they **choose** you, you**'ll be** a star.
Wenn sie dich wählen, bist du ... /
Wenn sie dich wählen, wirst du ... sein.

Linda If I **don't get** to the shop soon, they **won't have** those trendy new bags any more.

▸ *Unit 2 (p. 34) • P 7 (p. 41)*

Bedingungssätze (Typ 1)

Du kennst bereits Bedingungssätze vom Typ 1 (**„Was ist, wenn ...“-Sätze**).
Sie sagen aus, was unter bestimmten Bedingungen geschieht oder nicht geschieht:

***if*-Satz (Bedingung)**	**Hauptsatz (Folge)**
*If they **choose** you,*	*you**'ll be** a star.*
simple present	***will-future***

b) Conditional sentences (type 2)

If a film-maker **discovered** me, I **would be** famous.

Wenn ein Filmemacher mich entdecken würde, wäre ich berühmt / würde ich berühmt.

I **wouldn't live** here if I **was** rich and famous.

Ich würde nicht hier wohnen, wenn ich reich und berühmt wäre.

▸ *Unit 2 (p. 35) • P 8–10 (p. 41)*

Bedingungssätze (Typ 2)

Bedingungssätze vom Typ 2 sind **„Was wäre, wenn ...“-Sätze**.
Sie drücken aus, was unter bestimmten Bedingungen **sein würde**, aber doch eher unwahrscheinlich ist (oder sogar unmöglich):

Es ist unwahrscheinlich, dass Fiona von einem Filmemacher entdeckt werden wird. Also wird sie wahrscheinlich auch nicht berühmt.

***if*-Satz (Bedingung)**	**Hauptsatz (Folge)**
*If a film-maker **discovered** me,*	*I **would be** famous.*
simple past	***would + infinitive***

(Kurzform von *I/you/he/... would: I'd / you'd / he'd / ...*)

! Im *if*-Satz steht **kein *would***.
Also nicht:
If a film-maker ~~would discover~~ me, ...

If I **had** enough money, I could **buy** a new bike.
Wenn ich genug Geld hätte, könnte ich mir ein neues Rad kaufen.

Im Hauptsatz kann auch *could* („könnte“) stehen.

Vervollständige die Sätze in deinem Heft. Achte auf die richtige Form der Verben.

1 If the other girls ... (call) Latisha names, she wouldn't listen.
2 Latisha would forget the girls if she ... (be) Katrina.
3 Katrina ... (be) much happier if the girls ... (not call) her 'Fishface'.
4 If the girls ... (be) friendly to her, she ... (not be) upset.
5 If people ... (call) you 'Fishface', you ... (be) upset too. Right?
6 What would you do if classmates ... (call) you names?

Unit 3

GF 4 Relative clauses Relativsätze

The girl who plays for United U14s is Latisha.
Das Mädchen, das für die U14 von *United* spielt, ...

Anna is **an exchange student** who is staying with Latisha.
... eine Austauschschülerin, die bei Latisha wohnt.

Banglaboy is **a boy** who Latisha knows from the festival in Birmingham.
... ein Junge, den Latisha vom Festival ... kennt.

Mit Relativsätzen sagst du genauer, wen oder was du meinst.

◂ In Relativsätzen, die **Personen** beschreiben, verwendest du ***who***:
***the man / the woman / people** who* ...
der Mann, der ... / die Frau, die ... / Leute, die ...

Anna wants to go to **a shop** that sells cheap CDs.
... zu einem Laden, der billige CDs verkauft.

Mrs Byrd has cooked **a dish** that Anna likes.
... ein Gericht, das Anna mag.

◂ In Relativsätzen, die **Dinge** (und Tiere) beschreiben, verwendest du ***that***:
***the shop / the dish / an animal** that* ...
der Laden, der ... / das Gericht, das ... / ein Tier, das ...

... **a shop** which sells cheap CDs
The girl that plays for United U14s ...

Für Dinge (und Tiere) wird auch *which* verwendet. Und manchmal findest du auch *that* für Personen.

The girl **who plays** football ...

Das Mädchen, **das** Fußball **spielt** ...

! Beachte die unterschiedliche Wortstellung in englischen und deutschen Relativsätzen.

▸ *Unit 3 (p. 55)* • *P 4–6 (pp. 61–62)*

Wo brauchst du who, *wo brauchst du* that?

1 Anna is the German girl ... is staying with Latisha.
2 Latisha thinks jazz dance is a sport ... is really hard work.
3 What's the name of the player ... scored two goals in United U14s' last match?
4 Stewed chicken is a dish ... comes from Trinidad, isn't it?

GF 5 Contact clauses Relativsätze ohne Relativpronomen

Das Relativpronomen kann **Subjekt** oder **Objekt** sein.

1 An artist is somebody **who** paints pictures.
..., **der** Bilder malt.

1 Das Relativpronomen ist **Subjekt des Relativsatzes** (es steht direkt vor dem Verb):

	Subjekt	
An artist is somebody	***who***	*paints pictures.*
Ein Künstler ist jemand,	***der***	*Bilder malt.*
The Lowry is a museum	***that***	*has something for everybody.*
Das Lowry ist ein Museum,	***das***	*für jeden etwas hat.*

2 Beckham is the only player who Anna knows.
..., den Anna kennt.

2 Das Relativpronomen ist Objekt **des Relativsatzes**:

	Objekt	Subjekt	
Beckham is the only player	*who*	*Anna*	*knows.*
Beckham ist der einzige Spieler,	*den*	*Anna*	*kennt.*
Football is a sport	*that*	*Latisha*	*loves.*
Fußball ist ein Sport,	*den*	*Latisha*	*liebt.*

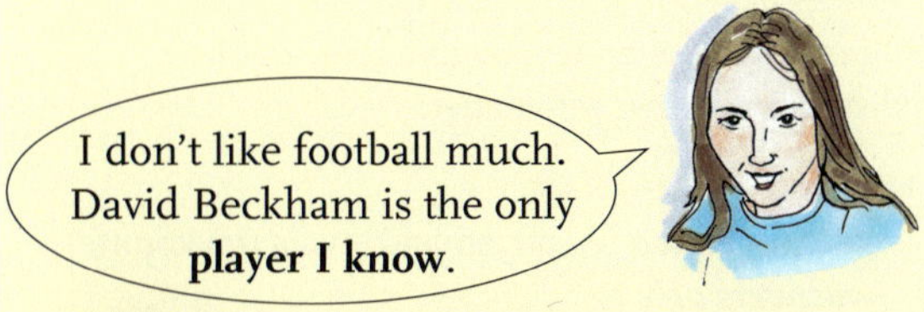

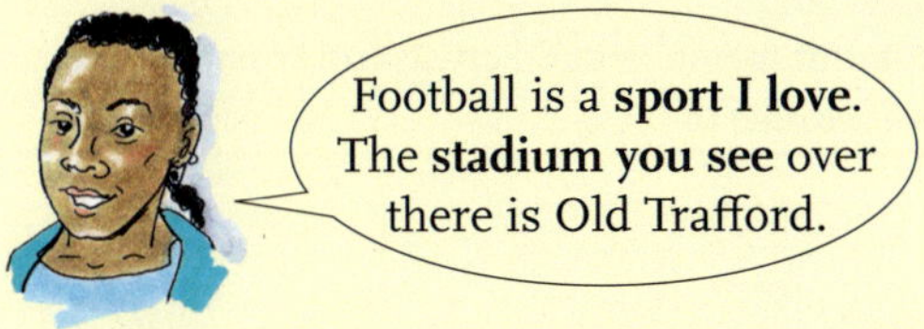

◄ Wenn *who* oder *that* **Objekt** des Relativsatzes ist, wird es manchmal **weggelassen** – wie in den Beispielen links.
Relativsätze ohne Relativpronomen nennt man *contact clauses.*

An artist is somebody [who paints] pictures.
(*not:* An artist is ~~somebody paints pictures~~.)

! Achtung:
Wenn das **Relativpronomen direkt vor dem Verb** steht, ist es Subjekt – dann darfst du es **nicht weglassen**!

The **boy Latisha is chatting** with is Banglaboy.
Der Junge, mit dem Latisha chattet, ist Banglaboy.

The **stadium they are looking** at is Old Trafford.

► *Unit 3 (p.56) • P 7 (p.62)*

! Beachte die Stellung der Präposition in Relativsätzen mit Verben wie *talk to, chat with, look at, stay with.*
Die Präposition steht an derselben Stelle wie im Hauptsatz:

Latisha is** chatting with **Banglaboy.
The boy ***Latisha is** chatting with **is Banglaboy.***

Wo kannst du who *und* that *weglassen? Schreib die Sätze als* contact clauses *in dein Heft.*

1 Anna is the girl who is staying with the Byrds.
2 Which is the museum that the whole family will love?
3 Football and jazz dance are sports that Latisha likes a lot.
4 David Beckham is a football star who everybody knows.
5 Lowry is an artist who came from Manchester.
6 Let's do something that we both want to do.

Unit 4

GF 6 Modals and their substitutes — Modale Hilfsverben und ihre Ersatzverben

a) REVISION *can – may – must*

can – may – must

Diese modalen Hilfsverben (*modal auxiliaries* oder kurz: *modals*) sagen, dass jemand etwas tun **kann, darf** oder **muss**:

- **„können“:** *can*
- **„dürfen“:** *can, may*
- **„müssen“:** *must*.

Latisha can play football very well.
Can/May I go to the match, Mum?
Latisha must do her homework first.

b) *(to) be able to – (to) be allowed to – (to) have to*

(to) be able to – (to) be allowed to – (to) have to

Wenn es um „können/dürfen/müssen“ in der Vergangenheit oder der Zukunft geht, werden meist **Ersatzverben** verwendet:

„können“: *(to) be able to*

- **Vergangenheit** (wenn jemand etwas tun **konnte**): ***was/were able to***
- **Zukunft** (wenn jemand etwas tun **können wird**): ***will be able to***

Robert was ill on Friday, but he was able to **go** to the disco on Saturday. ... konnte gehen ...

Jessica didn't have much time yesterday, but she will be able to **buy** a present for Ashley tomorrow. ... wird kaufen können ...

„dürfen“: *(to) be allowed to*

- **Vergangenheit** (wenn jemand etwas tun **durfte**): ***was/were allowed to***
- **Zukunft** (wenn jemand etwas tun **dürfen wird**): ***will be allowed to***

Emily wasn't allowed to **go** to Sam's party last month. ... durfte nicht gehen ...

She won't be allowed to **go** to Ashley's party on Saturday. ... wird nicht gehen dürfen...

„müssen“: *(to) have to*

- **Vergangenheit** (wenn jemand etwas tun **musste**): ***had to***
- **Zukunft** (wenn jemand etwas tun **müssen wird**): ***will have to***

Jessica had to **clean** her room yesterday. ... musste putzen ...

She can go to the party, but she will have to **be** home by ten. ... wird sein müssen ...

! Alle Ersatzverben werden auch im *simple present* verwendet.

Robert doesn't play an instrument, but he's able to DJ.

Emily I'm not allowed to **go** to parties!

Sam Hey Robert, I have to **talk** to you.

I could **hear** music, but I couldn't **see** anybody.

Zu *can* gibt es auch die Vergangenheitsform *could* („konnte“). Sie steht vor allem in verneinten Sätzen und Fragen und mit Verben der Wahrnehmung *(see, hear, ...)*.

▸ *Unit 4 (p. 71) • P 4–6 (p. 77)*

Vervollständige den Dialog mit Formen von be able to, be allowed to *und* have to.

Jessica My mother is so strict. Yesterday I wanted to buy a present for Ashley, but I ... (have to) tidy my room.
Emily My parents are strict too. I'm sure I ... (not be allowed to) go to Ashley's party.
Jessica Well, I'm sure I ... (have to) be home by ten again, as always.
Robert I ... (not be able to) go to the party because I'm going to drive to our cabin with my parents.

GF 7 Reflexive pronouns   Reflexivpronomen

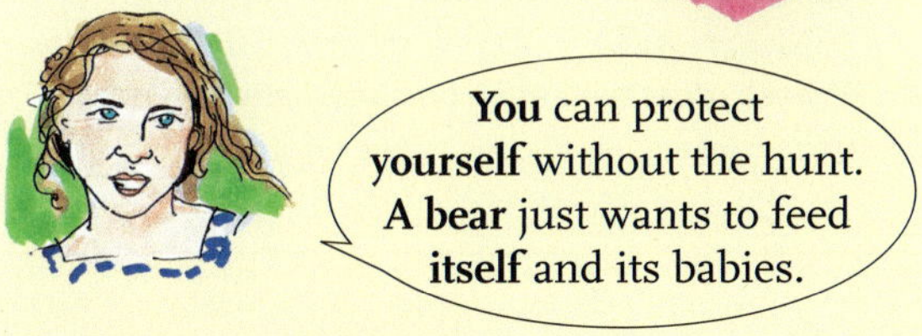

Reflexivpronomen *(ourselves, itself, yourself, ...)* bezeichnen dieselbe Person oder Sache wie das Subjekt *(we, a bear, you, ...)*:

Subjekt — Reflexivpronomen

We	*have to protect*	*ourselves*	*from the bears.*
A bear	*just wants to feed*	*itself*	*and its babies.*

Wir müssen uns vor den Bären schützen.
Ein Bär will nur sich und seine Babys ernähren.

Reflexive pronouns

Singular		Plural	
myself	(ich) mir/mich	**ourselves**	(wir) uns
yourself	(du) dir/dich	**yourselves**	(ihr) euch
himself	(er) sich	**themselves**	(sie) sich
herself	(sie) sich		
itself	(er/sie/es) sich		

! Es gibt eine Reihe von Verben, die im Deutschen mit „sich" gebraucht werden, im Englischen aber ohne Reflexivpronomen.

Beispiele:	
(to) argue	sich streiten
(to) feel	sich fühlen
(to) imagine sth.	sich etwas vorstellen
(to) relax	sich entspannen

(Weitere Beispiele ▸ *Vocabulary*, S. 168)

▸ *Unit 4 (p. 72)* • *P 8–9 (p. 78)*

Schreib die Sätze in dein Heft. In welchen Sätzen brauchst du ein Reflexivpronomen?

1 Do you know how you can protect ... from a bear?
2 If you see a bear, don't move ... quickly. Walk away slowly.
3 If I saw a bear, I would hide ... .
4 Bears just want to feed ... and their babies.

GF 8 Reflexive pronoun or *each other*? Reflexivpronomen oder *each other*?

Robert and Asif are taking photos of themselves.
Robert und Asif machen Fotos von sich (selbst).

Für **„sich"** im Sinne von **„sich selbst"** benutzt du die Pronomen auf ***-self/-selves***:
I – myself, he – himself, they – themselves usw.

◄ Robert und Asif machen Fotos von sich selbst – Robert fotografiert sich selbst, und Asif fotografiert sich selbst.

Now they are taking photos of each other.
Jetzt fotografieren sie sich gegenseitig. /
Jetzt machen sie Fotos voneinander.

▸ *Unit 4 (p. 73)* • *P 11 (p. 79)*

Für **„sich"** im Sinne von **„sich gegenseitig"** oder **„einander"** benutzt du ***each other***.

◄ Robert und Asif fotografieren sich gegenseitig – Robert fotografiert Asif, und Asif fotografiert Robert.

(Statt *each other* wird auch *one another* verwendet: *Now they are taking photos of one another.*)

Sieh dir die Bilder an. Schreib zu jedem Bild einen kurzen Satz. Brauchst du themselves *oder* each other?

1 (laugh at)
They're laughing ...

2 (teach – German)
They're teaching ...

3 (hurt)
They've hurt ...

4 (talk to)
They're ...

They understand each other ...

Unit 5

GF 9 The past perfect Das *past perfect*

a) Use

First Mika's family **lived** in Paris. ... lebte ...
They **moved** to London in 1994. ... zogen ...

Mika found it hard to settle down in London because he had lived in Paris for nine years.
..., weil er neun Jahre lang in Paris gelebt hatte.

He'd already written lots of songs when he released his first single at the age of 23.
Er hatte schon viele Songs geschrieben, ...

Gebrauch

◄ Du benutzt das *simple past* für **Handlungen, Ereignisse und Zustände in der Vergangenheit**.

◄ Mit dem ***past perfect*** (Plusquamperfekt, Vorvergangenheit) drückst du aus, dass eine Handlung noch **vor einer anderen Handlung in der Vergangenheit** stattgefunden hatte. Die Handlung im *past perfect* geschah zuerst:

2	1
*Mika **found** it hard ...*	*because he had lived ...*

1	2
He had already written ...	*when he **released** ...*

Past perfect
At the age of 12 he had written his first songs.
Mit 12 hatte er seine ersten Songs geschrieben.
*(= Mit 12 hatte er **bereits** Songs **geschrieben**.)*

Simple past
At the age of 12 he wrote his first songs.
Mit 12 schrieb er seine ersten Songs.
*(= **Erst als** er 12 Jahre alt war, schrieb er Songs.)*

! Beachte die Bedeutungsunterschiede zwischen *past perfect* und *simple past*.

b) Form

Mika had liked life in Paris.
He hadn't planned to become a pop singer.

Had Mika already moved when he started his music lessons? War Mika schon umgezogen, ...?

► *Unit 5 (p. 91) • P 4–5 (p. 95)*

Form

Das *past perfect* bildest du mit ***had*** (Kurzform: *'d*) und der 3. Form des Verbs. Die 3. Form des Verbs heißt **Partizip Perfekt** *(past participle)*.

! Beim *past perfect* musst du immer ***had*** verwenden, egal ob im Deutschen „hatte" oder „war" steht.

Simple past *oder* past perfect? *Sieh dir die Bilder an und vervollständige die Sätze.*

1 The band (start) to play when I arrived.

2 The band (start) to play when I arrived.

3 When his mum came home from work, Jason ... (make) tea.

4 When his mum came home from work, Jason ... (make) tea.

Grammatical terms (Grammatische Fachbegriffe)

adjective ['ædʒɪktɪv]	Adjektiv	*good, red, new, boring, ...*
adverb ['ædvɜːb]	Adverb	*always, badly, here, really, today*
adverb of frequency ['friːkwənsi]	Häufigkeitsadverb	*always, often, never, ...*
adverb of indefinite time [ɪnˌdefɪnət 'taɪm]	Adverb der unbestimmten Zeit	*already, ever, just, never, ...*
adverb of manner ['mænə]	Adverb der Art und Weise	*badly, happily, quietly, well, ...*
auxiliary [ɔːg'zɪliəri]	Hilfsverb	*be, have, do; will, can, must, ...*
comparison [kəm'pærɪsn]	Steigerung	*old – older – oldest*
conditional sentence [kənˌdɪʃənl 'sentəns]	Bedingungssatz	*I'd call him if I knew his number.*
conjunction [kən'dʒʌŋkʃn]	Konjunktion	*and, or, but; because, before, ...*
contact clause ['kɒntækt klɔːz]	Relativsatz ohne Relativpronomen	*She's the girl **I love**.*
future ['fjuːtʃə]	Zukunft, Futur	
***going to*-future**	Futur mit *going to*	***I'm going to watch** TV tonight.*
***if*-clause** ['ɪf klɔːz]	*if*-Satz, Nebensatz mit *if*	***If I see Jack**, I'll tell him.*
imperative [ɪm'perətɪv]	Imperativ (Befehlsform)	*Open your books. Don't talk.*
infinitive [ɪn'fɪnətɪv]	Infinitiv (Grundform des Verbs)	*(to) open, (to) see, (to) read, ...*
irregular verb [ɪˌregjələ 'vɜːb]	unregelmäßiges Verb	*(to) go – went – gone*
main clause	Hauptsatz	***I like Scruffy** because I like dogs.*
modal, modal auxiliary [ˌməʊdl‿ɔːg'zɪliəri]	modales Hilfsverb, Modalverb	*can, could, may, must, ...*
negative statement [ˌnegətɪv 'steɪtmənt]	verneinter Aussagesatz	*I don't like bananas.*
noun [naʊn]	Nomen, Substantiv	*Sophie, girl, brother, time, ...*
object ['ɒbdʒɪkt]	Objekt	*My sister is writing **a letter**.*
object form ['ɒbdʒɪkt fɔːm]	Objektform (der Personalpronomen)	*me, you, him, her, it, us, them*
past [pɑːst]	Vergangenheit	
past participle [ˌpɑːst 'pɑːtɪsɪpl]	Partizip Perfekt	*cleaned, planned, gone, seen, ...*
past perfect [ˌpɑːst 'pɜːfɪkt]	Plusquamperfekt, Vorvergangenheit	*He was late because he **had missed** the bus.*
past progressive [ˌpɑːst prə'gresɪv]	Verlaufsform der Vergangenheit	*At 7.30 I **was having** dinner.*
person ['pɜːsn]	Person	
personal pronoun [ˌpɜːsənl 'prəʊnaʊn]	Personalpronomen (persönliches Fürwort)	*I, you, he, she, it, we, they; me, you, him, her, it, us, them*
plural ['plʊərəl]	Plural, Mehrzahl	
positive statement [ˌpɒzətɪv 'steɪtmənt]	bejahter Aussagesatz	*I like oranges.*
possessive determiner [pəˌzesɪv dɪ'tɜːmɪnə]	Possessivbegleiter (besitzanzeigender Begleiter)	*my, your, his, her, its, our, their*
possessive form [pəˌzesɪv fɔːm]	*s*-Genitiv	*Jo's brother; my sister's room*
possessive pronoun [pəˌzesɪv 'prəʊnaʊn]	Possessivpronomen	*mine, yours, his, hers, ours, theirs*
preposition [ˌprepə'zɪʃn]	Präposition	*after, at, in, next to, under, ...*
present ['preznt]	Gegenwart	
present perfect [ˌpreznt 'pɜːfɪkt]	*present perfect*	*We**'ve made** a cake for you.*
present progressive [ˌpreznt prə'gresɪv]	Verlaufsform der Gegenwart	*The Hansons **are having** lunch.*
pronoun ['prəʊnaʊn]	Pronomen, Fürwort	
pronunciation [prəˌnʌnsi'eɪʃn]	Aussprache	
question ['kwestʃən]	Frage(satz)	
question tag ['kwestʃən tæg]	Frageanhängsel	*This place is great, **isn't it?***
question word ['kwestʃən wɜːd]	Fragewort	*what?, when?, where?, how?, ...*
regular verb [ˌregjələ 'vɜːb]	regelmäßiges Verb	*(to) help – helped – helped*
reflexive pronoun [rɪˌfleksɪv 'prəʊnaʊn]	Reflexivpronomen	*myself, yourself, themselves, ...*
relative clause [ˌrelətɪv 'klɔːz]	Relativsatz	*There's the girl **who helped me**.*
relative pronoun [ˌrelətɪv 'prəʊnaʊn]	Relativpronomen	*who, that, which*
short answer [ˌʃɔːt‿'ɑːnsə]	Kurzantwort	*Yes, I am. / No, I don't. / ...*

simple past [ˌsɪmpl ˈpɑːst]	einfache Form der Vergangenheit	*Jo **wrote** two letters yesterday.*
simple present [ˌsɪmpl ˈpreznt]	einfache Form der Gegenwart	*I always **go** to school by bike.*
singular [ˈsɪŋgjələ]	Singular, Einzahl	
spelling [ˈspelɪŋ]	Schreibweise, Rechtschreibung	
subject [ˈsʌbdʒɪkt]	Subjekt	***My sister** is writing a letter.*
subject form [ˈsʌbdʒɪkt fɔːm]	Subjektform (der Personalpronomen)	*I, you, he, she, it, we, they*
subordinate clause [səˌbɔːdɪnət ˈklɔːz]	Nebensatz	*I like Scruffy **because I like dogs**.*
verb [vɜːb]	Verb	*hear, open, help, go, …*
***will*-future**	Futur mit *will*	*I think it **will be** cold tonight.*
word order [ˈwɜːd‿ɔːdə]	Wortstellung	
yes/no question	Entscheidungsfrage	*Are you 13? Do you like comics?*

Lösungen der Grammar-File-Aufgaben

p.140 **Have** you ever **visited** the Natural History Museum? – Yes, **I have.**
When **did** you **go** there? – We **went** in the summer holidays last year. But I **haven't seen** the British Museum yet.
Oh, I **visited** that with my aunt and uncle a few months ago.

p.141
1 If the other girls **called** Latisha names, she wouldn't listen.
2 Latisha would forget the girls if she **was** Katrina.
3 Katrina **would be** much happier if the girls **didn't call** her 'Fishface'.
4 If the girls **were** friendly to her, she **wouldn't be** upset.
5 If people **called** you 'Fishface', you **would be** upset too. Right?
6 What would you do if classmates **called** you names?

p.142
1 Anna is the German girl **who** is staying with Latisha.
2 Latisha thinks jazz dance is a sport **that** is really hard work.
3 What's the name of the player **who** scored two goals in United U14s' last match?
4 Stewed chicken is a dish **that** comes from Trinidad, isn't it?

p.143
2 (Which is the museum the whole family will love?)
3 (Football and jazz dance are sports Latisha likes a lot.)
4 (David Beckham is a football star everybody knows.)
6 (Let's do something we both want to do.)

p.145/1 My mother is so strict. Yesterday I wanted to buy a present for Ashley, but I **had to** tidy my room.
My parents are strict too. I'm sure I **won't be allowed to** go to Ashley's party.
Well, I'm sure I **will have to** be home by ten again, as always.
I **won't be able to** go to the party because I'm going to drive to our cabin with my parents.

p.145/2
1 Do you know how you can protect **yourself** from a bear?
2 If you see a bear, don't move quickly. Walk away slowly.
3 If I saw a bear, I would hide.
4 Bears just want to feed **themselves** and their babies.

p.146
1 They're laughing at **each other**.
2 They're teaching **themselves** German.
3 They've hurt **themselves**.
4 They're talking to **each other**.

p.147
1 The band **started** to play when I arrived.
2 The band **had started** to play when I arrived.
3 When his mum came home from work, Jason **had made** tea.
4 When his mum came home from work, Jason **made** tea.

Diese Wörterverzeichnisse findest du in deinem Englischbuch:

- Das **Vocabulary** (Vokabelverzeichnis – S.150–171) enthält alle Wörter und Wendungen, die du lernen musst. Sie stehen in der Reihenfolge, in der sie in den Units vorkommen.
- Das **Dictionary** besteht aus zwei alphabetischen Wörterlisten zum Nachschlagen:
  Englisch – Deutsch: S.172–197
  Deutsch – Englisch: S.198–220.

So ist das Vocabulary aufgebaut:

- Hier siehst du, wo die Wörter vorkommen.
  p.54/A 1 = Seite 54, Abschnitt 1
  p.60/P 2 = Seite 60, Übung 2
- Die Lautschrift zeigt dir, wie ein Wort ausgesprochen und betont wird.
  (→ Englische Laute: S.220)
- Eingerückte Wörter lernst du am besten zusammen mit dem vorausgehenden Wort, weil die beiden zusammengehören.
- Diese Kästen solltest du dir besonders gut ansehen.

Tipps zum Wörterlernen findest du im Skills File auf Seite 125.

p.54/A 1	(to) **spot (-tt-)** [spɒt]	entdecken	I can't fin
	2 all	2 beide (2:2 unentschieden)	
p.60/P 2	(to) **score (a goal)** [skɔː], [ɡəʊl]	ein Tor schießen, einen Treffer erzielen	We won – Smith
	score [skɔː]	Spielstand; Punktestand	

A football match

What's the score now? – 2–0. *(you say: **two nil**)* — Wie steht e
What was the final score? – Chelsea 2, Arsenal 1. — Wie war der End
Our last match was a draw, 2–2. *(you say: **two all**)* — Unser letz

Word field: Sports

EQUIPMENT [ɪ'kwɪpmənt] Ausrüstung — LO

skis [skiːz]

Abkürzungen:

n = *noun*		*v* = *verb*	
adj = *adjective*		*adv* = *adverb*	
prep = *preposition*		*conj* = *conjunction*	
pl = *plural*		*no pl* = *no plural*	
p. = page		pp. = pages	
sb. = somebody		sth. = something	
jn. = jemanden		jm. = jemandem	
AE = *American English*		*BE* = *British English*	

infml = *informal* (umgangssprachlich, informell)

Symbole:

! Hier stehen Hinweise auf Besonderheiten, bei denen man leicht Fehler machen kann.

◄► ist das „Gegenteil"-Zeichen: **slow** ◄► **fast** (**slow** ist das Gegenteil von **fast**)

~ Die **Tilde** in den Beispielsätzen steht für das neue Wort.
Beispiel: **youth** – In her ~ my grandma was very beautiful.

Introduction

p.6	**youth** [juːθ]	Jugend	the time when you are young In her ~ my grandma was very beautiful.
	festival ['festɪvl]	Fest, Festival	*French:* le festival

Numbers

Im Englischen steht oft ein **Komma** in Zahlen, die größer als 1000 sind.

10,000 = ten thousand
10,400 = ten thousand four hundred
! 10.4 = ten **point** four (*deutsch:* 10,4 = zehn **Komma** vier)

1,100,000 = one million one hundred thousand
! 1.1 million[1] = one **point** one million (*deutsch:* 1,1 Millionen)

[1] ['mɪljən]

	the United Kingdom (UK) [ju,naɪtɪd 'kɪŋdəm], [ˌjuː 'keɪ]	das Vereinigte Königreich	! **the UK** = Great Britain (England, Scotland, Wales) and Northern Ireland *(Nordirland)*
	from **all over** the UK / the world / England	aus dem gesamten Vereinigten Königreich / aus der ganzen Welt / aus ganz England	Madonna is famous **all over** the world. (= auf der ganzen Welt)
	kind (of) [kaɪnd]	Art	What ~ **of** music do you like? – Rock music. ! Was für ein Auto ...? = What **kind of** car ...?
	national ['næʃnəl]	national, National-	**national ◄► international** *French:* national, e
	classical ['klæsɪkl]	klassisch	Do you like Mozart? – Oh yes! I love ~ music. *French:* classique
	concert ['kɒnsət]	Konzert	! Betonung auf der 1. Silbe: **concert** ['kɒnsət] *French:* le concert
	(to) **DJ** ['diː dʒeɪ]	(Musik/CDs/Platten) auflegen *(in der Disko)*	noun: **DJ (disc jockey)** – verb: (to) **DJ**
	steel drum [ˌstiːl 'drʌm]	Steeldrum	**steel drums** 
	steel [stiːl]	Stahl	
	drum [drʌm]	Trommel	! (to) **play the drums** *(pl)* = Schlagzeug spielen
p.7	**fiddle** ['fɪdl] *(infml)*	Fiedel, Geige	a **fiddle**  ! (to) **play the fiddle** = Geige spielen
	by the way [ˌbaɪ ðə 'weɪ]	übrigens; nebenbei (bemerkt)	**By the ~**, I've bought a new computer game.
	north [nɔːθ]	Norden; nach Norden; nördlich	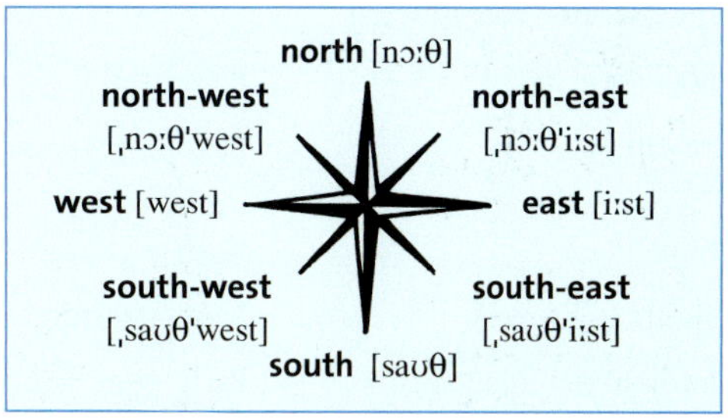
p.8	**hostel** ['hɒstl]	Herberge, Wohnheim	
	boss [bɒs]	Chef/in, Boss	
	gig [gɪg] *(infml)*	Gig, Auftritt	! (to) **do a gig** = einen Auftritt haben, ein Konzert geben
p.9	**mixture** ['mɪkstʃə]	Mischung	
	western ['westən]	westlich, West-	France is one of the biggest countries in ~ Europe.
p.10	**the United States (US)** [ju,naɪtɪd 'steɪts], [ˌjuː‿'es]	die Vereinigten Staaten (von Amerika)	
	How about ...?	Wie wär's mit ...?	= What about ...?
	workshop ['wɜːkʃɒp]	Workshop, Werkstatt	
	Nice to meet you.	Nett, dich kennenzulernen.	
p.11	**half an hour** [ˌhɑːf‿ən‿'aʊə]	eine halbe Stunde	! Word order: **half an hour** – **eine halbe Stunde**
	half [hɑːf], *pl* **halves** [hɑːvz]	Hälfte	I felt ill and spent ~ of the day in bed.

(to) **keep in touch** [tʌtʃ]	in Verbindung bleiben, Kontakt halten	It was nice to meet you. – Yes, let's **keep in ~**.
Wait and see!	Wart's ab!	What's for dinner this evening? – **Wait and ~!**
recording [rɪ'kɔ:dɪŋ]	Aufnahme, Aufzeichnung	
(to) **go with**	gehören zu, passen zu	The first text **goes ~** the third picture.
electric [ɪ'lektrɪk]	elektrisch, Elektro-	
flute [flu:t]	Querflöte	
recorder [rɪ'kɔ:də]	Blockflöte	
saxophone ['sæksəfəʊn]	Saxophon	
trombone [trɒm'bəʊn]	Posaune	
trumpet ['trʌmpɪt]	Trompete	
this way	so; auf diese Weise	Eat the right food. **This ~** you can stay healthy.
way	Art und Weise	A good ~ to make friends is to join a club.

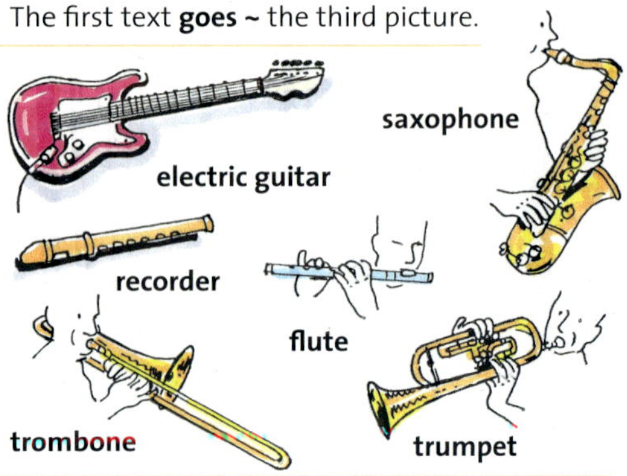

Unit 1: My London

p.12	**capital** ['kæpɪtl]	Hauptstadt	Berlin is the ~ of Germany. *French:* la capitale
	PS [,pi:_'es] (**postscript** ['pəʊstskrɪpt])	PS *(Nachschrift unter Briefen)*	
	big wheel [wi:l]	Riesenrad	
	wheel	Rad	A bike has two **~s**.
	high [haɪ]	hoch	What's the **~est** mountain in the world?
	sights *(pl)* [saɪts]	Sehenswürdigkeiten	I want to go to London. I want to see the ~.
	parliament ['pɑ:ləmənt]	Parlament	! Schreibung: **parliament** Betonung auf der 1. Silbe: **parliament** ['pɑ:ləmənt] *French:* le parlement
	sound file ['saʊnd faɪl]	Tondatei, Soundfile	
	although [ɔ:l'ðəʊ]	obwohl	I went to bed early ~ I wasn't really tired.
	royal ['rɔɪəl]	königlich	*French:* royal, e
	queen [kwi:n]	Königin	
	open-air [,əʊpən_'eə]	im Freien; Freilicht-	~-~ concerts / festivals / theatres
	air [eə]	Luft	*French:* l'air *(m)*
	(to) **dream (of, about)** [dri:m]	träumen (von)	verb: (to) **dream** – noun: **dream**

on („weiter")

You want to be a rock star? **Dream on**!	... Träum weiter!
It started to rain, but we **walked on**.	..., aber wir gingen weiter.
Read on. You'll find the information on the next few pages.	Lies weiter. ...
He stopped talking for a moment. Then he **went on**.	... Dann redete er weiter.

p.13	**natural history** [ˌnætʃrəl ˈhɪstri]	Naturkunde	
	dinosaur [ˈdaɪnəsɔː]	Dinosaurier	! Betonung und Aussprache: **<u>di</u>nosaur** [ˈdaɪnəsɔː]
	earthquake [ˈɜːθkweɪk]	Erdbeben	
	earth [ɜːθ]	Erde	What's the hottest country on ~? (= auf der Erde)
	trendy [ˈtrendi]	modisch, schick	
	second-hand [ˌsekənd ˈhænd]	gebraucht; aus zweiter Hand	! I bought it **second-hand**. = ... <u>aus</u> zweiter Hand
	dish [dɪʃ]	Gericht *(Speise)*	What's your favourite ~? – Spaghetti.
	lamb [læm]	Lamm	! Das „b" wird nicht gesprochen: **lamb** [læm]
	tip [tɪp]	Tipp	

Buildings and places in a town

		<u>In London:</u>
cathedral [kəˈθiːdrəl]	Kathedrale, Dom	**St. Paul's Cathedral** [sənt ˈpɔːlz]
circus [ˈsɜːkəs]	(runder) Platz	**Piccadilly Circus** [ˌpɪkədɪli ˈsɜːkəs]
column [ˈkɒləm]	Säule	**Nelson's Column** [ˌnelsnz ˈkɒləm]
lane [leɪn]	Gasse, Weg	**Brick Lane** [ˌbrɪk ˈleɪn]
lock [lɒk]	Schleuse	**Camden Lock** [ˌkæmdən ˈlɒk]
palace [ˈpæləs]	Palast, Schloss	**Buckingham Palace** [ˌbʌkɪŋəm ˈpæləs]
square [skweə]	Platz	**Leicester Square** ! [ˌlestə ˈskweə] **Trafalgar Square** [trəˌfælgə ˈskweə]

p.14/A 1	**single (ticket)** [ˈsɪŋgl]	einfache Fahrkarte *(nur Hinfahrt)*	**single (ticket)** ◄► **return (ticket)**
	Travelcard [ˈtrævlkɑːd]	Tagesfahrkarte *(der Londoner Verkehrsbetriebe)*	an all-day ticket
	public transport *(no pl)* [ˌpʌblɪk ˈtrænspɔːt]	öffentliche Verkehrsmittel, öffentlicher Personennahverkehr	It's cheaper to use ~ **transport** than to go by car. ! Betonung auf der 1. Silbe: **<u>trans</u>port** [ˈtrænspɔːt]
	rush hour [ˈrʌʃ_aʊə]	Hauptverkehrszeit	
	zone [zəʊn]	Zone, Bereich	*French:* la zone
	the Tube *(no pl)* [tjuːb] *(BE)*	die Londoner U-Bahn	the underground (in London)
	line [laɪn]	(U-Bahn-)Linie	*French:* la ligne
	mom [mɒm, *AE:* mɑːm] *(AE)*	Mama, Mutti; Mutter	= *BE* mum
	eastbound [ˈiːstbaʊnd]	Richtung Osten	**northbound** / **westbound** ← ↑ ↓ → **eastbound** / **southbound**
	(to) **change** [tʃeɪndʒ]	umsteigen	Take the Central Line eastbound and ~ to the Bakerloo Line southbound at Oxford Circus.
	platform [ˈplætfɔːm]	Bahnsteig, Gleis	The trains to London leave from ~ 3.

	central ['sentrəl]	Zentral-, Mittel-	❗ Betonung auf der 1. Silbe: **central** ['sentrəl]
p.15/A 3	(to) **listen for** sth.	auf etwas horchen, achten	I'm going to have a bath. Can you **listen** ~ the doorbell, please?
	detail ['di:teɪl]	Detail, Einzelheit	❗ Betonung und Aussprache: **detail** ['di:teɪl]
p.15/A 4	**once** [wʌns]	einst, früher einmal	**Once** we wrote letters. Now we send e-mails.
	across [ə'krɒs]	(quer) über	a bridge ~ a river 
p.16/A 5	**actually** ['æktʃuəli]	eigentlich; in Wirklichkeit	I wasn't ~ hungry, but I ate the pizza anyway. I'm not American, ~. I'm from Canada.
	mosque [mɒsk]	Moschee	
	special ['speʃl]	besondere(r, s)	I hope your birthday will be a ~ day.
	What's special about ...?	Was ist das Besondere an ...?	**What's ~ about** this place? – It's the oldest pub in Bristol.
	synagogue ['sɪnəgɒg]	Synagoge	❗ Betonung und Aussprache: **synagogue** ['sɪnəgɒg]
	meal [mi:l]	Mahlzeit, Essen	We like to eat a hot ~ in the evenings.
p.16/A 6	**mild** [maɪld]	mild	❗ Aussprache: **mild** [maɪld]
	spicy ['spaɪsi]	würzig, scharf gewürzt	**spicy ◄► mild**
	nut [nʌt]	Nuss	
	vegetable ['vedʒtəbl]	*(ein)* Gemüse	❗ **Vegetables are** good for me. = **Gemüse ist** gut ...
	menu ['menju:]	Speisekarte; Menü *(Computer)*	Look! There are 125 different pizzas on the ~. ❗ Ich nehme das **Menü**. = I'll have the **set meal**.
p.17/A 7	**strange** [streɪndʒ]	seltsam, sonderbar; fremd	He looked really ~ in a blouse and skirt. It was a ~ part of town, so I needed a map. *French:* étrange

Word field: Transport

p.20/P 2

1 **bus stop** ['bʌs stɒp]
2 **ticket machine** ['tɪkɪt mə,ʃi:n]
3 **bus pass** ['bʌs pɑ:s]
4 **gate** [geɪt] Flugsteig
5 **taxi** ['tæksi]
6 **tram** [træm]
7 **airport** ['eəpɔ:t]
8 **ferry** ['feri]

machine [mə'ʃi:n]	Maschine, Gerät	*French:* la machine
on foot	zu Fuß	We came here **on** ~. (= We walked here.) ❗ **on foot** – **by bike/car/train/...** (zu Fuß) (mit dem Rad/Auto/Zug/...)
ground [graʊnd]	(Erd-)Boden	This railway tunnel is 20 metres under the ~. ❗ Erdboden = **ground** – Fußboden = **floor**

p.22/P 6	**course** [kɔːs]	Kurs, Lehrgang	My mum does an English ~ on Friday evenings. *French:* le cours

Word field: Food

p.24/P 10

turkey ['tɜːki] Truthahn, Pute/Puter

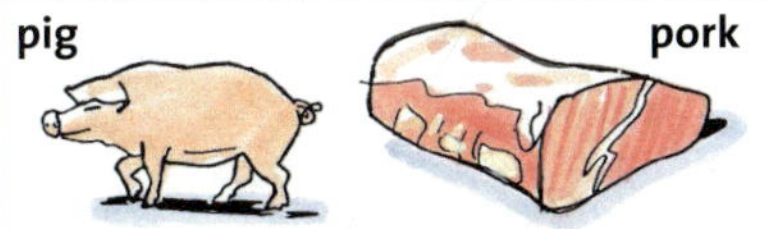

pork [pɔːk] Schweinefleisch

beef [biːf] Rindfleisch

1. **bacon** ['beɪkən] Schinkenspeck
2. **steak** [steɪk]
3. **pea** [piː]
4. **onion** ! ['ʌnjən]
5. **mushroom** ['mʌʃrʊm, -ruːm]
6. **egg** [eg]

p.24/P 11	**What an** interesting life!	Was für ein interessantes Leben!	! **What a** nice surprise! = **Was <u>für</u> eine** nette Überraschung!
p.25/P 13	**announcement** [ə'naʊnsmənt]	Durchsage, Ansage; Ankündigung, Bekanntgabe	Did she say Gate 15 or 50? I couldn't hear the ~.
p.25/P 14	**everyday** *(adj)* ['evrideɪ]	Alltags-; alltägliche(r, s)	Are you going to wear anything special tonight? – No, just my ~ clothes: jeans and a T-shirt.

Only a game

p.26	(to) **work** [wɜːk]	funktionieren	I need your help. My computer doesn't ~.
	helmet ['helmɪt]	Helm	**helmets**

around

herum... / umher...	We <u>walked</u> **around** till we found a nice café.	herumlaufen, umherspazieren
	It's fun to <u>run</u> and <u>jump</u> **around** in the park after school.	herumrennen; herumspringen
in ... umher, durch	We walked **around** <u>the town</u> and looked at the sights.	in der Stadt umher, durch die Stadt
	They rode their bikes **around** <u>the village</u>.	im Dorf umher, durch das Dorf
um ... (herum)	There was water all **around** them.	ganz um sie herum
	Let's run **around** the lake and see who is fastest.	um den See (herum)
	! *(auch zeitlich:)* I'll see you **around** six.	um sechs Uhr herum, gegen sechs

surprised (at sth.**)** [sə'praɪzd]	überrascht (über etwas)	I was ~ **at** the size of their house. It was bigger than I thought.
surprising [sə'praɪzɪŋ]	überraschend, erstaunlich	They played really badly. It's not ~ that they lost. ! It was **surprising**. = Es war überrasch**end**. She was **surprised**. = Sie war überrasch**t**.
(to) **surprise** sb. [sə'praɪz]	jn. überraschen	Don't tell Jo about the party. We want to ~ him. noun: **surprise** – verb: (to) **surprise**

(to) **be allowed to** do sth. [ə'laʊd]	etwas tun dürfen	**Are** you ~ **to** use dictionaries in your English tests?
sign [saɪn]	Schild; Zeichen	The ~ says it's only a mile to the city centre. I'll wait till you give me a ~. Then I'll come.
button ['bʌtn]	Knopf	 Which ~ do I push to turn the MP3 player on?
excited [ɪk'saɪtɪd]	aufgeregt, begeistert	**!** It was **exciting**. = Es war aufreg**end**. He was **excited**. = Er war aufreg**t**.
kind of scary [kaɪnd] *(infml)*	irgendwie unheimlich	**!** **kind of + noun:** What **kind of music** ... = Welche **Art** Musik ... **kind of + adjective:** **kind of scary** = **irgendwie** unheimlich
murder ['mɜːdə]	Mord	
(to) **murder** ['mɜːdə]	(er)morden	(to) kill
murderer ['mɜːdərə]	Mörder/in	**!** Mord = **murder** Mörder/in = **murderer**
p.27 **victim** ['vɪktɪm]	Opfer	
blood [blʌd]	Blut	
flower ['flaʊə]	Blume; Blüte	*French:* la fleur  
realistic [ˌriːə'lɪstɪk]	realistisch, wirklichkeitsnah	I want to see all the sights in London. – Be ~. We've only got two days.
plug [plʌg]	Stecker	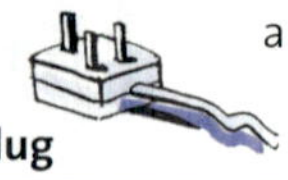 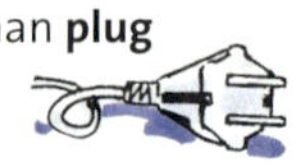
electricity [ɪˌlek'trɪsəti]	Strom, Elektrizität	noun: **electricity** – adjective: **electric** *French:* l'électricité *(f)* – électrique
flash [flæʃ]	Lichtblitz	
close (to) [kləʊs]	nahe (bei, an)	It's not far. The café is very ~ **to** our home.
shadow ['ʃædəʊ]	Schatten	I woke up and saw the ~ of a man on the wall. 
(to) **appear** [ə'pɪə]	erscheinen, auftauchen	(to) **appear** ◄► (to) **disappear**
knife [naɪf], *pl* **knives** [naɪvz]	Messer	**!** Stummes „k“: **knife** [naɪf] 
p.28 **light** [laɪt]	Licht	
we know **what to do**	wir wissen, was wir tun müssen; wir wissen, was zu tun ist	= we know what we have to do
whistle ['wɪsl]	(Triller-)Pfeife; Pfiff	verb: (to) **whistle** – noun: **whistle**

	ending ['endɪŋ]	Ende, (Ab-)Schluss *(einer Geschichte, eines Films usw.)*	Not every story can have a happy **~**.
	in my/your view [vju:]	meiner/deiner Ansicht nach	She doesn't like rap but **in my ~** it's fantastic.

How am I doing?

p.29	**How am I doing?**	Wie komme ich voran? *(Wie sind meine Fortschritte?)*	
	area ['eəriə]	Bereich; Gebiet, Gegend	Grammar is my problem **~**. I live in an **~** with a lot of restaurants.
	fact [fækt]	Tatsache, Fakt	I've found lots of interesting **~s** for my essay on the Music for Youth Festival. *French:* le fait

Unit 2: Island girl

p.30	**salmon** ['sæmən], *pl* **salmon**	Lachs	**!** Stummes „l": **salmon** ['sæmən]
	oil [ɔɪl]	Öl	
	huge [hju:dʒ]	riesig, sehr groß	

big – large – huge

big / large	**big** und **large** sind oft austauschbar.	a **big/large** family; a **big/large** house
	big ist umgangssprachlicher als **large**, daher solltest du in eher förmlichen Texten besser **large** schreiben.	
	large wird in der Regel nicht verwendet, um Menschen zu beschreiben.	a very **big** man
huge	**huge** bedeutet „riesig", „sehr groß".	a **huge** suitcase

	rock [rɒk]	Fels, Felsen	**rocks**
	farmer ['fɑ:mə]	Bauer/Bäuerin, Landwirt/in; (Fisch-)Züchter/in	
p.32/A 1	**electronic** [ɪˌlek'trɒnɪk]	elektronisch	*French:* électronique
	media *(pl)* ['mi:diə]	Medien	It's faster to use **~** like the phone or e-mail than to write letters.
	lonely ['ləʊnli]	einsam	I felt a bit **~**, alone in the big house.
	great-grandmother/-father	Urgroßmutter/-vater	
	post [pəʊst]	Post *(Briefe, Päckchen, ...)*	**!** die Post, das Postamt = the **post office**
	once [wʌns]	einmal	
	twice [twaɪs]	zweimal	**!** **once** (1x) – **twice** (2x) – **three times** (3x)
	(once/twice) **a** week	(einmal/zweimal) pro Woche	Our band practises **once ~ week**.

	(to) **imagine** sth. [ɪ'mædʒɪn]	sich etwas vorstellen	*French:* imaginer
	instant messages *(pl)* [ˌɪnstənt 'mesɪdʒɪz]	*Nachrichten, die man im Internet austauscht (in Echtzeit)*	
	message ['mesɪdʒ]	Nachricht	
	text message ['tekst ˌmesɪdʒ]	SMS	*French:* le texto, le SMS
	(to) **text** sb. [tekst]	jm. eine SMS schicken	Have a good trip. And ~ me when you get there.
p.32/A 2	**mate** [meɪt] *(infml)*	Freund/in, Kumpel	a good friend
	personal ['pɜːsənl]	persönliche(r, s)	*French:* personnel, le
	ringtone ['rɪŋtəʊn]	Klingelton	
	(to) **mix** [mɪks]	mischen, mixen	If you ~ blue and yellow, you get green.
p.33/A 3	(to) **take** [teɪk], **took** [tʊk], **taken** ['teɪkən]	dauern, *(Zeit)* brauchen	It **~s** about 15 minutes to get home from here. How long does the journey to Lyness **~**?
	(to) **pick** sb. **up** [ˌpɪk‿'ʌp]	jn. abholen	We can ~ you **up** at the station. ! (to) **pick sb. up** = jn. abholen (to) **pick sth. up** = etwas aufheben, hochheben
	timetable ['taɪmteɪbl]	Fahrplan	
	arrival (arr) [ə'raɪvl]	Ankunft	verb: (to) **arrive** – noun: **arrival** *French:* arriver – l'arrivée *(f)*
	departure (dep) [dɪ'pɑːtʃə]	Abfahrt, Abflug; Abreise	**arrival ◄► departure** *French:* le départ
	until [ən'tɪl]	bis	= till
p.33/A 5	**from** Monday **to** Friday	von Montag bis Freitag	
	ceilidh ['keɪli]	*Musik- und Tanzveranstaltung, vor allem in Schottland und Irland*	
p.34/A 6	**type** [taɪp] *(infml)*	Typ	*French:* le type
	(to) **go well**	gut (ver)laufen, gutgehen	Was the test difficult? – Yes, but it **went** ~.
	(to) **be able to** do sth. ['eɪbl]	etwas tun können; fähig sein/ in der Lage sein, etwas zu tun	Sarah **wasn't ~ to** come to my party last Friday. (= Sarah **couldn't** come ...)

„können" und „dürfen"

Du kennst bereits **can** für „können" und **can** und **may** für „dürfen":

Ananda **can** play hockey very well.	Ananda kann sehr gut Hockey spielen.
You **can/may** go to the disco, but please be home at 10.	Du darfst in die Disko gehen, ...

Wenn es um die **Vergangenheit** oder die **Zukunft** geht, verwende

- für **„können"** eine Form von **be able to** und
- für **„dürfen"** eine Form von **be allowed to**.

(to) **be able to**:	The museum was closed on Friday, but we **were able to** go on Saturday.[1]	..., aber wir konnten am Samstag hingehen.
	I **won't be able to** meet you tomorrow.	Ich werde dich morgen nicht treffen können.
(to) **be allowed to**:	**Were** you **allowed to** watch the film last night?	Durftest du den Film gestern Abend sehen?
	When I'm 18 **I'll be allowed to** drive.	Wenn ich 18 bin, werde ich Auto fahren dürfen.

[1] Es gibt auch eine Vergangenheitsform **could** („konnte"): It was so dark that we **couldn't** really see the sea.

rucksack ['rʌksæk]	Rucksack	! Aussprache: **rucksack** ['rʌksæk]

	(to) **expect** [ɪk'spekt]	erwarten	How many guests are you **~ing** to your party?
	not even	(noch) nicht einmal	I won't tell anybody, **not ~** my best friend. **!** • He **even** opened the letter. = Er hat den Brief **sogar** geöffnet! • He **didn't even** open the letter. = Er hat den Brief **nicht einmal** geöffnet!
	ponytail ['pəʊniteɪl]	Pferdeschwanz *(Frisur)*	a **ponytail** 
p.35/A 8	**upset (about)** [ˌʌp'set]	aufgebracht, gekränkt, mitgenommen (wegen)	John was ~ because his sister didn't remember his birthday.
	(to) **upset** sb. **(-tt-)** [ʌp'set], **upset, upset**	jn. ärgern, kränken, aus der Fassung bringen	It **~s** me when people are rude to me. The bad news about her father ~ her a lot.
	beauty ['bjuːti]	Schönheit	adjective: **beautiful** – noun: **beauty**
	(to) **call** sb. **names**	jn. mit Schimpfwörtern hänseln, jm. Schimpfwörter nachrufen	He felt upset because the other kids always **~ed him names** like Carrot-Nose or Rabbit-Ears.
	(to) **let** sb. **do** sth. **(-tt-)** [let], **let, let**	jm. erlauben, etwas zu tun; zulassen, dass jd. etwas tut	My parents never ~ me watch late films. You look hungry. **Let** me make you a sandwich.
	you **would** ... [wəd, wʊd]	du würdest ...	I don't want to leave my hometown. I ~ miss all my friends.
	stupid ['stjuːpɪd]	blöd, dumm	*French:* stupide
	bully ['bʊli]	(Schul-)Tyrann	verb: (to) **bully** – noun: **bully**
	(to) **forget (-tt-)** [fə'get], **forgot** [fə'gɒt], **forgotten** [fə'gɒtn]	vergessen	Tomorrow is Grandpa's birthday. Don't ~ it! (to) **forget** ◄► (to) **remember**
	just [dʒʌst]	einfach	I ~ can't find my keys. Do you know where I put them?

just

They call you names? **Just** don't listen to them.	... Hör **einfach** nicht hin.
It's **just** a game.	Es ist **nur/bloß** ein Spiel.
They're **just** leaving. / They've **just** left.	Sie gehen **gerade**. / Sie sind **gerade (eben)** gegangen.
Just then the phone rang.	**Genau in dem Moment / Gerade dann** klingelte das Telefon.
You look **just like** your mother.	Du siehst **genau wie** deine Mutter aus.

p.35/A 9	**feeling** ['fiːlɪŋ]	Gefühl	verb: (to) **feel** – noun: **feeling**
	entry ['entri]	Eintrag, Eintragung *(in Wörterbuch/Tagebuch)*	I've got a new dictionary. It has 200,000 **entries**. There's no ~ in Jane's diary for 12th June.
	above [ə'bʌv]	oben; über, oberhalb (von)	First look at the pictures ~. ↑ We live on a hill ~ the city.
	below [bɪ'ləʊ]	unten; unter, unterhalb (von)	Then look at the chart ~. ↓ I don't like the Tube. I feel scared ~ ground.
	translation [træns'leɪʃn]	Übersetzung	
	(to) **translate** [træns'leɪt]	übersetzen	We had to ~ the text from English into German.
	meaning ['miːnɪŋ]	Bedeutung	verb: (to) **mean** – noun: **meaning**

	correct [kə'rekt]	korrekt, richtig	verb: (to) **correct** – adjective: **correct** *French:* corriger – correct, e

Word field: Town and country

p.38/P 1

hilly ['hɪli] hügelig

bay [beɪ] Bucht

coast [kəʊst] Küste

canal [kə'næl]

car park ['kɑː pɑːk]

a **busy** street

busy ['bɪzi] belebt, verkehrsreich; hektisch

p.38/P 3	**stress** [stres]	Betonung	
p.39/P 4	**structure** ['strʌktʃə]	Struktur; Gliederung	! Betonung und Aussprache: **structure** ['strʌktʃə] *French:* la structure
	(to) **be called** [kɔːld]	heißen, genannt werden	Why **is** that rock ~ 'The Old Man of Hoy'?
	statement ['steɪtmənt]	Aussage, Feststellung	I'm afraid I don't agree with that ~.
p.41/P 9	**role** [rəʊl]	Rolle	What's your ~ in the play? – I'm the detective. *French:* le rôle
p.41/P 10	**million** ['mɪljən]	Million	! one **million** cars (eine Million Autos) – two **million** cars (zwei Millionen Autos) *But:* **millions of** cars (Millionen von Autos) *French:* le million
p.42/P 12	**kilometre (km)** ['kɪləmiːtə]	Kilometer	1,000 metres = 1 ~ *French:* le kilomètre
	centimetre (cm) ['sentɪmiːtə]	Zentimeter	100 ~s = 1 **metre** *French:* le centimètre

Orkney Star

p.44	**once more / once again**	noch einmal	The film was fantastic. I'd like to see it **once** ~.
	a **cup of** tea [kʌp]	eine Tasse Tee	
	you	man	How do ~ say 'once more' in German? (= Wie sagt man ...?)
	(to) **hit the windscreen** ['wɪndskriːn]	gegen/auf die Windschutz-scheibe schlagen/prallen	 A stone ~ **the windscreen**.
	Assembly [ə'sembli]	Versammlung *(morgendliche Schulversammlung, oft mit Andacht)*	

	head teacher [ˌhed 'tiːtʃə]	Schulleiter/in	
	(to) **believe** [bɪ'liːv]	glauben	That can't be true! I don't ~ it.
	you **might** need help [maɪt]	du könntest (vielleicht) Hilfe brauchen	If you wait outside Buckingham Palace, you ~ see the Queen.
	we **could** ... [kəd, kʊd]	wir könnten ...	! we **could** = **1.** wir konnten; **2.** wir könnten
	hairdresser ['heədresə]	Friseur/in	

at the hairdresser's / to the doctor's / ...

Wenn der **Ort** gemeint ist, an dem jemand seinen Beruf ausübt – z.B. ein Friseurgeschäft oder eine Arztpraxis – wird oft der ***s*-Genitiv** benutzt:

My father is **at the hairdresser's**.	Mein Vater ist beim Friseur.
She felt ill and went **to the doctor's**.	Sie fühlte sich krank und ging zum Arzt.
I met Grandpa **at the chemist's** this morning.	Ich habe Opa heute Morgen beim Apotheker getroffen.

p.45	(to) **cut (-tt-)** [kʌt], **cut, cut**	schneiden	
	(to) **blow** [bləʊ], **blew** [bluː], **blown** [bləʊn]	wehen, blasen	
	across [ə'krɒs]	hinüber, herüber	Look at that river. How can we get ~?
	anorak ['ænəræk]	Anorak, Windjacke	*French:* l'anorak *(m)*
	(to) **begin (-nn-)** [bɪ'gɪn], **began** [bɪ'gæn], **begun** [bɪ'gʌn]	beginnen, anfangen (mit)	It's time to ~. (= to start) (to) **begin** ◄► (to) **stop**
p.46	**clone** [kləʊn]	Klon	
	jealous (of) ['dʒeləs]	neidisch (auf); eifersüchtig (auf)	You get so much pocket money! I'm really ~. Sarah is ~ **of** her baby brother. She thinks her parents love him more.
	stew [stjuː]	Eintopf(gericht)	
	community hall [kə'mjuːnəti]	Gemeinschaftshalle, -saal, Gemeindehalle, -saal	
	(to) **grab (-bb-)** [græb]	schnappen, packen	I was late, so I **grabbed** my school bag and ran to the station.

How am I doing?

p.47	(to) **look** sth. **up** [ˌlʊk‿'ʌp]	etwas nachschlagen	**Look** ~ the meaning of 'stew' in your dictionary. Can you **look** ~ his new phone number for me?

Unit 3: World of sport

p.52	**final** ['faɪnl]	Finale, Endspiel	! Betonung und Aussprache: **final** ['faɪnl]
	final ['faɪnl]	letzte(r, s); End-	The hero saved the girl in the ~ minute of the film. *French:* final, e
	semi-final [ˌsemiˈfaɪnl]	Halbfinale	
	training session ['seʃn]	Trainingsstunde, -einheit	
p.53	(to) **be interested (in)** ['ɪntrəstɪd]	interessiert sein (an), sich interessieren (für)	! an **interesting** CD = eine interessante CD I'm **interested** in music. = Ich interessiere mich für Musik.

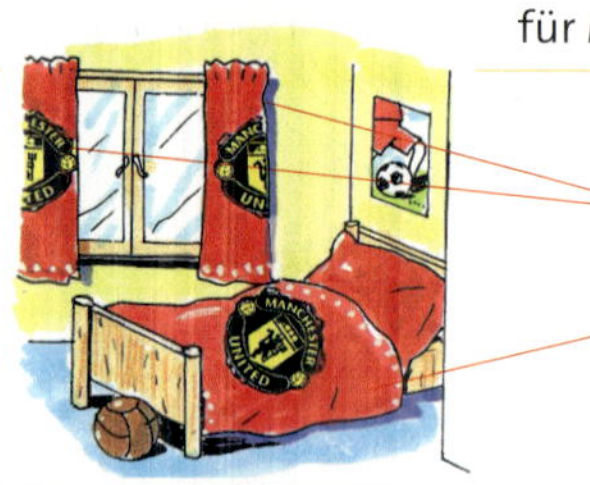

	bedspread ['bedspred]	Tagesdecke	
	curtain ['kɜːtn]	Vorhang	
	furniture *(no pl)* ['fɜːnɪtʃə]	Möbel	! Die **Möbel** <u>**sind**</u> neu. = The **furniture** <u>**is**</u> new. (*Never:* The ~~furnitures are~~ new.) <u>ein</u> Möbel(stück) = **a piece of furniture**

Words without a plural: furniture, hair, information, news, ...

<u>**This**</u> new **furniture** <u>**is**</u> very nice. <u>**Was it**</u> expensive?	<u>**Diese**</u> neuen **Möbel** <u>**sind**</u> sehr hübsch. <u>**Waren sie**</u> teuer?
I think your **hair** <u>**is**</u> too long. Why don't you cut <u>**it**</u>?	... deine **Haare** <u>**sind**</u> zu lang. Warum schneidest du <u>**sie**</u> nicht?
<u>**That's**</u> too much **homework**.	<u>**Das sind**</u> zu viele **Hausaufgaben**.
All <u>**this**</u> **information** <u>**is**</u> very interesting.	All <u>**diese**</u> **Informationen** <u>**sind**</u> sehr interessant.
OK, <u>**that's**</u> the bad **news**. And what <u>**is**</u> the good **news**?	OK, <u>**das ist/sind**</u> die schlechte(n) **Nachricht(en)**. Und was <u>**ist/sind**</u> die gute(n) **Nachricht(en)**?

p.54/A 1	(to) **train** [treɪn]	trainieren	*French:* entraîner
	supporter [səˈpɔːtə]	Anhänger/in, Fan	
	(to) **support** a team [səˈpɔːt]	eine Mannschaft unterstützen; Fan einer Mannschaft sein	Which football team do you ~? – Manchester United.
	(to) **spot** **(-tt-)** [spɒt]	entdecken	I can't find my key. If you ~ it, please tell me.
	draw [drɔː]	Unentschieden	I'm a bit upset that we didn't win, but at least it was a ~.
	2 all	2 beide (2:2 unentschieden)	
	(to) **score (a goal)** [skɔː], [gəʊl]	ein Tor schießen, einen Treffer erzielen	We won 3–2. – Oh, great! Who **~d**? – Smith **~d** all three **~s**.
	score [skɔː]	Spielstand; Punktestand	
	goal [gəʊl]	Tor *(im Sport)*	

A football match

What's the score now? – 2–0. *(you say:* ***two nil****)*	Wie steht es jetzt? – 2:0.
What was the final score? – Chelsea 2, Arsenal 1.	Wie war der Endstand? – 2:1.
Our last match was a draw, 2–2. *(you say:* ***two all****)*	Unser letztes Spiel war ein Unentschieden, 2:2.

coach [kəʊtʃ]	Trainer/in	

	atmosphere ['ætməsfɪə]	Atmosphäre	! Betonung und Aussprache: **atmosphere** ['ætməsfɪə] *French:* l'atmosphère *(f)*
	leotard ['liːətɑːd]	Gymnastikanzug; Turnanzug	
	tights *(pl)* [taɪts]	Strumpfhose	
p.55/A 4	**exchange student** [ɪks'tʃeɪndʒ ˌstjuːdnt]	Austauschschüler/in	
	(to) **enter** ['entə]	betreten; eintreten (in)	 (to) **enter** a room ◄► (to) **leave** a room
	bad timing ['taɪmɪŋ]	schlechtes Timing	
	appetite ['æpɪtaɪt]	Appetit	! Manchmal sagt man **Enjoy!**, wenn man gemeinsam isst. Aber nie ~~Good appetite~~!
	(to) **refer to** **(-rr-)** [rɪ'fɜː]	sich beziehen auf	This question **~s to** line 12 on page 46.
p.56/A 5	**whole** [həʊl]	ganze(r, s), gesamte(r, s)	the ~ day = all day
	artist ['ɑːtɪst]	Künstler/in	! **artist** = Künstler/in (*nicht:* ~~Artist/in~~) Betonung auf der 1. Silbe: **artist** ['ɑːtɪst] *French:* l'artiste *(m, f)*
	stadium ['steɪdiəm]	Stadion	
	(to) **make a deal** [diːl]	ein Abkommen/eine Abmachung treffen	Help me with my Maths, and I'll help you with English. – OK, it's a **deal**! (= Abgemacht!)
	(to) **paraphrase** ['pærəfreɪz]	umschreiben, anders ausdrücken	*French:* paraphraser
	general ['dʒenrəl]	allgemeine(r, s)	! Betonung auf der 1. Silbe: **general** ['dʒenrəl] *French:* général, e
p.57/A 8	(to) **beat** [biːt], **beat, beaten** ['biːtn]	schlagen; besiegen	I ~ my brother at tennis last Sunday.
	cup [kʌp]	Pokal	
	win [wɪn]	Sieg	verb: (to) **win** – noun: **win**
	in the end	schließlich, zum Schluss	No bus came, so **in the ~** we walked home. ! **at the end** of the lesson = am Ende / am Schluss der Stunde
	half-time [ˌhɑːf 'taɪm]	Halbzeit(pause)	the break between the first and the second half of a match ! the first **half** = die erste Halbzeit
	goalkeeper ['gəʊlkiːpə]	Torwart, Torfrau	
	shot [ʃɒt]	Schuss	
p.60/P 1	**difference** ['dɪfrəns]	Unterschied	! Betonung auf der 1. Silbe: **difference** ['dɪfrəns] adjective: **different** – noun: **difference** *French:* différent, e – la différence

Word field: Sports

p.60/P 2

EQUIPMENT [ɪ'kwɪpmənt] Ausrüstung

skis [ski:z]

table tennis bat [bæt]

badminton racket ['rækɪt]

running shoes

swimming trunks *(pl)* [trʌŋks] Badehose / **swimsuit** ['swɪmsu:t] Badeanzug

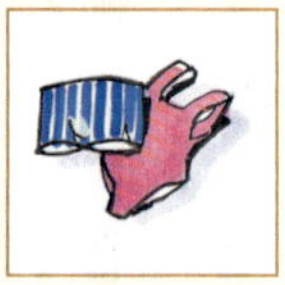

saddle ['sædl]

helmet, pads [pædz] (Knie-usw.)Schützer

helmet, pads Schulterpolster

LOCATION [ləʊ'keɪʃn] (Einsatz-)Ort, Platz

ski slope [sləʊp] Skipiste

sports hall

court [kɔ:t] Platz, Court

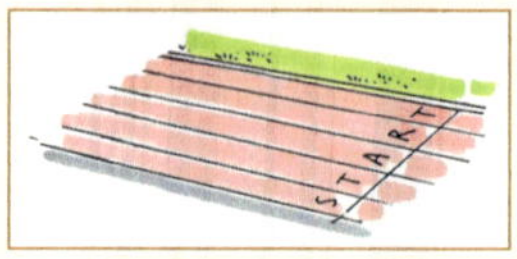

running track [træk] Laufbahn

(swimming) pool

bridle path ['braɪdl pɑ:θ] Reitweg

half-pipe ['hɑ:fpaɪp]

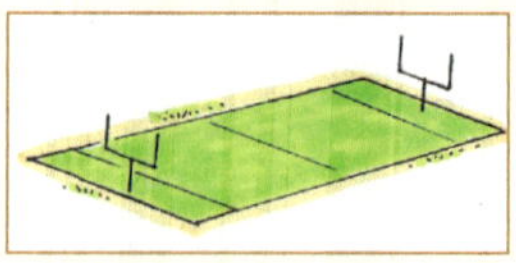

field

p.62/P 7	**pepper** ['pepə]	Pfeffer	
	salt [sɔ:lt]	Salz	**salt** and **pepper** *French:* le sel, le poivre
p.64/P 10	**order** ['ɔ:də]	Reihenfolge	*French:* l'ordre *(m)*
	(to) **end** [end]	enden; beenden	The road **~s** here. We'll have to walk now. A hot bath is a good way to ~ the day.
p.65/P 13	**about yourself** [jə'self, jɔ:'self]	über dich selbst	

Who needs legs?

p.66	**only** ['əʊnli]	erst	I'm not sixteen, I'm ~ fourteen. ! **only** = **1.** nur, bloß; **2.** erst
	(to) **grow up** [ˌgrəʊ‿'ʌp], **grew up** [ˌgruː‿'ʌp], **grown up** [ˌgrəʊn‿'ʌp]	erwachsen werden; aufwachsen	Dave wants to be a doctor when he **~s up**. When my grandparents were **~ing up**, they had no television.
	onto ['ɒntə, 'ɒntʊ]	auf (... hinauf)	The cat saw the dog and jumped ~ the table.
	(to) **take a ride**	eine Fahrt machen	
	ambulance ['æmbjələns]	Krankenwagen	! Betonung und Aussprache: **ambulance** ['æmbjələns] *French:* l'ambulance *(f)*
	athletics [æθ'letɪks]	Leichtathletik	I'm an ~ fan, I love sports like running and jumping. *French:* l'athlétisme *(m)*
	medal ['medl]	Medaille	! Betonung auf der 1. Silbe: **medal** ['medl] *French:* la médaille
	(to) **draw** [drɔː], **drew** [druː], **drawn** [drɔːn]	zeichnen	I'll ~ a little map to help you find my flat.
p.104	(to) **fight (for)** [faɪt], **fought** [fɔːt], **fought**	kämpfen (für, um)	Nathan had to ~ **for** his life after his accident.
	operation (on) [ˌɒpə'reɪʃn]	Operation (an)	He had an ~ **on** his knee after he was hurt in the match. *French:* l'opération *(f)*
	artificial [ˌɑːtɪ'fɪʃl]	künstlich, Kunst-	Are those flowers real or ~? ~ legs („Beinprothesen") *French:* artificiel, le
	sledge [sledʒ]	Schlitten	 a **sledge**
	disabled [dɪs'eɪbld]	(körper)behindert	
	talent ['tælənt]	Talent, Begabung	! Betonung auf der 1. Silbe: **talent** ['tælənt] *French:* le talent
	championship ['tʃæmpiənʃɪp]	Meisterschaft	*French:* le championnat
	(to) **represent** [ˌreprɪ'zent]	repräsentieren, vertreten	There were groups from all over Europe at the festival. A group from Frankfurt **~ed** Germany. *French:* représenter
	the Commonwealth ['kɒmənwelθ]	*Gemeinschaft der Länder des ehemaligen Britischen Weltreichs*	
	Paralympics [ˌpærə'lɪmpɪks]	*olympischer Wettkampf für Behindertensportler/innen*	

Unit 4: Growing up in Canada

p.68	(to) **date** sb. [deɪt]	mit jm. (aus)gehen; sich (regelmäßig) mit jm. treffen	Dad **~d** Mum for years before they got married.
	movie ['muːvi]	Film	film
	population [ˌpɒpju'leɪʃn]	Bevölkerung, Einwohner(zahl)	With a ~ of 2.5 million, Toronto is Canada's largest city. *French:* la population
	square km **(sq** km**)** [skweə]	Quadratkilometer	

	minus ['maɪnəs]	minus	**!** Aussprache: **minus** ['maɪnəs] 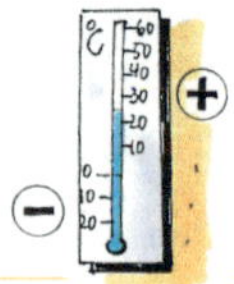
	plus [plʌs]	plus	
	Celsius (C) ['selsiəs]	Celsius	22 °**C** = 22 degrees **Celsius**
p.69	**sleepover** ['sli:pəʊvə]	Schlafparty	
	real late *(AE, infml)*	wirklich spät, richtig spät	= really late
	outdoor ['aʊtdɔ:]	im Freien, Außen-	~ activities; an ~ swimming pool („Freibad“)
	(to) **hunt** [hʌnt]	jagen	Do people still ~ lions in Africa?
	snowshoeing ['snəʊʃu:ɪŋ]	Schneeschuhwandern	two pairs of **snowshoes** 
	(to) **canoe** [kə'nu:]	paddeln, Kanu fahren	

Verbs and nouns with the same form

(to) **canoe**	paddeln, Kanu fahren	(to) **date**	mit jm. (aus)gehen	(to) **hunt**	jagen
canoe	Kanu, Paddelboot	**date**	Date, Verabredung	**hunt**	Jagd
(to) **colour**	kolorieren, färben; bunt an-, ausmalen	(to) **drive**	*(Auto)* fahren	(to) **link**	verbinden, verknüpfen
colour	Farbe	**drive**	(Auto-)Fahrt	**link**	Verbindung, Verknüpfung
(to) **cook**	kochen	(to) **fish**	fischen, angeln	(to) **sleep**	schlafen
cook	Koch/Köchin	**fish**	Fisch	**sleep**	Schlaf

p.70/A 1	(to) **turn** sth. **up/down** [tɜ:n]	etwas lauter/leiser stellen	Can you ~ **down** that music? It's too loud.
	lyrics *(pl)* ['lɪrɪks]	Liedtext(e), Songtext(e)	I like this song. What do the ~ mean in German?
	easy-going [ˌi:zi'gəʊɪŋ]	gelassen, locker	
	strict [strɪkt]	streng	Peter isn't allowed to watch TV after 8 o'clock. His parents are very ~ about that.
	(to) **waste** sth. **(on)** [weɪst]	etwas verschwenden, vergeuden (für)	'Don't ~ your time and money **on** computer games,' my dad said.
	latest ['leɪtɪst]	neueste(r, s)	The Kooks are great. Have you heard their ~ CD?
	cellphone ['selfəʊn] *(AE)*	Handy, Mobiltelefon	= *BE* mobile (phone) 
	adult ['ædʌlt]	Erwachsene(r)	Children pay 50 p, **~s** £ 1.50.
	old-fashioned [ˌəʊld'fæʃnd]	altmodisch	
	modern ['mɒdən]	modern	**!** Betonung auf der 1. Silbe: **modern** ['mɒdən] **modern** ◄► **old-fashioned** *French:* moderne
	(to) **laugh at** sb.	jn. auslachen, über jn. lachen	The other kids **~ed** ~ Jennifer because she had a funny accent.
	(to) **hang out** [ˌhæŋ‿'aʊt], **hung** [hʌŋ], **hung** *(infml)*	rumhängen, abhängen	
p.71/A 3	**(shopping) mall** [mɔ:l]	*(großes)* Einkaufszentrum	a big shopping centre
	by ten o'clock	bis (spätestens) zehn Uhr	Please be home ~ ten. (= not later than ten)

German „bis“

until / till („bis“)

I can stay up **until / till** eleven o'clock tonight.
We lived in Scotland **until / till** I was 12.

from ... to („von ... bis“)

We're open **from** Mondays **to** Saturdays.

by („bis spätestens“, „nicht später als“)

We need your report **by** Friday (= on or before Friday).
You must be home **by** 5.30 (= at or before 5.30).

	cabin ['kæbɪn]	Hütte	
	not ... until / not ... till	erst (um); nicht vor	! • The guests did**n't** leave **until/till** 3 am. Die Gäste gingen **erst um** 3 Uhr morgens. • I wo**n't** arrive **until/till** Monday night. Ich werde **erst** Montagnacht ankommen. / Ich werde **nicht vor** Montagnacht ankommen.
	guys *(pl)* [gaɪz] *(AE, infml)*	Leute	
p.72/A 6	**province** ['prɒvɪns]	Provinz	! Betonung auf der 1. Silbe: **province** ['prɒvɪns] *French:* la province
	traditional [trə'dɪʃənl]	traditionell	*French:* traditionel, le
	(to) **protect** sb. **(from)** [prə'tekt]	jn. (be)schützen (vor)	Wear a hat. It will ~ you **from** the sun. *French:* protéger

Reflexive pronouns (Reflexivpronomen)

I've hurt **myself**.	Ich habe	**mir**	wehgetan / **mich**	verletzt.
You've hurt **yourself**.	Du ...	**dir**	... / **dich**	...
He's hurt **himself**.	Er ...	**sich**	... / **sich**	...
She's hurt **herself**.	Sie ...	**sich**	... / **sich**	...
It's hurt **itself**.	Es ...	**sich**	... / **sich**	...
We've hurt **ourselves**.	Wir ...	**uns**	... / **uns**	...
You've hurt **yourselves**.	Ihr ...	**euch**	... / **euch**	...
They've hurt **themselves**.	Sie ...	**sich**	... / **sich**	...

! Aussprache/Betonung:
-self [-'self]
-selves [-'selvz]

	attack [ə'tæk]	Angriff	How can I protect my computer from virus **~s**? *French:* l'attaque *(f)*
	(to) **attack**	angreifen	If somebody **~s** us, we have to protect ourselves. *French:* attaquer
	exactly [ɪg'zæktli]	genau	You mean that man is a thief? – **Exactly**. *French:* exactement
	argument ['ɑːgjumənt]	Argument, Begründung; Streit	! **argument** = **1.** Argument – There are good **~s** for and against this idea. **2.** Streit – Mum and Dad had an ~ last night. Mum shouted a lot.
	(to) **blame** sb. **(for)** [bleɪm]	jm. die Schuld geben (an); jm. Vorwürfe machen (wegen)	Don't ~ me. It wasn't my mistake.
p.72/A 7	(to) **make a point**	ein Argument vorbringen	He **made** some interesting **~s** in the discussion.

	(to) **disagree (with)** [ˌdɪsəˈɡriː]	nicht übereinstimmen (mit); anderer Meinung sein (als)	I thought it was a good point, but the others **~d**. (to) **disagree** ◀▶ (to) **agree**
p.73/A 8	**leader** [ˈliːdə]	Leiter/in, (An-)Führer/in	
	microphone [ˈmaɪkrəfəʊn]	Mikrofon	! Aussprache: **microphone** [ˈmaɪkrəfəʊn] *French:* le microphone
	each other [iːtʃ‿ˈʌðə]	einander, sich (gegenseitig)	Paul likes Linda and Linda likes Paul. = Paul and Linda like **each ~**.
p.73/A 9	**chorus** [ˈkɔːrəs]	Refrain	! German „Chor“ = English **choir** [ˈkwaɪə]
p.76/P 1	**per cent (%)** [pəˈsent]	Prozent	Twenty **~ ~** of two hundred is forty. *French:* pour cent
	per [pɜː, pə]	pro	50 miles **~** hour = 50 miles an hour
	kilogram [ˈkɪləɡræm], **kilo** [ˈkiːləʊ] **(kg)**	Kilogramm, Kilo	We need two **kilograms/kilos of** oranges for the orange juice.

a 90-kilogram bear / a 14-hour flight / ...

a **90-kilogram** bear	ein 90 Kilogramm schwerer Bär
a **ten-kilometre** walk	eine Zehn-Kilometer-Wanderung
a **14-hour** flight	ein 14-stündiger Flug, ein 14-Stunden-Flug
a **24-hour** supermarket	ein Supermarkt, der 24 Stunden geöffnet ist
a **two-week** holiday	ein zweiwöchiger Urlaub

! Im Englischen steht das Nomen im Singular:
a **14-hour** flight
(*nicht:* a 14-~~hours~~ flight)

p.76/P 2	**(in)tolerant** [ˈtɒlərənt], [ɪnˈtɒlərənt]	(in)tolerant	! Betonung: **tolerant** [ˈtɒlərənt] **intolerant** [ɪnˈtɒlərənt]
	relaxed [rɪˈlækst]	locker, entspannt	
p.77/P 4	**rule** [ruːl]	Regel, Vorschrift	I don't understand the game. Can you explain the **~s**, please?
p.77/P 6	**crazy** [ˈkreɪzi]	verrückt	You want to go out in this rain? You must be **~**.
p.78/P 8	**strike** [straɪk]	Streik	! (to) **be on strike** = streiken, sich im Streik befinden (to) **go on strike** = streiken, in den Streik treten

Reflexiv im Deutschen – nicht reflexiv im Englischen

p.78/P 9

(to) **calm down**	sich beruhigen	(to) **prepare**	sich vorbereiten
(to) **clean one's teeth**	sich die Zähne putzen	(to) **refer to**	sich beziehen auf
(to) **feel**	sich fühlen; sich anfühlen	(to) **relax**	sich entspannen, sich ausruhen
(to) **get dressed**	sich anziehen	(to) **remember sth.**	sich an etwas erinnern; sich etwas merken
(to) **hide**	sich verstecken	(to) **sit down**	sich hinsetzen
(to) **imagine sth.**	sich etwas vorstellen	(to) **turn**	sich umdrehen
(to) **meet**	sich treffen	(to) **wonder**	sich fragen
(to) **move**	sich bewegen	(to) **worry**	sich Sorgen machen
(to) **open**	sich öffnen		

p.79/P 10	**walrus** [ˈwɔːlrəs]	Walross	
	blanket [ˈblæŋkɪt]	Decke *(zum Zudecken)*	

a **walrus** in a **blanket**

p. 80/P 13	(to) **brainstorm** ['breɪnstɔːm]	brainstormen *(so viele Ideen wie möglich sammeln)*	(to) collect as many ideas as possible
	silly ['sɪli]	albern, dumm	Maybe this is a ~ question, but can dogs understand different languages?
	(to) **revise** [rɪ'vaɪz]	überarbeiten; wiederholen	! (to) **revise** = **1.** überarbeiten – (to) ~ an essay, a text, a story **2.** wiederholen – (to) ~ vocabulary, grammar, ... *French:* réviser
	spelling ['spelɪŋ]	(Recht-)Schreibung, Schreibweise	Remember to check your ~ when you revise a text.

Two bear attacks

p. 81	(to) **camp** [kæmp]	zelten	We asked the farmer if we could ~ in his field.
	while [waɪl]	während	Somebody stole my bike ~ I was in the shop.
	(to) **escape (from** sb./sth.**)** [ɪ'skeɪp]	fliehen (vor jm./aus etwas); entkommen	A lion **~d from** its cage at London Zoo last night. The thief **~d** in a fast sports car.
	(to) **warn** sb. **(about** sth.**)** [wɔːn]	jn. (vor etwas) warnen	The doctor **~ed** him **about** the dangers of smoking.
p. 82	(to) **paddle** ['pædl]	paddeln	
	rapids *(pl)* ['ræpɪdz]	Stromschnellen	

They're **paddling** through the **rapids.**

Unit 5: A teen magazine

pp. 88/89	(to) **announce** [ə'naʊns]	ankündigen, bekanntgeben	The form teacher **~d** the names of the winners. verb: (to) **announce** – noun: **announcement** *French:* annoncer
	That's up to you.	Das liegt bei dir. / Das kannst/musst du (selbst) entscheiden.	Will I be on the football team? – **That's ~ ~ you**. If you practise hard, you'll have a good chance.
	section ['sekʃn]	Abschnitt, Teil, (Themen-)Bereich	! Betonung auf der 1. Silbe: **section** ['sekʃn] *French:* la section
	editor ['edɪtə]	Redakteur/in	
	(to) **produce** [prə'djuːs]	produzieren, herstellen	Germany **~s** millions of cars every year. *French:* produire
	(to) **publish** ['pʌblɪʃ]	veröffentlichen	J. K. Rowling **~ed** her first Harry Potter book in 1997. *French:* publier
	drawing ['drɔːɪŋ]	Zeichnung	verb: (to) **draw** – noun: **drawing**
	(to) **contact** sb. ['kɒntækt]	sich mit jm. in Verbindung setzen; mit jm. Kontakt aufnehmen	If you want to ~ me, you can phone me or send me an e-mail. ! Betonung auf der 1. Silbe: **contact** ['kɒntækt]
	office ['ɒfɪs]	Büro	Dad works in a factory and mum works in an ~.

	success [sək'ses]	Erfolg	The party was a big ~. Everybody enjoyed it. *French:* le succès
	successful [sək'sesfl]	erfolgreich	The band was very ~ in the UK, but not in Canada or the US.
	headphones *(pl)* ['hedfəʊnz]	Kopfhörer	
	monitor ['mɒnɪtə]	Bildschirm, Monitor	
	How do they **feel about ...?**	Was halten sie von ...?	I don't like Jim's friends. **How** do you ~ ~ them?
p. 90	(to) **skim** a text **(-mm-)** [skɪm]	einen Text überfliegen *(um den Inhalt grob zu erfassen)*	
	useful ['juːsfl]	nützlich	If you don't know a city well, it's ~ to have a street map.
	main [meɪn]	Haupt-	the ~ idea = the most important idea
	bold print [ˌbəʊld 'prɪnt]	Fettdruck	The names of cities with over a million people are in **bold** ~ on this map.
	caption ['kæpʃn]	Bildunterschrift	
	(to) **wake up** [ˌweɪk_'ʌp], **woke** [wəʊk], **woken** ['wəʊkən]	aufwachen	Yesterday I didn't ~ ~ till 8 o'clock and was late for school.
	(to) **wake** sb. **(up)**, **woke, woken**	jn. (auf)wecken	This morning my mother **woke** me ~ at 7. 
	(radio, pop) station ['steɪʃn]	(Radio-, Pop-)Sender	
	so that	sodass, damit	I'm saving money ~ ~ I can buy a new bike.
	silence ['saɪləns]	Stille; Schweigen	There was ~ when the teacher walked into the classroom. *French:* le silence 
p. 91	**riddle** ['rɪdl]	Rätsel	
	leather ['leðə]	Leder	
	pipe [paɪp]	Pfeife	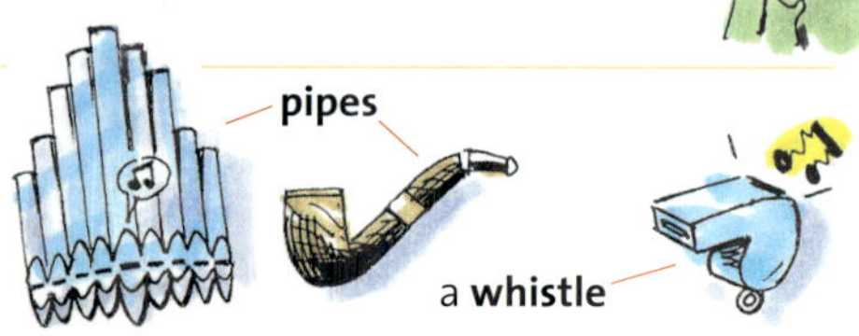
	(to) **stick out of** sth. [stɪk], **stuck, stuck** [stʌk]	aus etwas herausragen, herausstehen	A long pipe **stuck** ~ **of** the old man's mouth.
	(to) **keep** [kiːp], **kept, kept** [kept]	(be)halten; aufbewahren	**Keep** your eyes open when you're on the road. You can ~ the book, I don't need it any more. Where do you ~ your drawings? – In my dossier.
	(to) **squeeze** [skwiːz]	drücken; (aus)pressen	She said thank you and **~d** my arm. For one glass of juice, ~ three or four oranges. 
	(to) **settle down** [ˌsetl 'daʊn]	sich eingewöhnen	Have you **~d down** at your new school yet?
	(to) **be good at** sth.	gut in etwas sein; etwas gut können	(to) **be good at** sth. ◄► (to) **be bad at** sth.

	(to) **decide (on)** [dɪ'saɪd]	beschließen; sich entscheiden (für)	Have you **~d** what project you would like to do? We've **~d on** a project about Toronto. (= We've **~d** to do a project about Toronto.) *French:* décider
	age [eɪdʒ]	Alter	I'm 14. What ~ are you? – 15. At the ~ of 28, my cousin got a job – at last.
	(to) **be sold out**	ausverkauft sein, vergriffen sein	The concert tickets **were ~ out** in only three hours.
p. 92	**vacation** [və'keɪʃn, *AE:* veɪ'keɪʃn] *(AE)*	Urlaub, Ferien	= *BE* holiday
	(to) **get** sth. **off the ground**	etwas auf den Weg bringen; etwas auf die Beine stellen	
	(to) **have a crush on** sb. [krʌʃ]	in jn. verknallt sein	Look, he's smiling at you again. I think he **has a ~ on** you.
	that far/good/bad/...	so weit/gut/schlecht/...	I knew you could sing, but I didn't know you were **~ good**. (= so good)
	least [li:st]	am wenigsten	Which article do you like best, and which do you like ~?
p. 93/P 1	**album** ['ælbəm]	Album	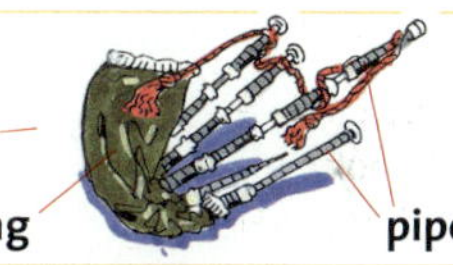
	bagpipes *(pl)* ['bægpaɪps]	Dudelsack	
	career [kə'rɪə]	Karriere	
	musician [mju:'zɪʃn]	Musiker/in	 These **musicians** are **recording** a new **album.**
	opera ['ɒprə]	Oper	
	record ['rekɔ:d]	Schallplatte	
	(to) **record** [rɪ'kɔ:d]	*(Musik)* aufnehmen, aufzeichnen	
	(to) **release** [rɪ'li:s]	*(CD, Film usw.)* herausbringen, auf den Markt bringen	
	single ['sɪŋgl]	Single	
	track [træk]	Stück, Titel, Track *(auf einer CD)*	Now we'll hear a ~ from their new album.
	tune [tju:n]	Melodie	
	musical instrument [ˌmju:zɪkl‿'ɪnstrəmənt]	Musikinstrument	**!** Betonung auf der 1. Silbe: **instrument** ['ɪnstrəmənt]
p. 95/P 4	(to) **go wrong**	schiefgehen	(to) **go wrong** („schiefgehen") ◄► (to) **go well** („gutgehen")
	the night/week/... before	in der Nacht/Woche/... zuvor	She went back to work last Monday although she had been very ill **the week ~**.
p. 96/P 6	**biography** [baɪ'ɒgrəfi]	Biografie	**!** Betonung auf der 2. Silbe: **biography** [baɪ'ɒgrəfi] *French:* la biographie
	company ['kʌmpəni]	Firma, Gesellschaft	
	copy ['kɒpi]	Exemplar	I haven't got the book in German, but I've got an English ~.
	capital letter [ˌkæpɪtl 'letə]	Großbuchstabe	**CAPITAL LETTERS**
	tense [tens]	(grammatische) Zeit, Tempus	

Das Dictionary besteht aus zwei alphabetischen Wörterlisten:

Englisch – Deutsch (S.172–197)
Deutsch – Englisch (S.198–220).

Das **English – German Dictionary** enthält den Wortschatz der Bände 1 bis 3 von *English G 21.*
Wenn du wissen möchtest, was ein Wort bedeutet, wie man es ausspricht oder wie es genau geschrieben wird, kannst du hier nachschlagen.

Im **English – German Dictionary** werden folgende **Abkürzungen und Symbole** verwendet:

jm. = jemandem	sb. = somebody	*pl = plural*	*AE = American English*
jn. = jemanden	sth. = something	*no pl = no plural*	*infml = informal*

° Mit diesem Kringel sind Wörter markiert, die nicht zum Lernwortschatz gehören.
► Der Pfeil verweist auf Kästchen im Vocabulary (S.150–171), in denen du weitere Informationen zu diesem Wort findest.

Die **Fundstellenangaben** zeigen, wo ein Wort zum ersten Mal vorkommt.
Die Ziffern in Klammern bezeichnen Seitenzahlen:

I = Band 1 • II = Band 2 • III = Band 3
III Intro (6) = Band 3, Introduction, Seite 6
III Intro (6/151) = Band 3, Introduction, Seite 151 (im Vocabulary, zu Seite 6)
III 1 (12) = Band 3, Unit 1, Seite 12
III 1 (12/152) = Band 3, Unit 1, Seite 152 (im Vocabulary, zu Seite 12)

Tipps zur Arbeit mit einem English – German Dictionary findest du im Skills File auf Seite 126.

A

a [ə]
1. ein, eine I
2. once/twice a week einmal/zweimal pro Woche III 2 (32)
a bit ein bisschen, etwas II • **a few** ein paar, einige II • **a lot (of)** eine Menge, viel, viele II • **He likes her a lot.** Er mag sie sehr. I

able ['eɪbl]**: be able to do sth.** etwas tun können; fähig sein / in der Lage sein, etwas zu tun III 2 (34)
► S.158 „können" und „dürfen"

°aboriginals *(pl)* [ˌæbə'rɪdʒənlz] Ureinwohner/innen

about [ə'baʊt]
1. über I
2. ungefähr II
ask about sth. nach etwas fragen I • **This is about Mr Green.** Es geht um Mr Green. I • **How about ...?** Wie wär's mit ...? III Intro (10)
What about ...? 1. Was ist mit ...? / Und ...? I; **2.** Wie wär's mit ...? I
What are you talking about? Wovon redest du? I • **°What are the pages about?** Wovon handeln die Seiten? • **What was the best thing about ...?** Was war das Beste an ...? II • **°Say what you like about ...** Sag, was du an ... magst

above [ə'bʌv]
1. oben III 2 (35)
2. über, oberhalb (von) III 2 (35)

abroad [ə'brɔːd] im Ausland II
go abroad ins Ausland gehen/fahren II

accent ['æksənt] Akzent II

accident ['æksɪdənt] Unfall II

across [ə'krɒs]
1. (quer) über III 1 (15)
2. hinüber, herüber III 2 (45)

act [ækt] aufführen, spielen I
°Act out ... Spiele/Spielt ... vor.

activity [æk'tɪvəti] Aktivität, Tätigkeit I

actor ['æktə] Schauspieler/in II

actually ['æktʃuəli] eigentlich; in Wirklichkeit III 1 (16)

°adapt [ə'dæpt] adaptieren, anpassen; bearbeiten

add (to) [æd] hinzufügen, ergänzen, addieren (zu) I • **°add up** addieren, zusammenzählen

adjective ['ædʒɪktɪv] Adjektiv I

adult ['ædʌlt] Erwachsene(r) III 4 (70)

adverb ['ædvɜːb] Adverb I

afraid [ə'freɪd]
1. be afraid (of) Angst haben (vor) I
2. I'm afraid leider II

after ['ɑːftə] nach *(zeitlich)* I
after that danach I

after ['ɑːftə] nachdem II

afternoon [ˌɑːftə'nuːn] Nachmittag I • **in the afternoon** nachmittags, am Nachmittag I • **on Friday afternoon** freitagnachmittags, am Freitagnachmittag I

again [ə'gen] wieder; noch einmal I
once again noch einmal III 2 (44)

against [ə'genst] gegen I

age [eɪdʒ] Alter III 5 (91)

ago [ə'gəʊ]**: a minute ago** vor einer Minute I

agree (on) [ə'griː] sich einigen (auf) I • **agree with sb./sth.** jm./etwas zustimmen; mit jm./etwas übereinstimmen II

air [eə] Luft III 1 (12/152)

airport ['eəpɔːt] Flughafen III 1 (20/154)

album ['ælbəm] Album III 5 (93)

all [ɔːl] alle; alles I • **2 all** 2 beide (2:2 unentschieden) III 3 (54) • **all around the castle** ganz um die Burg herum II • **all day** den ganzen Tag (lang) I • **all over the world** auf der ganzen Welt III Intro (6/151) • **all right** [ɔːl 'raɪt] gut, in Ordnung II • **all the time** die ganze Zeit I • **all we have to do now ...** alles, was wir jetzt (noch) tun müssen, ... II • **from all around Wales** aus ganz Wales II
from all over England/the UK aus ganz England/aus dem

gesamten Vereinigten Königreich III Intro (6) • **This is all wrong.** Das ist ganz falsch. I
all-day ticket [ˌɔːl deɪ 'tɪkɪt] Tagesfahrkarte III 1 (14/153)
allowed [ə'laʊd]**: be allowed to do sth.** etwas tun dürfen III 1 (26)
► S.158 „können" und „dürfen"
almost ['ɔːlməʊst] fast, beinahe II
alone [ə'ləʊn] allein I
along the road [ə'lɒŋ] entlang der Straße / die Straße entlang II
alphabet ['ælfəbet] Alphabet I
°**alphabetical** [ˌælfə'betɪkl] alphabetisch
already [ɔːl'redi] schon, bereits II
also ['ɔːlsəʊ] auch II
°**alternative** [ɔːl'tɜːnətɪv] alternative(r, s), Alternativ-
although [ɔːl'ðəʊ] obwohl III 1 (12)
always ['ɔːlweɪz] immer I
am [ˌeɪ_'em]**: 7 am** 7 Uhr morgens/vormittags I
amazing [ə'meɪzɪŋ] erstaunlich, unglaublich II
ambulance ['æmbjələns] Krankenwagen III 3 (66)
American football [əˌmerɪkən 'fʊtbɔːl] Football I
an [ən] ein, eine I • *siehe* **a**
and [ənd, ænd] und I
angel ['eɪndʒl] Engel II
angry (about sth./with sb.) ['æŋgri] wütend, böse (über etwas/auf jn.) II
animal ['ænɪml] Tier II
announce [ə'naʊns] ankündigen, bekanntgeben III 5 (88/89)
announcement [ə'naʊnsmənt] Durchsage, Ansage; Ankündigung, Bekanntgabe III 1 (25)
anorak ['ænəræk] Anorak, Windjacke III 2 (45)
another [ə'nʌðə] ein(e) andere(r, s); noch ein(e) I • **another 45p** weitere 45 Pence, noch 45 Pence II **one another** einander, sich (gegenseitig) III 4 (146)
answer ['ɑːnsə] antworten; beantworten I
answer (to) ['ɑːnsə] Antwort (auf) I
any ['eni]**: any ...?** (irgend)welche ...? I • **not (...) any** kein, keine I • **not (...) any more** nicht mehr II
anybody ['enibɒdi] (irgend)jemand II • **not (...) anybody** niemand II
anything ['eniθɪŋ] (irgend)etwas II • **not (...) anything** nichts II
anyway ['eniweɪ]
1. sowieso I
2. trotzdem II
anywhere ['eniweə] irgendwo(hin) II • **not (...) anywhere** nirgendwo(hin) II
appear [ə'pɪə] erscheinen, auftauchen III 1 (27)
appetite ['æpɪtaɪt] Appetit III 3 (55)
apple ['æpl] Apfel I
appointment [ə'pɔɪntmənt] Termin, Verabredung I
April ['eɪprəl] April I
°**aquatic** [ə'kwætɪk] Wasser-
are [ɑː] bist; sind; seid I • **How are you?** Wie geht es dir/Ihnen/euch? II • **The pencils are 35p.** Die Bleistifte kosten 35 Pence. I • **You're joking, aren't you?** Du machst Witze, nicht wahr? / Das ist nicht dein Ernst, oder? II
area ['eəriə] Bereich; Gebiet, Gegend III 1 (29)
argue ['ɑːgjuː] sich streiten, sich zanken I
argument ['ɑːgjumənt]
1. Argument, Begründung III 4 (72)
2. Streit III 4 (72)
arm [ɑːm] Arm I
armchair ['ɑːmtʃeə] Sessel I
around [ə'raʊnd] in ... umher, durch; um ... (herum) III 1 (26/155) • **all around the castle** ganz um die Burg herum II • **around six** um sechs Uhr herum, gegen sechs III 1 (26/155) • **around the lake** um den See (herum) III 1 (26/155) **around the town** in der Stadt umher, durch die Stadt III 1 (26/155) **from all around Wales** aus ganz Wales II • **look around** sich umsehen III 1 (26) • **walk/run/jump around** herumgehen/-rennen/-springen, umhergehen/-rennen/-springen III 1 (26/155)
► S.155 around
arrival (arr) [ə'raɪvl] Ankunft III 2 (33)
arrive [ə'raɪv] ankommen, eintreffen II
art [ɑːt] Kunst I
article ['ɑːtɪkl] (Zeitungs-)Artikel I
artificial [ˌɑːtɪ'fɪʃl] künstlich, Kunst- III 3 (104)
artist ['ɑːtɪst] Künstler/in III 3 (56)
as [əz, æz]
1. als, während II
2. **as a child** als Kind II
3. **as you can see** wie du sehen kannst II
4. **as big/exciting as** so groß/aufregend wie II • **as soon as** sobald, sowie II • °**as well** auch
ask [ɑːsk] fragen I • **ask about sth.** nach etwas fragen I • **ask questions** Fragen stellen I • **ask sb. for sth.** jn. um etwas bitten II **ask sb. the way** jn. nach dem Weg fragen II
asleep [ə'sliːp]**: be asleep** schlafen I
Assembly [ə'sembli] Versammlung *(morgendliche Schulversammlung, oft mit Andacht)* III 2 (44)
°**assistant** [ə'sɪstənt] Assistent/in
at [ət, æt]**: at 7 Hamilton Street** in der Hamiltonstraße 7 I • **at 8.45** um 8.45 I • **at 16** mit 16, im Alter von 16 Jahren II • **at break** in der Pause *(zwischen Schulstunden)* II **at home** daheim, zu Hause I • **at last** endlich, schließlich I • **at least** zumindest, wenigstens I **at night** nachts, in der Nacht I **at school** in der Schule I • **at that table** an dem Tisch (dort) / an den Tisch (dort) I • **at the back (of the room)** hinten, im hinteren Teil (des Zimmers) II • **at the bottom (of)** unten, am unteren Ende (von) II **at the chemist's/hairdresser's** beim Apotheker/Friseur III 2 (44/161) **at the end (of)** am Ende (von) I **at the moment** im Moment, gerade II • **at the Shaws' house** im Haus der Shaws/bei den Shaws zu Hause I • **at the station** am Bahnhof I • **at the top (of)** oben, am oberen Ende, an der Spitze (von) I **at the weekend** am Wochenende I • **at work** bei der Arbeit / am Arbeitsplatz I
ate [et, eɪt] *siehe* **eat**
athletics [æθ'letɪks] Leichtathletik III 3 (66)
°**Atlantic** [ət'læntɪk]**: the Atlantic** der Atlantische Ozean, Atlantik
atmosphere ['ætməsfɪə] Atmosphäre III 3 (54)
attack [ə'tæk] angreifen III 4 (72/167)
attack [ə'tæk] Angriff III 4 (72)
attraction [ə'trækʃn] Attraktion, Anziehungspunkt II
audience ['ɔːdiəns] Publikum; Zuschauer/innen, Zuhörer/innen II
August ['ɔːgəst] August I
aunt [ɑːnt] Tante I • **auntie** ['ɑːnti] Tante II
°**autograph** ['ɔːtəgrɑːf] Autogramm
autumn ['ɔːtəm] Herbst I
away [ə'weɪ] weg, fort I
awful ['ɔːfl] furchtbar, schrecklich II
°**Aye.** [aɪ] Ja. *(besonders in Schottland und Irland gebräuchlich)*

B

baby ['beɪbi] Baby I • **have a baby** ein Baby/Kind bekommen II
back [bæk]
°**1.** Rücken
2. at the back (of) hinten, im hinteren Teil (von) II
back (to) [bæk] zurück (nach) I
back door [ˌbæk 'dɔː] Hintertür II
background ['bækgraʊnd] Hintergrund II • **background file** *etwa:* Hintergrundinformation(en) II
bacon ['beɪkən] Schinkenspeck III 1 (24/155)
bad [bæd] schlecht, schlimm I
be bad at sth. schlecht in etwas sein; etwas schlecht können III 5 (91/170) • **bad timing** schlechtes Timing III 3 (55)
badminton ['bædmɪntən] Badminton, Federball I • **badminton racket** ['rækɪt] Badmintonschläger III 3 (60/164)
bag [bæg] Tasche, Beutel, Tüte I
°**baggy** ['bægi] weit (geschnitten) *(Kleidung)*
bagpipes *(pl)* ['bægpaɪps] Dudelsack III 5 (93)
ball [bɔːl] Ball I
°**ballet** ['bæleɪ] Ballett
banana [bə'nɑːnə] Banane I
band [bænd] Band, (Musik-)Gruppe I
°**Bangladeshi** [ˌbæŋglə'deʃi] bangladeschisch
bank [bæŋk] Bank, Sparkasse I
bank robber ['bæŋk ˌrɒbə] Bankräuber/in I
bar [bɑː] Bar II
baseball ['beɪsbɔːl] Baseball I
baseball cap Baseballmütze II
basket ['bɑːskɪt] Korb I • **a basket of apples** ein Korb Äpfel I
basketball ['bɑːskɪtbɔːl] Basketball I
bat [bæt]**: table tennis bat** Tischtennisschläger III 3 (60/164)
bath [bɑːθ] Bad, Badewanne II
have a bath baden, ein Bad nehmen II
bathroom ['bɑːθruːm] Badezimmer I
bay [beɪ] Bucht III 2 (38/160)
be [biː], **was/were, been** sein I
beach [biːtʃ] Strand II • **on the beach** am Strand II
bear [beə] Bär II
beard [bɪəd] Bart II
beat [biːt], **beat, beaten** schlagen; besiegen III 3 (57)
beaten ['biːtn] *siehe* **beat**
beautiful ['bjuːtɪfl] schön I
beauty ['bjuːti] Schönheit III 2 (35)
became [bɪ'keɪm] *siehe* **become**
because [bɪ'kɒz] weil I
become [bɪ'kʌm], **became, become** werden II
bed [bed] Bett I • **Bed and Breakfast (B&B)** [ˌbed‿ən 'brekfəst] Frühstückspension I • **go to bed** ins Bett gehen I
bedroom ['bedruːm] Schlafzimmer I
bedspread ['bedspred] Tagesdecke III 3 (53)
beef [biːf] Rindfleisch III 1 (24/155)
been [biːn] *siehe* **be**
before [bɪ'fɔː] vor *(zeitlich)* I
before [bɪ'fɔː] bevor II
before [bɪ'fɔː] (vorher) schon mal II
the night/week/... before in der Nacht/Woche/... zuvor III 5 (95)
began [bɪ'gæn] *siehe* **begin**
begin (-nn-) [bɪ'gɪn], **began, begun** beginnen, anfangen (mit) III 2 (45)
beginning [bɪ'gɪnɪŋ] Beginn, Anfang; Einleitung II
begun [bɪ'gʌn] *siehe* **begin**
behind [bɪ'haɪnd] hinter II
believe [bɪ'liːv] glauben III 2 (44)
bell [bel] Klingel, Glocke I
belong (to) [bɪ'lɒŋ] gehören (zu) II
below [bɪ'ləʊ]
1. unten III 2 (35/159)
2. unter, unterhalb (von) III 2 (35/159)
best [best] am besten II • **the best ...** der/die/das beste ...; die besten I • **like sth. best** etwas am liebsten mögen III 3 (57) • **What was the best thing about ...?** Was war das Beste an ...? II
better ['betə] besser I • **like sth. better** etwas lieber mögen II
between [bɪ'twiːn] zwischen II
big [bɪg] groß I
▸ S.157 big – large – huge
big wheel [ˌbɪg 'wiːl] Riesenrad III 1 (12)
bike [baɪk] Fahrrad I • **ride a bike** Rad fahren I
bin [bɪn] Mülltonne II
biography [baɪ'ɒgrəfi] Biografie III 5 (96)
biology [baɪ'ɒlədʒi] Biologie I
bird [bɜːd] Vogel I
birthday ['bɜːθdeɪ] Geburtstag I
for his birthday zu seinem Geburtstag III 3 (66) • **Happy birthday.** Herzlichen Glückwunsch zum Geburtstag. I • **My birthday is in May.** Ich habe im Mai Geburtstag. I • **My birthday is on 13th June.** Ich habe am 13. Juni Geburtstag. I
When's your birthday? Wann hast du Geburtstag? I
biscuit ['bɪskɪt] Keks, Plätzchen I
bit [bɪt]**: a bit** ein bisschen, etwas II
black [blæk] schwarz I
black bear ['blæk beə] Schwarzbär III 4 (76)
blame sb. (for) [bleɪm] jm. die Schuld geben (an); jm. Vorwürfe machen (wegen) III 4 (72)
blanket ['blæŋkɪt] Decke *(zum Zudecken)* III 4 (79)
bleep [bliːp] piepsen II
bleep [bliːp] Piepton II
blew [bluː] *siehe* **blow**
blood [blʌd] Blut III 1 (27)
blouse [blaʊz] Bluse II
blow [bləʊ], **blew, blown** wehen, blasen III 2 (45)
blown [bləʊn] *siehe* **blow**
blue [bluː] blau I
board [bɔːd] (Wand-)Tafel I • **on the board** an der/die Tafel I
boat [bəʊt] Boot, Schiff I
body ['bɒdi] Körper I
bold print [ˌbəʊld 'prɪnt] Fettdruck III 5 (90)
book [bʊk] Buch I
booklet ['bʊklət] Broschüre II
boot [buːt] Stiefel I
boring ['bɔːrɪŋ] langweilig I
born [bɔːn]**: be born** geboren sein/werden II
boss [bɒs] Chef/in, Boss III Intro (8)
both [bəʊθ] beide I
bottle ['bɒtl] Flasche I • **a bottle of milk** eine Flasche Milch I
bottom ['bɒtəm] unteres Ende II
at the bottom (of) unten, am unteren Ende (von) II
bought [bɔːt] *siehe* **buy**
bowl [bəʊl] Schüssel I • **a bowl of cornflakes** eine Schale Cornflakes I
box [bɒks] Kasten, Kästchen, Kiste I
boy [bɔɪ] Junge I
°**bracket** ['brækɪt] Klammer *(in Texten)*
brainstorm ['breɪnstɔːm] brainstormen *(so viele Ideen wie möglich sammeln)* III 4 (80)
bread *(no pl)* [bred] Brot I
break [breɪk] Pause I • **at break** in der Pause *(zwischen Schulstunden)* II
breakfast ['brekfəst] Frühstück I
have breakfast frühstücken I
bridge [brɪdʒ] Brücke I
bridle path ['braɪdl pɑːθ] Reitweg III 3 (60/164)
bright [braɪt] hell, leuchtend II

bring [brɪŋ], **brought, brought** (mit-, her)bringen I
British ['brɪtɪʃ] britisch; Brite, Britin II
°**brochure** ['brəʊʃə] Prospekt, Broschüre
broken ['brəʊkən] gebrochen; zerbrochen, kaputt II
brother ['brʌðə] Bruder I
brought [brɔːt] *siehe* **bring**
brown [braʊn] braun I
°**budget** ['bʌdʒɪt] Budget • °**be on a budget** mit wenig Geld auskommen müssen
budgie ['bʌdʒi] Wellensittich I
build [bɪld], **built, built** bauen II
building ['bɪldɪŋ] Gebäude II
built [bɪlt] *siehe* **build**
bully ['bʊli] einschüchtern, tyrannisieren II
bully ['bʊli] (Schul-)Tyrann III 2 (35)
bunk (bed) [bʌŋk] Etagenbett, Koje II
bus [bʌs] Bus I
business: Mind your own business. [ˌmaɪnd jər‿əʊn 'bɪznəs] Das geht dich nichts an! / Kümmere dich um deine eigenen Angelegenheiten! II
bus pass ['bʌs pɑːs] Bus-Monatskarte III 1 (20/154)
bus stop ['bʌs stɒp] Bushaltestelle III 1 (20/154)
busy ['bɪzi] belebt, verkehrsreich; hektisch III 2 (38/160)
but [bət, bʌt] aber I
button ['bʌtn] Knopf III 1 (26)
buy [baɪ], **bought, bought** kaufen I
°**buzz** [bʌz] *hier:* den Summer/die Glocke betätigen
by [baɪ]
1. von I
2. an; (nahe) bei II
by car/bike/... mit dem Auto/Rad/... II • °**by hand** von Hand, mit der Hand • **by ten o'clock** bis (spätestens) zehn Uhr III 4 (71) • **by the way** [ˌbaɪ ðə 'weɪ] übrigens; nebenbei (bemerkt) III Intro (7)
► S.167 German „bis"
Bye. [baɪ] Tschüs! I

C

cabin ['kæbɪn] Hütte III 4 (71)
café ['kæfeɪ] *(kleines)* Restaurant, Imbissstube, Café I
cage [keɪdʒ] Käfig I
cake [keɪk] Kuchen, Torte I
calendar ['kælɪndə] Kalender I
call [kɔːl] rufen; anrufen; nennen I
call sb. names jn. mit Schimpfwörtern hänseln, jm. Schimpfwörter nachrufen III 2 (35)
call [kɔːl] Anruf, Telefongespräch I
make a call ein Telefongespräch führen II
called [kɔːld]: **be called** heißen, genannt werden III 2 (39)
calm down [ˌkɑːm 'daʊn] sich beruhigen II
came [keɪm] *siehe* **come**
camel ['kæml] Kamel II
camera ['kæmərə] Kamera, Fotoapparat I
°**cameraman/-woman** ['kæmrəmən, -wʊmən] Kameramann/-frau
camp [kæmp] zelten III 4 (81)
can [kən, kæn]
1. können I
2. dürfen I
Can I help you? Kann ich Ihnen helfen? / Was kann ich für Sie tun? *(im Geschäft)* I
► S.158 „können" und „dürfen"
canal [kə'næl] Kanal III 2 (38/160)
canoe [kə'nuː] paddeln, Kanu fahren III 4 (69)
canoe [kə'nuː] Kanu, Paddelboot III 4 (69/166)
cap [kæp] Mütze, Kappe II
capital ['kæpɪtl] Hauptstadt III 1 (12)
capital letter [ˌkæpɪtl 'letə] Großbuchstabe III 5 (96)
caption ['kæpʃn] Bildunterschrift III 5 (90)
car [kɑː] Auto I • **car park** Parkplatz III 2 (38/160)
caravan ['kærəvæn] Wohnwagen II
card [kɑːd] (Spiel-, Post-)Karte I
career [kə'rɪə] Karriere III 5 (93)
careful ['keəfl]
1. vorsichtig II
2. sorgfältig II
caretaker ['keəteɪkə] Hausmeister/Hausmeisterin II
car park ['kɑː pɑːk] Parkplatz III 2 (38/160)
carrot ['kærət] Möhre, Karotte I
cartoon [kɑː'tuːn] Cartoon (Zeichentrickfilm; Bilderwitz) II
case [keɪs] Fall II
castle ['kɑːsl] Burg, Schloss II
cat [kæt] Katze I
catch [kætʃ], **caught, caught** fangen; erwischen II
cathedral [kə'θiːdrəl] Kathedrale, Dom III 1 (12/153)
°**Catholic** ['kæθlɪk] katholisch; Katholik/in
caught [kɔːt] *siehe* **catch**
CD [ˌsiː'diː] CD I • **CD player** CD-Spieler I
ceilidh ['keɪli] *Musik- und Tanzveranstaltung, vor allem in Schottland und Irland* III 2 (33)
cellphone ['selfəʊn] *(AE)* Handy, Mobiltelefon III 4 (70)
Celsius (C) ['selsiəs] Celsius III 4 (68)
cent (c) [sent] Cent I
centimetre (cm) ['sentɪmiːtə] Zentimeter III 2 (42/160)
central ['sentrəl] Zentral-, Mittel- III 1 (14)
centre ['sentə] Zentrum, Mitte I
century ['sentʃəri] Jahrhundert II
°**chain** [tʃeɪn] Kette
chair [tʃeə] Stuhl I
champion ['tʃæmpiən] Meister/in, Champion I
championship ['tʃæmpiənʃɪp] Meisterschaft III 3 (104)
chance [tʃɑːns] Chance, Möglichkeit, Aussicht II
change [tʃeɪndʒ]
1. Wechselgeld I
°**2.** (Ver-)Änderung
change [tʃeɪndʒ]
1. umsteigen III 1 (14)
°**2.** (ver)ändern
channel ['tʃænl] Kanal, Sender II
charity ['tʃærəti] Wohlfahrtsorganisation II
°**chart** [tʃɑːt] Schaubild, Diagramm, Tabelle • °**charts** *(pl)* Hitliste, Charts
chat (-tt-) [tʃæt] chatten, plaudern II
chat [tʃæt] Chat, Unterhaltung II
chat room ['tʃæt ruːm] Chatroom III 3 (55)
cheap [tʃiːp] billig, preiswert II
check [tʃek] (über)prüfen, kontrollieren I
checkpoint ['tʃekpɔɪnt] Kontrollpunkt *(hier: zur Selbstüberprüfung)* I
cheer [tʃɪə] jubeln, Beifall klatschen II
cheese [tʃiːz] Käse I
chemist ['kemɪst] Drogerie, Apotheke II • **at the chemist's** beim Apotheker III 2 (44/161)
chicken ['tʃɪkɪn] Huhn; (Brat-)Hähnchen I
child [tʃaɪld], *pl* **children** ['tʃɪldrən] Kind I
chips *(pl)* [tʃɪps] Pommes frites I
chocolate ['tʃɒklət] Schokolade I
°**choice** [tʃɔɪs] (Aus-)Wahl, Entscheidung
choir ['kwaɪə] Chor I
choose [tʃuːz], **chose, chosen** (sich) aussuchen, (aus)wählen I
chorus ['kɔːrəs] Refrain III 4 (73)

chose [tʃəʊz] *siehe* **choose**
chosen ['tʃəʊzn] *siehe* **choose**
church [tʃɜːtʃ] Kirche I
cinema ['sɪnəmə] Kino II • **go to the cinema** ins Kino gehen II
°**circle** ['sɜːkl] Kreis
circus ['sɜːkəs]
1. Zirkus III 3 (56)
2. (runder) Platz III 1 (12/153)
city ['sɪti] Stadt, Großstadt I
city centre [ˌsɪti 'sentə] Stadtzentrum, Innenstadt I
°**clan** [klæn] Clan, Sippe
°**clapshot** ['klæpʃɒt] *schottisches Eintopfgericht*
class [klɑːs] (Schul-)Klasse I
class teacher Klassenlehrer/in I
classical ['klæsɪkl] klassisch III Intro (6)
classmate ['klɑːsmeɪt] Klassenkamerad/in, Mitschüler/in I
classroom ['klɑːsruːm] Klassenzimmer I
°**clause** [klɔːz] (Teil-, Glied-)Satz
clean [kliːn] sauber II
clean [kliːn] sauber machen, putzen I • **I clean my teeth.** Ich putze mir die Zähne. I
cleaner ['kliːnə] Putzfrau, -mann II
clear [klɪə] klar, deutlich I
clever ['klevə] klug, schlau I
click on sth. [klɪk] etwas anklicken II
climb [klaɪm] klettern; hinaufklettern (auf) I • **Climb a tree.** Klettere auf einen Baum. I
clinic ['klɪnɪk] Klinik II
clock [klɒk] (Wand-, Stand-, Turm-)Uhr I
clone [kləʊn] Klon III 2 (46)
°**clone** [kləʊn] klonen
close (to) [kləʊs] nahe (bei, an) III 1 (27) • **That was close.** Das war knapp. II
close [kləʊz] schließen, zumachen I
closed [kləʊzd] geschlossen II
°**closing phrase** ['kləʊzɪŋ freɪz] Schlussworte *(am Briefende)*
clothes *(pl)* [kləʊðz, kləʊz] Kleider, Kleidung(sstücke) II
cloud [klaʊd] Wolke II
cloudy ['klaʊdi] bewölkt II
club [klʌb] Klub; Verein I
coach [kəʊtʃ] Trainer/in III 3 (54)
coast [kəʊst] Küste III 2 (38/160)
cola ['kəʊlə] Cola I
cold [kəʊld] kalt I • **be cold** frieren I
cold [kəʊld] Erkältung II • **have a cold** erkältet sein, eine Erkältung haben II

°**collage** ['kɒlɑːʒ] Collage
collect [kə'lekt] sammeln I
collector [kə'lektə] Sammler/in II
°**colony** ['kɒləni] Kolonie
colour ['kʌlə] Farbe I • **What colour is ...?** Welche Farbe hat ...? I
colour ['kʌlə] kolorieren, färben; bunt an-, ausmalen III 4 (69/166)
column ['kɒləm] Säule III 1 (12/153)
°**combine** [kəm'baɪn] kombinieren, verbinden
come [kʌm]**, came, come** kommen I • **come home** nach Hause kommen I • **come in** hereinkommen I • **Come on. 1.** Na los, komm. II; **2.** Ach komm! / Na hör mal! II
comic ['kɒmɪk] Comic-Heft I
Commonwealth ['kɒmənwelθ]**: the Commonwealth** *Gemeinschaft der Länder des ehemaligen Britischen Weltreichs* III 3 (104)
community [kə'mjuːnəti]**: community centre** Gemeinschaftszentrum, Gemeindezentrum III 4 (68)
community hall Gemeinschaftshalle, -saal, Gemeindehalle, -saal III 2 (46)
company ['kʌmpəni] Firma, Gesellschaft III 5 (96)
°**compare** [kəm'peə] vergleichen
comparison [kəm'pærɪsn] Steigerung; Vergleich II • °**make comparisons** Vergleiche anstellen, vergleichen
°**competition** [ˌkɒmpə'tɪʃn] Wettbewerb, Wettkampf
°**complete** [kəm'pliːt] vollständig, komplett
°**complete** [kəm'pliːt] vervollständigen, ergänzen
°**compromise** ['kɒmprəmaɪz] Kompromiss
computer [kəm'pjuːtə] Computer I
concert ['kɒnsət] Konzert III Intro (6)
contact sb. ['kɒntækt] sich mit jm. in Verbindung setzen; mit jm. Kontakt aufnehmen III 5 (88/89)
°**continue** [kən'tɪnjuː] fortsetzen; weitermachen (mit)
°**conversation** [ˌkɒnvə'seɪʃn] Unterhaltung, Gespräch
°**convincing** [kən'vɪnsɪŋ] überzeugend
cook [kʊk] kochen, zubereiten II
cook [kʊk] Koch/Köchin III 4 (69/166)
cooker ['kʊkə] Herd I
cool [kuːl]
1. kühl II
2. cool I
copy ['kɒpi] kopieren II

copy ['kɒpi]
1. Kopie II
2. Exemplar III 5 (96)
corner ['kɔːnə] Ecke I • **on the corner of Sand Street and London Road** Sand Street, Ecke London Road II
cornflakes ['kɔːnfleɪks] Cornflakes I
correct [kə'rekt] berichtigen, korrigieren II
correct [kə'rekt] korrekt, richtig III 2 (35)
°**cost** [kɒst]**, cost, cost** kosten
could [kəd, kʊd]**: he could ...**
1. er konnte ... II
2. er könnte ... III 2 (44)
► S.158 „können" und „dürfen"
count [kaʊnt] zählen II
counter ['kaʊntə] Spielstein II
country ['kʌntri] Land *(auch als Gegensatz zur Stadt)* II • **in the country** auf dem Land II
course [kɔːs] Kurs, Lehrgang III 1 (22)
course: of course [əv 'kɔːs] natürlich, selbstverständlich I
court [kɔːt] Platz, Court *(für Squash, Badminton)* III 3 (60/164)
cousin ['kʌzn] Cousin, Cousine I
cover ['kʌvə]
1. (CD-)Hülle I
°**2. inside cover** Umschlaginnenseite
cow [kaʊ] Kuh II
crazy ['kreɪzi] verrückt III 4 (77)
°**crew** [kruː] Besatzung, (Schiffs-)Mannschaft
°**cricket** ['krɪkɪt] Kricket
crisps *(pl)* [krɪsps] Kartoffelchips I
crocodile ['krɒkədaɪl] Krokodil II
cross [krɒs] überqueren; (sich) kreuzen II
°**crosse** [krɒs] *Sportgerät für Lacrosse*
crush [krʌʃ]**: have a crush on sb.** in jn. verknallt sein III 5 (92)
°**culture** ['kʌltʃə] Kultur
cup [kʌp]
1. Tasse III 2 (44) • **a cup of tea** eine Tasse Tee III 2 (44)
2. Pokal III 3 (57)
cupboard ['kʌbəd] (Küchen-)Schrank I
curtain ['kɜːtn] Vorhang III 3 (53)
customer ['kʌstəmə] Kunde, Kundin II
cut (-tt-) [kʌt]**, cut, cut** schneiden III 2 (45) • **cut sth. off** etwas abschneiden, abtrennen III 3 (66)
cycle ['saɪkl] (mit dem) Rad fahren II • **cycle path** Radweg II

D

dad [dæd] Papa, Vati; Vater I
dance [dɑːns] tanzen I
dance [dɑːns] Tanz I
dancer ['dɑːnsə] Tänzer/in II
dancing ['dɑːnsɪŋ] Tanzen I
dancing lessons Tanzstunden, Tanzunterricht I
danger ['deɪndʒə] Gefahr I
dangerous ['deɪndʒərəs] gefährlich II
dark [dɑːk] dunkel I
date [deɪt]
1. Datum I
2. Date, Verabredung III 4 (69/166)
date sb. [deɪt] mit jm. (aus)gehen; sich (regelmäßig) mit jm. treffen III 4 (68)
daughter ['dɔːtə] Tochter I
day [deɪ] Tag I • **°a day out** ein Tagesausflug • **one day** eines Tages I • **days of the week** Wochentage I • **that day** an jenem Tag III 3 (66)
dead [ded] tot I
deal [diːl]: **It's a deal!** Abgemacht! III 3 (56/163) • **make a deal** ein Abkommen/eine Abmachung treffen III 3 (56)
dear [dɪə] Schatz, Liebling I
Oh dear! Oje! II
dear [dɪə]: **Dear Jay ...** Lieber Jay, ... I
December [dɪ'sembə] Dezember I
decide (on) [dɪ'saɪd] beschließen; sich entscheiden (für) III 5 (91)
deer, *pl* **deer** [dɪə] Reh, Hirsch II
°definition [ˌdefɪ'nɪʃn] Definition
degree [dɪ'griː] Grad II
delicious [dɪ'lɪʃəs] köstlich, lecker II
department store [dɪ'pɑːtmənt stɔː] Kaufhaus II
departure (dep) [dɪ'pɑːtʃə] Abfahrt, Abflug; Abreise III 2 (33)
describe sth. (to sb.) [dɪ'skraɪb] (jm.) etwas beschreiben II
description [dɪ'skrɪpʃn] Beschreibung II
design [dɪ'zaɪn] entwerfen, gestalten II
°designer [dɪ'zaɪnə] Designer/in
desk [desk] Schreibtisch I
detail ['diːteɪl] Detail, Einzelheit III 1 (15)
detective [dɪ'tektɪv] Detektiv/in I
°dialogue ['daɪəlɒg] Dialog
diary ['daɪəri] Tagebuch; Terminkalender I • **°keep a diary** ein Tagebuch führen
dice, *pl* **dice** [daɪs] Würfel II
°dictate [dɪk'teɪt] diktieren
dictionary ['dɪkʃənri] Wörterbuch, *(alphabetisches)* Wörterverzeichnis I
did [dɪd] *siehe* **do** • **Did you know ...?** Wusstest du ...? I • **we didn't go** ['dɪdnt] wir gingen nicht / wir sind nicht gegangen I
die (of) *(-ing form:* **dying**) [daɪ] sterben (an) II
difference ['dɪfrəns] Unterschied III 3 (60)
different (from) ['dɪfrənt] verschieden, unterschiedlich; anders (als) I
difficult ['dɪfɪkəlt] schwierig, schwer I
dining room ['daɪnɪŋ ruːm] Esszimmer I
dinner ['dɪnə] Abendessen, Abendbrot I • **have dinner** Abendbrot essen I
dinosaur ['daɪnəsɔː] Dinosaurier III 1 (13)
direct question [dəˌrekt 'kwestʃən] direkte Frage II
directions *(pl)* [də'rekʃnz] Wegbeschreibung(en) II
°director [də'rektə] Regisseur/in
dirty ['dɜːti] schmutzig II
disabled [dɪs'eɪbld] (körper)behindert III 3 (104)
disagree (with) [ˌdɪsə'griː] nicht übereinstimmen (mit); anderer Meinung sein (als) III 4 (72)
disappear [ˌdɪsə'pɪə] verschwinden II
disc jockey (DJ) ['dɪsk dʒɒki, 'diː dʒeɪ] Diskjockey III Intro (6/151)
disco ['dɪskəʊ] Disko I
discover [dɪ'skʌvə] entdecken; herausfinden II
°discus ['dɪskəs] Diskuswerfen
°discuss [dɪ'skʌs] diskutieren, besprechen
discussion [dɪ'skʌʃn] Diskussion II
dish [dɪʃ] Gericht *(Speise)* III 1 (13)
dishwasher ['dɪʃwɒʃə] Geschirrspülmaschine I
°dive [daɪv]: **take a dive** eintauchen; einen Kopfsprung machen
°divide (into) [dɪ'vaɪd] auf-, einteilen (in)
divorced [dɪ'vɔːst] geschieden I
DJ ['diː dʒeɪ] Diskjockey III Intro (6/151)
DJ ['diː dʒeɪ] (Musik/CDs/Platten) auflegen *(in der Disko)* III Intro (6)
do [duː], **did, done** tun, machen I
Do you like ...? Magst du ...? I
do a gig einen Auftritt haben, ein Konzert geben III Intro (8/151) • **do a good job** gute Arbeit leisten II
do a project ein Projekt machen, durchführen II • **do an exercise** eine Übung machen II • **do sport** Sport treiben I
°dock [dɒk] Hafen; Dock
doctor ['dɒktə] Doktor; Arzt/Ärztin II • **to the doctor's** zum Arzt III 2 (44/161)
°documentary [ˌdɒkju'mentri] Dokumentarfilm, -beitrag
dog [dɒg] Hund I
°dollar ['dɒlə] Dollar
done [dʌn] *siehe* **do**
don't [dəʊnt]: **Don't listen to Dan.** Hör/Hört nicht auf Dan. I • **I don't like ...** Ich mag ... nicht. / Ich mag kein(e) ... I
door [dɔː] Tür I
doorbell ['dɔːbel] Türklingel I
dossier ['dɒsieɪ] Mappe, Dossier *(des Sprachenportfolios)* I
double ['dʌbl] zweimal, doppelt, Doppel- I
double-click ['dʌblklɪk] doppelklicken II
down [daʊn] hinunter, herunter, nach unten I • **down there** dort unten II • **fall down** hinfallen II
download [ˌdaʊn'ləʊd] runterladen, downloaden II
downstairs [ˌdaʊn'steəz] unten; nach unten I
°dragon ['drægən] Drache
drama ['drɑːmə] Schauspiel, darstellende Kunst I
drank [dræŋk] *siehe* **drink**
draw [drɔː] Unentschieden III 3 (54)
▶ S.162 A football match
draw [drɔː], **drew, drawn** zeichnen III 3 (66)
drawing ['drɔːɪŋ] Zeichnung III 5 (88/89)
drawn [drɔːn] *siehe* **draw**
dream [driːm] Traum I • **dream house** Traumhaus I
dream (of, about) [driːm] träumen (von) III 1 (12) • **dream on** weiterträumen III 1 (13/152)
dress [dres] Kleid I
dressed [drest]: **get dressed** sich anziehen I
drew [druː] *siehe* **draw**
drink [drɪŋk] Getränk I
drink [drɪŋk], **drank, drunk** trinken I
drive [draɪv], **drove, driven** *(ein Auto/mit dem Auto)* fahren II
drive [draɪv] (Auto-)Fahrt III 4 (69/166)
driven ['drɪvn] *siehe* **drive**
driver ['draɪvə] Fahrer/in II
drop (-pp-) [drɒp]
1. fallen lassen I
2. fallen I

drove [drəʊv] *siehe* **drive**
drum [drʌm] Trommel III Intro (6)
play the drums Schlagzeug spielen III Intro (6/151)
drunk [drʌŋk] *siehe* **drink**
°**dump** [dʌmp] Müllabladeplatz, Deponie
°**during** *(prep)* ['djʊərɪŋ] während
dustbin ['dʌstbɪn] Mülltonne II
DVD [ˌdiː viː' diː] DVD I

E

each [iːtʃ] jeder, jede, jedes (einzelne) I • **each other** einander, sich (gegenseitig) III 4 (73)
ear [ɪə] Ohr I
earache ['ɪəreɪk] Ohrenschmerzen II
early ['ɜːli] früh I
earring ['ɪərɪŋ] Ohrring I
earth [ɜːθ] Erde III 1 (13/153) • **on earth** auf der Erde III 1 (13/153)
earthquake ['ɜːθkweɪk] Erdbeben III 1 (13)
east [iːst] Osten; nach Osten; östlich III Intro (7/151)
eastbound ['iːstbaʊnd] Richtung Osten III 1 (14)
easy ['iːzi] leicht, einfach I
easy-going [ˌiːzi'gəʊɪŋ] gelassen, locker III 4 (70)
eat [iːt], **ate, eaten** essen I
eaten ['iːtn] *siehe* **eat**
editor ['edɪtə] Redakteur/in III 5 (88/89)
e-friend ['iːfrend] Brieffreund/in *(im Internet)* I
°**e.g.** [ˌiː 'dʒiː] *(from Latin: exempli gratia)* z.B.
egg [eg] Ei III 1 (24/155)
°**either ... or ...** ['aɪðə ... ɔː, 'iːðə ... ɔː] entweder ... oder
electric [ɪ'lektrɪk] elektrisch, Elektro- III Intro (11)
°**electrician** [ɪˌlek'trɪʃn] Elektriker/in
electricity [ɪˌlek'trɪsəti] Strom, Elektrizität III 1 (27)
electronic [ɪˌlek'trɒnɪk] elektronisch III 2 (32)
elephant ['elɪfənt] Elefant I
elevator ['elɪveɪtə] *(AE)* Fahrstuhl, Aufzug II
else [els]: **What else do you know ...?** Was weißt du sonst noch ...? II
e-mail ['iːmeɪl] E-Mail I
empty ['empti] leer I
°**encyclopedia** [ɪnˌsaɪklə'piːdiə] Enzyklopädie, Lexikon
end [end] Ende, Schluss I • **at the end (of)** am Ende (von) I • **in the end** schließlich, zum Schluss III 3 (57)
end [end] enden; beenden III 3 (64)
ending ['endɪŋ] Ende, (Ab-)Schluss *(einer Geschichte, eines Films usw.)* III 1 (28)
enemy ['enəmi] Feind/in II
energy ['enədʒi] Energie; Kraft II
engineer [ˌendʒɪ'nɪə] Ingenieur/in II
English ['ɪŋglɪʃ] Englisch; englisch I
enjoy [ɪn'dʒɔɪ] genießen II
enough [ɪ'nʌf] genug I
enter ['entə]
1. betreten; eintreten (in) III 3 (55)
2. enter sth. etwas eingeben, eintragen II
°**entertainment** [ˌentə'teɪnmənt] Unterhaltung, Entertainment
entry ['entri] Eintrag, Eintragung *(in Wörterbuch/Tagebuch)* III 2 (35)
equipment [ɪ'kwɪpmənt] Ausrüstung III 3 (60/164)
escape (from sb./sth.) [ɪ'skeɪp] fliehen (vor jm./aus etwas); entkommen III 4 (81)
essay (about, on) ['eseɪ] Aufsatz (über) I
°**etc. (et cetera)** [ˌet 'setərə] usw.
euro (€) ['jʊərəʊ] Euro I
even ['iːvn] sogar II • **not even** (noch) nicht einmal III 2 (34)
evening ['iːvnɪŋ] Abend I • **in the evening** abends, am Abend I
on Friday evening freitagabends, am Freitagabend I
°**event** [ɪ'vent] Ereignis; Veranstaltung
ever? ['evə] je? / jemals? / schon mal? II
every ['evri] jeder, jede, jedes I
everybody ['evribɒdi] jeder, alle II
everyday *(adj)* ['evrideɪ] Alltags-; alltägliche(r, s) III 1 (25)
°**everyone** ['evriwʌn] jeder, alle
everything ['evriθɪŋ] alles I
everywhere ['evriweə] überall I
exactly [ɪg'zæktli] genau III 4 (72)
example [ɪg'zɑːmpl] Beispiel I
for example zum Beispiel I
°**except** [ɪk'sept] außer, bis auf
exchange [ɪks'tʃeɪndʒ] (Schüler-)Austausch III 3 (55/163) • **exchange student** Austauschschüler/in III 3 (55)
excited [ɪk'saɪtɪd] aufgeregt, begeistert III 1 (26)
exciting [ɪk'saɪtɪŋ] aufregend, spannend II
Excuse me, ... [ɪk'skjuːz miː] Entschuldigung, ... / Entschuldigen Sie, ... I
exercise ['eksəsaɪz] Übung, Aufgabe I • **exercise book** ['eksəsaɪz bʊk] Schulheft, Übungsheft I
expect [ɪk'spekt] erwarten III 2 (34)
expensive [ɪk'spensɪv] teuer I
explain sth. to sb. [ɪk'spleɪn] jm. etwas erklären, erläutern II
explanation [ˌeksplə'neɪʃn] Erklärung II
explore [ɪk'splɔː] erkunden, erforschen I
explorer [ɪk'splɔːrə] Entdecker/in, Forscher/in II
extra ['ekstrə] zusätzlich I
eye [aɪ] Auge I
°**e-zine** ['iːziːn] elektronisches Magazin, elektronische Zeitschrift

F

face [feɪs] Gesicht I
fact [fækt] Tatsache, Fakt III 1 (29)
factory ['fæktri] Fabrik II
fair [feə] fair, gerecht II
fall [fɔːl], **fell, fallen** fallen, stürzen; hinfallen II • **fall down** hinfallen II • **fall off** herunterfallen (von) II
fallen ['fɔːlən] *siehe* **fall**
family ['fæməli] Familie I
family tree (Familien-)Stammbaum I
famous (for) ['feɪməs] berühmt (für, wegen) II
fan [fæn] Fan I
fantastic [fæn'tæstɪk] fantastisch, toll I
far [fɑː] weit (entfernt) I • **so far** bis jetzt, bis hierher I
farm [fɑːm] Bauernhof, Farm II
farmer ['fɑːmə] Bauer/Bäuerin, Landwirt/in; (Fisch-)Züchter/in III 2 (30)
fashion ['fæʃn] Mode II
fast [fɑːst] schnell II • **fast food** Fastfood III 2 (40)
father ['fɑːðə] Vater I
favourite ['feɪvərɪt] Favorit/in; Liebling III 2 (40); Lieblings- I
February ['februəri] Februar I
fed [fed] *siehe* **feed** • **be fed up (with sth.)** [ˌfed‿'ʌp] die Nase voll haben (von etwas) II
feed [fiːd], **fed, fed** füttern I
feel [fiːl], **felt, felt** fühlen; sich fühlen; sich anfühlen II • **How do they feel about ...?** Was halten sie von ...? III 5 (88/89)
feeling ['fiːlɪŋ] Gefühl III 2 (35)
feet [fiːt] *Plural von „foot“*
fell [fel] *siehe* **fall**
felt [felt] *siehe* **feel**

felt tip ['felt tɪp] Filzstift I
°**female** ['fi:meɪl] weiblich
ferry ['feri] Fähre III 1 (20/154)
festival ['festɪvl] Fest, Festival III Intro (6)
few: a few [ə 'fju:] ein paar, einige II
°**fewer** ['fju:ə] weniger
fiddle ['fɪdl] *(infml)* Fiedel, Geige III Intro (7) • **play the fiddle** Geige spielen III Intro (7/151)
field [fi:ld] Feld, Acker, Weide II; Sportplatz, Spielfeld III 3 (60/164)
in the field auf dem Feld II
fight (for) [faɪt], **fought, fought** kämpfen (für, um) III 3 (104) • **fight sth.** etwas bekämpfen III 4 (81)
°**file** [faɪl] (Akten-)Ordner, Hefter
file [faɪl]: **background file** *etwa:* Hintergrundinformation(en) II
grammar file *Grammatikanhang* I
skills file *Anhang mit Lern- und Arbeitstechniken* I • **sound file** Tondatei, Soundfile III 1 (12)
°**fill in** [ˌfɪl_'ɪn]
1. einsetzen
2. ausfüllen
film [fɪlm] filmen III 2 (44)
film [fɪlm] Film I
°**film crew** ['fɪlm kru:] Filmcrew, Filmteam
°**film researcher** [rɪ'sɜ:tʃə] Filmrechercheur/in
film star ['fɪlm stɑ:] Filmstar I
final ['faɪnl] letzte(r, s); End- III 3 (52/162) • **final score** Endstand *(beim Sport)* III 3 (54/162)
► S.162 A football match
final ['faɪnl] Finale, Endspiel III 3 (52)
°**finally** ['faɪnəli] schließlich, endlich
find [faɪnd], **found, found** finden I
find out (about) herausfinden (über) I
finder ['faɪndə] Finder I
fine [faɪn]
1. gut, schön; in Ordnung II
2. *(gesundheitlich)* gut II
I'm/He's fine. Es geht mir/ihm gut. II
finger ['fɪŋgə] Finger I
finish ['fɪnɪʃ] beenden, zu Ende machen; enden I
fire ['faɪə] Feuer, Brand II
fireman ['faɪəmən] Feuerwehrmann II
firewoman ['faɪəˌwʊmən] Feuerwehrfrau II
fireworks *(pl)* ['faɪəwɜ:ks] Feuerwerk(skörper) II
first [fɜ:st]
1. erste(r, s) I
2. zuerst, als Erstes I
be first der/die Erste sein I
°**First Nations** [ˌfɜ:st 'neɪʃnz] *indianische Ureinwohner/innen Kanadas*
fish, *pl* **fish** [fɪʃ] Fisch I
fish [fɪʃ] fischen, angeln III 4 (69/166)
fit (-tt-) [fɪt] passen I
fit [fɪt] fit III 2 (41)
flash [flæʃ] Lichtblitz III 1 (27)
flat [flæt] Wohnung I
flavour ['fleɪvə] Geschmack, Geschmacksrichtung II
flew [flu:] *siehe* **fly**
flight [flaɪt] Flug II
floor [flɔ:] Fußboden I
flow chart ['fləʊ tʃɑ:t] Flussdiagramm I
flower ['flaʊə] Blume; Blüte III 1 (27)
flown [fləʊn] *siehe* **fly**
flute [flu:t] Querflöte III Intro (11)
fly [flaɪ], **flew, flown** fliegen II
fog [fɒg] Nebel II
foggy ['fɒgi] neblig II
folk (music) [fəʊk] Folk *(englische, schottische, irische oder nordamerikanische Volksmusik des 20. Jahrhunderts)* III Intro (6)
follow ['fɒləʊ] folgen; verfolgen I
the following ... die folgenden ... II
food [fu:d]
1. Essen; Lebensmittel I
2. Futter I
foot [fʊt], *pl* **feet** [fi:t] Fuß I • **on foot** zu Fuß III 1 (20)
football ['fʊtbɔ:l] Fußball I
football boots ['fʊtbɔ:l bu:ts] Fußballschuhe, -stiefel I
football pitch ['fʊtbɔ:l pɪtʃ] Fußballplatz, -feld II
football shirt ['fʊtbɔ:l ʃɜ:t] (Fußball-)Trikot III 3 (54)
for [fə, fɔ:] für I • **for breakfast/ lunch/dinner** zum Frühstück/ Mittagessen/Abendbrot I • **for example** zum Beispiel I • **for his birthday** zu seinem Geburtstag III 3 (66) • **for lots of reasons** aus vielen Gründen I • **for miles** meilenweit II • **for three days** drei Tage (lang) I • **just for fun** nur zum Spaß I • **What for?** Wofür? II • **What's for homework?** Was haben wir als Hausaufgabe auf? I
foreground ['fɔ:graʊnd] Vordergrund II
°**foreign** ['fɒrən] fremd, ausländisch
forest ['fɒrɪst] Wald II
forget (-tt-) [fə'get], **forgot, forgotten** vergessen III 2 (35)
forgot [fə'gɒt] *siehe* **forget**
forgotten [fə'gɒtn] *siehe* **forget**
fork [fɔ:k] Gabel III 1 (27/156)
form [fɔ:m]
1. (Schul-)Klasse I • **form teacher** Klassenlehrer/in I
°2. Form
°**form** [fɔ:m] bilden
fought [fɔ:t] *siehe* **fight**
found [faʊnd] *siehe* **find**
fox [fɒks] Fuchs II
free [fri:]
1. frei I • **free time** Freizeit, freie Zeit I
2. kostenlos I
°**freight train** ['freɪt treɪn] Güterzug
French [frentʃ] Französisch I
°**French Canadians** [ˌfrentʃ kə'neɪdiənz] Franko-Kanadier/innen
Friday ['fraɪdeɪ, 'fraɪdi] Freitag I
fridge [frɪdʒ] Kühlschrank I
friend [frend] Freund/in I
friendly ['frendli] freundlich II
frog [frɒg] Frosch II
from [frəm, frɒm]
1. aus I
2. von I
from all around Wales aus ganz Wales II • **from all over England/ the UK** aus ganz England/aus dem gesamten Vereinigten Königreich III Intro (6) • **from Monday to Friday** von Montag bis Freitag III 2 (33)
from my point of view aus meiner Sicht; von meinem Standpunkt aus gesehen II • **I'm from ...** Ich komme aus ... / Ich bin aus ... I
Where are you from? Wo kommst du her? I
► S.167 German „bis"
front [frʌnt]: **in front of** vor *(räumlich)* I • **to the front** nach vorn I
front door [ˌfrʌnt 'dɔ:] Wohnungstür, Haustür I
°**front page** [ˌfrʌnt 'peɪdʒ] Titelseite
fruit [fru:t] Obst, Früchte; Frucht I
fruit salad ['fru:t ˌsæləd] Obstsalat I
full [fʊl] voll I
fun [fʌn] Spaß I • **have fun** Spaß haben, sich amüsieren I • **Have fun!** Viel Spaß! I • **just for fun** nur zum Spaß I • **Riding is fun.** Reiten macht Spaß. I
funny ['fʌni] witzig, komisch I
furniture *(no pl)* ['fɜ:nɪtʃə] Möbel III 3 (53) • **a piece of furniture** ein Möbelstück III 3 (53/162)
► S.162 Words without a plural
°**fusion** ['fju:ʒn] *aus der Verschmelzung verschiedener Musikrichtungen entstandener Musikstil*
future ['fju:tʃə] Zukunft I

G

°Gaelic ['gælɪk, 'geɪlɪk] Gälisch, gälisch
game [geɪm] Spiel I • **a game of football** ein Fußballspiel II
°gap [gæp] Lücke
garage ['gærɑːʒ] Garage II
garden ['gɑːdn] Garten I
gate [geɪt] Flugsteig III 1 (20/154)
gave [geɪv] *siehe* **give**
gear: sports gear *(no pl)* ['spɔːts gɪə] Sportausrüstung, Sportsachen II
general ['dʒenrəl] allgemeine(r, s) III 3 (56)
geography [dʒi'ɒgrəfi] Geografie, Erdkunde I
German ['dʒɜːmən] Deutsch; deutsch; Deutsche(r) I
Germany ['dʒɜːməni] Deutschland I
get (-tt-) [get], **got, got**
1. bekommen, kriegen II
2. holen, besorgen II
3. gelangen, (hin)kommen I
4. get angry/hot/... wütend/heiß/... werden II
5. get off (the train/bus) (aus dem Zug/Bus) aussteigen I • **get on (the train/bus)** (in den Zug/Bus) einsteigen I
6. get up aufstehen I
get dressed sich anziehen I
get ready (for) sich fertig machen (für), sich vorbereiten (auf) I • **get sth. off the ground** etwas auf den Weg bringen; etwas auf die Beine stellen III 5 (92) • **get things ready** Dinge fertig machen, vorbereiten I
getting by in English [,getɪŋ 'baɪ] *etwa:* auf Englisch zurechtkommen I
°gherkin ['gɜːkɪn] (Essig-)Gurke
gig [gɪg] *(infml)* Gig, Auftritt III Intro (8) • **do a gig** einen Auftritt haben, ein Konzert geben III Intro (8/151)
giraffe [dʒə'rɑːf] Giraffe II
girl [gɜːl] Mädchen I
°girlfriend ['gɜːlfrend] Freundin
give [gɪv], **gave, given** geben I
given ['gɪvn] *siehe* **give**
°glad [glæd] froh
glass [glɑːs] Glas I • **a glass of water** ein Glas Wasser I
glasses *(pl)* ['glɑːsɪz] (eine) Brille I
glue [gluː] (auf-, ein)kleben II
glue [gluː] Klebstoff I
glue stick ['gluː stɪk] Klebestift I
go [gəʊ], **went, gone** gehen I; fahren II • **go abroad** ins Ausland gehen/fahren II • **go by car/train/bike/...** mit dem Auto/Zug/Rad/... fahren II • **°go crazy** durchdrehen, verrückt werden • **go for a walk** spazieren gehen, einen Spaziergang machen II • **go home** nach Hause gehen I • **go on 1.** weitermachen I; weiterreden III 1 (13/152); **2.** angehen *(Licht)* III 1 (27) • **go on a trip** einen Ausflug machen II • **go on holiday** in Urlaub fahren II • **go out** weg-, raus-, ausgehen I • **go riding** reiten gehen I • **go shopping** einkaufen gehen I • **go surfing** wellenreiten gehen, surfen gehen II **go swimming** schwimmen gehen I • **go to bed** ins Bett gehen I **go to the cinema** ins Kino gehen II • **go well** gut (ver)laufen, gutgehen III 2 (34) • **go with** gehören zu, passen zu III Intro (11) • **go wrong** schiefgehen III 5 (95) • **Let's go.** Auf geht's! I
goal [gəʊl] Tor *(im Sport)* III 3 (54)
goalkeeper ['gəʊlkiːpə] Torwart, Torfrau III 3 (57)
gold [gəʊld] Gold III 3 (104)
golf [gɒlf] Golf III 3 (57)
gone [gɒn] *siehe* **go**
good [gʊd]
1. gut I • **be good at sth.** gut in etwas sein; etwas gut können III 5 (91) • **Good afternoon.** Guten Tag. *(nachmittags)* I • **Good luck (with ...)!** Viel Glück (bei/mit ...)! I **Good morning.** Guten Morgen. I
2. brav II
Goodbye. [,gʊd'baɪ] Auf Wiedersehen. I • **say goodbye** sich verabschieden I
got [gɒt] *siehe* **get**
got [gɒt]: **I've got ...** Ich habe ... I **I haven't got a chair.** Ich habe keinen Stuhl. I
grab (-bb-) [græb] schnappen, packen III 2 (46)
grammar ['græmə] Grammatik I
grammar file *Grammatikanhang* I
grandchild ['græntʃaɪld], *pl* **grandchildren** ['-tʃɪldrən] Enkel/in I
granddaughter ['grændɔːtə] Enkelin II
grandfather ['grænfɑːðə] Großvater I
grandma ['grænmɑː] Oma I
grandmother ['grænmʌðə] Großmutter I
grandpa ['grænpɑː] Opa I
grandparents ['grænpeərənts] Großeltern I
grandson ['grænsʌn] Enkel II
granny ['græni] Oma II
great [greɪt] großartig, toll I
great-grandfather [,greɪt 'grænfɑːðə] Urgroßvater III 2 (32)
great-grandmother [,greɪt 'grænmʌðə] Urgroßmutter III 2 (32)
green [griːn] grün I
°greeting ['griːtɪŋ] Gruß, Begrüßung
grew [gruː] *siehe* **grow**
grey [greɪ] grau II
ground [graʊnd]
1. (Erd-)Boden III 1 (20)
°2. (Sport-)Platz
get sth. off the ground etwas auf den Weg bringen; etwas auf die Beine stellen III 5 (92)
group [gruːp] Gruppe I • **group word** Oberbegriff II
grow [grəʊ], **grew, grown**
1. wachsen II
2. *(Getreide usw.)* anbauen, anpflanzen II
grow up erwachsen werden; aufwachsen III 3 (66)
grown [grəʊn] *siehe* **grow**
grumble ['grʌmbl] murren, nörgeln I
guess [ges] raten, erraten, schätzen II • **Guess what!** Stell dir vor! / Stellt euch vor! II
°guess [ges] Vermutung, Schätzung
guest [gest] Gast I
°guide book ['gaɪd bʊk] Reiseführer
guinea pig ['gɪni pɪg] Meerschweinchen I
guitar [gɪ'tɑː] Gitarre I • **play the guitar** Gitarre spielen I
gun [gʌn] (Schuss-)Waffe II
guys *(pl)* [gaɪz] *(AE, infml)* Leute III 4 (71)

H

had [hæd] *siehe* **have**
°haggis ['hægɪs] *gefüllter Schafsmagen*
hair *(no pl)* [heə] Haar, Haare I
► S.162 Words without a plural
hairdresser ['heədresə] Friseur/in III 2 (44) • **at the hairdresser's** beim Friseur III 2 (44/161)
half [hɑːf], *pl* **halves** [hɑːvz]
1. Hälfte III Intro (11/151)
2. Halbzeit III 3 (57/163)
the first half die erste Halbzeit III 3 (57/163)
half [hɑːf]: **half an hour** eine halbe Stunde III Intro (11) • **half past 11** halb zwölf (11.30 / 23.30) I
half-pipe ['hɑːfpaɪp] Halfpipe *(halbierte Röhre für Inlineskater)* III 3 (60/164)

half-time [ˌhɑːf ˈtaɪm] Halbzeit(pause) III 3 (57)
hall [hɔːl]
1. Flur, Diele I
2. Halle, Saal III 2 (46/161)
halves [hɑːvz] *Plural von „half"*
hamburger [ˈhæmbɜːgə] Hamburger I
hamster [ˈhæmstə] Hamster I
hand [hænd] Hand I
hang [hæŋ], **hung, hung:**
°hang down herunterhängen
hang out *(infml)* rumhängen, abhängen III 4 (70) • **°hang sth. up** etwas aufhängen
happen (to) [ˈhæpən] geschehen, passieren (mit) I
happy [ˈhæpi] glücklich, froh I
Happy birthday. Herzlichen Glückwunsch zum Geburtstag. I
happy ending Happyend II
harbour [ˈhɑːbə] Hafen II
hard [hɑːd] hart; schwer, schwierig II • **work hard** hart arbeiten II
hat [hæt] Hut II
hate [heɪt] hassen, gar nicht mögen I
have [həv, hæv], **had, had** haben, besitzen II • **have a baby** ein Baby/Kind bekommen II • **have a bath** baden, ein Bad nehmen II
have a cold erkältet sein, eine Erkältung haben II • **have a crush on sb.** in jn. verknallt sein III 5 (92) • **Have a good time!** Viel Spaß! / Viel Vergnügen! III 1 (21)
have a party eine Party feiern/veranstalten II • **have a sauna** in die Sauna gehen II • **have a shower** (sich) duschen I • **have a sore throat** Halsschmerzen haben II
have a temperature Fieber haben II • **have breakfast** frühstücken I
have dinner Abendbrot essen I
have ... for breakfast ... zum Frühstück essen/trinken I • **have fun** Spaß haben, sich amüsieren I
Have fun! Viel Spaß! I • **have to do** tun müssen I
have got: I've got ... [aɪv ˈgɒt] Ich habe ... I • **I haven't got a chair.** [ˈhævnt gɒt] Ich habe keinen Stuhl. I
he [hiː] er I
head [hed] Kopf I • **°head of state** Staatsoberhaupt • **°running head** Leitwort *(am Kopf einer Wörterbuchseite)*
headache [ˈhedeɪk] Kopfschmerzen II
°heading [ˈhedɪŋ] Überschrift
headphones *(pl)* [ˈhedfəʊnz] Kopfhörer III 5 (88/89)
head teacher [ˌhed ˈtiːtʃə] Schulleiter/in III 2 (44)
healthy [ˈhelθi] gesund II
hear [hɪə], **heard, heard** hören I
heard [hɜːd] *siehe* **hear**
heart [hɑːt] Herz II
hedgehog [ˈhedʒhɒg] Igel II
held [held] *siehe* **hold**
helicopter [ˈhelɪkɒptə] Hubschrauber, Helikopter II
Hello. [həˈləʊ] Hallo. / Guten Tag. I
helmet [ˈhelmɪt] Helm III 1 (26)
help [help] helfen I • **Can I help you?** Kann ich Ihnen helfen? / Was kann ich für Sie tun? *(im Geschäft)* I
help [help] Hilfe I
her [hə, hɜː]
1. ihr, ihre I
2. sie; ihr I
here [hɪə]
1. hier I
2. hierher I
Here you are. Bitte sehr. / Hier bitte. I
hero [ˈhɪərəʊ], *pl* **heroes** [ˈhɪərəʊz] Held, Heldin II
hers [hɜːz] ihrer, ihre, ihrs II
herself [həˈself, hɜːˈself] sich (selbst) III 4 (72/167)
Hi! [haɪ] Hallo! I • **Say hi to Dilip for me.** Grüß Dilip von mir. I
hid [hɪd] *siehe* **hide**
hidden [ˈhɪdn] *siehe* **hide**
hide [haɪd], **hid, hidden** sich verstecken; *(etwas)* verstecken I
high [haɪ] hoch III 1 (12)
°high-tech companies [ˌhaɪtek ˈkʌmpəniz] Hightech-Firmen
hill [hɪl] Hügel II
hilly [ˈhɪli] hügelig III 2 (38/160)
him [hɪm] ihn; ihm I
himself [hɪmˈself] sich (selbst) III 4 (72/167)
hip hop [ˈhɪp hɒp] Hiphop III Intro (6)
hippo [ˈhɪpəʊ] Flusspferd II
his [hɪz]
1. sein, seine I
2. seiner, seine, seins II
history [ˈhɪstri] Geschichte I
hit (-tt-) [hɪt], **hit, hit** schlagen I
hit the windscreen gegen/auf die Windschutzscheibe schlagen/prallen III 2 (44)
hit [hɪt] Hit III 4 (73)
hobby [ˈhɒbi] Hobby I
hockey [ˈhɒki] Hockey I
hockey pitch [ˈhɒki pɪtʃ] Hockeyplatz, -feld II
hockey shoes [ˈhɒki ʃuːz] Hockeyschuhe I
hold [həʊld], **held, held** halten II
°hold up hochhalten
hole [həʊl] Loch I
holiday(s) [ˈhɒlədeɪ(z)] Ferien I
be on holiday in Urlaub sein; Ferien haben/machen II • **go on holiday** in Urlaub fahren II
home [həʊm] Heim, Zuhause I
at home daheim, zu Hause I
come home nach Hause kommen I • **get home** nach Hause kommen I • **go home** nach Hause gehen I
°homeless [ˈhəʊmləs] obdachlos
homework *(no pl)* [ˈhəʊmwɜːk] Hausaufgabe(n) I • **do homework** die Hausaufgabe(n) machen I
What's for homework? Was haben wir als Hausaufgabe auf? I
► S.162 Words without a plural
Hooray! [huˈreɪ] Hurra! II
hope [həʊp] hoffen II
hope [həʊp] Hoffnung III 3 (66)
horrible [ˈhɒrəbl] scheußlich, grauenhaft II
horse [hɔːs] Pferd I
hospital [ˈhɒspɪtl] Krankenhaus II
hostel [ˈhɒstl] Herberge, Wohnheim III Intro (8)
hot [hɒt] heiß I • **hot chocolate** heiße Schokolade I • **hot-water bottle** Wärmflasche II
hotel [həʊˈtel] Hotel II
hotline [ˈhɒtlaɪn] Hotline II
hour [ˈaʊə] Stunde II • **a 14-hour flight** ein 14-stündiger Flug, ein 14-Stunden-Flug III 4 (76/168) • **a 24-hour supermarket** ein Supermarkt, der 24 Stunden geöffnet ist III 4 (76/168) • **half an hour** eine halbe Stunde III Intro (11)
house [haʊs] Haus I • **at the Shaws' house** im Haus der Shaws/bei den Shaws zu Hause I
how [haʊ] wie I • **How about ...?** Wie wär's mit ...? III Intro (10)
How am I doing? Wie komme ich voran? *(Wie sind meine Fortschritte?)* III 1 (29) • **How are you?** Wie geht es dir/Ihnen/euch? II
How do they feel about ...? Was halten sie von ...? III 5 (88/89) • **How do you know ...?** Woher weißt/kennst du ...? I • **how many?** wie viele? I • **how much?** wie viel? I
How much is/are ...? Was kostet/kosten ...? / Wie viel kostet/kosten ...? I

huge [hjuːdʒ] riesig, sehr groß III 2 (30)
► S.157 big – large – huge

hundred ['hʌndrəd] hundert I

hung [hʌŋ] *siehe* **hang**

hungry ['hʌŋgri] hungrig I • **be hungry** Hunger haben, hungrig sein I

hunt [hʌnt] jagen III 4 (69)

hunt [hʌnt] Jagd III 4 (69/166)

hunter ['hʌntə] Jäger/in III 4 (72)

hurry ['hʌri] eilen; sich beeilen II **hurry up** sich beeilen I

hurry ['hʌri]: **be in a hurry** in Eile sein, es eilig haben I

hurt [hɜːt], **hurt, hurt** wehtun; verletzen I

hurt [hɜːt] verletzt II

husband ['hʌzbənd] Ehemann II

hutch [hʌtʃ] (Kaninchen-)Stall I

I

I [aɪ] ich I • **I'm** [aɪm] ich bin I **I'm from ...** Ich komme aus ... / Ich bin aus ... I • **I'm ... years old.** Ich bin ... Jahre alt. I • **I'm sorry.** Entschuldigung. / Tut mir leid. I

ice [aɪs] Eis II

ice cream [ˌaɪs 'kriːm] (Speise-)Eis I

ice hockey ['aɪs hɒki] Eishockey III Intro (11)

ice rink ['aɪs rɪŋk] Schlittschuhbahn II

idea [aɪ'dɪə] Idee, Einfall I

if [ɪf]
1. falls, wenn II
2. ob II

ill [ɪl] krank II

°**imaginary** [ɪ'mædʒɪnəri] imaginär *(nur in der Vorstellung vorhanden, nicht wirklich)*

imagine sth. [ɪ'mædʒɪn] sich etwas vorstellen III 2 (32)

°**immigration** [ˌɪmɪ'greɪʃn] Immigration, Einwanderung

important [ɪm'pɔːtnt] wichtig II **important to sb.** wichtig für jn. III 4 (70)

impossible [ɪm'pɒsəbl] unmöglich II

°**improve** [ɪm'pruːv] verbessern

in [ɪn] in I • **in 1948** im Jahr 1948 II • **in ... Street** in der ...straße I **in English** auf Englisch I • **in front of** vor *(räumlich)* I • **in here** hier drinnen I • **in my/your view** meiner/deiner Ansicht nach III 1 (28) • **in other places** an anderen Orten, anderswo III 1 (13) • °**in the 1970s** in den 70er-Jahren *(des 20. Jahrhunderts)* • **in the afternoon** nachmittags, am Nachmittag I • **in the country** auf dem Land II • **in the end** schließlich, zum Schluss III 3 (57) • **in the evening** abends, am Abend I • **in the field** auf dem Feld II • **in the morning** am Morgen, morgens I **in the photo** auf dem Foto I • **in the picture** auf dem Bild I • **in the sky** am Himmel II • **in there** dort drinnen I • °**in the world** auf der Welt • **in time** rechtzeitig II

°**incorrect** [ˌɪnkə'rekt] falsch

°**independent** [ˌɪndɪ'pendənt] unabhängig

°**Indians** *(pl)* ['ɪndiənz] Indianer/innen

indirect question [ˌɪndərekt 'kwestʃən] indirekte Frage II

infinitive [ɪn'fɪnətɪv] Infinitiv *(Grundform des Verbs)* I

information (about/on) *(no pl)* [ˌɪnfə'meɪʃn] Information(en) (über) I
► S.162 Words without a plural

inside [ˌɪn'saɪd]
1. innen (drin), drinnen I
2. nach drinnen II
3. **inside the car** ins Auto (hinein), ins Innere des Autos II

°**inside cover** [ˌɪnsaɪd 'kʌvə] Umschlaginnenseite

install [ɪn'stɔːl] installieren, einrichten II

installation [ˌɪnstə'leɪʃn] Installation, Einrichtung II

instant messages *(pl)* [ˌɪnstənt 'mesɪdʒɪz] *Nachrichten, die man im Internet austauscht (in Echtzeit)* III 2 (32)

instructions *(pl)* [ɪn'strʌkʃnz] (Gebrauchs-)Anweisung(en), Anleitung(en) II

instrument ['ɪnstrəmənt] Instrument II

°**interest sb.** ['ɪntrəst] jn. interessieren

interested: be interested (in) ['ɪntrəstɪd] interessiert sein (an), sich interessieren (für) III 3 (53)

interesting ['ɪntrəstɪŋ] interessant I

international [ˌɪntə'næʃnəl] international III Intro (6/151)

internet ['ɪntənet] Internet I

interview ['ɪntəvjuː] interviewen, befragen II

interview ['ɪntəvjuː] Interview II

into ['ɪntə, 'ɪntʊ] in ... (hinein) I

intolerant [ɪn'tɒlərənt] intolerant III 4 (76)

°**introduce** [ˌɪntrə'djuːs] vorstellen

introduction [ˌɪntrə'dʌkʃn] Einführung, Einleitung III (3)

°**Inuit** ['ɪnuɪt, 'ɪnjuɪt] Inuit

invitation (to) [ˌɪnvɪ'teɪʃn] Einladung (zu) I

invite (to) [ɪn'vaɪt] einladen (zu) I

irregular [ɪ'regjələ] unregelmäßig I

is [ɪz] ist I

island ['aɪlənd] Insel II

°**issue** ['ɪʃuː] Thema, (Streit-)Frage

it [ɪt] er/sie/es I • **It's £1.** Er/Sie/Es kostet 1 Pfund. I • **It says here: ...** Hier steht: ... / Es heißt hier: ... II

IT [ˌaɪ 'tiː], **information technology** [tek'nɒlədʒi] IT, Informationstechnologie II

°**italics** [ɪ'tælɪks]: **in italics** kursiv; in Kursivschrift

its [ɪts] sein/seine; ihr/ihre I

itself [ɪt'self] sich (selbst) III 4 (72/167)

J

jacket ['dʒækɪt] Jacke, Jackett II

January ['dʒænjuəri] Januar I

°**javelin** ['dʒævlɪn] Speerwerfen

jazz [dʒæz] Jazz I

jealous (of) ['dʒeləs] neidisch (auf); eifersüchtig (auf) III 2 (46)

jeans *(pl)* [dʒiːnz] Jeans I

jewellery ['dʒuːəlri] Schmuck II

job [dʒɒb] Aufgabe, Job I

join sb. [dʒɔɪn] sich jm. anschließen; bei jm. mitmachen II • °**join up (with)** sich zusammentun (mit)

joke [dʒəʊk] Witz I

joke [dʒəʊk] scherzen, Witze machen II

journey ['dʒɜːni] Reise, Fahrt II

judo ['dʒuːdəʊ] Judo I • **do judo** Judo machen I

jug [dʒʌg] Krug I • **a jug of milk** ein Krug Milch I

juice [dʒuːs] Saft I

July [dʒu'laɪ] Juli I

°**jumble** ['dʒʌmbl] gebrauchte Sachen, Trödel

jumble sale ['dʒʌmbl seɪl] Wohltätigkeitsbasar I

jump [dʒʌmp] springen II

June [dʒuːn] Juni I

junior ['dʒuːniə] Junioren-, Jugend- I

just [dʒʌst]
1. (einfach) nur, bloß I
2. einfach III 2 (35) • **I just can't find them.** Ich kann sie einfach nicht finden. III 2 (35/159)

3. gerade (eben), soeben II
just then genau in dem Moment; gerade dann II
4. just like you genau wie du II
▶ S.159 just

K

kangaroo [ˌkæŋgəˈruː] Känguru II
keep [kiːp], **kept, kept** (be)halten; aufbewahren III 5 (91) • **keep in touch** in Verbindung bleiben, Kontakt halten III Intro (11) • **keep sth. warm/cool/open/...** etwas warm/kühl/offen/... halten II • **°keep a diary** ein Tagebuch führen
°keep fit fit bleiben
kept [kept] *siehe* **keep**
key [kiː] Schlüssel I • **key word** Stichwort, Schlüsselwort I
keyboard [ˈkiːbɔːd] Keyboard *(elektronisches Tasteninstrument)* III Intro (7)
kid [kɪd] Kind, Jugendliche(r) I
kill [kɪl] töten I
kilogram (kg) [ˈkɪləgræm], **kilo** [ˈkiːləʊ] Kilogramm, Kilo III 4 (76)
a 90-kilogram bear ein 90 Kilogramm schwerer Bär III 4 (76/168)
kilometre (km) [ˈkɪləmiːtə] Kilometer III 2 (42) • **a ten-kilometre walk** eine Zehn-Kilometer-Wanderung III 4 (76/168)
°kilt [kɪlt] Kilt, Schottenrock
kind (of) [kaɪnd] Art III Intro (6)
What kind of car ...? Was für ein Auto ...? III Intro (6/151)
kind of scary [kaɪnd] *(infml)* irgendwie unheimlich III 1 (26)
king [kɪŋ] König I
kitchen [ˈkɪtʃɪn] Küche I
kite [kaɪt] Drachen I
knee [niː] Knie I
knew [njuː] *siehe* **know**
knife [naɪf], *pl* **knives** [naɪvz] Messer III 1 (27)
knock (on) [nɒk] (an)klopfen (an) I
know [nəʊ], **knew, known**
1. wissen I
2. kennen I
know about sth. von etwas wissen; über etwas Bescheid wissen II • **How do you know ...?** Woher weißt du ...? / Woher kennst du ...? I • **I don't know.** Ich weiß es nicht. I • **..., you know.** ..., wissen Sie. / ..., weißt du. I • **You know what, Sophie?** Weißt du was, Sophie? I
known [nəʊn] *siehe* **know**

kph (kilometres per hour) [ˌkeɪ piː‿ˈeɪtʃ] km/h (Stundenkilometer, Kilometer pro Stunde) III 4 (76)

L

°label [ˈleɪbl] beschriften, etikettieren
°lacrosse [ləˈkrɒs] Lacrosse *(Sportart)*
°ladder [ˈlædə] *(die)* Leiter
laid [leɪd] *siehe* **lay**
lake [leɪk] (Binnen-)See II
lamb [læm] Lamm III 1 (13)
lamp [læmp] Lampe I
land [lænd] Land, Grund und Boden II • **on land** auf dem Land III 1 (20)
land [lænd] landen II
lane [leɪn] Gasse, Weg III 1 (12/153)
language [ˈlæŋgwɪdʒ] Sprache I
large [lɑːdʒ] groß II
▶ S.157 big – large – huge
lasagne [ləˈzænjə] Lasagne I
°laser [ˈleɪzə] Laser
last [lɑːst] letzte(r, s) I • **the last day** der letzte Tag I • **at last** endlich, schließlich I
late [leɪt] spät; zu spät I • **be late** zu spät sein/kommen I • **Sorry, I'm late.** Entschuldigung, dass ich zu spät bin/komme. I
later [ˈleɪtə] später I
latest [ˈleɪtɪst] neueste(r, s) III 4 (70)
laugh [lɑːf] lachen I • **laugh at sb.** jn. auslachen, über jn. lachen III 4 (70) • **laugh out loud** laut lachen II
laughter [ˈlɑːftə] Gelächter II
lay the table [leɪ], **laid, laid** den Tisch decken I
°layout [ˈleɪaʊt] Layout, Seitengestaltung
leader [ˈliːdə] (An-)Führer/in, Leiter/in III 4 (73)
learn [lɜːn] lernen I • **learn sth. about sth.** etwas über etwas erfahren, etwas über etwas herausfinden II
least [liːst] am wenigsten III 5 (92)
at least zumindest, wenigstens I
leather [ˈleðə] Leder III 5 (91)
leave [liːv], **left, left**
1. (weg)gehen; abfahren II
2. verlassen II
3. zurücklassen II
left [left] *siehe* **leave**
left [left] linke(r, s) II • **look left** nach links schauen II • **on the left** links, auf der linken Seite I • **turn left** (nach) links abbiegen II
leg [leg] Bein I

leisure centre [ˈleʒə sentə] Freizeitzentrum, -park II
lemonade [ˌleməˈneɪd] Limonade I
leotard [ˈliːətɑːd] Gymnastikanzug; Turnanzug III 3 (54)
lesson [ˈlesn] (Unterrichts-)Stunde I • **lessons** *(pl)* [ˈlesnz] Unterricht I
let (-tt-) [let], **let, let** lassen II
Let's ... Lass uns ... / Lasst uns ... I
Let's go. Auf geht's! I • **Let's look at the list.** Sehen wir uns die Liste an. / Lasst uns die Liste ansehen. I
let sb. do sth. jm. erlauben, etwas zu tun; zulassen, dass jd. etwas tut III 2 (35)
letter [ˈletə]
1. Buchstabe I
2. letter (to) Brief (an) II
lettuce [ˈletɪs] (Kopf-)Salat II
library [ˈlaɪbrəri] Bibliothek, Bücherei I
life [laɪf], *pl* **lives** [laɪvz] Leben I
lift [lɪft] Fahrstuhl, Aufzug II
light [laɪt] Licht III 1 (28)
like [laɪk] wie I • **just like you** genau wie du II • **What was the weather like?** Wie war das Wetter? II • **°like that / like this** so
like [laɪk] mögen, gernhaben I
like sth. better etwas lieber mögen II • **like sth. best** etwas am liebsten mögen III 3 (57) • **I like swimming/dancing/...** Ich schwimme/tanze/... gern. I • **I'd like ... (= I would like ...)** Ich hätte gern ... / Ich möchte gern ... I • **I'd like to go (= I would like to go)** Ich würde gern gehen / Ich möchte gehen I • **I wouldn't like to go** Ich würde nicht gern gehen / Ich möchte nicht gehen I • **Would you like ...?** Möchtest du ...? / Möchten Sie ...? I • **°Say what you like about ...** Sag, was du an ... magst
line [laɪn]
1. Zeile II
2. (U-Bahn-)Linie III 1 (14)
link [lɪŋk] verbinden, verknüpfen I
link [lɪŋk] Verbindung, Verknüpfung III 4 (69/166)
linking word [ˈlɪŋkɪŋ wɜːd] Bindewort II
lion [ˈlaɪən] Löwe II
list [lɪst] Liste I
list [lɪst] auflisten, aufzählen II
listen (to) [ˈlɪsn] zuhören; sich *etwas* anhören I • **listen for sth.** auf etwas horchen, achten III 1 (15)
listener [ˈlɪsnə] Zuhörer/in II
little [ˈlɪtl] klein I

live [lɪv] leben, wohnen I
live music [laɪv] Livemusik II
lives [laɪvz] *Plural von „life"*
living room ['lɪvɪŋ ruːm] Wohnzimmer I
°**local** ['ləʊkl] lokal, örtlich, Lokal-
location [ləʊ'keɪʃn] (Einsatz-)Ort, Platz III 3 (60/164)
lock [lɒk] Schleuse III 1 (12/153)
lock up [ˌlɒk_'ʌp] abschließen II
logo ['ləʊgəʊ], *pl* **logos** Logo, Markenzeichen III 2 (32)
lonely ['ləʊnli] einsam III 2 (32)
long [lɒŋ] lang I • **a long time** lange III 1 (13)
look [lʊk]
1. schauen, gucken I
2. look different/great/old anders/toll/alt aussehen I
look after sth./sb. auf etwas/jn. aufpassen; sich um etwas/jn. kümmern II • **look around** sich umsehen III 1 (26) • **look at** ansehen, anschauen I • **look for** suchen II **look left/right** nach links/rechts schauen II • **look round** sich umsehen I • **look sth. up** etwas nachschlagen III 2 (47) • **look up (from)** hochsehen, aufschauen (von) II
°**loon** [luːn] Seetaucher
lose [luːz], **lost, lost** verlieren II
lost [lɒst] *siehe* **lose** • °**we're lost** wir haben uns verirrt/verlaufen
lot [lɒt]: **a lot (of)** eine Menge, viel, viele II • **Thanks a lot!** Vielen Dank! I • **He likes her a lot.** Er mag sie sehr. I • **lots more** viel mehr I • **lots of ...** eine Menge ..., viele ..., viel ... I
loud [laʊd] laut I
love [lʌv] lieben, sehr mögen II
love [lʌv]
1. Liebe II
2. Liebes, Liebling III 2 (33)
Love ... Liebe Grüße, ... *(Briefschluss)* I
luck [lʌk]: **Good luck (with ...)!** Viel Glück (bei/mit ...)! I
luckily ['lʌkɪli] zum Glück, glücklicherweise II
lucky ['lʌki]: **be lucky (with)** Glück haben (mit) II
lunch [lʌntʃ] Mittagessen I
lunch break Mittagspause I
lyrics *(pl)* ['lɪrɪks] Liedtext(e), Songtext(e) III 4 (70)

M

machine [mə'ʃiːn] Maschine, Gerät III 1 (20)
mad [mæd] verrückt I • **be mad about sth.** verrückt nach/auf etwas sein III 3 (104)
made [meɪd] *siehe* **make**
magazine [ˌmægə'ziːn] Zeitschrift, Magazin I
mail [meɪl] schicken, senden *(per Post oder E-Mail)* I • **mail sb.** jn. anmailen II
main [meɪn] Haupt- III 5 (90)
make [meɪk], **made, made** machen; bauen I • **make a call** ein Telefongespräch führen II • **make a deal** ein Abkommen/eine Abmachung treffen III 3 (56) • **make a mess** alles durcheinanderbringen, alles in Unordnung bringen I • **make a point** ein Argument vorbringen III 4 (72) • °**make comparisons** Vergleiche anstellen, vergleichen °**make notes** (sich) Notizen machen • °**make sth. up** sich etwas ausdenken • °**What makes a game a good game?** Was macht ein Spiel zu einem guten Spiel?
make-up ['meɪkʌp] Make-up II
mall [mɔːl], **shopping mall** *(großes)* Einkaufszentrum III 4 (71)
man [mæn], *pl* **men** [men] Mann I
manager ['mænɪdʒə] Manager/in III 5 (96)
many ['meni] viele I • **how many?** wie viele? I
map [mæp] Landkarte, Stadtplan II
March [mɑːtʃ] März I
mark sth. up [ˌmɑːk_'ʌp] etwas markieren, kennzeichnen II
°**marked** [mɑːkt] markiert
market ['mɑːkɪt] Markt II
marmalade ['mɑːməleɪd] (Orangen-)Marmelade I
married (to) ['mærɪd] verheiratet (mit) I
match [mætʃ] Spiel, Wettkampf I
°**match** [mætʃ]
1. passen zu
2. zuordnen
°**Match the letters and numbers.** Ordne die Buchstaben den Zahlen zu.
mate [meɪt] *(infml)* Freund/in, Kumpel III 2 (32)
°**material** [mə'tɪəriəl] Material, Stoff
maths [mæθs] Mathematik I
matter ['mætə]: **What's the matter?** Was ist los? / Was ist denn? II
may [meɪ] dürfen I
► S.158 „können" und „dürfen"

May [meɪ] Mai I
maybe ['meɪbi] vielleicht I
me [miː] mir; mich I • **Me too.** Ich auch. I • **more than me** mehr als ich II • **That's me.** Das bin ich. I **Why me?** Warum ich? I
meal [miːl] Mahlzeit, Essen III 1 (16)
set meal Menü III 1 (16/154)
mean [miːn], **meant, meant**
1. bedeuten II
2. meinen *(sagen wollen)* II
meaning ['miːnɪŋ] Bedeutung III 2 (35)
meant [ment] *siehe* **mean**
meat [miːt] Fleisch I
medal ['medl] Medaille III 3 (66)
media *(pl)* ['miːdiə] Medien III 2 (32)
mediation [ˌmiːdi'eɪʃn] Vermittlung, Sprachmittlung, Mediation II
medium ['miːdiəm] mittel(groß) II
meet [miːt], **met, met**
1. treffen; kennenlernen I
2. sich treffen I
Nice to meet you. Nett, dich kennenzulernen. III Intro (10)
men [men] *Plural von „man"*
menu ['menjuː]
1. Speisekarte III 1 (16)
2. Menü *(Computer)* III 1 (16)
mess [mes]: **be a mess** sehr unordentlich sein; fürchterlich aussehen *(Zimmer)* II • **make a mess** alles durcheinanderbringen, alles in Unordnung bringen I
message ['mesɪdʒ] Nachricht III 2 (32)
met [met] *siehe* **meet**
°**method** ['meθəd] Methode, Art und Weise
metre ['miːtə] Meter II
mice [maɪs] *Plural von „mouse"*
microphone ['maɪkrəfəʊn] Mikrofon III 4 (73)
middle (of) ['mɪdl] Mitte I; Mittelteil II
might [maɪt]: **you might need help** du könntest (vielleicht) Hilfe brauchen III 2 (44)
mild [maɪld] mild III 1 (16)
mile [maɪl] Meile *(= ca. 1,6 km)* II • **for miles** meilenweit II
milk [mɪlk] Milch I
million ['mɪljən] Million III Intro (6/150); III 2 (41)
mime [maɪm] pantomimisch darstellen, vorspielen II
°**mime** [maɪm] Pantomime
mind map ['maɪnd mæp] Mindmap („Gedankenkarte", „Wissensnetz") I
Mind your own business. [ˌmaɪnd jər_əʊn 'bɪznəs] Das geht dich

nichts an! / Kümmere dich um deine eigenen Angelegenheiten! II
mine [maɪn] meiner, meine, meins II
mini- ['mɪni] Mini- II
mints *(pl)* [mɪnts] Pfefferminzbonbons I
minus ['maɪnəs] minus III 4 (68)
minute ['mɪnɪt] Minute I • **Wait a minute.** Warte mal! / Moment mal! II
mirror ['mɪrə] Spiegel II
miss [mɪs]
1. vermissen II
2. verpassen II
3. Miss a turn. Einmal aussetzen. II
Miss White [mɪs] Frau White *(unverheiratet)* I
missing ['mɪsɪŋ]: **be missing** fehlen II • **°the missing information/ words** die fehlenden Informationen/Wörter
mistake [mɪ'steɪk] Fehler I
mix [mɪks] mischen, mixen III 2 (32)
°mix up durcheinanderbringen
°be mixed up durcheinander/ in der falschen Reihenfolge sein
mix [mɪks] Mix, Mischung III 4 (73)
mixture ['mɪkstʃə] Mischung III Intro (9)
°mobile ['məʊbaɪl] Mobile
mobile (phone) ['məʊbaɪl] Mobiltelefon, Handy I
model ['mɒdl] Modell*(-flugzeug, -schiff usw.)* I; (Foto-)Modell II
modern ['mɒdən] modern III 4 (70/166)
mole [məʊl] Maulwurf II
mom [mɒm, *AE:* mɑ:m] *(AE)* Mama, Mutti; Mutter III 1 (14)
moment ['məʊmənt] Moment, Augenblick II • **at the moment** im Moment, gerade II
Monday ['mʌndeɪ, 'mʌndi] Montag I • **Monday morning** Montagmorgen I
money ['mʌni] Geld I
monitor ['mɒnɪtə] Bildschirm, Monitor III 5 (88/89)
monkey ['mʌŋki] Affe II
monster ['mɒnstə] Monster, Ungeheuer III 2 (42)
month [mʌnθ] Monat I
moon [mu:n] Mond II
more [mɔ:] mehr I • **lots more** viel mehr I • **more boring (than)** langweiliger (als) II • **more quickly (than)** schneller (als) II • **more than** mehr als II • **more than me** mehr als ich II • **no more music** keine Musik mehr I • **not (...) any more** nicht mehr II • **once more** noch einmal III 2 (44) • **one more** noch ein(e), ein(e) weitere(r, s) I
morning ['mɔ:nɪŋ] Morgen, Vormittag I • **in the morning** morgens, am Morgen I • **Monday morning** Montagmorgen I • **on Friday morning** freitagmorgens, am Freitagmorgen I
mosque [mɒsk] Moschee III 1 (16)
most [məʊst] (der/die/das) meiste ...; am meisten II • **most people** die meisten Leute I • **(the) most boring** der/die/das langweiligste ...; am langweiligsten II
mother ['mʌðə] Mutter I
mountain ['maʊntən] Berg II
mouse [maʊs], *pl* **mice** [maɪs] Maus I
mouth [maʊθ] Mund I
move [mu:v]
1. bewegen; sich bewegen II
Move back one space. Geh ein Feld zurück. II • **Move on one space.** Geh ein Feld vor. II
2. move (to) umziehen (nach, in) II
move in einziehen II • **move out** ausziehen II
movement ['mu:vmənt] Bewegung II
movie ['mu:vi] Film III 4 (68)
MP3 player [ˌempi:'θri: ˌpleɪə] MP3-Spieler I
Mr ... ['mɪstə] Herr ... I
Mrs ... ['mɪsɪz] Frau ... I
Ms ... [mɪz, məz] Frau ... II
much [mʌtʃ] viel I • **how much?** wie viel? I • **How much is/are ...?** Was kostet/kosten ...? / Wie viel kostet/kosten ...? I • **like/love sth. very much** etwas sehr mögen/ sehr lieben II
°multi-cultural [ˌmʌlti'kʌltʃərəl] multikulturell
multiple choice [ˌmʌltɪpl 'tʃɔɪs] Multiple-Choice II
mum [mʌm] Mama, Mutti; Mutter I
°mummy ['mʌmi] Mumie
murder ['mɜ:də] Mord III 1 (26)
murder ['mɜ:də] (er)morden III 1 (26/156)
murderer ['mɜ:dərə] Mörder/in III 1 (26/156)
museum [mju'zi:əm] Museum I
mushroom ['mʌʃrʊm, -ru:m] Pilz III 1 (24/155)
music ['mju:zɪk] Musik I
musical ['mju:zɪkl] Musical I
musical instrument [ˌmju:zɪkl‿'ɪnstrəmənt] Musikinstrument III 5 (93)
musician [mju:'zɪʃn] Musiker/in III 5 (93)
must [mʌst] müssen I
mustn't do ['mʌsnt] nicht tun dürfen II
my [maɪ] mein/e I • **My name is ...** Ich heiße ... / Mein Name ist ... I
It's my turn. Ich bin dran / an der Reihe. I
myself [maɪ'self] mir/mich (selbst) III 4 (72/167)
mystery ['mɪstri] Rätsel, Geheimnis II

N

name [neɪm] Name I • **call sb. names** jn. mit Schimpfwörtern hänseln, jm. Schimpfwörter nachrufen III 2 (35) • **My name is ...** Ich heiße ... / Mein Name ist ... I
What's your name? Wie heißt du? I
name [neɪm] nennen; benennen II
°nation: First Nations [ˌfɜ:st 'neɪʃnz] *indianische Ureinwohner/innen Kanadas*
national ['næʃnəl] national, National- III Intro (6)
natural history [ˌnætʃrəl 'hɪstri] Naturkunde III 1 (13)
near [nɪə] in der Nähe von, nahe (bei) I
neat [ni:t] gepflegt II • **neat and tidy** schön ordentlich II
°necessary ['nesəsəri] nötig, notwendig
need [ni:d] brauchen, benötigen I
°need to do tun müssen
needn't do ['ni:dnt] nicht tun müssen, nicht zu tun brauchen II
neighbour ['neɪbə] Nachbar/in I
nervous ['nɜ:vəs] nervös, aufgeregt I
°net [net] Netz
°network ['netwɜ:k] (Wörter-)Netz
never ['nevə] nie, niemals I
new [nju:] neu I
news *(no pl)* [nju:z] Nachrichten II
► S.162 Words without a plural
newspaper ['nju:speɪpə] Zeitung I
next [nekst]: **be next** der/die Nächste sein I • **the next morning/day** am nächsten Morgen/Tag I • **the next photo** das nächste Foto I • **What have we got next?** Was haben wir als Nächstes? I
next to [nekst] neben I

nice [naɪs] schön, nett I • **Nice to meet you.** Nett, dich kennenzulernen. III Intro (10)
night [naɪt] Nacht, später Abend I
at night nachts, in der Nacht I
on Friday night freitagnachts, Freitagnacht I
nil [nɪl] null III 3 (54/162)
► S.162 A football match
no [nəʊ] nein I
no [nəʊ] kein, keine I • **no more music** keine Musik mehr I • **No way!** Auf keinen Fall! / Kommt nicht in Frage! II
nobody ['nəʊbədi] niemand II
nod (-dd-) [nɒd] nicken (mit) II
noise [nɔɪz] Geräusch; Lärm I
noisy ['nɔɪzi] laut, lärmend II
°**noodle** ['nu:dl] Nudel
north [nɔ:θ] Norden; nach Norden; nördlich III Intro (7)
northbound ['nɔ:θbaʊnd] Richtung Norden III 1 (14/153)
north-east [ˌnɔ:θ'i:st] Nordosten; nach Nordosten; nordöstlich III Intro (7/151)
°**northern** ['nɔ:ðən] Nord-, nördlich
north-west [ˌnɔ:θ'west] Nordwesten; nach Nordwesten; nordwestlich III Intro (7/151)
nose [nəʊz] Nase I
not [nɒt] nicht I • **not (...) any** kein, keine I • **not (...) any more** nicht mehr II • **not (...) anybody** niemand II • **not (...) anything** nichts II • **not (...) anywhere** nirgendwo(hin) II • **not even** (noch) nicht einmal III 2 (34) • **not ... till / not ... until** erst (um); nicht vor III 4 (71) • **not (...) yet** noch nicht II
note [nəʊt] Mitteilung, Notiz I
°**make notes** sich Notizen machen
take notes sich Notizen machen I
nothing ['nʌθɪŋ] nichts II
°**notice** ['nəʊtɪs] Notiz, Mitteilung
November [nəʊ'vembə] November I
now [naʊ] nun, jetzt I
number ['nʌmbə] Zahl, Ziffer, Nummer I
► S.150 Numbers
nut [nʌt] Nuss III 1 (16)

O

o [əʊ] null I
°**obvious** ['ɒbviəs] offensichtlich
°**och** [ɒk] ach *(besonders in Schottland und Irland gebräuchlich)*
o'clock [ə'klɒk]: **eleven o'clock** elf Uhr I
October [ɒk'təʊbə] Oktober I
°**odd** [ɒd]: **What word is the odd one out?** Welches Wort passt nicht dazu? / Welches Wort gehört nicht dazu?
of [əv, ɒv] von I • **of the summer holidays** der Sommerferien I
of course [əv 'kɔ:s] natürlich, selbstverständlich I
off [ɒf]: **cut sth. off** etwas abschneiden, abtrennen III 3 (66) • **fall off** herunterfallen (von) II • **get off (the train/bus)** (aus dem Zug/Bus) aussteigen I • **get sth. off the ground** etwas auf den Weg bringen; etwas auf die Beine stellen III 5 (92) • **take sth. off** etwas ausziehen *(Kleidung)* II; etwas absetzen *(Hut, Helm)* III 1 (27) • **take 10c off** 10 Cent abziehen I • **turn sth. off** etwas ausschalten II
office ['ɒfɪs] Büro III 5 (88/89)
°**official** [ə'fɪʃl] offiziell
often ['ɒfn] oft, häufig I
Oh dear! [əʊ 'dɪə] Oje! II
Oh well ... [əʊ 'wel] Na ja ... / Na gut ... I
oil [ɔɪl] Öl III 2 (30)
°**oil rig** ['ɔɪl rɪg] Ölbohrinsel; Ölförderturm
°**oil terminal** ['ɔɪl ˌtɜ:mɪnəl] Ölhafen
OK [əʊ'keɪ] okay, gut, in Ordnung I
old [əʊld] alt I • **How old are you?** Wie alt bist du? I • **I'm ... years old.** Ich bin ... Jahre alt. I • **thirteen-year-old** Dreizehnjährige(r) III 4 (76)
old-fashioned [ˌəʊld'fæʃnd] altmodisch III 4 (70)
on [ɒn]
1. auf I
2. weiter III 1 (13/152)
3. *(Radio, Licht usw.)* an, eingeschaltet II • **go on** angehen III 1 (27)
on 13th June am 13. Juni I • **on earth** auf der Erde III 1 (13/153)
on foot zu Fuß III 1 (20) • **on Friday** am Freitag I • **on Friday afternoon** freitagnachmittags, am Freitagnachmittag I • **on Friday evening** freitagabends, am Freitagabend I • **on Friday morning** freitagmorgens, am Freitagmorgen I • **on Friday night** freitagnachts, Freitagnacht I • **on the beach** am Strand II • **on the board** an die Tafel I • **on the corner of Sand Street and London Road** Sand Street, Ecke London Road II • **on the left** links, auf der linken Seite I
on the phone am Telefon I • **on the plane** im Flugzeug II • **on the radio** im Radio I • **on the right** rechts, auf der rechten Seite I • **on the train** im Zug I • **on TV** im Fernsehen I • **What page are we on?** Auf welcher Seite sind wir? I
be on holiday in Urlaub sein; Ferien haben/machen II • **go on holiday** in Urlaub fahren II
straight on geradeaus weiter II
► S.152 on („weiter")
once [wʌns]
1. einst, früher einmal III 1 (15)
2. einmal III 2 (32)
once more / once again noch einmal III 2 (44)
one [wʌn] eins, ein, eine I • **one another** einander, sich (gegenseitig) III 4 (146) • **one day** eines Tages I • **one more** noch ein/e, ein/e weitere(r, s) I • **a new one** ein neuer / eine neue / ein neues II • **my old ones** meine alten II
onion ['ʌnjən] Zwiebel III 1 (24/155)
online [ˌɒn'laɪn] online, Online- III 2 (41)
only ['əʊnli]
1. nur, bloß I; erst III 3 (66)
2. **the only guest** der einzige Gast I
onto ['ɒntə, 'ɒntʊ] auf (... hinauf) III 3 (66)
open ['əʊpən]
1. öffnen, aufmachen I
2. sich öffnen I
open ['əʊpən] offen, geöffnet II
open-air im Freien; Freilicht- III 1 (12) • **open-top bus** oben offener (Doppeldecker-)Bus III 1 (20)
°**opening sentence** [ˌəʊpənɪŋ 'sentəns] Einleitungssatz
opera ['ɒprə] Oper III 5 (93)
operation (on) [ˌɒpə'reɪʃn] Operation (an) III 3 (104)
opposite ['ɒpəzɪt] gegenüber (von) II
opposite ['ɒpəzɪt] Gegenteil I
or [ɔ:] oder I • °**either ... or ...** ['aɪðə ... ɔ:, 'i:ðə ... ɔ:] entweder ... oder
orange ['ɒrɪndʒ] orange(farben) I
orange ['ɒrɪndʒ] Orange, Apfelsine I
orange juice ['ɒrɪndʒ dʒu:s] Orangensaft I
order ['ɔ:də] Reihenfolge III 3 (64)
°**word order** Wortstellung
organ ['ɔ:gən] Orgel II
°**organize** ['ɔ:gənaɪz] organisieren
°**original** [ə'rɪdʒənl] Original
other ['ʌðə] andere(r, s) I • **the others** die anderen I • **the other way round** anders herum II

Ouch! [aʊtʃ] Autsch! I
our ['aʊə] unser, unsere I
ours ['aʊəz] unserer, unsere, unseres II
ourselves [aʊə'selvz] uns (selbst) III 4 (72/167)
out [aʊt] heraus, hinaus; draußen II
be out weg sein, nicht da sein I
out of ... aus ... (heraus/hinaus) I
°a day out ein Tagesausflug
outdoor ['aʊtdɔː] im Freien, Außen- III 4 (69)
outfit ['aʊtfɪt] Outfit *(Kleidung; Ausrüstung)* II
outside [ˌaʊt'saɪd]
1. draußen I
2. nach draußen II
3. outside his room vor seinem Zimmer; außerhalb seines Zimmers I
over ['əʊvə]
1. über, oberhalb von I
2. über, mehr als II
3. be over vorbei/zu Ende sein I
all over the world auf der ganzen Welt III Intro (6/151) • **from all over England/the UK** aus ganz England/aus dem gesamten Vereinigten Königreich III Intro (6) • **over there** da drüben, dort drüben I
over to ... hinüber zu/nach ... II
own [əʊn]**: our own pool** unser eigenes Schwimmbad II
°owner ['əʊnə] Besitzer/in

P

pack [pæk] packen, einpacken II
packet ['pækɪt] Päckchen, Packung, Schachtel I • **a packet of mints** ein Päckchen/eine Packung Pfefferminzbonbons I
paddle ['pædl] paddeln III 4 (82)
paddle ['pædl] Paddel III 4 (82/169)
pads *(pl)* [pædz] *(Knie- usw.)* Schützer *(für Inlineskater)*; Schulterpolster *(beim American Football)* III 3 (60/164)
page [peɪdʒ] (Buch-, Heft-)Seite I
What page are we on? Auf welcher Seite sind wir? I
paid [peɪd] *siehe* **pay**
paint [peɪnt] malen, anmalen I
painter ['peɪntə] Maler/in II
pair [peə]**: a pair (of)** ein Paar II
palace ['pæləs] Palast, Schloss III 1 (12/153)
paper ['peɪpə]
1. Papier I
2. Zeitung II
paragraph ['pærəgrɑːf] Absatz *(in einem Text)* II
Paralympics [ˌpærə'lɪmpɪks] *olympischer Wettkampf für Behindertensportler/innen* III 3 (104)
paramedic [ˌpærə'medɪk] Sanitäter/in II
paraphrase ['pærəfreɪz] umschreiben, anders ausdrücken III 3 (56)
parcel ['pɑːsl] Paket I
parents ['peərənts] Eltern I
park [pɑːk] Park I
parliament ['pɑːləmənt] Parlament III 1 (12)
parrot ['pærət] Papagei I
part [pɑːt] Teil I
partner ['pɑːtnə] Partner/in I
party ['pɑːti] Party I • **have a party** eine Party feiern/veranstalten II
pass [pɑːs] (herüber)reichen, weitergeben I • **pass round** herumgeben I • **°pass sth. on** etwas weitergeben
past [pɑːst] Vergangenheit II
past [pɑːst] vorbei (an), vorüber (an) II • **half past 11** halb zwölf (11.30 / 23.30) I • **quarter past 11** Viertel nach 11 (11.15 / 23.15) I
path [pɑːθ] Pfad, Weg II • **bridle path** ['braɪdl pɑːθ] Reitweg III 3 (60/164)
pay (for sth.) [peɪ]**, paid, paid** etwas bezahlen II
PE [ˌpiː‿'iː]**, Physical Education** [ˌfɪzɪkəl‿edʒu'keɪʃn] Sportunterricht, Turnen I
pea [piː] Erbse III 1 (24/155)
pen [pen] Kugelschreiber, Füller I
pence (p) *(pl)* [pens] Pence *(Plural von „penny")* I
pencil ['pensl] Bleistift I
pencil case ['pensl keɪs] Federmäppchen I
pencil sharpener ['pensl ʃɑːpnə] Bleistiftanspitzer I
penny ['peni] *kleinste britische Münze* I
people ['piːpl] Menschen, Leute I
pepper ['pepə] Pfeffer III 3 (62)
per [pɜː, pə] pro III 4 (76)
per cent (%) [pə'sent] Prozent III 4 (76)
person ['pɜːsn] Person II
personal ['pɜːsənl] persönliche(r, s) III 2 (32)
pet [pet] Haustier I • **pet shop** Tierhandlung I
phone [fəʊn] Telefon I • **on the phone** am Telefon I • **phone call** Anruf, Telefongespräch I • **phone number** Telefonnummer I
phone [fəʊn] anrufen II
photo ['fəʊtəʊ] Foto I • **in the photo** auf dem Foto I • **take photos** Fotos machen, fotografieren I
°photocopy ['fəʊtəʊkɒpi] Fotokopie
photographer [fə'tɒgrəfə] Fotograf/in II
phrase [freɪz] Ausdruck, (Rede-) Wendung I
piano [pi'ænəʊ] Klavier, Piano I
play the piano Klavier spielen I
pick up [ˌpɪk‿'ʌp]**: pick sb. up** jn. abholen III 2 (33) • **pick sth. up** etwas hochheben, aufheben II
picnic ['pɪknɪk] Picknick II
picture ['pɪktʃə] Bild I • **in the picture** auf dem Bild I
pie [paɪ] Obstkuchen; Pastete II
piece [piːs]**: a piece of** ein Stück I
a piece of paper ein Stück Papier I
pig [pɪg] Schwein III 1 (24/155)
pink [pɪŋk] pink(farben), rosa I
pipe [paɪp] Pfeife III 5 (91)
pirate ['paɪrət] Pirat, Piratin I
pitch [pɪtʃ]**: football/hockey pitch** Fußball-/Hockeyplatz, -feld II
pizza ['piːtsə] Pizza I
place [pleɪs] Ort, Platz I • **in other places** an anderen Orten, anderswo III 1 (13) • **°take place** stattfinden
°placemat ['pleɪsmæt] Set, Platzdeckchen
plan [plæn] Plan I
plan (-nn-) [plæn] planen II
plane [pleɪn] Flugzeug II • **on the plane** im Flugzeug II
planet ['plænɪt] Planet II
plate [pleɪt] Teller I • **a plate of chips** ein Teller Pommes frites I
platform ['plætfɔːm] Bahnsteig, Gleis III 1 (14)
play [pleɪ] spielen I • **play a trick on sb.** jm. einen Streich spielen II
play the drums Schlagzeug spielen III Intro (6/151) • **play the fiddle** Geige spielen III Intro (7/151) • **play the guitar** Gitarre spielen I • **play the piano** Klavier spielen I
play [pleɪ] Theaterstück I
player ['pleɪə] Spieler/in I
playlist ['pleɪlɪst] Titelliste *(von zu spielenden Songs)* III 5 (92)
please [pliːz] bitte *(in Fragen und Aufforderungen)* I
plug [plʌg] Stecker III 1 (27)
plus [plʌs] plus III 4 (68/166)
pm [ˌpiː‿'em]**: 7 pm** 7 Uhr abends/ 19 Uhr I
pocket ['pɒkɪt] Tasche *(an Kleidungsstück)* II • **pocket money** Taschengeld II

poem ['pəʊɪm] Gedicht I
point [pɔɪnt] Punkt II • **make a point** ein Argument vorbringen III 4 (72) • **point of view** [ˌpɔɪnt_əv 'vjuː] Standpunkt II • **from my point of view** aus meiner Sicht; von meinem Standpunkt aus gesehen II • **10.4 (ten point four)** 10,4 (zehn Komma vier) III Intro (6/150) ► S.150 Numbers
point (at/to sth.) [pɔɪnt] zeigen, deuten (auf etwas) II
police *(pl)* [pə'liːs] Polizei I
policeman, -woman [pə'liːsmən, -wʊmən] Polizist, Polizistin II
police station [pə'liːs steɪʃn] Polizeiwache, Polizeirevier II
poltergeist ['pəʊltəgaɪst] Poltergeist I
ponytail ['pəʊniteɪl] Pferdeschwanz *(Frisur)* III 2 (34)
poor [pɔː, pʊə] arm I • **poor Sophie** (die) arme Sophie I
pop (music) [pɒp] Pop(musik) III Intro (6)
popcorn ['pɒpkɔːn] Popcorn II
°**popular** ['pɒpjələ] populär, beliebt
population [ˌpɒpju'leɪʃn] Bevölkerung, Einwohner(zahl) III 4 (68)
pork [pɔːk] Schweinefleisch III 1 (24/155)
possible ['pɒsəbl] möglich II
post [pəʊst] Post *(Briefe, Päckchen, ...)* III 2 (32)
postcard ['pəʊstkɑːd] Postkarte II
poster ['pəʊstə] Poster I
post office ['pəʊst_ɒfɪs] Postamt II
potato [pə'teɪtəʊ], *pl* **potatoes** Kartoffel I
pound (£) [paʊnd] Pfund *(britische Währung)* I
practice ['præktɪs] *hier:* Übungsteil I
practise ['præktɪs] üben; trainieren I
prepare [prɪ'peə] vorbereiten; sich vorbereiten II • **prepare for** sich vorbereiten auf II
present ['preznt]
1. Gegenwart I
2. Geschenk I
present sth. (to sb.) [prɪ'zent] (jm.) etwas präsentieren, vorstellen I
presentation [ˌprezn'teɪʃn] Präsentation, Vorstellung I
presenter [prɪ'zentə] Moderator/in II
°**president** ['prezɪdənt] Präsident/in
pretty ['prɪti] hübsch I
pretty cool/good/... ['prɪti] ziemlich cool/gut/... II
price [praɪs] (Kauf-)Preis I
°**prince** [prɪns] Prinz
print: bold print [ˌbəʊld 'prɪnt] Fettdruck III 5 (90)
print sth. out [ˌprɪnt_'aʊt] etwas ausdrucken II
prize [praɪz] Preis, Gewinn I
probably ['prɒbəbli] wahrscheinlich II
problem ['prɒbləm] Problem II
produce [prə'djuːs] produzieren, herstellen III 5 (88/89)
°**profile** ['prəʊfaɪl] Porträt, Beschreibung
programme ['prəʊgræm] Programm I
project (about, on) ['prɒdʒekt] Projekt (über, zu) I
promise ['prɒmɪs] versprechen II
°**pronounce** [prə'naʊns] aussprechen
pronunciation [prəˌnʌnsi'eɪʃn] Aussprache I
proof *(no pl)* [pruːf] Beweis(e) II
protect sb. (from) [prə'tekt] jn. (be)schützen (vor) III 4 (72)
proud (of sb./sth.) [praʊd] stolz (auf jn./etwas) II
province ['prɒvɪns] Provinz III 4 (72)
PS [ˌpiː_'es] **(postscript** ['pəʊstskrɪpt]**)** PS *(Nachschrift unter Briefen)* III 1 (12)
pub [pʌb] Kneipe, Lokal II
public ['pʌblɪk] öffentliche(r, s) III 1 (14/153) • **public transport** *(no pl)* öffentliche Verkehrsmittel, öffentlicher Personennahverkehr III 1 (14)
publish ['pʌblɪʃ] veröffentlichen III 5 (88/89)
pull [pʊl] ziehen I
pullover ['pʊləʊvə] Pullover II
°**punk** [pʌŋk] Punk, Punker/in
punk (rock) [pʌŋk] Punk(rock) III Intro (6)
purple ['pɜːpl] violett; lila I
purse [pɜːs] Geldbörse II
push [pʊʃ] drücken, schieben, stoßen I
put (-tt-) [pʊt], **put, put** legen, stellen, *(etwas wohin)* tun I • **put sth. on** etwas anziehen *(Kleidung)* II; etwas aufsetzen *(Hut, Helm)* III 1 (26) • °**Put up your hand.** Heb deine Hand. / Hebt eure Hand.
puzzled ['pʌzld] verwirrt II
pyjamas *(pl)* [pə'dʒɑːməz] Schlafanzug II

Q

quarter ['kwɔːtə]**: quarter past 11** Viertel nach 11 (11.15 / 23.15) I **quarter to 12** Viertel vor 12 (11.45 / 23.45) I
queen [kwiːn] Königin III 1 (12)
question ['kwestʃn] Frage I • **ask questions** Fragen stellen
°**question word** ['kwestʃn wɜːd] Fragewort
quick [kwɪk] schnell I
quiet ['kwaɪət] leise, still, ruhig I
quite quickly/well/... [kwaɪt] ziemlich schnell/gut/... II
quiz [kwɪz], *pl* **quizzes** ['kwɪzɪz] Quiz, Ratespiel I
°**quotation marks** [kwəʊ'teɪʃn mɑːks] Anführungszeichen, -striche

R

rabbit ['ræbɪt] Kaninchen I
°**race** [reɪs] Rennen
°**race boats** [reɪs] mit Booten an Rennen teilnehmen
racket ['rækɪt]**: badminton racket** Badmintonschläger III 3 (60/164)
radio ['reɪdiəʊ] Radio I • **on the radio** im Radio I
railway ['reɪlweɪ] Eisenbahn II
rain [reɪn] Regen II
rain [reɪn] regnen II
rainy ['reɪni] regnerisch II
ran [ræn] *siehe* **run**
rang [ræŋ] *siehe* **ring**
rap [ræp] Rap *(rhythmischer Sprechgesang)* I
rap (-pp-) [ræp] rappen III Intro (6)
rapids *(pl)* ['ræpɪdz] Stromschnellen III 4 (82)
rapper ['ræpə] Rapper/in III 4 (70)
RE [ˌɑːr_'iː]**, Religious Education** [rɪˌlɪdʒəs_edʒu'keɪʃn] Religion, Religionsunterricht I
read [riːd]**, read, read** lesen I **read on** weiterlesen III 1 (13/152) °**read out** vorlesen • °**Read out loud.** Lies laut vor. • °**Read the poem to a partner.** Lies das Gedicht einem Partner/einer Partnerin vor.
read [red] *siehe* **read**
reader ['riːdə] Leser/in II
ready ['redi] bereit, fertig I • **get ready (for)** sich fertig machen (für), sich vorbereiten (auf) I • **get things ready** Dinge fertig machen, vorbereiten I

real [rɪəl] echt, wirklich I • **real late** *(AE, infml)* wirklich spät, richtig spät III 4 (69)
realistic [ˌriːə'lɪstɪk] realistisch, wirklichkeitsnah III 1 (27)
really ['rɪəli] wirklich I
reason ['riːzn] Grund, Begründung I • **for lots of reasons** aus vielen Gründen I
record [rɪ'kɔːd] *(Musik)* aufnehmen, aufzeichnen III 5 (93)
record ['rekɔːd] Schallplatte III 5 (93)
recorder [rɪ'kɔːdə] Blockflöte III Intro (11)
recording [rɪ'kɔːdɪŋ] Aufnahme, Aufzeichnung III Intro (11)
recycled [ˌriː'saɪkld] wiederverwertet, wiederverwendet, recycelt II
recycling [ˌriː'saɪklɪŋ] Wiederverwertung, Recycling II
red [red] rot I
refer to (-rr-) [rɪ'fɜː] sich beziehen auf III 3 (55)
reggae ['regeɪ] Reggae III Intro (6)
rehearsal [rɪ'hɜːsl] Probe *(am Theater)* I
rehearse [rɪ'hɜːs] proben *(am Theater)* I
°**relationship** [rɪ'leɪʃnʃɪp] Beziehung
relax [rɪ'læks] (sich) entspannen, sich ausruhen II
relaxed [rɪ'lækst] locker, entspannt III 4 (76)
release [rɪ'liːs] *(CD, Film usw.)* herausbringen, auf den Markt bringen III 5 (93)
°**religious** [rɪ'lɪdʒəs] religiös
remember sth. [rɪ'membə] **1.** sich an etwas erinnern I **2.** sich etwas merken I °**Remember ...** Denk dran, ...
report (on) [rɪ'pɔːt] Bericht, Reportage (über) I
report (to sb.) [rɪ'pɔːt] (jm.) berichten II
represent [ˌreprɪ'zent] repräsentieren, vertreten III 3 (104)
°**research** *(no pl)* [rɪ'sɜːtʃ, 'riːsɜːtʃ] Nachforschung(en), Erkundigung(en)
°**researcher** [rɪ'sɜːtʃə]**: film researcher** Filmrechercheur/in
°**reserve** [rɪ'zɜːv] Reservat, Schutzgebiet
°**responsible (for)** [rɪ'spɒnsəbl] verantwortlich (für)
rest [rest] Rest II
restaurant ['restrɒnt] Restaurant II
result [rɪ'zʌlt] Ergebnis, Resultat I
return ticket [rɪ'tɜːn ˌtɪkɪt] Rückfahrkarte II

revise [rɪ'vaɪz] **1.** überarbeiten III 4 (80) **2.** wiederholen III 4 (80)
revision [rɪ'vɪʒn] Wiederholung *(des Lernstoffs)* I
°**rewrite** [ˌriː'raɪt]**, rewrote, rewritten** umschreiben, neu schreiben
°**rewritten** [ˌriː'rɪtn] *siehe* **rewrite**
°**rewrote** [ˌriː'rəʊt] *siehe* **rewrite**
rhino ['raɪnəʊ] Nashorn II
rich [rɪtʃ] reich II
ridden ['rɪdn] *siehe* **ride**
riddle ['rɪdl] Rätsel III 5 (91)
ride [raɪd]**, rode, ridden** reiten I **go riding** ['raɪdɪŋ] reiten gehen I **ride a bike** Rad fahren I
ride [raɪd]**: (bike) ride** (Rad-)Fahrt, (Rad-)Tour II • **take a ride** eine Fahrt machen III 3 (66)
riding boots *(pl)* ['raɪdɪŋ buːts] Reitstiefel III 3 (66)
riding hat ['raɪdɪŋ hæt] Reitkappe, Reiterhelm III 3 (66)
right [raɪt] richtig I • **all right** [ɔːl 'raɪt] gut, in Ordnung II • **be right** Recht haben I • **That's right.** Das ist richtig. / Das stimmt. I • **You need a school bag, right?** Du brauchst eine Schultasche, stimmt's? / nicht wahr? I
right [raɪt] rechte(r, s) II • **look right** nach rechts schauen II • **on the right** rechts, auf der rechten Seite I • **turn right** (nach) rechts abbiegen II
right [raɪt]**: right after lunch** direkt/gleich nach dem Mittagessen I **right now** jetzt sofort; jetzt gerade I • **right behind you** direkt/genau hinter dir II
ring [rɪŋ] Ring II
ring [rɪŋ]**, rang, rung** klingeln, läuten II
ringtone ['rɪŋtəʊn] Klingelton III 2 (32)
river ['rɪvə] Fluss II
road [rəʊd] Straße I • **Park Road** [ˌpɑːk 'rəʊd] Parkstraße I
°**roadie** ['rəʊdi] *(infml)* Roadie *(Helfer einer Band, zuständig für Auf- und Abbau der Anlage)*
°**road manager** ['rəʊd ˌmænɪdʒə] *Begleiter/in einer Band auf Tournee (organisiert z.B. die Reiseunterkünfte)*
rock [rɒk] Fels, Felsen III 2 (30)
rock (music) [rɒk] Rock(musik) III Intro (6)
rode [rəʊd] *siehe* **ride**
role [rəʊl] Rolle III 2 (41)
role play ['rəʊl pleɪ] Rollenspiel II

roll [rəʊl] Brötchen I
Roman ['rəʊmən] römisch; Römer, Römerin II
room [ruːm, rʊm] Raum, Zimmer I
°**root** [ruːt] Wurzel
round [raʊnd] rund II
round [raʊnd] um ... (herum); in ... umher II • **the other way round** anders herum II
°**route** [ruːt] Route, Weg
royal ['rɔɪəl] königlich III 1 (12)
rubber ['rʌbə] Radiergummi I
rubbish ['rʌbɪʃ] (Haus-)Müll, Abfall II
rucksack ['rʌksæk] Rucksack III 2 (34)
rude [ruːd] unhöflich, unverschämt II
rule [ruːl] Regel, Vorschrift III 4 (77)
ruler ['ruːlə] Lineal I
run [rʌn] (Wett-)Lauf II
run (-nn-) [rʌn]**, ran, run** laufen, rennen I
°**runaway** ['rʌnəweɪ] Ausreißer/in
rung [rʌŋ] *siehe* **ring**
runner ['rʌnə] Läufer/in II
°**running head** [ˌrʌnɪŋ 'hed] Leitwort *(am Kopf einer Wörterbuchseite)*
running shoes ['rʌnɪŋ ʃuːz] Laufschuhe III 3 (60/164)
running track ['rʌnɪŋ træk] Laufbahn *(Sport)* III 3 (60/164)
rush hour ['rʌʃ_aʊə] Hauptverkehrszeit III 1 (14)

S

sad [sæd] traurig II
saddle ['sædl] Sattel III 3 (60/164)
safe (from) [seɪf] sicher, in Sicherheit (vor) II
said [sed] *siehe* **say**
sail [seɪl] segeln II
salad ['sæləd] Salat *(als Gericht oder Beilage)* I
salmon ['sæmən]**,** *pl* **salmon** Lachs III 2 (30)
salt [sɔːlt] Salz III 3 (62/164)
same [seɪm]**: the same ...** der-/die-/dasselbe ...; dieselben ... I • **be/look the same** gleich sein/aussehen I
sandal ['sændl] Sandale II
sandwich ['sænwɪtʃ, 'sænwɪdʒ] Sandwich, *(zusammengeklapptes)* belegtes Brot I
sang [sæŋ] *siehe* **sing**
sat [sæt] *siehe* **sit**
Saturday ['sætədeɪ, 'sætədi] Samstag, Sonnabend I
sauna ['sɔːnə] Sauna II • **have a sauna** in die Sauna gehen II

sausage ['sɒsɪdʒ] (Brat-, Bock-) Würstchen, Wurst I
save [seɪv]
1. retten II
2. sparen II
saw [sɔː] *siehe* **see**
saxophone ['sæksəfəʊn] Saxophon III Intro (11)
say [seɪ], **said, said** sagen I • **It says here: ...** Hier steht: ... / Es heißt hier: ... II • **say goodbye** sich verabschieden I • **Say hi to Dilip for me.** Grüß Dilip von mir. I **say sorry** sich entschuldigen II
scan (-nn-) [skæn]
°**1.** (ein)scannen
2. scan a text einen Text schnell nach bestimmten Wörtern/Informationen absuchen II
scared [skeəd] verängstigt II • **be scared (of)** Angst haben (vor) I
scary ['skeəri] unheimlich; gruselig I
scene [siːn] Szene I
school [skuːl] Schule I • **at school** in der Schule I
school bag ['skuːl bæg] Schultasche I
school subject ['sʌbdʒɪkt] Schulfach I
science ['saɪəns] Naturwissenschaft I
°**scientist** ['saɪəntɪst] (Natur-)Wissenschaftler/in
score [skɔː] Spielstand; Punktestand III 3 (54/162) • **final score** Endstand *(beim Sport)* III 3 (54/162) **What's the score?** Wie steht es? *(beim Sport)* III 3 (54/162)
► S.162 A football match
score (a goal) [skɔː] ein Tor schießen, einen Treffer erzielen III 3 (54)
°**Scots** *(pl)* [skɒts] Schotten
°**Scottish** ['skɒtɪʃ] schottisch
sea [siː] Meer, *(die)* See I
search (for) [sɜːtʃ] suchen (nach) II
°**search engine** ['sɜːtʃ_ˌendʒɪn] Suchmaschine
second ['sekənd] zweite(r, s) I
second-hand [ˌsekənd 'hænd] gebraucht; aus zweiter Hand III 1 (13)
°**secretly** ['siːkrətli] heimlich, insgeheim
section ['sekʃn] Abschnitt, Teil, (Themen-)Bereich III 5 (88/89)
see [siː], **saw, seen**
1. sehen I
2. see sb. jn. besuchen, jn. aufsuchen II
See? Siehst du? I • **See you.** Tschüs. / Bis bald. I • **Wait and see!** Wart's ab! III Intro (11)

°**seem (to do)** [siːm] (zu tun) scheinen
seen [siːn] *siehe* **see**
sell [sel], **sold, sold** verkaufen I
be sold out ausverkauft sein, vergriffen sein III 5 (91)
semi-final [ˌsemi'faɪnl] Halbfinale III 3 (52)
send [send], **sent, sent** senden, schicken II
sent [sent] *siehe* **send**
sentence ['sentəns] Satz I
September [sep'tembə] September I
series, *pl* **series** ['sɪəriːz] (Sende-) Reihe, Serie II
set a trap (for sb.) (-tt-) [set], **set, set** (jm.) eine Falle stellen II
set meal [ˌset 'miːl] Menü III 1 (16/154)
settle down [ˌsetl 'daʊn] sich eingewöhnen III 5 (91)
°**settler** ['setlə] Siedler/in
°**sex** [seks] Geschlecht
shadow ['ʃædəʊ] Schatten III 1 (27)
share sth. (with) [ʃeə] sich etwas teilen (mit) I
she [ʃiː] sie I
sheep, *pl* **sheep** [ʃiːp] Schaf II
shelf [ʃelf], *pl* **shelves** [ʃelvz] Regal(brett) I
shine [ʃaɪn], **shone, shone** scheinen *(Sonne)* II
ship [ʃɪp] Schiff I
shirt [ʃɜːt] Hemd I
shiver ['ʃɪvə] zittern II
shoe [ʃuː] Schuh I
shone [ʃɒn] *siehe* **shine**
shop [ʃɒp] Laden, Geschäft I
shop (-pp-) [ʃɒp] einkaufen (gehen) I
shop assistant ['ʃɒp_əˌsɪstənt] Verkäufer/in I
shopping ['ʃɒpɪŋ] (das) Einkaufen I
go shopping einkaufen gehen I
shopping list Einkaufsliste I
shopping mall ['ʃɒpɪŋ mɔːl] *(großes)* Einkaufszentrum III 4 (71)
shop window [ˌʃɒp 'wɪndəʊ] Schaufenster II
short [ʃɔːt] kurz I
°**shortbread** ['ʃɔːtbred] *schottischer Butterkeks*
shorts *(pl)* [ʃɔːts] Shorts, kurze Hose I
shot [ʃɒt]
1. Schuss III 3 (57)
°**2.** Szene *(beim Filmen)*
winning shot Siegtreffer, Siegesschuss III 3 (57)
°**shot put** ['ʃɒt pʊt] Kugelstoßen
°**should** [ʃəd, ʃʊd]: **you should** du solltest

shoulder ['ʃəʊldə] Schulter I
shout [ʃaʊt] schreien, rufen I
shout at sb. jn. anschreien I
show [ʃəʊ] Show, Vorstellung I
show [ʃəʊ], **showed, shown** zeigen I
shower ['ʃaʊə] Dusche I • **have a shower** (sich) duschen I
shown [ʃəʊn] *siehe* **show**
shut up [ˌʃʌt_'ʌp], **shut, shut** den Mund halten II
shy [ʃaɪ] schüchtern, scheu II
side [saɪd] Seite II
sights *(pl)* [saɪts] Sehenswürdigkeiten III 1 (12)
sign [saɪn] Schild; Zeichen III 1 (26)
silence ['saɪləns] Stille; Schweigen III 5 (90)
silent letter [ˌsaɪlənt 'letə] „stummer" Buchstabe *(nicht gesprochener Buchstabe)* II
silly ['sɪli] albern, dumm III 4 (80)
sing [sɪŋ], **sang, sung** singen I
singer ['sɪŋə] Sänger/in II
single ['sɪŋgl] ledig, alleinstehend I
single ['sɪŋgl] Single III 5 (93)
single (ticket) ['sɪŋgl] einfache Fahrkarte *(nur Hinfahrt)* III 1 (14)
sink [sɪŋk] Spüle, Spülbecken I
sister ['sɪstə] Schwester I
sit (-tt-) [sɪt], **sat, sat** sitzen; sich setzen I • **sit down** sich hinsetzen II • **Sit with me.** Setz dich zu mir. / Setzt euch zu mir. I
°**situation** [ˌsɪtʃu'eɪʃn] Situation
size [saɪz] Größe I
skate [skeɪt] Inliner/Skateboard fahren I; Schlittschuh laufen, eislaufen II
skateboard ['skeɪtbɔːd] Skateboard I
skates *(pl)* [skeɪts] Inliner I
sketch [sketʃ] Sketch I
ski [skiː] Ski III 3 (60/164) • **ski slope** ['skiː sləʊp] Skipiste III 3 (60/164)
ski [skiː] Ski laufen/fahren III 3 (60)
skills file ['skɪlz faɪl] *Anhang mit Lern- und Arbeitstechniken* I
skim a text (-mm-) [skɪm] einen Text überfliegen *(um den Inhalt grob zu erfassen)* III 5 (90)
skirt [skɜːt] Rock II
ski slope ['skiː sləʊp] Skipiste III 3 (60/164)
sky [skaɪ] Himmel II • **in the sky** am Himmel II
°**skyscraper** ['skaɪskreɪpə] Wolkenkratzer
slave [sleɪv] Sklave, Sklavin II
sledge [sledʒ] Schlitten III 3 (104)
sleep [sliːp] Schlaf III 4 (69/166)

sleep [sliːp]**, slept, slept** schlafen I
sleepover ['sliːpəʊvə] Schlafparty III 4 (69)
slept [slept] *siehe* **sleep**
slow [sləʊ] langsam II
small [smɔːl] klein II
smell [smel] riechen II
smell [smel] Geruch II
smile [smaɪl] lächeln I • **smile at sb.** jn. anlächeln II
smile [smaɪl] Lächeln II
smoke [sməʊk] rauchen II
smoke [sməʊk] Rauch II
snack [snæk] Snack, Imbiss II
snake [sneɪk] Schlange I
snow [snəʊ] Schnee II
snowshoe ['snəʊʃuː] Schneeschuh III 4 (69/166)
snowshoeing ['snəʊʃuːɪŋ] Schneeschuhwandern III 4 (69)
so [səʊ]
1. also; deshalb, daher I • **So?** Und? / Na und? II
2. so sweet so süß I • **so far** bis jetzt, bis hierher I
3. so that sodass, damit III 5 (90)
4. I think so. Ich glaube (ja). I
I don't think so. Das finde/glaube ich nicht. I • **Do you really think so?** Meinst du wirklich? / Glaubst du das wirklich? II
soap [səʊp] Seife I
°**social networking websites** [ˌsəʊʃl 'netwɜːkɪŋ ˌwebsaɪts] soziale Netzwerkdienste *(Websites, die gegenseitige Vernetzungen unterstützen, z.B. Weblogs und Internet-Communitys)*
sock [sɒk] Socke, Strumpf I
sofa ['səʊfə] Sofa I
software ['sɒftweə] Software II
sold [səʊld] *siehe* **sell** • **be sold out** ausverkauft sein, vergriffen sein III 5 (91)
some [səm, sʌm] einige, ein paar I
some cheese/juice/money etwas Käse/Saft/Geld I
somebody ['sʌmbədi] jemand I
Find/Ask somebody who ... Finde/Frage jemanden, der ... II
something ['sʌmθɪŋ] etwas I
something to eat etwas zu essen I
sometimes ['sʌmtaɪmz] manchmal I
somewhere ['sʌmweə] irgendwo(hin) II
son [sʌn] Sohn I
song [sɒŋ] Lied, Song I
soon [suːn] bald I • **as soon as** sobald, sowie II

sore [sɔː]**: be sore** wund sein, wehtun II • **have a sore throat** Halsschmerzen haben II
sorry ['sɒri]**: (I'm) sorry.** Entschuldigung. / Tut mir leid. I • **Sorry, I'm late.** Entschuldigung, dass ich zu spät bin/komme. I • **Sorry?** Wie bitte? I • **say sorry** sich entschuldigen II
sound [saʊnd] klingen, sich *(gut usw.)* anhören I
sound [saʊnd] Laut; Klang I
°**sound assistant** ['saʊnd‿ əˌsɪstənt] Tonassistent/in
sound file ['saʊnd faɪl] Tondatei, Soundfile III 1 (12)
soup [suːp] Suppe II
°**source** [sɔːs] (Informations-)Quelle
south [saʊθ] Süden; nach Süden; südlich III Intro (7/151)
southbound ['saʊθbaʊnd] Richtung Süden III 1 (14/153)
south-east [ˌsaʊθ'iːst] Südosten; nach Südosten; südöstlich III Intro (7/151)
south-west [ˌsaʊθ'west] Südwesten; nach Südwesten; südwestlich III Intro (7/151)
°**souvenir** [ˌsuːvə'nɪə] Andenken, Souvenir
space [speɪs]
°**1.** Weltraum
2. Move back one space. Geh ein Feld zurück. II • **Move on one space.** Geh ein Feld vor. II
spaghetti [spə'geti] Spaghetti II
speak (to) [spiːk]**, spoke, spoken** sprechen (mit), reden (mit) II
special ['speʃl] besondere(r, s) III 1 (16) • **What's special about ...?** Was ist das Besondere an ...? III 1 (16/154)
°**speech bubble** ['spiːtʃ bʌbl] Sprechblase
spell [spel] buchstabieren I
spelling ['spelɪŋ] (Recht-)Schreibung, Schreibweise III 4 (80)
spend [spend]**, spent, spent: spend money (on)** Geld ausgeben (für) II • **spend time (on)** Zeit verbringen (mit) II
spent [spent] *siehe* **spend**
spicy ['spaɪsi] würzig, scharf gewürzt III 1 (16)
spoke [spəʊk] *siehe* **speak**
spoken ['spəʊkən] *siehe* **speak**
spoon [spuːn] Löffel III 1 (27/156)
sport [spɔːt] Sport; Sportart I
do sport Sport treiben I
sports gear *(no pl)* ['spɔːts gɪə] Sportausrüstung, Sportsachen II

sports hall ['spɔːts hɔːl] Sporthalle III 3 (60/164)
°**sportsman/-woman** ['spɔːtsmən, 'spɔːtswʊmən] Sportler/in
spot (-tt-) [spɒt] entdecken III 3 (54)
spring [sprɪŋ] Frühling I
spy [spaɪ] Spion/in I
square [skweə] Platz *(in der Stadt)* II
square km (sq km) [skweə] Quadratkilometer III 4 (68)
squeeze [skwiːz] drücken; (aus-)pressen III 5 (91)
squirrel ['skwɪrəl] Eichhörnchen II
stadium ['steɪdiəm] Stadion III 3 (56)
stage [steɪdʒ] Bühne I
stairs *(pl)* [steəz] Treppe; Treppenstufen I
stamp [stæmp] Briefmarke I
stand [stænd]**, stood, stood** stehen; sich (hin)stellen II • **stand up** aufstehen II
star [stɑː]
1. Stern II
2. (Film-, Pop-)Star I
start [stɑːt] starten, anfangen, beginnen (mit) I
start [stɑːt] Start, Anfang, Beginn II
state [steɪt] Staat III Intro (10)
statement ['steɪtmənt] Aussage, Feststellung III 2 (39)
station ['steɪʃn]
1. Bahnhof I • **at the station** am Bahnhof I
2. (radio/pop) station (Radio-/Pop-)Sender III 5 (90)
statue ['stætʃuː] Statue II
stay [steɪ] bleiben; wohnen, übernachten II • **stay out** draußen bleiben, wegbleiben III 4 (71)
steak [steɪk] Steak III 1 (24/155)
steal [stiːl]**, stole, stolen** stehlen II
steel [stiːl] Stahl III Intro (6)
steel drum [ˌstiːl 'drʌm] Steeldrum III Intro (6)
step [step] Schritt
stew [stjuː] Eintopf(gericht) III 2 (46)
°**stewed chicken** [stjuːd] geschmortes Hühnchen
°**stick** [stɪk] Stock, Stange
stick [stɪk]**, stuck, stuck:**
1. stick out of sth. aus etwas herausragen, herausstehen III 5 (91)
°**2. stick up one's nose** die Nase rümpfen
still [stɪl] (immer) noch I
stole [stəʊl] *siehe* **steal**
stolen ['stəʊlən] *siehe* **steal**
stomach ['stʌmək] Magen II
stomach ache Magenschmerzen, Bauchweh II
stone [stəʊn] Stein II

stood [stʊd] *siehe* **stand**
stop (-pp-) [stɒp]
1. aufhören I
2. anhalten I
Stop that! Hör auf damit! / Lass das! I
storm [stɔːm] Sturm; Gewitter II
stormy ['stɔːmi] stürmisch II
story ['stɔːri] Geschichte, Erzählung I
straight [streɪt]
°1. gerade, aufrecht
2. **straight on** geradeaus weiter II
strange [streɪndʒ] seltsam, sonderbar; fremd III 1 (17)
strawberry ['strɔːbəri] Erdbeere II
street [striːt] Straße I • **at 7 Hamilton Street** in der Hamiltonstraße 7 I
stress [stres] Betonung III 2 (38)
°**stressed** [strest] betont
°**stretch sth. out** [ˌstretʃ‿'aʊt] etwas ausstrecken
strict [strɪkt] streng III 4 (70)
strike [straɪk] Streik III 4 (78) • **be on strike** streiken, sich im Streik befinden III 4 (78/168) • **go on strike** streiken, in den Streik treten III 4 (78/168)
strong [strɒŋ] stark II
structure ['strʌktʃə] Struktur; Gliederung III 2 (39)
structure ['strʌktʃə] strukturieren, aufbauen II
stuck [stʌk] *siehe* **stick** • °**they stuck up their nose** sie rümpften die Nase
student ['stjuːdənt] Schüler/in; Student/in I
studio ['stjuːdiəʊ] Studio I
study skills *(pl)* ['stʌdi skɪlz] Lern- und Arbeitstechniken I
stuff [stʌf] Zeug, Kram II
stupid ['stjuːpɪd] blöd, dumm III 2 (35)
subject ['sʌbdʒɪkt] Schulfach I
subway ['sʌbweɪ]: **the subway** *(AE)* die U-Bahn II
success [sək'ses] Erfolg III 5 (88/89)
successful [sək'sesfl] erfolgreich III 5 (88/89/170)
suddenly ['sʌdnli] plötzlich, auf einmal I
sugar ['ʃʊgə] Zucker II
°**suggest** [sə'dʒest] vorschlagen, empfehlen
suitcase ['suːtkeɪs] Koffer II
°**sum** [sʌm] Summe
°**summarize** ['sʌməraɪz] zusammenfassen
summer ['sʌmə] Sommer I
sun [sʌn] Sonne II
Sunday ['sʌndeɪ, 'sʌndi] Sonntag I
sung [sʌŋ] *siehe* **sing**
sunglasses *(pl)* ['sʌnglɑːsɪz] (eine) Sonnenbrille I
sunny ['sʌni] sonnig II
supermarket ['suːpəmɑːkɪt] Supermarkt II
support a team [sə'pɔːt] eine Mannschaft unterstützen; Fan einer Mannschaft sein III 3 (54/162)
supporter [sə'pɔːtə] Anhänger/in, Fan III 3 (54)
suppose [sə'pəʊz] annehmen, vermuten II
sure [ʃʊə, ʃɔː] sicher I
surf the internet [sɜːf] im Internet surfen II
surfboard ['sɜːfbɔːd] Surfbrett II
surfing ['sɜːfɪŋ]: **go surfing** wellenreiten gehen, surfen gehen II
surprise [sə'praɪz] Überraschung II
surprise sb. [sə'praɪz] jn. überraschen III 1 (26/155)
surprised (at sth.) [sə'praɪzd] überrascht (über etwas) III 1 (26)
surprising [sə'praɪzɪŋ] überraschend, erstaunlich III 1 (26/155)
survey (on) ['sɜːveɪ] Umfrage, Untersuchung (über) II
survival [sə'vaɪvl] Überleben II
survive [sə'vaɪv] überleben II
swam [swæm] *siehe* **swim**
°**swap (-pp-)** [swɒp] tauschen
sweatshirt ['swetʃɜːt] Sweatshirt I
°**swede** [swiːd] Steck-, Kohlrübe
sweet [swiːt] süß I
sweetheart ['swiːthɑːt] Liebling, Schatz II
sweets *(pl)* [swiːts] Süßigkeiten I
swim (-mm-) [swɪm], **swam, swum** schwimmen I • **go swimming** schwimmen gehen I
swimmer ['swɪmə] Schwimmer/in II
swimming pool ['swɪmɪŋ puːl] Schwimmbad, Schwimmbecken I
swimming trunks *(pl)* ['swɪmɪŋ trʌŋks] Badehose III 3 (60/164)
swimsuit ['swɪmsuːt] Badeanzug III 3 (60/164)
swum [swʌm] *siehe* **swim**
syllable ['sɪləbl] Silbe I
synagogue ['sɪnəgɒg] Synagoge III 1 (16)

T

table ['teɪbl] Tisch I
table tennis ['teɪbl tenɪs] Tischtennis I • **table tennis bat** Tischtennisschläger III 3 (60/164)
take [teɪk], **took, taken**
1. nehmen I
2. (weg-, hin)bringen I
3. dauern, *(Zeit)* brauchen III 2 (33)
°**take a dive** eintauchen; einen Kopfsprung machen • **take notes** sich Notizen machen I • **take photos** Fotos machen, fotografieren I • °**take place** stattfinden
take a ride eine Fahrt machen III 3 (66) • **take sth. off** etwas ausziehen *(Kleidung)* II; etwas absetzen *(Hut, Helm)* III 1 (27) • **take 10c off** 10 Cent abziehen I • **take sth. out** etwas herausnehmen I
°**Take turns.** Wechselt euch ab.
I'll take it. *(beim Einkaufen)* Ich nehme es (ihn, sie). / Ich werde es (ihn, sie) nehmen. I
°**take** [teɪk] Einstellung, Take *(beim Filmen)*
taken ['teɪkən] *siehe* **take**
talent ['tælənt] Talent, Begabung III 3 (104)
talk [tɔːk]: **talk (about)** reden (über), sich unterhalten (über) I
talk (to) reden (mit), sich unterhalten (mit) I
°**talk** [tɔːk]: **give a talk** einen Vortrag/ein Referat halten
tank [tæŋk] Tank III 2 (31)
°**tartan** ['tɑːtn] Schottenstoff *(mit Schottenmuster)*
taught [tɔːt] *siehe* **teach**
taxi ['tæksi] Taxi III 1 (20/154)
tea [tiː] Tee; *(auch:) leichte Nachmittags- oder Abendmahlzeit* I
teach [tiːtʃ], **taught, taught** unterrichten, lehren I
teacher ['tiːtʃə] Lehrer/in I
team [tiːm] Team, Mannschaft I
teaspoon ['tiːspuːn] Teelöffel III 1 (27/156)
°**technology** [tek'nɒlədʒi] Technologie
teddy bear ['tedi beə] Teddybär III 2 (44)
teen [tiːn] Teenager-, Jugend- III 5 (88)
teenager ['tiːneɪdʒə] Teenager, Jugendliche(r) II
teeth [tiːθ] *Plural von „tooth"*
telephone ['telɪfəʊn] Telefon I
telephone number Telefonnummer I
television (TV) ['telɪvɪʒn] Fernsehen I
tell (about) [tel], **told, told** erzählen (von), berichten (über) I • **Tell me your names.** Sagt mir eure Namen. I • **tell sb. the way** jm. den Weg beschreiben II • **tell sb. to do**

sth. jn. auffordern, etwas zu tun; jm. sagen, dass er/sie etwas tun soll II
temperature ['temprətʃə] Temperatur II • **have a temperature** Fieber haben II
tennis ['tenɪs] Tennis I
tense [tens] (grammatische) Zeit, Tempus III 5 (96)
term [tɜːm] Trimester II
°**terminal** ['tɜːmɪnəl]: **oil terminal** Ölhafen
terrible ['terəbl] schrecklich, furchtbar I
°**territory** ['terətriː] Revier, Gebiet, Territorium
test [test] Klassenarbeit, Test, Prüfung II
°**test** [test] prüfen, testen
text [tekst] Text I
text message ['tekst ˌmesɪdʒ] SMS III 2 (32)
text sb. [tekst] jm. eine SMS schicken III 2 (32/158)
than [ðæn, ðən] als II • **more than** mehr als II • **more than me** mehr als ich II
Thank you. ['θæŋk juː] Danke (schön). I • **Thanks.** [θæŋks] Danke. I • **Thanks a lot!** Vielen Dank! I • **Thanks very much!** Danke sehr! / Vielen Dank! II
that [ðət, ðæt]
1. das (dort) I
2. jene(r, s) I
°**like that** so • **that day** an jenem Tag III 3 (66) • **That's me.** Das bin ich. I • **That's right.** Das ist richtig. / Das stimmt. I • **That's up to you.** Das liegt bei dir./Das kannst/musst du (selbst) entscheiden. III 5 (88/89) • **that's why** deshalb, darum I • **That way ...** So ... / Auf diese Weise ... III 3 (56)
that [ðət, ðæt] der, die, das; die *(Relativpronomen)* III 3 (55)
that [ðət, ðæt] dass I • **so that** sodass, damit III 5 (90)
that far/good/bad/... [ðæt] so weit/gut/schlecht/... III 5 (92)
the [ðə, ði] der, die, das; die I
theatre ['θɪətə] Theater II
their [ðeə] ihr, ihre *(Plural)* I
theirs [ðeəz] ihrer, ihre, ihrs II
them [ðəm, ðem] sie; ihnen I
themselves [ðəm'selvz] sich (selbst) III 4 (72/167)
then [ðen] dann, danach I
there [ðeə]
1. da, dort I
2. dahin, dorthin I
down there dort unten II • **in there** dort drinnen I • **over there** da drüben, dort drüben I • **up there** dort oben III 1 (12) • **there are** es sind (vorhanden); es gibt I **there's** es ist (vorhanden); es gibt I • **there isn't a ...** es ist kein/e ...; es gibt kein/e ... I
thermometer [θə'mɒmɪtə] Thermometer II
these [ðiːz] diese, die (hier) I
they [ðeɪ] sie *(Plural)* I
thief [θiːf], *pl* **thieves** [θiːvz] Dieb/in II
thing [θɪŋ] Ding, Sache I • **What was the best thing about ...?** Was war das Beste an ...? II
think [θɪŋk], **thought, thought** glauben, meinen, denken I • **I think so.** Ich glaube (ja). I • **I don't think so.** Das finde/glaube ich nicht. I • **think about 1.** nachdenken über II; **2.** denken über, halten von II • **think of 1.** denken über, halten von II; **2.** denken an; sich ausdenken II
third [θɜːd] dritte(r, s) I
thirsty ['θɜːsti] durstig I • **be thirsty** Durst haben, durstig sein I
this [ðɪs]
1. dies (hier) I
2. diese(r, s) I
This is Isabel. Hier spricht Isabel. / Hier ist Isabel. *(am Telefon)* II
this morning/afternoon/evening heute Morgen/Nachmittag/Abend I • **this way 1.** hier entlang, in diese Richtung II; **2.** so; auf diese Weise III Intro (11)
those [ðəʊz] die (da), jene (dort) I
thought [θɔːt] *siehe* **think**
thousand ['θaʊznd] tausend I
threw [θruː] *siehe* **throw**
throat [θrəʊt] Hals, Kehle II • **have a sore throat** Halsschmerzen haben II
through [θruː] durch II
throw [θrəʊ], **threw, thrown** werfen I
thrown [θrəʊn] *siehe* **throw**
Thursday ['θɜːzdeɪ, 'θɜːzdi] Donnerstag I
°**tick** [tɪk] Häkchen
ticket ['tɪkɪt]
1. Eintrittskarte I
2. Fahrkarte II
all-day ticket Tagesfahrkarte III 1 (14/153) • **return ticket** Rückfahrkarte II • **single ticket** einfache Fahrkarte *(nur Hinfahrt)* III 1 (14)
ticket machine ['tɪkɪt məˌʃiːn] Fahrkartenautomat III 1 (20/154)
tide [taɪd] Gezeiten, Ebbe und Flut II • **the tide is in** es ist Flut II **the tide is out** es ist Ebbe II
tidy ['taɪdi] aufräumen I
tidy ['taɪdi] ordentlich, aufgeräumt II
tiger ['taɪgə] Tiger II
tights *(pl)* [taɪts] Strumpfhose III 3 (54)
till [tɪl] bis *(zeitlich)* I • **not ... till** erst (um); nicht vor III 4 (71)
► S.167 German „bis"
time [taɪm]
1. Zeit; Uhrzeit I • **a long time** lange III 1 (13) • **in time** rechtzeitig II • **What's the time?** Wie spät ist es? I
2. time(s) Mal(e); -mal II
timeline ['taɪmlaɪn] Zeitstrahl III 3 (66)
timetable ['taɪmteɪbl]
1. Stundenplan I
2. Fahrplan III 2 (33)
timing ['taɪmɪŋ]: **bad timing** schlechtes Timing III 3 (55)
tip [tɪp] Tipp III 1 (13)
tired ['taɪəd] müde I
title ['taɪtl] Titel, Überschrift I
to [tə, tu]
1. zu, nach I • **an e-mail to** eine E-Mail an I • **to Jenny's** zu Jenny I • **to the doctor's** zum Arzt III 2 (44/161) • **to the front** nach vorn I • **I've never been to Bath.** Ich bin noch nie in Bath gewesen. II • **write to** schreiben an I
2. quarter to 12 Viertel vor 12 (11.45 / 23.45) I • **from Monday to Friday** von Montag bis Freitag III 2 (33)
3. something to eat etwas zu essen I • **try to do** versuchen, zu tun I • **we know what to do** wir wissen, was wir tun müssen; wir wissen, was zu tun ist III 1 (28)
4. um zu I
► S.167 German „bis"
toast [təʊst] Toast(brot) I
tobacco [tə'bækəʊ] Tabak II
today [tə'deɪ] heute I
toe [təʊ] Zeh I
together [tə'geðə] zusammen I
toilet ['tɔɪlət] Toilette I
told [təʊld] *siehe* **tell**
tolerant ['tɒlərənt] tolerant III 4 (76)
tomato [tə'mɑːtəʊ], *pl* **tomatoes** Tomate II
tomorrow [tə'mɒrəʊ] morgen I
tomorrow's weather das Wetter von morgen II
°**tongue-twister** ['tʌŋtwɪstə] Zungenbrecher

tonight [tə'naɪt] heute Nacht, heute Abend I • **tonight's programme** das Programm von heute Abend; das heutige Abendprogramm II
too [tuː]**: from Bristol too** auch aus Bristol I • **Me too.** Ich auch. I
too much/big/... [tuː] zu viel/groß/ ... I
took [tʊk] *siehe* **take**
tooth [tuːθ], *pl* **teeth** [tiːθ] Zahn I
toothache ['tuːθeɪk] Zahnschmerzen II
top [tɒp]
1. Spitze, oberes Ende I • **at the top (of)** oben, am oberen Ende, an der Spitze (von) I
2. Top, Oberteil I
topic ['tɒpɪk] Thema, Themenbereich I • **topic sentence** *Satz, der in das Thema eines Absatzes einführt* II
tornado [tɔː'neɪdəʊ] Tornado, Wirbelsturm II
tortoise ['tɔːtəs] Schildkröte I
°**tossing the caber** [ˌtɒsɪŋ ðə 'keɪbə] Baumstammwerfen
touch [tʌtʃ] berühren, anfassen II
touch [tʌtʃ]**: keep in touch** in Verbindung bleiben, Kontakt halten III Intro (11)
tour (of the house) [tʊə] Rundgang, Tour (durch das Haus) I
tourist ['tʊərɪst] Tourist/in II
tourist information Fremdenverkehrsamt II
towards sb./sth. [tə'wɔːdz] auf jn./ etwas zu II
tower ['taʊə] Turm I
town [taʊn] Stadt I
track [træk]
1. Stück, Titel, Track *(auf einer CD)* III 5 (93)
2. running track Laufbahn *(Sport)* III 3 (60/164)
traditional [trə'dɪʃənl] traditionell III 4 (72)
traffic ['træfɪk] Verkehr II
train [treɪn] Zug I • **on the train** im Zug I
train [treɪn] trainieren III 3 (54)
trainers *(pl)* ['treɪnəz] Turnschuhe II
training session ['treɪnɪŋ ˌseʃn] Trainingsstunde, -einheit III 3 (52)
tram [træm] Straßenbahn III 1 (20/154)
translate [træns'leɪt] übersetzen III 2 (35/159)
translation [træns'leɪʃn] Übersetzung III 2 (35)
transport *(no pl)* ['trænspɔːt] Verkehrsmittel III 1 (14/153) • **public transport** *(no pl)* öffentliche Verkehrsmittel, öffentlicher Personennahverkehr III 1 (14)
trap [træp] Falle II
travel (-ll-) ['trævl] reisen II
Travelcard ['trævlkɑːd] Tagesfahrkarte *(der Londoner Verkehrsbetriebe)* III 1 (14)
tree [triː] Baum I
trendy ['trendi] modisch, schick III 1 (13)
trick [trɪk]
1. (Zauber-)Kunststück, Trick I • **do tricks** (Zauber-)Kunststücke machen I
2. Streich II • **play a trick on sb.** jm. einen Streich spielen II
trip [trɪp] Reise; Ausflug I • **go on a trip** einen Ausflug machen II
trombone [trɒm'bəʊn] Posaune III Intro (11)
trouble ['trʌbl] Schwierigkeiten, Ärger II • **be in trouble** in Schwierigkeiten sein; Ärger kriegen II
trousers *(pl)* ['traʊzəz] Hose II
true [truː] wahr II
trumpet ['trʌmpɪt] Trompete III Intro (11)
try [traɪ]
1. versuchen I
2. probieren, kosten I
try and do sth. / try to do sth. versuchen, etwas zu tun I • **try on** anprobieren *(Kleidung)* I
T-shirt ['tiːʃɜːt] T-Shirt I
tube [tjuːb]**: the Tube** *(no pl)* die Londoner U-Bahn III 1 (14)
Tuesday ['tjuːzdeɪ, 'tjuːzdi] Dienstag I
tune [tjuːn] Melodie III 5 (93)
tunnel ['tʌnl] Tunnel II
turkey ['tɜːki] Truthahn, Pute/Puter III 1 (24/155)
turn [tɜːn]
1. sich umdrehen II • **turn left/ right** (nach) links/rechts abbiegen II • **turn to sb.** sich jm. zuwenden; sich an jn. wenden II
2. turn sth. on etwas einschalten I
turn sth. off etwas ausschalten II
turn sth. up/down etwas lauter/ leiser stellen III 4 (70)
turn [tɜːn]**: (It's) my turn.** Ich bin dran / an der Reihe. I • **Miss a turn.** Einmal aussetzen. II • °**Take turns.** Wechselt euch ab. • **Whose turn is it?** Wer ist dran / an der Reihe? II
TV [tiː'viː] Fernsehen I • **on TV** im Fernsehen I • **watch TV** fernsehen I
twice [twaɪs] zweimal III 2 (32/157)
twin [twɪn]**: twin brother** Zwillingsbruder I • **twins** *(pl)* Zwillinge I
twin town Partnerstadt I
type [taɪp] *(infml)* Typ III 2 (34)

U

uncle ['ʌŋkl] Onkel I
unconscious [ʌn'kɒnʃəs] bewusstlos II
uncool [ˌʌn'kuːl] *(infml)* uncool III 2 (34)
under ['ʌndə] unter I
underground ['ʌndəgraʊnd]**: the underground** die U-Bahn II
°**underline** [ˌʌndə'laɪn] unterstreichen
°**underlined** [ˌʌndə'laɪnd] unterstrichen
understand [ˌʌndə'stænd], **understood, understood** verstehen, begreifen I
understood [ˌʌndə'stʊd] *siehe* **understand**
unfair [ˌʌn'feə] unfair, ungerecht III 2 (40)
unfriendly [ʌn'frendli] unfreundlich III 2 (40)
unhappy [ʌn'hæpi] unglücklich III 2 (40)
unhealthy [ʌn'helθi] ungesund III 2 (40)
uniform ['juːnɪfɔːm] Uniform I
unit ['juːnɪt] Kapitel, Lektion I
united: the United Kingdom (UK) [juˌnaɪtɪd 'kɪŋdəm], [ˌjuː 'keɪ] das Vereinigte Königreich *(Großbritannien und Nordirland)* III Intro (6)
the United States (US) [juˌnaɪtɪd 'steɪts], [ˌjuː‿'es] die Vereinigten Staaten (von Amerika) III Intro (10)
unsafe [ʌn'seɪf] nicht sicher, gefährlich III 2 (40)
untidy [ʌn'taɪdi] unordentlich III 2 (40)
until [ən'tɪl] bis III 2 (33) • **not ... until** erst (um); nicht vor III 4 (71)
► S.167 German „bis"
up [ʌp] hinauf, herauf, nach oben I
up (the hill) (den Hügel) hinauf II
up there dort oben III 1 (12)
That's up to you. Das liegt bei dir. / Das kannst/musst du (selbst) entscheiden. III 5 (88/89)
°**update** [ˌʌp'deɪt] aktualisieren, auf den neuesten Stand bringen
upset (about) [ˌʌp'set] aufgebracht, gekränkt, mitgenommen (wegen) III 2 (35)

upset sb. **(-tt-)** [ʌp'set], **upset, upset** jn. ärgern, kränken, aus der Fassung bringen III 2 (35/159)
upstairs [ˌʌp'steəz] oben; nach oben I
us [əs, ʌs] uns I
use [ju:z] benutzen, verwenden I
°**used** [ju:zd] gebraucht
useful ['ju:sfl] nützlich III 5 (90)
usually ['ju:ʒuəli] meistens, gewöhnlich, normalerweise I

V

vacation [və'keɪʃn, *AE:* veɪ'keɪʃn] *(AE)* Urlaub, Ferien III 5 (92)
valley ['væli] Tal II • **valley floor** Talboden II
vegetable ['vedʒtəbl] *(ein)* Gemüse III 1 (16)
°**velodrome** ['velədrəʊm] Radrennbahn
°**venue** ['venju:] Veranstaltungsort, Austragungsort
°**version** ['vɜ:ʃn, 'vɜ:ʒn] Version
very ['veri] sehr I • **like/love sth. very much** etwas sehr mögen/ sehr lieben II • **Thanks very much!** Danke sehr! / Vielen Dank! II
victim ['vɪktɪm] Opfer III 1 (27)
video ['vɪdiəʊ] Video III 1 (12)
view [vju:] Aussicht, Blick II • **in my/your view** meiner/deiner Ansicht nach III 1 (28) • **point of view** Standpunkt II • **from my point of view** aus meiner Sicht; von meinem Standpunkt aus gesehen II
°**Viking** ['vaɪkɪŋ] Wikinger/in
village ['vɪlɪdʒ] Dorf I
°**virtual reality (VR)** [ˌvɜ:tʃuəl ri'æləti] virtuelle Realität *(am Rechner o. im Internet künstlich erzeugter Raum)*
virus ['vaɪrəs] Virus I
visit ['vɪzɪt] besuchen, aufsuchen II
visit ['vɪzɪt] Besuch II
visitor ['vɪzɪtə] Besucher/in, Gast I
vocabulary [və'kæbjələri] Vokabelverzeichnis, Wörterverzeichnis I
voice [vɔɪs] Stimme I
volleyball ['vɒlibɔ:l] Volleyball I
vowel sound ['vaʊəl saʊnd] Vokallaut II

W

wait (for) [weɪt] warten (auf) I
I can't wait to see ... ich kann es kaum erwarten, ... zu sehen I
Wait a minute. Warte mal! / Moment mal! II • **Wait and see!** Wart's ab! III Intro (11)
waiter ['weɪtə] Kellner II
waitress ['weɪtrəs] Kellnerin II
wake [weɪk], **woke, woken:**
1. wake sb. (up) jn. (auf)wecken III 5 (90/170)
2. wake up aufwachen III 5 (90)
walk [wɔ:k] (zu Fuß) gehen I
walk on weitergehen III 1 (13/152)
walk [wɔ:k] Spaziergang II • **go for a walk** spazieren gehen, einen Spaziergang machen II
wall [wɔ:l] Wand; Mauer II
walrus ['wɔ:lrəs] Walross III 4 (79)
want [wɒnt] (haben) wollen I
want to do tun wollen I
wardrobe ['wɔ:drəʊb] Kleiderschrank I
warm [wɔ:m] warm II
warn sb. (about sth.) [wɔ:n] jn. (vor etwas) warnen III 4 (81)
was [wəz, wɒz]: **I/he/she/it was** *siehe* **be**
wash [wɒʃ] waschen I; (auf-) wischen *(Fußboden)* II • **I wash my face.** Ich wasche mir das Gesicht. I
waste (on) [weɪst] verschwenden, vergeuden (für) III 4 (70)
watch [wɒtʃ] beobachten, sich *etwas* ansehen; zusehen I
°**watch for sth.** auf etwas achten, nach etwas Ausschau halten
watch TV fernsehen I
watch [wɒtʃ] Armbanduhr I
water ['wɔ:tə] Wasser I
wave [weɪv] winken II
way [weɪ]
1. Weg II • **ask sb. the way** jn. nach dem Weg fragen II • **on the way (to)** auf dem Weg (zu/nach) II • **tell sb. the way** jm. den Weg beschreiben II
2. Richtung II • **the other way round** anders herum II • **the wrong way** in die falsche Richtung II • **this way** hier entlang, in diese Richtung II • **which way?** in welche Richtung? / wohin? II
3. Art und Weise III Intro (11/152)
that way so; auf diese Weise III 3 (56) • **this way** so; auf diese Weise III Intro (11)
4. by the way übrigens; nebenbei (bemerkt) III Intro (7) • **No way!** Auf keinen Fall! / Kommt nicht in Frage! II
we [wi:] wir I
weak [wi:k] schwach II
wear [weə], **wore, worn** tragen, anhaben *(Kleidung)* I
weather ['weðə] Wetter II
webcam ['webkæm] Webcam, Internetkamera II
website ['websaɪt] Website II
Wednesday ['wenzdeɪ, 'wenzdi] Mittwoch I
°**wee** [wi:] *(infml)* klein *(besonders in Schottland gebräuchlich)*
week [wi:k] Woche I • **days of the week** Wochentage I • **a two-week holiday** ein zweiwöchiger Urlaub III 4 (76/168)
weekend [ˌwi:k'end] Wochenende I
at the weekend am Wochenende I
welcome ['welkəm]
1. Welcome (to Bristol). Willkommen (in Bristol). I
2. You're welcome. Gern geschehen. / Nichts zu danken. I
welcome sb. (to) ['welkəm] jn. begrüßen, willkommen heißen (in) I
They welcome you to ... Sie heißen dich in ... willkommen I
well [wel]
1. gut II • **go well** gut (ver)laufen, gutgehen III 2 (34) • **You did well.** Das hast du gut gemacht. II
Oh well ... Na ja ... / Na gut ... I
Well, ... Nun, ... / Also, ... I
2. *(gesundheitlich)* gut; gesund, wohlauf II
°**3. as well** auch
°**wellies** *(pl)* ['weliz] *(infml)* Gummistiefel *(Plural)*
Welsh [welʃ] walisisch; Walisisch II
went [went] *siehe* **go**
were [wə, wɜ:]: **we/you/they were** *siehe* **be**
west [west] Westen; nach Westen; westlich III Intro (7/151)
westbound ['westbaʊnd] Richtung Westen III 1 (14/153)
western ['westən] westlich, West- III Intro (9)
what [wɒt]
1. was I
2. welche(r, s) I
we know what to do wir wissen, was wir tun müssen; wir wissen, was zu tun ist III 1 (28) • **What about ...? 1.** Was ist mit ...? / Und ...? I; **2.** Wie wär's mit ...? I • **What an interesting life!** Was für ein interessantes Leben! III 1 (24)
°**What are the pages about?** Wovon handeln die Seiten? • **What are you talking about?** Wovon redest du? I • **What colour is ...?** Welche Farbe hat ...? I • **What else do you know ...?** Was weißt du sonst noch ...? II • **What for?**

Wofür? II • **What have we got next?** Was haben wir als Nächstes? I • **What kind of car ...?** Was für ein Auto ...? III Intro (6/151) **What page are we on?** Auf welcher Seite sind wir? I • **What's for homework?** Was haben wir als Hausaufgabe auf? I • **What's for lunch?** Was gibt es zum Mittagessen? III 1 (25) • **What's the matter?** Was ist los? / Was ist denn? II **What's the time?** Wie spät ist es? I • **What's wrong with you?** Was fehlt dir? II • **What's your name?** Wie heißt du? I • **What was the weather like?** Wie war das Wetter? II

wheel [wi:l] Rad III 1 (12) • **big wheel** Riesenrad III 1 (12)

wheelchair ['wi:ltʃeə] Rollstuhl I

when [wen] wann I • **When's your birthday?** Wann hast du Geburtstag? I

when [wen]
1. wenn I
2. als I

where [weə]
1. wo I
2. wohin I
Where are you from? Wo kommst du her? I

which [wɪtʃ] welche(r, s) I • **Which picture ...?** Welches Bild ...? I **which way?** in welche Richtung? / wohin? II

which [wɪtʃ] der, die, das; die *(Relativpronomen)* III 3 (142)

while *(conj)* [waɪl] während III 4 (81)

whisky ['wɪski] Whisky II

whisper ['wɪspə] flüstern I

whistle ['wɪsl] pfeifen II

whistle ['wɪsl] (Triller-)Pfeife; Pfiff III 1 (28)

white [waɪt] weiß I

who [hu:]
1. wer I
2. wen / wem II

who [hu:] der, die, das; die *(Relativpronomen)* III 3 (55)

whole [həʊl] ganze(r, s), gesamte(r, s) III 3 (56)

whose? [hu:z] wessen? II **Whose are these?** Wem gehören diese? II • **Whose turn is it?** Wer ist dran? / Wer ist an der Reihe? II

why [waɪ] warum I • **Why me?** Warum ich? I • **that's why** deshalb, darum I

wife [waɪf], *pl* **wives** [waɪvz] Ehefrau II

wild [waɪld] wild II

will [wɪl]: **you'll be cold (= you will be cold)** du wirst / ihr werdet frieren II

win (-nn-) [wɪn], **won, won** gewinnen I

win [wɪn] Sieg III 3 (57)

wind [wɪnd] Wind I

window ['wɪndəʊ] Fenster I

windscreen ['wɪndskri:n] Windschutzscheibe III 2 (44)

windy ['wɪndi] windig I

winner ['wɪnə] Gewinner/in, Sieger/in II

winning shot [ˌwɪnɪŋ 'ʃɒt] Siegtreffer, Siegesschuss III 3 (57)

winter ['wɪntə] Winter I

with [wɪð]
1. mit I
2. bei I
go with gehören zu, passen zu III Intro (11) • **Sit with me.** Setz dich zu mir. / Setzt euch zu mir. I

without [wɪ'ðaʊt] ohne I

wives [waɪvz] *pl von „wife"* II

woke [wəʊk] *siehe* **wake**

woken ['wəʊkən] *siehe* **wake**

wolf [wʊlf], *pl* **wolves** [wʊlvz] Wolf II

woman ['wʊmən], *pl* **women** ['wɪmɪn] Frau I

won [wʌn] *siehe* **win**

wonder ['wʌndə] sich fragen, gern wissen wollen II

won't [wəʊnt]: **you won't be cold (= you will not be cold)** du wirst nicht frieren/ ihr werdet nicht frieren II

wood [wʊd] Holz II

woodpecker ['wʊdpekə] Specht II

woods *(pl)* [wʊdz] Wald, Wälder II

°**wool** [wʊl] Wolle

word [wɜ:d] Wort I • **word building** Wortbildung II • **word field** Wortfeld III Intro (11) • °**word order** Wortstellung

wore [wɔ:] *siehe* **wear**

work [wɜ:k]
1. arbeiten I
2. funktionieren III 1 (26)
work hard hart arbeiten II • **work on sth.** an etwas arbeiten I

work [wɜ:k] Arbeit I • **at work** bei der Arbeit / am Arbeitsplatz I

worker ['wɜ:kə] Arbeiter/in II

worksheet ['wɜ:kʃi:t] Arbeitsblatt I

workshop ['wɜ:kʃɒp] Workshop, Werkstatt III Intro (10)

world [wɜ:ld] Welt I • **all over the world** auf der ganzen Welt III Intro (6/151) • °**in the world** auf der Welt

worn [wɔ:n] *siehe* **wear**

worry ['wʌri] Sorge, Kummer II

worry (about) ['wʌri] sich Sorgen machen (wegen, um) I • **Don't worry.** Mach dir keine Sorgen. I

worse [wɜ:s] schlechter, schlimmer II

worst [wɜ:st]: **(the) worst** am schlechtesten, schlimmsten; der/die/das schlechteste, schlimmste II

would [wəd, wʊd]: **you would ...** du würdest ... III 2 (35) • **I'd like ... (= I would like ...)** Ich hätte gern ... / Ich möchte gern ... I • **Would you like ...?** Möchtest du ...? / Möchten Sie ...? I • **I'd like to go (= I would like to go)** ich würde gern gehen / ich möchte gehen I • **I wouldn't like to go** ich würde nicht gern gehen / ich möchte nicht gehen I

write [raɪt], **wrote, written** schreiben I • **write down** aufschreiben I • **write to** schreiben an I °**write sth. up** etwas (schriftlich) ausarbeiten

writer ['raɪtə] Schreiber/in; Schriftsteller/in II

written ['rɪtn] *siehe* **write**

wrong [rɒŋ] falsch, verkehrt I **be wrong** 1. falsch sein I; 2. sich irren, Unrecht haben II • **go wrong** schiefgehen III 5 (95) • **the wrong way** in die falsche Richtung II • **What's wrong with you?** Was fehlt dir? II

wrote [rəʊt] *siehe* **write**

Y

yard [jɑ:d] Hof II • **in the yard** auf dem Hof II

yawn [jɔ:n] gähnen II

year [jɪə]
1. Jahr I
2. Jahrgangsstufe I
thirteen-year-old Dreizehnjährige(r) III 4 (76)

yellow ['jeləʊ] gelb I

yes [jes] ja I

yesterday ['jestədeɪ, 'jestədi] gestern I • **yesterday morning/afternoon/evening** gestern Morgen/Nachmittag/Abend I • **yesterday's homework** die Hausaufgaben von gestern II

yet [jet]: **not (...) yet** noch nicht II **yet?** schon? II

yoga ['jəʊgə] Yoga I

you [ju:]
1. du; Sie I
2. man III 2 (44)

3. ihr I • **you two** ihr zwei I
4. dir; dich; euch I
young [jʌŋ] jung I
your [jɔː]
1. dein/e I
2. Ihr I
3. euer/eure I
yours [jɔːz]
1. deiner, deine, deins II
2. Ihrer, Ihre, Ihrs II
3. eurer, eure, eures II
yourself [jə'self, jɔː'self] dir/dich (selbst) III 4 (72/167) • **about yourself** über dich selbst III 3 (65)
yourselves [jə'selvz, jɔː'selvz] euch (selbst) III 4 (72/167)
youth [juːθ] Jugend III Intro (6)

Z

zebra ['zebrə] Zebra II
zero ['zɪərəʊ] null I
zone [zəʊn] Zone, Bereich III 1 (14)

Das **German – English Dictionary** enthält den **Lernwortschatz** der Bände 1 bis 3 von *English G 21*. Es kann dir eine erste Hilfe sein, wenn du vergessen hast, wie etwas auf Englisch heißt.

Wenn du wissen möchtest, wo das englische Wort zum ersten Mal in *English G 21* vorkommt, dann kannst du im **English – German Dictionary** (S. 172–197) nachschlagen.

Im **German – English Dictionary** werden folgende **Abkürzungen** und **Symbole** verwendet:

jm. = jemandem	sb. = somebody	*pl = plural*	*BE = British English*	*infml = informal*
jn. = jemanden	sth. = something	*no pl = no plural*	*AE = American English*	

▸ Der Pfeil verweist auf Kästchen im Vocabulary (S. 150–171), in denen du weitere Informationen findest.

Tipps zur Arbeit mit einem German – English Dictionary findest du im Skills File auf Seite 127.

A

abbiegen: (nach) links/rechts abbiegen turn left/right [tɜ:n]
Abend evening ['i:vnɪŋ]; *(später Abend)* night [naɪt] • **am Abend, abends** in the evening
Abendbrot, -essen dinner ['dɪnə] **Abendbrot essen** have dinner **zum Abendbrot** for dinner
aber but [bət, bʌt]
abfahren *(wegfahren)* leave [li:v]
Abfahrt *(Abreise)* departure (dep) [dɪ'pɑ:tʃə]
Abfall rubbish ['rʌbɪʃ]
Abflug departure (dep) [dɪ'pɑ:tʃə]
Abgemacht! It's a deal! [di:l]
abhängen *(rumhängen)* hang out [ˌhæŋ_'aʊt] *(infml)*
abholen: jn. abholen pick sb. up [ˌpɪk_'ʌp]
Abkommen: ein Abkommen treffen make a deal [di:l]
Abmachung: eine Abmachung treffen make a deal [di:l]
Abreise departure [dɪ'pɑ:tʃə]
Absatz *(in einem Text)* paragraph ['pærəgrɑ:f]
abschließen *(Raum)* lock up [ˌlɒk_'ʌp]
abschneiden: etwas abschneiden cut sth. off [ˌkʌt_'ɒf]
Abschnitt section ['sekʃn]
abschreiben *(kopieren)* copy ['kɒpi]
absetzen: etwas absetzen *(Hut, Helm)* take sth. off [ˌteɪk_'ɒf]
abtrennen: etwas abtrennen cut sth. off [ˌkʌt_'ɒf]
abwarten: Wart's ab! Wait and see!
abziehen: 10 Cent abziehen take 10c off [ˌteɪk_'ɒf]
achten: auf etwas achten *(horchen)* listen for sth. ['lɪsn]
Acker field [fi:ld]
addieren (zu) add (to) [æd]
Adjektiv adjective ['ædʒɪktɪv]
Adverb adverb ['ædvɜ:b]
Affe monkey ['mʌŋki]
Aktivität activity [æk'tɪvəti]
Akzent accent ['æksənt]
albern silly ['sɪli]
Album album ['ælbəm]
alle *(die ganze Gruppe)* all [ɔ:l]
allein alone [ə'ləʊn]
alleinstehend single ['sɪŋgl]
alles everything ['evriθɪŋ]; all [ɔ:l]
alles, was wir jetzt (noch) tun müssen, ... all we have to do now ...
allgemeine(r, s) general ['dʒenrəl]
alltägliche(r, s), Alltags- everyday ['evrideɪ]
Alphabet alphabet ['ælfəbet]
als 1. *(zeitlich)* when [wen]; *(während)* as [əz, æz]
2. als Kind as a child
3. größer/teurer als bigger/more expensive than [ðæn, ðən] • **mehr als** more than • **mehr als ich** more than me
also *(daher, deshalb)* so [səʊ]
Also, ... Well, ... [wel]
alt old [əʊld]
Alter age [eɪdʒ]
altmodisch old-fashioned [ˌəʊld-'fæʃnd]
am 1. am Bahnhof at the station **am Himmel** in the sky • **am oberen Ende (von)** at the top (of) **am Strand** on the beach • **am Telefon** on the phone • **am unteren Ende (von)** at the bottom (of) ['bɒtəm]
2. *(nahe bei)* **am Meer** by the sea
3. *(zeitlich)* **am 13. Juni** on 13th June • **am Morgen/Nachmittag/Abend** in the morning/afternoon/evening • **am Ende (von)** at the end (of) • **am Freitag** on Friday **am Freitagmorgen** on Friday morning • **am nächsten Morgen/Tag** the next morning/day • **am Wochenende** at the weekend
amüsieren: sich amüsieren have fun [hæv 'fʌn]
an 1. an anderen Orten *(anderswo)* in other places • **an dem/den Tisch (dort)** at that table • **an der Spitze** at the top (of) • **an der/die Tafel** on the board • **an jenem Tag** that day • **schreiben an** write to
2. *(nahe bei)* **an der See** by the sea
3. Was war das Beste an ...? What was the best thing about ...?
4. an sein *(Radio, Licht usw.)* be on
anbauen *(Getreide usw.)* grow [grəʊ]
andere(r, s) other ['ʌðə] • **die anderen** the others • **ein(e) andere(r, s) ...** another ... [ə'nʌðə]
anders (als) different (from) ['dɪfrənt] **anders ausdrücken** *(umschreiben)* paraphrase ['pærəfreɪz] • **anders herum** the other way round
anderswo in other places
Anfang beginning [bɪ'gɪnɪŋ]; start [stɑ:t]
anfangen (mit) begin [bɪ'gɪn]; start [stɑ:t]
anfassen touch [tʌtʃ]
anfühlen: sich gut anfühlen feel good [fi:l]
Anführer/in leader ['li:də]
angehen *(Licht)* go on
angeln fish [fɪʃ]
angreifen attack [ə'tæk]
Angriff attack [ə'tæk]
Angst haben (vor) be afraid (of) [ə'freɪd]; be scared (of) [skeəd]
anhaben *(Kleidung)* wear [weə]
anhalten stop [stɒp]
Anhänger/in *(Fan)* supporter [sə'pɔ:tə]
anhören 1. sich etwas anhören listen to sth. ['lɪsn]
2. sich gut anhören sound good [saʊnd]
anklicken: etwas anklicken click on sth. [klɪk]

anklopfen (an) knock (on) [nɒk]
ankommen arrive [ə'raɪv]
ankündigen announce [ə'naʊns]
Ankündigung announcement [ə'naʊnsmənt]
Ankunft arrival (arr) [ə'raɪvl]
anlächeln: jn. anlächeln smile at sb. [smaɪl]
Anleitung(en) *(Gebrauchsanweisungen)* instructions *(pl)* [ɪn'strʌkʃnz]
anmailen: jn. anmailen mail sb. [meɪl]
anmalen paint [peɪnt]; *(bunt ausmalen)* colour ['kʌlə]
annehmen *(vermuten)* suppose [sə'pəʊz]
Anorak anorak ['ænəræk]
anpflanzen *(Getreide usw.)* grow [grəʊ]
anprobieren *(Kleidung)* try on [,traɪ_'ɒn]
Anruf call [kɔ:l]; phone call ['fəʊn kɔ:l]
anrufen call [kɔ:l]; phone [fəʊn]
Ansage *(Durchsage)* announcement [ə'naʊnsmənt]
anschauen look at [lʊk]
anschließen: sich jm. anschließen join sb. [dʒɔɪn]
anschreien shout at [ʃaʊt]
ansehen: sich etwas ansehen look at sth. [lʊk]; watch sth. [wɒtʃ]
Ansicht: meiner/deiner Ansicht nach in my/your view [vju:]
Antwort (auf) answer (to) ['ɑ:nsə]
antworten answer ['ɑ:nsə]
Anweisung(en) *(Gebrauchsanweisungen)* instructions *(pl)* [ɪn'strʌkʃnz]
anziehen: etwas anziehen *(Kleidung)* put sth. on [,pʊt_'ɒn] • **sich anziehen** get dressed [get 'drest]
Apfel apple ['æpl]
Apfelsine orange ['ɒrɪndʒ]
Apotheke chemist ['kemɪst]
Apotheker: beim Apotheker at the chemist's ['kemɪsts]
► S.161 at the hairdresser's / to the doctor's
Appetit appetite ['æpɪtaɪt]
April April ['eɪprəl]
Arbeit work [wɜ:k] • **bei der Arbeit/am Arbeitsplatz** at work
arbeiten (an) work (on) [wɜ:k]
Arbeiter/in worker ['wɜ:kə]
Arbeitsblatt worksheet ['wɜ:kʃi:t]
Arbeits- und Lerntechniken study skills ['stʌdi skɪlz]
Ärger *(Schwierigkeiten)* trouble ['trʌbl] • **Ärger kriegen** be in trouble
ärgern: jn. ärgern *(kränken)* upset sb. [ʌp'set]
Argument argument ['ɑ:gjumənt]
ein Argument vorbringen make a point
arm poor [pɔ:, pʊə]
Arm arm [ɑ:m]
Armbanduhr watch [wɒtʃ]
Art 1. *(Sorte)* kind (of) [kaɪnd]
2. Art und Weise way [weɪ]
Artikel article ['ɑ:tɪkl]
Arzt/Ärztin doctor ['dɒktə] • **zum Arzt** to the doctor's
► S.161 at the hairdresser's / to the doctor's
Atmosphäre atmosphere ['ætməsfɪə]
Attraktion attraction [ə'trækʃn]
auch: auch aus Bristol from Bristol too [tu:]; also from Bristol ['ɔ:lsəʊ]
Ich auch. Me too.
auf on [ɒn] • **auf (... hinauf)** onto ['ɒntə, 'ɒntʊ] • **auf dem Bild/Foto** in the picture/photo • **auf dem Feld** in the field • **auf dem Hof** in the yard • **auf dem Land** *(im Gegensatz zur Stadt)* in the country; *(nicht auf dem Wasser)* on land **auf dem Weg (zu/nach)** on the way (to) • **auf der Erde** on earth **auf der ganzen Welt** all over the world • **auf diese Weise** that way; this way • **auf einmal** suddenly ['sʌdnli] • **auf Englisch** in English **Auf geht's!** Let's go. • **auf jn./etwas zu** towards sb./sth. [tə'wɔ:dz] **Auf keinen Fall!** No way! • **Auf welcher Seite sind wir?** What page are we on? • **Auf Wiedersehen.** Goodbye. [,gʊd'baɪ]
aufbewahren keep [ki:p]
auffordern: jn. auffordern, etwas zu tun tell sb. to do sth.
aufführen *(Szene, Dialog)* act [ækt]
Aufgabe *(im Schulbuch)* exercise ['eksəsaɪz]; *(Job)* job [dʒɒb]
aufgebracht (wegen) upset (about) [,ʌp'set]
aufgeräumt *(ordentlich)* tidy ['taɪdi]
aufgeregt *(nervös)* nervous ['nɜ:vəs]; *(begeistert)* excited [ɪk'saɪtɪd]
aufheben: etwas aufheben *(hochheben)* pick sth. up [,pɪk_'ʌp]
aufhören stop [stɒp]
auflegen *(Musik/CDs/Platten; in der Disko)* DJ ['di: dʒeɪ]
auflisten list [lɪst]
aufmachen open ['əʊpən]
Aufnahme *(Aufzeichnung)* recording [rɪ'kɔ:dɪŋ]
aufnehmen 1. *(aufzeichnen; Musik)* record [rɪ'kɔ:d]
2. mit jm. Kontakt aufnehmen contact sb. ['kɒntækt]
aufpassen: auf etwas/jn. aufpassen look after sth./sb. [,lʊk_'ɑ:ftə]
aufräumen tidy ['taɪdi]
aufregend exciting [ɪk'saɪtɪŋ]
Aufsatz essay ['eseɪ]
aufschauen (von) look up (from) [,lʊk_'ʌp]
aufschreiben write down [,raɪt 'daʊn]
aufsetzen: etwas aufsetzen *(Hut, Helm)* put sth. on
aufstehen *(sich erheben)* stand up [,stænd_'ʌp]; get up [,get_'ʌp]; *(aus dem Bett)* get up
aufsuchen: jn. aufsuchen see sb. [si:]
auftauchen *(erscheinen)* appear [ə'pɪə]
Auftritt *(Konzert)* gig [gɪg] *(infml)*
einen Auftritt haben *(ein Konzert geben)* do a gig
aufwachen wake up [,weɪk_'ʌp]
aufwachsen grow up [,grəʊ_'ʌp]
aufwecken: jn. aufwecken wake sb. (up) [,weɪk_'ʌp]
aufwischen *(Fußboden)* wash [wɒʃ]
aufzählen *(auflisten)* list [lɪst]
aufzeichnen *(Musik)* record [rɪ'kɔ:d]
Aufzeichnung *(Aufnahme)* recording [rɪ'kɔ:dɪŋ]
Aufzug lift [lɪft] *(BE)*; elevator ['elɪveɪtə] *(AE)*
Auge eye [aɪ]
Augenblick moment ['məʊmənt]
August August ['ɔ:gəst]
aus: Ich komme/bin aus ... I'm from ... [frəm, frɒm] • **aus ... (heraus/hinaus)** out of ... ['aʊt_əv] • **aus der ganzen Welt** from all over the world • **aus dem Zug/Bus aussteigen** get off the train/bus **aus ganz Wales** from all around Wales/from all over Wales • **aus meiner Sicht** from my point of view • **aus vielen Gründen** for lots of reasons • **aus zweiter Hand** *(gebraucht)* second-hand [,sekənd 'hænd]
ausdenken: sich etwas ausdenken think of sth. [θɪŋk]
Ausdruck *((Rede-)Wendung)* phrase [freɪz]
ausdrucken: etwas ausdrucken print sth. out [,prɪnt_'aʊt]
ausdrücken: anders ausdrücken *(umschreiben)* paraphrase ['pærəfreɪz]
Ausflug trip [trɪp] • **einen Ausflug machen** go on a trip
ausgeben: Geld ausgeben (für) spend money (on) [spend]
ausgehen *(weg-, rausgehen)* go out
mit jm. ausgehen *(regelmäßig)* date sb. [deɪt]
auslachen: jn. auslachen laugh at sb. [lɑ:f]

Ausland: im Ausland abroad [əˈbrɔːd] **ins Ausland gehen/fahren** go abroad
ausmalen *(bunt anmalen, kolorieren)* colour [ˈkʌlə]
auspressen squeeze [skwiːz]
ausruhen: sich ausruhen relax [rɪˈlæks]
Ausrüstung equipment [ɪˈkwɪpmənt]
Aussage statement [ˈsteɪtmənt]
ausschalten: etwas ausschalten turn sth. off [ˌtɜːn_ˈɒf]
aussehen: anders/toll/alt aussehen look different/great/old [lʊk] **fürchterlich aussehen** be a mess [mes] • **gleich aussehen** look the same
außerhalb seines Zimmers outside his room [ˌaʊtˈsaɪd]
aussetzen: Einmal aussetzen. Miss a turn. [tɜːn]
Aussicht *(Blick)* view [vjuː]
Aussprache pronunciation [prəˌnʌnsiˈeɪʃn]
aussteigen (aus dem Zug/Bus) get off (the train/bus) [ˌget_ˈɒf]
aussuchen: (sich) etwas aussuchen choose sth. [tʃuːz]
Austausch *(Schüleraustausch)* exchange [ɪksˈtʃeɪndʒ]
Austauschschüler/in exchange student [ɪksˈtʃeɪndʒ ˌstjuːdnt]
ausverkauft sein be sold out [ˌsəʊld_ˈaʊt]
auswählen choose [tʃuːz]
ausziehen 1. *(aus Wohnung)* move out [ˌmuːv_ˈaʊt] **2. etwas ausziehen** *(Kleidung)* take sth. off [ˌteɪk_ˈɒf]
Auto car [kɑː]
Autofahrt drive [draɪv]
Autsch! Ouch! [aʊtʃ]

B

Baby baby [ˈbeɪbi] • **ein Baby bekommen** have a baby
Badeanzug swimsuit [ˈswɪmsuːt]
Badehose swimming trunks *(pl)* [trʌŋks]
baden *(ein Bad nehmen)* have a bath [bɑːθ]
Badewanne bath [bɑːθ]
Badezimmer bathroom [ˈbɑːθruːm]
Badminton badminton [ˈbædmɪntən]
Badmintonschläger badminton racket [ˈrækɪt]
Bahnhof station [ˈsteɪʃn] • **am Bahnhof** at the station
Bahnsteig *(Gleis)* platform [ˈplætfɔːm]
bald soon [suːn]
Ball ball [bɔːl]
Banane banana [bəˈnɑːnə]
Band *(Musikgruppe)* band [bænd]
Bank *(Sparkasse)* bank [bæŋk]
Bankräuber/in bank robber [ˈrɒbə]
Bär bear [beə]
Bar bar [bɑː]
Bart beard [bɪəd]
Baseball baseball [ˈbeɪsbɔːl]
Baseballmütze baseball cap [kæp]
Basketball basketball [ˈbɑːskɪtbɔːl]
Bauchweh stomach ache [ˈstʌmək_eɪk]
bauen build [bɪld]
Bauer/Bäuerin farmer [ˈfɑːmə]
Bauernhof farm [fɑːm]
Baum tree [triː]
beantworten answer [ˈɑːnsə]
bedeuten mean [miːn]
Bedeutung meaning [ˈmiːnɪŋ]
beeilen: sich beeilen hurry [ˈhʌri]; hurry up [ˌhʌri_ˈʌp]
beenden finish [ˈfɪnɪʃ]; end [end]
Begabung talent [ˈtælənt]
begeistert excited [ɪkˈsaɪtɪd]
Beginn beginning [bɪˈgɪnɪŋ]; start [stɑːt]
beginnen (mit) begin [bɪˈgɪn]; start [stɑːt]
begreifen understand [ˌʌndəˈstænd]
Begründung *(Grund)* reason [ˈriːzn]; *(Argument)* argument [ˈɑːgjumənt]
behalten keep [kiːp]
behindert disabled [dɪsˈeɪbld]
bei: bei den Shaws zu Hause at the Shaws' house • **bei der Arbeit** at work • **Englisch bei Mr Kingsley** English with Mr Kingsley • **beim Apotheker** at the chemist's **beim Friseur** at the hairdresser's
► S.161 at the hairdresser's / to the doctor's
beide both [bəʊθ] • **2 beide** *(2:2 unentschieden)* 2 all
► S.162 A football match
Beifall klatschen cheer [tʃɪə]
Bein leg [leg] • **etwas auf die Beine stellen** get sth. off the ground
beinahe almost [ˈɔːlməʊst]
Beispiel example [ɪgˈzɑːmpl] • **zum Beispiel** for example
bekämpfen fight [faɪt]
Bekanntgabe announcement [əˈnaʊnsmənt]
bekanntgeben announce [əˈnaʊns]
bekommen get [get] • **ein Baby bekommen** have a baby
belebt *(Straße; Ort)* busy [ˈbɪzi]
benennen name [neɪm]
benötigen need [niːd]
benutzen use [juːz]
beobachten watch [wɒtʃ]
Bereich area [ˈeəriə]; section [ˈsekʃn]
bereit ready [ˈredi]
bereits already [ɔːlˈredi]
Berg mountain [ˈmaʊntən]
Bericht (über) report (on) [rɪˈpɔːt]
berichten (über) tell (about) [tel] **(jm.) etwas berichten** report sth. (to sb.) [rɪˈpɔːt]
berichtigen correct [kəˈrekt]
beruhigen: sich beruhigen calm down [ˌkɑːm ˈdaʊn]
berühmt (für, wegen) famous (for) [ˈfeɪməs]
berühren touch [tʌtʃ]
Bescheid: über etwas Bescheid wissen know about sth. [nəʊ]
beschließen decide [dɪˈsaɪd]
beschreiben: (jm.) etwas beschreiben describe sth. (to sb.) [dɪˈskraɪb] **jm. den Weg beschreiben** tell sb. the way
Beschreibung description [dɪˈskrɪpʃn]
beschützen: jn. beschützen (vor) protect sb. (from) [prəˈtekt]
besiegen beat [biːt]
besondere(r, s) special [ˈspeʃl] • **Was ist das Besondere an ...?** What's special about ...?
besorgen *(holen)* get [get]
besser better [ˈbetə]
beste: am besten (the) best [best] **der/die/das beste ...; die besten ...** the best ... • **Was war das Beste an ...?** What was the best thing about ...?
Besuch visit [ˈvɪzɪt]
besuchen: jn. besuchen visit sb. [ˈvɪzɪt]; see sb. [siː]
Besucher/in visitor [ˈvɪzɪtə]
Betonung stress [stres]
betreten *(eintreten in)* enter [ˈentə]
Bett bed [bed]
Beutel bag [bæg]
Bevölkerung population [ˌpɒpjuˈleɪʃn]
bevor before [bɪˈfɔː]
bewegen: sich bewegen move [muːv]
Bewegung movement [ˈmuːvmənt]
Beweis(e) proof *(no pl)* [pruːf]
bewölkt cloudy [ˈklaʊdi]
bewusstlos unconscious [ʌnˈkɒnʃəs]
bezahlen: etwas bezahlen pay for sth. [peɪ]
beziehen: sich beziehen auf refer to [rɪˈfɜː]
Bibliothek library [ˈlaɪbrəri]
Bild picture [ˈpɪktʃə] • **auf dem Bild** in the picture
Bildschirm monitor [ˈmɒnɪtə]
Bildunterschrift caption [ˈkæpʃn]
billig cheap [tʃiːp]
Bindewort linking word [ˈlɪŋkɪŋ wɜːd]
Biografie biography [baɪˈɒgrəfi]

Biologie biology [baɪ'ɒlədʒi]
bis *(zeitlich)* until [ən'tɪl]; till [tɪl]
Bis bald. See you. ['si: ju:] • **bis jetzt / bis hierher** so far • **bis (spätestens) zehn Uhr** by ten o'clock • **von Montag bis Freitag** from Monday to Friday
► S.167 German „bis"
bisschen: ein bisschen a bit [bɪt]
bitte 1. *(in Fragen und Aufforderungen)* please [pli:z]
2. Bitte sehr. / Hier bitte. Here you are.
3. Bitte, gern geschehen. You're welcome. ['welkəm]
4. Wie bitte? Sorry? ['sɒri]
bitten: jn. um etwas bitten ask sb. for sth. [ɑ:sk]
blasen *(wehen)* blow [bləʊ]
blau blue [blu:]
bleiben stay [steɪ] • **in Verbindung bleiben** keep in touch [tʌtʃ]
Bleistift pencil ['pensl]
Bleistiftanspitzer pencil sharpener ['pensl ʃɑ:pnə]
Blick *(Aussicht)* view [vju:]
Blockflöte recorder [rɪ'kɔ:də]
blöd stupid ['stju:pɪd]
bloß just [dʒʌst]; only ['əʊnli]
Blume flower ['flaʊə]
Bluse blouse [blaʊz]
Blut blood [blʌd]
Blüte flower ['flaʊə]
Boden *(Erdboden)* ground [graʊnd]
Boot boat [bəʊt]
böse sein (über etwas/auf jn.) be angry (about sth./with sb.) ['æŋgri]
Boss boss [bɒs]
brainstormen *(so viele Ideen wie möglich sammeln)* brainstorm ['breɪnstɔ:m]
Brand fire ['faɪə]
brauchen need [ni:d]; *(Zeit brauchen, dauern)* take [teɪk] • **nicht zu tun brauchen** needn't do ['ni:dnt]
braun brown [braʊn]
brav good [gʊd]
Brief (an) letter (to) ['letə]
Brieffreund/in *(im Internet)* e-friend ['i:frend]
Briefmarke stamp [stæmp]
Brille: (eine) Brille glasses *(pl)* ['glɑ:sɪz]
bringen: (mit-, her)bringen bring [brɪŋ] • **(weg-, hin)bringen** take [teɪk] • **auf den Markt bringen** *(CD, Film usw.)* release [rɪ'li:s] • **etwas auf den Weg bringen** get sth. off the ground
britisch; Brite, Britin British ['brɪtɪʃ]
Broschüre booklet ['bʊklət]
Brot bread *(no pl)* [bred]
Brötchen roll [rəʊl]
Brücke bridge [brɪdʒ]
Bruder brother ['brʌðə]
Buch book [bʊk]
Bücherei library ['laɪbrəri]
Buchstabe letter ['letə]
buchstabieren spell [spel]
Bucht bay [beɪ]
Bühne stage [steɪdʒ]
bunt an-, ausmalen colour ['kʌlə]
Burg castle ['kɑ:sl]
Büro office ['ɒfɪs]
Bus bus [bʌs]
Bushaltestelle bus stop ['bʌs stɒp]
Bus-Monatskarte bus pass ['bʌs pɑ:s]

C

Café café ['kæfeɪ]
Cartoon cartoon [kɑ:'tu:n]
CD CD [ˌsi:'di:] • **CD-Spieler** CD player [ˌsi:'di: ˌpleɪə]
Celsius Celsius (C) ['selsiəs]
Cent cent (c) [sent]
Champion champion ['tʃæmpiən]
Chance *(Gelegenheit; Aussicht)* chance [tʃɑ:ns]
Chat *(Unterhaltung)* chat [tʃæt]
Chatroom chat room ['tʃæt ru:m]
chatten chat [tʃæt]
Chef/in boss [bɒs]
Chor choir ['kwaɪə]
Cola cola ['kəʊlə]
Comic-Heft comic ['kɒmɪk]
Computer computer [kəm'pju:tə]
cool cool [ku:l]
Cornflakes cornflakes ['kɔ:nfleɪks]
Court *(für Squash, Badminton)* court [kɔ:t]
Cousin, Cousine cousin ['kʌzn]

D

da, dahin *(dort, dorthin)* there [ðeə]
da drüben over there [ˌəʊvə 'ðeə]
daheim at home [ət 'həʊm]
daher so [səʊ]
damit *(sodass)* so that
danach *(zeitlich)* after that [ˌɑ:ftə 'ðæt]
Danke. Thank you. ['θæŋk ju:]; Thanks. • **Danke sehr!** Thanks very much! • **Vielen Dank!** Thanks a lot!
dann then [ðen]
darstellende Kunst drama ['drɑ:mə]
darum that's why ['ðæts ˌwaɪ]
das 1. *(Artikel)* the [ðə, ði]
2. *(Relativpronomen)* **das Mädchen, das ...** the girl who ... / the girl that ... • **das Auto, das ...** the car that ... / the car which ...
das (dort) *(Singular)* that [ðət, ðæt]; *(Plural)* those [ðəʊz] • **Das bin ich.** That's me. • **Das liegt bei dir. / Das kannst/musst du (selbst) entscheiden.** That's up to you.
dass that [ðət, ðæt]
dasselbe the same [seɪm]
Date *(Verabredung)* date [deɪt]
Datum date [deɪt]
dauern *(Zeit brauchen)* take [teɪk]
Decke *(zum Zudecken)* blanket ['blæŋkɪt]
decken: den Tisch decken lay the table [ˌleɪ ðə 'teɪbl]
dein(e) ... your ... [jɔ:]
deiner, deine, deins yours [jɔ:z]
denken think [θɪŋk] • **denken an** think of • **Was denkst du über ...?** What do you think about/of ...?
der 1. *(Artikel)* the [ðə, ði]
2. *(Relativpronomen)* **der Mann, der ...** the man who ... / the man that ... • **der Laden, der ...** the shop that ... / the shop which ...
derselbe the same [seɪm]
deshalb so [səʊ]; that's why ['ðæts ˌwaɪ]
Detail detail ['di:teɪl]
Detektiv/in detective [dɪ'tektɪv]
deuten (auf etwas) *(zeigen)* point (at/to sth.) [pɔɪnt]
deutlich clear [klɪə]
Deutsch; deutsch; Deutsche(r) German ['dʒɜ:mən]
Deutschland Germany ['dʒɜ:məni]
Dezember December [dɪ'sembə]
dich you [ju:] • **dich (selbst)** *(Reflexivpronomen)* yourself [jə'self, jɔ:'self]
► S.167 Reflexive pronouns
die 1. *(Artikel)* the [ðə, ði]
2. *(Relativpronomen)* **die Frau, die ...** the woman who ... / the woman that ... • **die Jacke, die ...** the jacket that ... / the jacket which ...
die (dort) *(Singular)* that [ðət, ðæt]; *(Plural)* those [ðəʊz] • **die (hier)** *(Singular)* this [ðɪs]; *(Plural)* these [ði:z]
Dieb/in thief [θi:f], *pl* thieves [θi:vz]
Diele hall [hɔ:l]
Dienstag Tuesday ['tju:zdeɪ, 'tju:zdi]
(siehe auch unter „Freitag")
dies (hier); diese(r, s) *(Singular)* this [ðɪs]; *(Plural)* these [ði:z]
dieselbe(n) the same [seɪm]
Ding thing [θɪŋ]
Dinosaurier dinosaur ['daɪnəsɔ:]

dir you [juː] • **dir (selbst)** *(Reflexivpronomen)* yourself [jə'self, jɔː'self]
▸ S.167 Reflexive pronouns
direkt: direkt hinter dir right behind you • **direkte Frage** direct question [də,rekt 'kwestʃən]
Diskjockey disc jockey ['dɪsk dʒɒki]; DJ ['diː dʒeɪ]
Disko disco ['dɪskəʊ]
Diskussion discussion [dɪ'skʌʃn]
Doktor doctor ['dɒktə]
Dom cathedral [kə'θiːdrəl]
Donnerstag Thursday ['θɜːzdeɪ, 'θɜːzdi] *(siehe auch unter „Freitag")*
doppelklicken double-click ['dʌblklɪk]
doppelt, Doppel- double ['dʌbl]
Dorf village ['vɪlɪdʒ]
dort, dorthin there [ðeə] • **dort drinnen** in there • **dort drüben** over there • **dort oben** up there **dort unten** down there
Dossier dossier ['dɒsieɪ]
downloaden download [,daʊn'ləʊd]
Drachen kite [kaɪt]
dran: Ich bin dran. It's my turn. [tɜːn] **Wer ist dran** Whose turn is it? [huːz]
draußen outside [,aʊt'saɪd]; out [aʊt] **nach draußen** outside • **draußen bleiben** stay out
Dreizehnjährige(r) thirteen-year-old
drinnen inside [,ɪn'saɪd] • **dort drinnen** in there [,ɪn 'ðeə] • **hier drinnen** in here [,ɪn 'hɪə] • **nach drinnen** inside
dritte(r, s) third [θɜːd]
Drogerie chemist ['kemɪst]
drüben: da/dort drüben over there [,əʊvə 'ðeə]
drücken push [pʊʃ]; *(pressen)* squeeze [skwiːz]
du you [juː]
Dudelsack bagpipes *(pl)* ['bæɡpaɪps]
dumm stupid ['stjuːpɪd]; *(albern)* silly ['sɪli]
dunkel dark [dɑːk]
durch through [θruː]; *(in ... umher)* around [ə'raʊnd] • **durch die Stadt** around the town
▸ S.155 around
durcheinander: alles durcheinanderbringen make a mess [,meɪk_ə 'mes]
durchführen: ein Projekt durchführen do a project
Durchsage announcement [ə'naʊnsmənt]
dürfen can [kən, kæn]; may [meɪ]; be allowed to [ə'laʊd] • **nicht dürfen** mustn't ['mʌsnt]
▸ S.158 „können" und „dürfen"
Durst haben, durstig sein be thirsty ['θɜːsti]
Dusche shower ['ʃaʊə]
duschen; sich duschen have a shower ['ʃaʊə]
DVD DVD [,diː viː 'diː]

E

Ebbe und Flut *(Gezeiten)* tide [taɪd] **es ist Ebbe** the tide is out
echt real [rɪəl]
Ecke corner ['kɔːnə] • **Sand Street, Ecke London Road** on the corner of Sand Street and London Road
Ehefrau wife [waɪf], *pl* wives [waɪvz]
Ehemann husband ['hʌzbənd]
Ei egg [eɡ]
Eichhörnchen squirrel ['skwɪrəl]
eifersüchtig (auf) jealous (of) ['dʒeləs]
eigene(r, s): unser eigenes Schwimmbad our own pool [əʊn]
eigentlich *(in Wirklichkeit)* actually ['æktʃuəli]
Eile: in Eile sein be in a hurry ['hʌri]
eilen *(sich beeilen)* hurry ['hʌri]
eilig: es eilig haben be in a hurry ['hʌri]
ein(e) a, an [ə, ən]; one [wʌn] **ein(e) andere(r, s) ...** another ... [ə'nʌðə] • **eine Menge** a lot (of) [lɒt]; lots (of) [lɒts] • **ein neuer / eine neue / ein neues** a new one [wʌn] • **ein paar** some [səm, sʌm] **eines Tages** one day
einander *(sich gegenseitig)* one another [,wʌn_ə'nʌðə]; each other [iːtʃ_'ʌðə]
einfach *(nicht schwierig)* easy ['iːzi] **einfach (nur)** just [dʒʌst] • **einfache Fahrkarte** *(nur Hinfahrt)* single (ticket) ['sɪŋɡl]
Einfall *(Idee)* idea [aɪ'dɪə]
eingeben: etwas eingeben *(in den Computer)* enter sth. ['entə]
eingeschaltet sein *(Radio, Licht usw.)* be on
eingewöhnen: sich eingewöhnen settle down [,setl 'daʊn]
einige some [səm, sʌm]; *(einige wenige)* a few [fjuː]
einigen: sich einigen (auf) agree (on) [ə'ɡriː]
einkaufen: einkaufen gehen go shopping [,ɡəʊ 'ʃɒpɪŋ]
Einkaufen shopping ['ʃɒpɪŋ]
Einkaufszentrum (shopping) mall [mɔːl]
einladen (zu) invite (to) [ɪn'vaɪt]
Einladung (zu) invitation (to) [,ɪnvɪ'teɪʃn]
einmal once [wʌns] • **auf einmal** suddenly ['sʌdnli] • **Einmal aussetzen.** Miss a turn. [tɜːn] • **früher einmal** once • **(noch) nicht einmal** not even • **noch einmal** once more/once again
einpacken pack [pæk]
eins, ein, eine one ['wʌn]
einsam lonely ['ləʊnli]
einschalten *(Computer usw.)* turn on [,tɜːn_'ɒn]
einschüchtern bully ['bʊli]
einst *(früher einmal)* once [wʌns]
einsteigen (in den Zug/Bus) get on (the train/bus) [,ɡet_'ɒn]
Eintopf(gericht) stew [stjuː]
Eintrag *(in Wörterbuch/Tagebuch)* entry ['entri]
eintragen: etwas eintragen *(in Formular)* enter sth. ['entə]
Eintragung *(in Tagebuch)* entry ['entri]
eintreffen *(ankommen)* arrive [ə'raɪv]
eintreten (in) enter ['entə]
Eintrittskarte ticket ['tɪkɪt]
Einwohner(zahl) population [,pɒpju'leɪʃn]
Einzelheit detail ['diːteɪl]
einziehen *(in Wohnung)* move in [,muːv_'ɪn]
einzig: der einzige Gast the only guest ['əʊnli]
Eis ice [aɪs]; *(Speiseeis)* ice cream [,aɪs 'kriːm]
Eisenbahn railway ['reɪlweɪ]
Eishockey ice hockey ['aɪs hɒki]
eislaufen skate [skeɪt]
Elefant elephant ['elɪfənt]
elektrisch, Elektro- electric [ɪ'lektrɪk]
Elektrizität electricity [ɪ,lek'trɪsəti]
elektronisch electronic [ɪ,lek'trɒnɪk]
Eltern parents ['peərənts]
E-Mail (an) e-mail (to) ['iːmeɪl]
End- *(letzte/r/s)* final ['faɪnl]
Ende **1.** end [end]; *(einer Geschichte, eines Films usw.)* ending ['endɪŋ] **am Ende (von)** at the end (of) • **zu Ende machen** finish ['fɪnɪʃ] • **zu Ende sein** be over ['əʊvə] **2. oberes Ende** *(Spitze)* top [tɒp] **am oberen Ende** at the top **3. unteres Ende** bottom ['bɒtəm] **am unteren Ende** at the bottom ['bɒtəm]
enden finish ['fɪnɪʃ]; end [end]
endlich at last [ət 'lɑːst]
Endspiel final ['faɪnl]
Endstand *(beim Sport)* final score [,faɪnl 'skɔː]
▸ S.162 A football match

Energie energy ['enədʒi]
Engel angel ['eɪndʒl]
Englisch; englisch English ['ɪŋglɪʃ]
Enkel grandson ['grænsʌn]; grandchild ['græntʃaɪld], *pl* grandchildren ['græntʃɪldrən]
Enkelin granddaughter ['grændɔːtə]; grandchild ['græntʃaɪld], *pl* grandchildren ['græntʃɪldrən]
entdecken discover [dɪ'skʌvə]; spot [spɒt]
Entdecker/in *(Forscher/in)* explorer [ɪk'splɔːrə]
entkommen escape [ɪ'skeɪp]
entlang der Straße / die Straße entlang along the street [ə'lɒŋ]
entscheiden: sich entscheiden (für) decide (on) [dɪ'saɪd] • **Das kannst/musst du (selbst) entscheiden.** That's up to you.
entschuldigen: sich entschuldigen say sorry ['sɒri]
Entschuldigung 1. *(Tut mir leid)* I'm sorry. ['sɒri] • **Entschuldigung, dass ich zu spät komme.** Sorry, I'm late. **2. Entschuldigung, ...** *(Darf ich mal stören?)* Excuse me, ... [ɪk'skjuːz miː]
entspannen; sich entspannen relax [rɪ'læks]
entspannt relaxed [rɪ'lækst]
entwerfen design [dɪ'zaɪn]
er 1. *(männliche Person)* he [hiː] **2.** *(Ding, Tier)* it [ɪt]
Erbse pea [piː]
Erdbeben earthquake ['ɜːθkweɪk]
Erdbeere strawberry ['strɔːbəri]
Erde earth [ɜːθ] • **auf der Erde** on earth
Erdkunde geography [dʒi'ɒgrəfi]
erfahren: etwas über etwas erfahren learn sth. about sth. [lɜːn]
Erfolg success [sək'ses]
erfolgreich successful [sək'sesfl]
erforschen explore [ɪk'splɔː]
ergänzen add (to) [æd]
Ergebnis result [rɪ'zʌlt]
erinnern: sich erinnern (an) remember [rɪ'membə]
erkältet sein have a cold [kəʊld]
Erkältung cold [kəʊld] • **eine Erkältung haben** have a cold
erklären: jm. etwas erklären explain sth. to sb. [ɪk'spleɪn]
Erklärung explanation [ˌeksplə'neɪʃn]
erkunden explore [ɪk'splɔː]
erlauben: jm. erlauben, etwas zu tun let sb. do sth. [let]
erläutern: jm. etwas erläutern explain sth. to sb. [ɪk'spleɪn]
ermorden murder ['mɜːdə]
erraten guess [ges]
erscheinen *(auftauchen)* appear [ə'pɪə]
erst only ['əʊnli] • **erst Montag** *(nicht vor Montag)* not until/not till Monday • **erst um 3** *(nicht vor 3)* not until/not till 3 o'clock
erstaunlich surprising [sə'praɪzɪŋ]; amazing [ə'meɪzɪŋ]
erste(r, s) first [fɜːst] • **als Erstes** first • **der erste Tag** the first day **der/die Erste sein** be first
erwachsen werden grow up [ˌgrəʊ_'ʌp]
Erwachsene(r) adult ['ædʌlt]
erwarten expect [ɪk'spekt] • **ich kann es kaum erwarten, ... zu sehen** I can't wait to see ... [weɪt]
erwischen *(fangen)* catch [kætʃ]
erzählen (von) tell (about) [tel]
Erzählung story ['stɔːri]
erzielen: einen Treffer erzielen *(ein Tor schießen)* score (a goal) [skɔː], [gəʊl]
es it [ɪt] • **es gibt** *(es ist vorhanden)* there's; *(es sind vorhanden)* there are
Essen food [fuːd]; *(Mahlzeit)* meal [miːl]
essen eat [iːt] • **Abendbrot essen** have dinner • **Toast zum Frühstück essen** have toast for breakfast
Esszimmer dining room ['daɪnɪŋ ruːm]
Etagenbett bunk (bed) [bʌŋk]
etwas something ['sʌmθɪŋ]; *(irgendetwas)* anything ['eniθɪŋ]; *(ein bisschen)* a bit [bɪt] • **etwas Käse/Saft** some cheese/juice [səm, sʌm]
euch you [juː] • **euch (selbst)** yourselves [jə'selvz, jɔː'selvz]
► S.167 Reflexive pronouns
euer, eure ... your ... [jɔː]
eurer, eure, eures yours [jɔːz]
Euro euro ['jʊərəʊ]
Exemplar copy ['kɒpi]

F

Fabrik factory ['fæktri]
fähig sein, etwas zu tun be able to do sth. ['eɪbl]
Fähre ferry ['feri]
fahren go [gəʊ]; *(ein Auto/mit dem Auto)* drive [draɪv] • **in Urlaub fahren** go on holiday • **mit dem Auto/Zug/Rad/... fahren** go by car/train/bike/... • **Inliner/Skateboard fahren** skate [skeɪt] • **Rad fahren** cycle ['saɪkl]; ride a bike [ˌraɪd_ə 'baɪk]
Fahrer/in driver ['draɪvə]
Fahrkarte ticket ['tɪkɪt] • **einfache Fahrkarte** *(nur Hinfahrt)* single (ticket) ['sɪŋgl]
Fahrkartenautomat ticket machine ['tɪkɪt məˌʃiːn]
Fahrplan timetable ['taɪmteɪbl]
Fahrrad bike [baɪk]
Fahrstuhl lift [lɪft] *(BE)*; elevator ['elɪveɪtə] *(AE)*
Fahrt: (Auto-)Fahrt drive [draɪv] **(Rad-)Fahrt** (bike) ride [raɪd] **eine Fahrt machen** take a ride
fair fair [feə]
Fakt fact [fækt]
Fall 1. *(Kriminalfall)* case [keɪs] **2. Auf keinen Fall!** No way! [ˌnəʊ 'weɪ]
Falle trap [træp] • **(jm.) eine Falle stellen** set a trap (for sb.) [set]
fallen fall [fɔːl]; drop [drɒp]
fallen lassen drop [drɒp]
falls if [ɪf]
falsch wrong [rɒŋ] • **in die falsche Richtung** the wrong way
Familie family ['fæməli]
Fan fan [fæn]; *(Unterstützer/in)* supporter [sə'pɔːtə] • **Fan einer Mannschaft sein** support a team [sə'pɔːt]
fangen catch [kætʃ]
fantastisch fantastic [fæn'tæstɪk]
Farbe colour ['kʌlə] • **Welche Farbe hat ...?** What colour is ...?
färben *(bunt an-, ausmalen)* colour
Farm farm [fɑːm]
Fassung: jn. aus der Fassung bringen upset sb. [ʌp'set]
fast almost ['ɔːlməʊst]
Fastfood fast food [ˌfɑːst 'fuːd]
Favorit/in favourite ['feɪvərɪt]
Februar February ['februəri]
Federball badminton ['bædmɪntən]
Federmäppchen pencil case ['pensl keɪs]
fehlen *(nicht da sein)* be missing ['mɪsɪŋ] • **Was fehlt dir?** *(bei Krankheit)* What's wrong with you?
Fehler mistake [mɪ'steɪk]
feiern: eine Party feiern have a party
Feind/in enemy ['enəmi]
Feld 1. field [fiːld] • **auf dem Feld** in the field **2.** *(bei Brettspielen)* **Geh ein Feld vor.** Move on one space. [speɪs] **Geh ein Feld zurück.** Move back one space.
Fels, Felsen rock [rɒk]
Fenster window ['wɪndəʊ]
Ferien holidays ['hɒlədeɪz] *(BE)*; vacation [və'keɪʃn, *AE:* veɪ'keɪʃn] *(AE)* **Ferien haben/machen** be on holiday

Fernsehen television ['telɪvɪʒn]; TV [tiː'viː] • **im Fernsehen** on TV
fernsehen watch TV [ˌwɒtʃ tiː'viː]
fertig *(bereit)* ready ['redi] • **sich fertig machen (für)** *(sich vorbereiten)* get ready (for) • **Dinge fertig machen (für)** get things ready (for)
Fest, Festival festival ['festɪvl]
Feststellung *(Aussage)* statement ['steɪtmənt]
Fettdruck bold print [ˌbəʊld 'prɪnt]
Feuer fire ['faɪə]
Feuerwehrfrau firewoman ['faɪəˌwʊmən]
Feuerwehrmann fireman ['faɪəmən]
Feuerwerk(skörper) fireworks *(pl)* ['faɪəwɜːks]
Fieber haben have a temperature ['temprətʃə]
Fiedel fiddle ['fɪdl] *(infml)*
Film film [fɪlm]; movie ['muːvi]
filmen film [fɪlm]
Filmstar film star ['fɪlm stɑː]
Filzstift felt tip ['felt tɪp]
Finale final ['faɪnl]
finden *(entdecken)* find [faɪnd]
Finger finger ['fɪŋgə]
Firma company ['kʌmpəni]
Fisch fish, *pl* fish [fɪʃ]
fischen fish [fɪʃ]
fit fit [fɪt]
Flasche bottle ['bɒtl] • **eine Flasche Milch** a bottle of milk
Fleisch meat [miːt]
fliegen fly [flaɪ]
fliehen (vor jm./aus etwas) escape (from sb./sth.) [ɪ'skeɪp]
Flug flight [flaɪt]
Flughafen airport ['eəpɔːt]
Flugsteig gate [geɪt]
Flugzeug plane [pleɪn] • **im Flugzeug** on the plane
Flur hall [hɔːl]
Fluss river ['rɪvə]
Flussdiagramm flow chart ['fləʊ tʃɑːt]
Flusspferd hippo ['hɪpəʊ]
flüstern whisper ['wɪspə]
Flut: Ebbe und Flut *(Gezeiten)* tide [taɪd] • **es ist Flut** the tide is in
folgen follow ['fɒləʊ] • **die folgenden ...** the following ...
Folk *(englische, schottische, irische oder nordamerikanische Volksmusik des 20. Jahrhunderts)* folk (music) [fəʊk]
Football American football [əˌmerɪkən 'fʊtbɔːl]
Forscher/in *(Entdecker/in)* explorer [ɪk'splɔːrə]
fort away [ə'weɪ]

Foto photo ['fəʊtəʊ] • **auf dem Foto** in the photo • **Fotos machen** take photos
Fotoapparat camera ['kæmərə]
Fotograf/in photographer [fə'tɒgrəfə]
fotografieren take photos [teɪk 'fəʊtəʊz]
Frage question ['kwestʃn] • **Fragen stellen** ask questions • **Kommt nicht in Frage!** No way!
fragen ask [ɑːsk] • **nach etwas fragen** ask about sth. • **jn. nach dem Weg fragen** ask sb. the way
sich fragen wonder ['wʌndə]
Französisch French [frentʃ]
Frau woman ['wʊmən], *pl* women ['wɪmɪn] • **Frau Brown** Mrs Brown ['mɪsɪz]; Ms Brown [mɪz, məz] • **Frau White** *(unverheiratet)* Miss White [mɪs]
frei free [friː] • **freie Zeit** free time
im Freien *(Außen-)* outdoor ['aʊtdɔː]; *(Freilicht-)* open-air [ˌəʊpən_'eə]
Freilicht- open-air [ˌəʊpən_'eə]
Freitag Friday ['fraɪdeɪ, 'fraɪdi]
freitagabends, am Freitagabend on Friday evening • **freitagnachts, Freitagnacht** on Friday night
Freizeit free time [ˌfriː 'taɪm]
Freizeitzentrum, -park leisure centre ['leʒə sentə]
fremd strange [streɪndʒ]
Fremdenverkehrsamt tourist information ['tʊərɪst_ɪnfəˌmeɪʃn]
Freund/in friend [frend]; *(Kumpel)* mate [meɪt] *(infml)*
freundlich friendly ['frendli]
frieren be cold [kəʊld]
Friseur/in hairdresser ['heədresə]
beim Friseur at the hairdresser's
► S.161 at the hairdresser's / to the doctor's
froh happy ['hæpi]
Frosch frog [frɒg]
Frucht, Früchte fruit [fruːt]
früh early ['ɜːli]
früher *(einst, früher einmal)* once [wʌns]
Frühling spring [sprɪŋ]
Frühstück breakfast ['brekfəst]
zum Frühstück for breakfast
frühstücken have breakfast
Frühstückspension Bed and Breakfast (B&B) [ˌbed_ən 'brekfəst]
Fuchs fox [fɒks]
fühlen; sich fühlen feel [fiːl]
führen: ein Telefongespräch führen make a call ['kɔːl]
Führer/in *(Leiter/in, Anführer/in)* leader ['liːdə]
Füller pen [pen]
funktionieren work [wɜːk]

für for [fə, fɔː] • **Was für ein Auto ...?** What kind of car ...? • **Was für ein interessantes Leben!** What an interesting life!
furchtbar terrible ['terəbl]; awful ['ɔːfl]
fürchterlich aussehen be a mess [mes]
Fuß foot [fʊt], *pl* feet [fiːt] • **zu Fuß** on foot
Fußball football ['fʊtbɔːl]
Fußballplatz, -feld football pitch ['fʊtbɔːl pɪtʃ]
Fußballschuhe, -stiefel football boots ['fʊtbɔːl buːts]
Fußballspiel: ein Fußballspiel a game of football [geɪm]
Fußballtrikot football shirt ['fʊtbɔːl ʃɜːt]
Fußboden floor [flɔː]
Futter food [fuːd]
füttern feed [fiːd]

G

Gabel fork [fɔːk]
gähnen yawn [jɔːn]
ganze(r, s) whole [həʊl] • **auf der ganzen Welt** all over the world
aus der ganzen Welt from all over the world • **aus ganz Wales** from all around Wales/from all over Wales • **Das ist ganz falsch.** This is all wrong. • **den ganzen Tag (lang)** all day • **die ganze Zeit** all the time • **ganz um die Burg herum** all around the castle
Garage garage ['gærɑːʒ]
Garten garden ['gɑːdn]
Gasse lane [leɪn]
Gast guest [gest]; *(Besucher/in)* visitor ['vɪzɪtə]
Gebäude building ['bɪldɪŋ]
geben give [gɪv] • **ein Konzert geben** do a gig • **es gibt** *(es ist vorhanden)* there's; *(es sind vorhanden)* there are • **jm. die Schuld geben (an)** blame sb. (for) [bleɪm]
Was gibt es zum Mittagessen? What's for lunch?
Gebiet *(Bereich; Gegend)* area ['eəriə]
geboren sein/werden be born [bɔːn]
gebraucht *(aus zweiter Hand)* second-hand [ˌsekənd 'hænd]
gebrochen *(Arm, Bein)* broken ['brəʊkən]
Geburtstag birthday ['bɜːθdeɪ]
Ich habe im Mai / am 13. Juni Geburtstag. My birthday is in May / on 13th June. • **Wann hast du Geburtstag?** When's your birthday?

zu seinem Geburtstag for his birthday
Gedicht poem ['pəʊɪm]
Gefahr danger ['deɪndʒə]
gefährlich dangerous ['deɪndʒərəs]; *(nicht sicher)* unsafe [ʌn'seɪf]
Gefühl feeling ['fi:lɪŋ]
gegen against [ə'genst] • **gegen sechs** *(um sechs Uhr herum)* around six
Gegend *(Gebiet)* area ['eəriə]
Gegenteil opposite ['ɒpəzɪt]
gegenüber (von) opposite ['ɒpəzɪt]
Gegenwart present ['preznt]
Geheimnis *(Rätsel)* mystery ['mɪstri]
gehen 1. go [gəʊ]; *(zu Fuß gehen)* walk [wɔ:k]; *(weggehen)* leave [li:v] **Auf geht's!** Let's go. • **einkaufen gehen** go shopping; shop [ʃɒp] **Geh ein Feld vor.** Move on one space. [speɪs] • **Geh ein Feld zurück.** Move back one space. • **in die Sauna gehen** have a sauna • **ins Ausland gehen** go abroad • **ins Bett gehen** go to bed • **ins Kino gehen** go to the cinema • **mit jm. (aus)gehen** *(regelmäßig)* date sb. [deɪt] • **nach Hause gehen** go home • **reiten/schwimmen gehen** go riding/swimming • **spazieren gehen** go for a walk [wɔ:k]
2. Es geht mir/ihm gut. I'm/He's fine. [faɪn] • **Wie geht es dir/Ihnen/euch?** How are you?
3. Es geht um Mr Green. This is about Mr Green.
4. Das geht dich nichts an! Mind your own business. [ˌmaɪnd jər‿ˌəʊn 'bɪznəs]
gehören 1. jm. gehören/zu jm. gehören belong to [bɪ'lɒŋ] • **Wem gehören diese?** Whose are these?
2. gehören zu *(passen zu)* go with
Geige fiddle ['fɪdl] *(infml)* • **Geige spielen** play the fiddle
gekränkt (wegen) upset (about) [ˌʌp'set]
Gelächter laughter ['lɑ:ftə]
gelangen *(hinkommen)* get [get]
gelassen *(locker)* easy-going [ˌi:zi'gəʊɪŋ]
gelb yellow ['jeləʊ]
Geld money ['mʌni] • **Geld ausgeben (für)** spend money (on) [spend]
Geldbörse purse [pɜ:s]
Gelegenheit *(Chance, Möglichkeit)* chance [tʃɑ:ns]
Gemeindehalle, -saal community hall [kə'mju:nəti]
Gemeindezentrum community centre [kə'mju:nəti]
Gemeinschaftshalle, -saal community hall [kə'mju:nəti]
Gemeinschaftszentrum community centre [kə'mju:nəti]
Gemüse: *(ein)* **Gemüse** vegetable ['vedʒtəbl]
genannt werden *(heißen)* be called [kɔ:ld]
genau exactly [ɪg'zæktli] • **genau hinter dir** right behind you **genau in dem Moment** just then **genau wie du** just like you
genießen enjoy [ɪn'dʒɔɪ]
genug enough [ɪ'nʌf]
geöffnet open ['əʊpən]
Geografie geography [dʒi'ɒgrəfi]
gepflegt neat [ni:t]
gerade at the moment; *(soeben)* just [dʒʌst] • **gerade dann** *(genau in dem Moment)* just then • **jetzt gerade** *(in diesem Moment)* right now [raɪt 'naʊ]
geradeaus weiter straight on [streɪt‿'ɒn]
Gerät *(Maschine)* machine [mə'ʃi:n]
Geräusch noise [nɔɪz]
gerecht fair [feə]
Gericht *(Speise)* dish [dɪʃ]
gern: Ich hätte gern … / Ich möchte gern … I'd like … (= I would like …) **Ich schwimme/tanze/… gern.** I like swimming/dancing/… • **Ich würde gern gehen** I'd like to go • **Ich würde nicht gern gehen** I wouldn't like to go • **Gern geschehen.** You're welcome. ['welkəm]
gernhaben like [laɪk]
Geruch smell [smel]
gesamte(r, s) whole [həʊl] • **aus dem gesamten Vereinigten Königreich** from all over the UK
Geschäft *(Laden)* shop [ʃɒp]
geschehen (mit) happen (to) ['hæpən]
Geschenk present ['preznt]
Geschichte 1. story ['stɔ:ri]
2. *(vergangene Zeiten)* history ['hɪstri]
geschieden divorced [dɪ'vɔ:st]
Geschirrspülmaschine dishwasher ['dɪʃwɒʃə]
geschlossen closed [kləʊzd]
Geschmack(srichtung) flavour ['fleɪvə]
Gesellschaft *(Firma)* company ['kʌmpəni]
Gesicht face [feɪs]
gestalten design [dɪ'zaɪn]
gestern yesterday ['jestədeɪ, 'jestədi] **gestern Morgen/Nachmittag/Abend** yesterday morning/afternoon/evening • **die Hausaufgaben von gestern** yesterday's homework
gesund healthy ['helθi]
Getränk drink [drɪŋk]
Gewinn *(Preis)* prize [praɪz]
gewinnen win [wɪn]
Gewinner/in winner ['wɪnə]
Gewitter storm [stɔ:m]
gewöhnlich usually ['ju:ʒuəli]
gewürzt *(würzig, scharf gewürzt)* spicy ['spaɪsi]
Gezeiten *(Ebbe und Flut)* tide [taɪd]
Gig *(Auftritt, Konzert)* gig [gɪg] *(infml)*
Giraffe giraffe [dʒə'rɑ:f]
Gitarre guitar [gɪ'tɑ:] • **Gitarre spielen** play the guitar
Glas glass [glɑ:s] • **ein Glas Wasser** a glass of water
glauben think [θɪŋk]; believe [bɪ'li:v] **Das glaube ich nicht. / Ich glaube nicht.** I don't think so. • **Ich glaube (ja).** I think so. • **Glaubst du das wirklich?** Do you really think so?
gleich 1. gleich sein/aussehen be/look the same [seɪm]
2. gleich nach dem Mittagessen right after lunch [raɪt]
Gleis *(Bahnsteig)* platform ['plætfɔ:m]
Gliederung *(Struktur)* structure ['strʌktʃə]
Glocke bell [bel]
Glück: Glück haben (mit) be lucky (with) ['lʌki] • **Viel Glück (bei/mit …)!** Good luck (with …)! [gʊd 'lʌk] • **zum Glück** *(glücklicherweise)* luckily ['lʌkɪli]
glücklich happy ['hæpi]
glücklicherweise luckily ['lʌkɪli]
Gold gold [gəʊld]
Golf golf [gɒlf]
Grad degree [dɪ'gri:]
Grammatik grammar ['græmə]
grau grey [greɪ]
grauenhaft horrible ['hɒrəbl]
groß big [bɪg]; large [lɑ:dʒ]; *(riesig)* huge [hju:dʒ]
► S.157 big – large – huge
großartig great [greɪt]
Großbuchstabe capital letter [ˌkæpɪtl 'letə]
Größe *(Schuhgröße usw.)* size [saɪz]
Großeltern grandparents ['grænpeərənts]
Großmutter grandmother ['grænmʌðə]
Großstadt city ['sɪti]
Großvater grandfather ['grænfɑ:ðə]
grün green [gri:n]
Grund reason ['ri:zn] • **aus vielen Gründen** for lots of reasons

Gruppe group [gruːp]; *(Musikgruppe)* band [bænd]
gruselig scary ['skeəri]
Gruß: Liebe Grüße, ... *(Briefschluss)* Love ... [lʌv]
Grüß Dilip von mir. Say hi to Dilip for me.
gucken look [lʊk]
gut good [gʊd]; *(okay)* OK [əʊ'keɪ]; *(in Ordnung)* all right [ɔːl 'raɪt]; *(gesundheitlich gut, wohlauf)* well [wel]; fine [faɪn] • **Es geht mir/ihm gut.** I'm/He's fine. • **gut in etwas sein/etwas gut können** be good at sth. • **gute Arbeit leisten** do a good job • **Guten Morgen.** Good morning. • **Guten Tag.** Hello.; *(nachmittags)* Good afternoon.
gut (ver)laufen *(gutgehen, klappen)* go well • **Das hast du gut gemacht.** You did well.
gutgehen *(gut (ver)laufen, klappen)* go well
Gymnastikanzug leotard ['liːətɑːd]

H

Haar, Haare hair *(no pl)* [heə]
► S.162 Words without a plural
haben have got ['hæv gɒt]; have [həv, hæv] • **Ich habe keinen Stuhl.** I haven't got a chair. • **Ich habe am 13. Juni/im Mai Geburtstag.** My birthday is on 13th June/in May. **Wann hast du Geburtstag?** When's your birthday? • **haben wollen** want [wɒnt] • **Was haben wir als Hausaufgabe auf?** What's for homework?
Hafen harbour ['hɑːbə]
Hähnchen chicken ['tʃɪkɪn]
halb: eine halbe Stunde half an hour [ˌhɑːf‿ən‿'aʊə] • **halb zwölf** half past 11
Halbfinale semi-final [ˌsemi'faɪnl]
Halbzeit half [hɑːf] • **die erste Halbzeit** the first half • **Halbzeit(pause)** half-time [ˌhɑːf 'taɪm]
Halfpipe *(halbierte Röhre für Inline-skater)* half-pipe ['hɑːfpaɪp]
Hälfte half [hɑːf], *pl* halves [hɑːvz]
Halle hall [hɔːl]
Hallo! Hi! [haɪ]; Hello. [hə'ləʊ]
Hals throat [θrəʊt]
Halsschmerzen haben have a sore throat [sɔː 'θrəʊt]
halten 1. hold [həʊld]
2. *(aufbewahren)* keep [kiːp] **etwas warm/kühl/offen/... halten** keep sth. warm/cool/open/...
3. *(behalten)* keep • **Kontakt halten** keep in touch [tʌtʃ]
4. Halt den Mund! Shut up. [ˌʃʌt‿'ʌp]
5. Was hältst du von ...? What do you think about/of ...? / How do you feel about ...?
Hamburger hamburger ['hæmbɜːgə]
Hamster hamster ['hæmstə]
Hand hand [hænd] • **aus zweiter Hand** *(gebraucht)* second-hand
Handy mobile (phone) ['məʊbaɪl] *(BE)*; cellphone ['selfəʊn] *(AE)*
hänseln: jn. mit Schimpfwörtern hänseln call sb. names
Happyend happy ending [ˌhæpi‿'endɪŋ]
hart hard [hɑːd] • **hart arbeiten** work hard
hassen hate [heɪt]
häufig often ['ɒfn]
Haupt- main [meɪn]
Hauptstadt capital ['kæpɪtl]
Hauptverkehrszeit rush hour ['rʌʃ‿aʊə]
Haus house [haʊs] • **im Haus der Shaws / bei den Shaws zu Hause** at the Shaws' house • **nach Hause gehen** go home [həʊm] • **nach Hause kommen** come home; get home • **zu Hause** at home
Hausaufgabe(n) homework *(no pl)* ['həʊmwɜːk] • **die Hausaufgabe(n) machen** do homework • **Was haben wir als Hausaufgabe auf?** What's for homework?
► S.162 Words without a plural
Hausmeister/in caretaker ['keəteɪkə]
Haustier pet [pet]
Haustür front door [ˌfrʌnt 'dɔː]
Heim home [həʊm]
heiß hot [hɒt]
heißen 1. *(genannt werden)* be called [kɔːld] • **Ich heiße ...** My name is ... • **Wie heißt du?** What's your name?
2. Sie heißen dich in ... willkommen They welcome you to ... ['welkəm]
Held/in hero ['hɪərəʊ], *pl* heroes ['hɪərəʊz]
helfen help [help]
Helikopter helicopter ['helɪkɒptə]
hell *(leuchtend)* bright [braɪt]
Helm helmet ['helmɪt]
Hemd shirt [ʃɜːt]
herauf up [ʌp]
heraus out [aʊt] • **aus ... heraus** out of ... ['aʊt‿əv]
herausbringen *(CD, Film usw. auf den Markt bringen)* release [rɪ'liːs]
herausfinden find out [ˌfaɪnd‿'aʊt]; *(entdecken)* discover [dɪ'skʌvə]
etwas über etwas herausfinden learn sth. about sth. [lɜːn]
herausnehmen take out [ˌteɪk‿'aʊt]
herausragen aus etwas stick out of sth. [stɪk]
herausstehen aus etwas *(herausragen)* stick out of sth. [stɪk]
Herberge hostel ['hɒstl]
herbringen bring [brɪŋ]
Herbst autumn ['ɔːtəm]
Herd cooker ['kʊkə]
hereinkommen come in [ˌkʌm‿'ɪn]
Herr Brown Mr Brown ['mɪstə]
herstellen produce [prə'djuːs]
herüber across [ə'krɒs]
herum: anders herum the other way round [raʊnd] • **um ... herum** round, around • **ganz um die Burg herum** all around the castle • **um sechs Uhr herum** *(gegen sechs)* around six
► S.155 around
herum-: etwas herumgeben pass sth. round [raʊnd] • **herumgehen** walk around • **herumrennen** run around • **herumspringen** jump around
► S.155 around
herunter down [daʊn]
herunterfallen (von) fall off [ˌfɔːl‿'ɒf]
Herz heart [hɑːt]
Herzlichen Glückwunsch zum Geburtstag. Happy birthday. [ˌhæpi 'bɜːθdeɪ]
heute today [tə'deɪ] • **heute Morgen/Nachmittag/Abend** this morning/afternoon/evening **heute Nacht** tonight [tə'naɪt] **das Programm von heute** today's programme
heutig: das heutige Programm today's programme
hier here [hɪə] • **Hier bitte.** *(Bitte sehr.)* Here you are. • **hier drinnen** in here [ˌɪn 'hɪə] • **hier entlang** this way ['ðɪs weɪ] • **Hier spricht Isabel. / Hier ist Isabel.** *(am Telefon)* This is Isabel. • **Hier steht: ... / Es heißt hier: ...** *(im Text)* It says here: ...
hierher here [hɪə]
Hilfe help [help]
Himmel sky [skaɪ] • **am Himmel** in the sky
hinauf up [ʌp] • **den Hügel hinauf** up the hill
hinaufklettern (auf) climb [klaɪm] **Klettere auf einen Baum.** Climb a tree.
hinaus out [aʊt] • **aus ... hinaus** out of ... ['aʊt‿əv]
hinein: in ... hinein into ... ['ɪntə, 'ɪntʊ]
hinfallen fall [fɔːl]; fall down

hinkommen *(gelangen)* get [get]
hinsetzen: sich hinsetzen sit down [ˌsɪt 'daʊn]
hinstellen: sich hinstellen stand [stænd]
hinten (im Zimmer) at the back (of the room) [bæk]
hinter behind [bɪ'haɪnd] • **im hinteren Teil (des Zimmers)** at the back (of the room) [bæk]
Hintergrund background ['bækgraʊnd]
Hintertür back door
hinüber across [ə'krɒs] • **hinüber zu/nach ...** over to ... ['əʊvə]
hinunter down [daʊn]
hinzufügen (zu) add (to) [æd]
Hiphop hip hop ['hɪp hɒp]
Hirsch deer, *pl* deer [dɪə]
Hit hit [hɪt]
Hobby hobby ['hɒbi], *pl* hobbies
hoch high [haɪ]
hochheben: etwas hochheben pick sth. up [ˌpɪk_'ʌp]
hochsehen (von) look up (from) [ˌlʊk_'ʌp]
Hockey hockey ['hɒki]
Hockeyplatz, -feld hockey pitch [pɪtʃ]
Hockeyschuhe hockey shoes [ʃu:z]
Hof yard [jɑ:d] • **auf dem Hof** in the yard
hoffen hope [həʊp]
Hoffnung hope [həʊp]
holen *(besorgen)* get [get]
Holz wood [wʊd]
horchen: auf etwas horchen listen for sth.
hören hear [hɪə] • **Na hör mal!** Come on. [ˌkʌm_'ɒn]
Hose trousers *(pl)* ['traʊzəz]
Hotel hotel [həʊ'tel]
Hotline hotline ['hɒtlaɪn]
hübsch pretty ['prɪti]
Hubschrauber helicopter ['helɪkɒptə]
Hügel hill [hɪl]
hügelig hilly ['hɪli]
Huhn chicken ['tʃɪkɪn]
Hülle cover ['kʌvə]
Hund dog [dɒg]
hundert hundred ['hʌndrəd]
Hunger haben, hungrig sein be hungry ['hʌŋgri]
Hurra! Hooray! [hu'reɪ]
Hut hat [hæt]
Hütte cabin ['kæbɪn]

I

ich I [aɪ] • **Ich auch.** Me too. [ˌmi: 'tu:] • **Das bin ich.** That's me. **Warum ich?** Why me?
Idee idea [aɪ'dɪə]
Igel hedgehog ['hedʒhɒg]
ihm him; *(bei Dingen, Tieren)* it
ihn him; *(bei Dingen, Tieren)* it
ihnen them [ðəm, ðem]
Ihnen *(höfliche Anrede)* you [ju:]
ihr *(Plural von „du")* you [ju:]
ihr: Hilf ihr. Help her. [hə, hɜ:]
ihr(e) ... *(besitzanzeigend)* *(zu „she")* her ... [hə, hɜ:]; *(zu „they")* their ... [ðeə]
Ihr(e) ... *(höfliche Anrede)* your ... [jɔ:]
ihrer, ihre, ihrs *(zu „she")* hers [hɜ:z]; *(zu „they")* theirs [ðeəz]
Ihrer, Ihre, Ihrs *(höfliche Anrede)* yours [jɔ:z]
im: im Alter von 16 Jahren at 16 **im Ausland** abroad [ə'brɔ:d] • **im Fernsehen** on TV • **im Flugzeug** on the plane • **im Freien** *(Frei-licht-)* open-air • **im Haus der Shaws** at the Shaws' house • **im hinteren Teil (des Zimmers)** at the back (of the room) [bæk] • **im Internet surfen** surf the internet **im Jahr 1948** in 1948 • **im Mai** in May • **im Moment** at the moment • **im Radio** on the radio **im Zug** on the train
Imbiss snack [snæk]
immer always ['ɔ:lweɪz] • **immer noch** still [stɪl]
in in • **in ... (hinein)** into ... ['ɪntə, 'ɪntʊ] • **in ... umher** *(durch)* around **in den Zug/Bus einsteigen** get on the train/bus • **in der Stadt umher** around the town • **in der ...straße** in ... Street • **in der Hamiltonstraße 7** at 7 Hamilton Street • **in der Nacht** at night • **in der Nähe von** near • **in der Pause** *(zwischen Schulstunden)* at break • **in der Schule** at school • **in die falsche Richtung** the wrong way • **in die Sauna gehen** have a sauna • **in Eile sein** be in a hurry • **ins Bett gehen** go to bed • **ins Kino gehen** go to the cinema • **in Schwierigkeiten sein** be in trouble ['trʌbl] **in Urlaub fahren** go on holiday **in Urlaub sein** be on holiday • **in Verbindung bleiben** keep in touch [tʌtʃ] • **in welche Richtung?** which way? • **in Wirklichkeit** *(eigentlich)* actually ['æktʃuəli] • **Ich bin noch nie in Bath gewesen.** I've never been to Bath.
indirekte Frage indirect question [ˌɪndərekt 'kwestʃən]
Infinitiv infinitive [ɪn'fɪnətɪv]
Information(en) (über) information (about/on) *(no pl)* [ˌɪnfə'meɪʃn]
► S.162 Words without a plural
Informationstechnologie (IT) information technology (IT) [tek'nɒlədʒi], [ˌaɪ 'ti:]
Ingenieur/in engineer [ˌendʒɪ'nɪə]
Inliner skates [skeɪts] • **Inliner fahren** skate
innen (drin) inside [ˌɪn'saɪd]
Innenstadt city centre [ˌsɪti 'sentə]
Insel island ['aɪlənd]
Installation installation [ˌɪnstə'leɪʃn]
installieren install [ɪn'stɔ:l]
Instrument instrument ['ɪnstrəmənt]
interessant interesting ['ɪntrəstɪŋ]
interessieren: sich interessieren (für) be interested (in) ['ɪntrəstɪd]
interessiert sein (an) be interested (in) ['ɪntrəstɪd]
international international [ˌɪntə'næʃnəl]
Internet internet ['ɪntənet] • **im Internet surfen** surf the internet
Interview interview ['ɪntəvju:]
interviewen interview ['ɪntəvju:]
intolerant intolerant [ɪn'tɒlərənt]
irgendetwas anything ['eniθɪŋ]
irgendjemand anybody ['enibɒdi]
irgendwelche any ['eni]
irgendwie unheimlich kind of scary [kaɪnd] *(infml)*
irgendwo(hin) somewhere ['sʌmweə]; anywhere ['eniweə]
irren: sich irren be wrong [rɒŋ]
IT (Informationstechnologie) IT (information technology) [ˌaɪ 'ti:], [tek'nɒlədʒi]

J

ja yes [jes]
Jacke, Jackett jacket ['dʒækɪt]
Jagd hunt [hʌnt]
jagen hunt [hʌnt]
Jäger/in hunter ['hʌntə]
Jahr year [jɪə]
Jahrgangsstufe year [jɪə]
Jahrhundert century ['sentʃəri]
Januar January ['dʒænjuəri]
Jazz jazz [dʒæz]
je? *(jemals?)* ever? ['evə]
Jeans jeans *(pl)* [dʒi:nz]
jede(r, s) ... *(Begleiter)* **1.** every ... ['evri] **2.** *(jeder einzelne)* each ... [i:tʃ]
jeder *(alle)* everybody ['evribɒdi]
jemals? ever? ['evə]

jemand somebody ['sʌmbədi]; *(irgendjemand)* anybody ['enibɒdi]
jene(r, s) *(Singular)* that [ðət, ðæt]; *(Plural)* those [ðəʊz] • **an jenem Tag** that day
jetzt now [naʊ] • **jetzt gerade, jetzt sofort** right now
Job job [dʒɒb]
jubeln cheer [tʃɪə]
Judo judo ['dʒu:dəʊ] • **Judo machen** do judo
Jugend youth [ju:θ]
Jugend- junior ['dʒu:niə]; *(Teenager-)* teen [ti:n]
Jugendliche(r) kid [kɪd]; teenager ['ti:neɪdʒə]
Juli July [dʒu'laɪ]
jung young [jʌŋ]
Junge boy [bɔɪ]
Juni June [dʒu:n]
Junioren- junior ['dʒu:niə]

K

Käfig cage [keɪdʒ]
Kalender calendar ['kælɪndə]
kalt cold [kəʊld]
Kamel camel ['kæml]
Kamera camera ['kæmərə]
kämpfen (für, um) fight (for) [faɪt]
Kanal 1. canal [kə'næl] 2. *(Fernsehsender)* channel ['tʃænl]
Känguru kangaroo [ˌkæŋgə'ru:]
Kaninchen rabbit ['ræbɪt]
Kanu canoe [kə'nu:] • **Kanu fahren** canoe [kə'nu:]
Kappe cap [kæp]
kaputt broken ['brəʊkən]
Karotte carrot ['kærət]
Karriere career [kə'rɪə]
Karte *(Post-, Spielkarte)* card [kɑ:d]
Kartoffel potato [pə'teɪtəʊ], *pl* -toes
Kartoffelchips crisps *(pl)* [krɪsps]
Käse cheese [tʃi:z]
Kästchen, Kasten box [bɒks]
Kathedrale cathedral [kə'θi:drəl]
Katze cat [kæt]
kaufen buy [baɪ]
Kaufhaus department store [dɪ'pɑ:tmənt stɔ:]
Kehle throat [θrəʊt]
kein(e) no; not a; not (...) any • **Ich habe keinen Stuhl.** I haven't got a chair. • **Ich mag kein(e) ...** I don't like ... • **keine Musik mehr** no more music
Keks biscuit ['bɪskɪt]
Kellner waiter ['weɪtə]
Kellnerin waitress ['weɪtrəs]
kennen know [nəʊ]
kennenlernen meet [mi:t]
kennzeichnen mark up [ˌmɑ:k_'ʌp]
Keyboard *(elektronisches Tasteninstrument)* keyboard ['ki:bɔ:d]
Kilogramm, Kilo kilogram (kg) ['kɪləgræm], kilo ['ki:ləʊ] • **ein 90 Kilogramm schwerer Bär** a 90-kilogram bear
Kilometer kilometre (km) ['kɪləmi:tə] **eine Zehn-Kilometer-Wanderung** a ten-kilometre walk
Kind child [tʃaɪld], *pl* children ['tʃɪldrən]; kid [kɪd]
Kino cinema ['sɪnəmə] • **ins Kino gehen** go to the cinema
Kirche church [tʃɜ:tʃ]
Kiste box [bɒks]
Klang sound [saʊnd]
klar clear [klɪə]
Klasse class [klɑ:s]; form [fɔ:m]
Klassenkamerad/in classmate ['klɑ:smeɪt]
Klassenlehrer/in class teacher; form teacher ['ti:tʃə]
Klassenzimmer classroom ['klɑ:sru:m]
Klassik *(Musik)* classical music ['klæsɪkl]
klassisch classical ['klæsɪkl]
klatschen: Beifall klatschen cheer [tʃɪə]
Klavier piano [pi'ænəʊ] • **Klavier spielen** play the piano
kleben: (auf-, ein)kleben glue [glu:]
Klebestift glue stick ['glu: stɪk]
Klebstoff glue [glu:]
Kleid dress [dres]
Kleider *(Kleidungsstücke)* clothes *(pl)* [kləʊðz, kləʊz]
Kleiderschrank wardrobe ['wɔ:drəʊb]
Kleidung(sstücke) clothes *(pl)* [kləʊðz, kləʊz]
klein little ['lɪtl]; small [smɔ:l]
Kleinstadt town [taʊn]
klettern climb [klaɪm] • **Klettere auf einen Baum.** Climb a tree.
Klingel bell [bel]
klingeln ring [rɪŋ]
Klingelton ringtone ['rɪŋtəʊn]
klingen sound [saʊnd]
Klinik clinic ['klɪnɪk]
Klon clone [kləʊn]
klopfen (an) knock (on) [nɒk]
Klub club [klʌb]
klug clever ['klevə]
km/h *(Stundenkilometer, Kilometer pro Stunde)* kph (kilometres per hour)
knapp: Das war knapp. That was close. [kləʊs]
Kneipe pub [pʌb]
Knie knee [ni:]
Knopf button ['bʌtn]
Koch cook [kʊk]
kochen cook [kʊk]
Köchin cook [kʊk]
Koffer suitcase ['su:tkeɪs]
Koje *(Etagenbett)* bunk (bed) [bʌŋk]
kolorieren colour ['kʌlə]
komisch *(witzig)* funny ['fʌni]
Komma: 10,4 (zehn Komma vier) 10.4 (ten point four)
► S.150 Numbers
kommen come [kʌm]; *(hinkommen)* get [get] • **Ich komme aus ...** I'm from ... • **Wo kommst du her?** Where are you from? • **nach Hause kommen** come home; get home • **zu spät kommen** be late **Kommt nicht in Frage!** No way! **Ach komm!** Come on. [ˌkʌm_'ɒn] **Na los, komm.** Come on.
König king [kɪŋ]
Königin queen [kwi:n]
königlich royal ['rɔɪəl]
Königreich: das Vereinigte Königreich *(Großbritannien und Nordirland)* the United Kingdom (UK) [juˌnaɪtɪd 'kɪŋdəm], [ˌju: 'keɪ]
können can [kən, kæn]; be able to ['eɪbl] • **etwas gut/schlecht können** be good/bad at sth.
► S.158 „können" und „dürfen"
könnte(n): ich/er könnte ... I/he could ... [kəd, kʊd] • **du könntest (vielleicht) Hilfe brauchen** you might need help [maɪt]
konnte(n): ich/er konnte ... I/he could ... [kəd, kʊd]
Kontakt: Kontakt halten keep in touch [tʌtʃ] • **mit jm. Kontakt aufnehmen** contact sb. ['kɒntækt]
kontrollieren *(prüfen)* check [tʃek]
Konzert concert ['kɒnsət] • **ein Konzert geben** *(einen Auftritt haben)* do a gig *(infml)*
Kopf head [hed]
Kopfhörer headphones *(pl)* ['hedfəʊnz]
Kopfschmerzen headache ['hedeɪk]
kopieren copy ['kɒpi]
Korb basket ['bɑ:skɪt] • **ein Korb Äpfel** a basket of apples
Körper body ['bɒdi]
korrekt correct [kə'rekt]
korrigieren correct [kə'rekt]
kosten *(Essen probieren)* try [traɪ]
kosten: Er/Sie/Es kostet 1 Pfund. It's £1. • **Sie kosten 35 Pence.** They are 35 p. • **Wie viel kostet/kosten ...?** How much is/are ...?
kostenlos free [fri:]
köstlich delicious [dɪ'lɪʃəs]
Kraft *(Energie)* energy ['enədʒi]
Kram stuff [stʌf]

krank ill [ɪl]
kränken: jn. kränken *(aus der Fassung bringen)* upset sb. [ʌp'set]
Krankenhaus hospital ['hɒspɪtl]
Krankenwagen ambulance ['æmbjələns]
kreuzen; sich kreuzen cross [krɒs]
kriegen get [get]
Krokodil crocodile ['krɒkədaɪl]
Krug jug [dʒʌg] • **ein Krug Orangensaft** a jug of orange juice
Küche kitchen ['kɪtʃɪn]
Kuchen cake [keɪk]
Küchenschrank cupboard ['kʌbəd]
Kugelschreiber pen [pen]
Kuh cow [kaʊ]
kühl cool [ku:l]
Kühlschrank fridge [frɪdʒ]
Kummer worry ['wʌri]
kümmern 1. sich um etwas/jn. kümmern look after sth./sb. [ˌlʊk‿'ɑ:ftə] **2. Kümmere dich um deine eigenen Angelegenheiten!** Mind your own business. [ˌmaɪnd jər‿əʊn 'bɪznəs]
Kumpel mate [meɪt] *(infml)*
Kunde, Kundin customer ['kʌstəmə]
Kunst art [ɑ:t]
Künstler/in artist ['ɑ:tɪst]
künstlich artificial [ˌɑ:tɪ'fɪʃl]
Kurs *(Lehrgang)* course [kɔ:s]
kurz short [ʃɔ:t] • **kurze Hose** shorts *(pl)* [ʃɔ:ts]
Küste coast [kəʊst]

L

lächeln smile [smaɪl]
lachen laugh [lɑ:f] • **laut lachen** laugh out loud • **über jn. lachen** laugh at sb.
Lachs salmon ['sæmən], *pl* salmon
Laden *(Geschäft)* shop [ʃɒp]
Lage: in der Lage sein, etwas zu tun be able to do sth. ['eɪbl]
Lamm lamb [læm]
Lampe lamp [læmp]
Land *(auch als Gegensatz zur Stadt)* country ['kʌntri]; *(Grund und Boden)* land [lænd] • **auf dem Land** *(im Gegensatz zur Stadt)* in the country; *(nicht auf dem Wasser)* on land
landen land [lænd]
Landkarte map [mæp]
Landwirt/in farmer ['fɑ:mə]
lang long [lɒŋ] • **drei Tage lang** for three days • **lange** a long time
langsam slow [sləʊ]
langweilig boring ['bɔ:rɪŋ]
Lärm noise [nɔɪz]
lärmend noisy ['nɔɪzi]
Lasagne lasagne [lə'zænjə]
lassen let [let] • **Lass uns ... / Lasst uns ...** Let's ... • **Lass das!** Stop that!
Lauf run [rʌn]
Laufbahn *(Sport)* running track [træk]
laufen run [rʌn]
Läufer/in runner ['rʌnə]
Laufschuhe running shoes
laut loud [laʊd]; *(lärmend)* noisy ['nɔɪzi] • **laut lachen** laugh out loud • **etwas lauter stellen** turn sth. up [tɜ:n]
Laut sound [saʊnd]
läuten ring [rɪŋ]
leben live [lɪv]
Leben life [laɪf], *pl* lives [laɪvz]
Lebensmittel food [fu:d]
lecker delicious [dɪ'lɪʃəs]
Leder leather ['leðə]
ledig single ['sɪŋgl]
leer empty ['empti]
legen *(hin-, ablegen)* put [pʊt]
lehren teach [ti:tʃ]
Lehrer/in teacher ['ti:tʃə]
Lehrgang *(Kurs)* course [kɔ:s]
leicht *(nicht schwierig)* easy ['i:zi]
Leichtathletik athletics [æθ'letɪks]
leider I'm afraid [ə'freɪd]
leidtun: Tut mir leid. I'm sorry. ['sɒri]
leise quiet ['kwaɪət] • **etwas leiser stellen** turn sth. down [tɜ:n]
Leiter/in *(Anführer/in)* leader ['li:də]
Lektion *(im Schulbuch)* unit ['ju:nɪt]
lernen learn [lɜ:n]
Lern- und Arbeitstechniken study skills ['stʌdi skɪlz]
lesen read [ri:d]
Leser/in reader ['ri:də]
letzte(r, s) last [lɑ:st]; final ['faɪnl]
leuchtend bright [braɪt]
Leute people ['pi:pl]; guys [gaɪz] *(AE, infml)*
Licht light [laɪt]
Lichtblitz flash [flæʃ]
Liebe love [lʌv]
Liebe Grüße, ... *(Briefschluss)* Love ... [lʌv]
lieben love [lʌv]
Lieber Jay, ... Dear Jay ... [dɪə]
lieber: etwas lieber mögen like sth. better
Liebling dear [dɪə]; love [lʌv]; sweetheart ['swi:thɑ:t]; *(Favorit/in)* favourite ['feɪvərɪt]
Lieblings-: meine Lieblingsfarbe my favourite colour ['feɪvərɪt]
liebsten: etwas am liebsten mögen like sth. best
Lied song [sɒŋ]
Liedtext(e) lyrics *(pl)* ['lɪrɪks]
liegen: Das liegt bei dir. *(Das kannst/musst du (selbst) entscheiden.)* That's up to you.
lila purple ['pɜ:pl]
Limonade lemonade [ˌlemə'neɪd]
Lineal ruler ['ru:lə]
Linie: (U-Bahn-)Linie line [laɪn]
linke(r, s) left [left] • **links, auf der linken Seite** on the left • **(nach) links abbiegen** turn left • **nach links schauen** look left
Liste list [lɪst]
Livemusik live music [laɪv]
Loch hole [həʊl]
locker *(entspannt)* relaxed [rɪ'lækst]; *(gelassen)* easy-going [ˌi:zi'gəʊɪŋ]
Löffel spoon [spu:n]
Logo logo ['ləʊgəʊ], *pl* logos
Lokal *(Kneipe)* pub [pʌb]
Löwe lion ['laɪən]
Luft air [eə]

M

machen do [du:]; make [meɪk] • **die Hausaufgabe(n) machen** do homework • **einen Ausflug machen** go on a trip • **einen Spaziergang machen** go for a walk • **eine Fahrt machen** take a ride • **eine Übung machen** do an exercise
Ferien machen be on holiday
Fotos machen take photos • **jm. Vorwürfe machen (wegen)** blame sb. (for) • **Judo machen** do judo
sich Notizen machen take notes
sich Sorgen machen (wegen, um) worry (about) ['wʌri] • **(Zauber-) Kunststücke machen** do tricks
Reiten macht Spaß. Riding is fun.
Mädchen girl [gɜ:l]
Magazin *(Zeitschrift)* magazine [ˌmægə'zi:n]
Magen stomach ['stʌmək]
Magenschmerzen stomach ache ['stʌmək‿eɪk]
Magst du ...? Do you like ...?
Mahlzeit meal [mi:l]
Mai May [meɪ]
Make-up make-up ['meɪkʌp]
Mal(e); -mal time(s) [taɪm], [taɪmz]
malen paint [peɪnt]
Maler/in painter ['peɪntə]
Mama mum [mʌm] *(BE)*; mom [mɒm, *AE:* mɑ:m] *(AE)*
man you
Manager/in manager ['mænɪdʒə]
manchmal sometimes ['sʌmtaɪmz]
Mann man [mæn], *pl* men [men]
Mannschaft team [ti:m]

Mappe *(des Sprachenportfolios)* dossier ['dɒsieɪ]
Markenzeichen *(Logo)* logo ['ləʊgəʊ], *pl* logos
markieren mark up [ˌmɑːk_'ʌp]
Markt market ['mɑːkɪt] • **auf den Markt bringen** *(CD, Film usw. herausbringen)* release [rɪ'liːs]
Marmelade *(Orangenmarmelade)* marmalade ['mɑːməleɪd]
März March [mɑːtʃ]
Maschine machine [mə'ʃiːn]
Mathematik maths [mæθs]
Mauer wall [wɔːl]
Maulwurf mole [məʊl]
Maus mouse [maʊs], *pl* mice [maɪs]
Medaille medal ['medl]
Mediation *(Sprachmittlung)* mediation [ˌmiːdi'eɪʃn]
Medien media *(pl)* ['miːdiə]
Meer sea [siː]
Meerschweinchen guinea pig ['gɪni pɪg]
mehr more [mɔː] • **mehr als** more than • **mehr als ich** more than me • **nicht mehr** not (...) any more • **viel mehr** lots more **keine Musik mehr** no more music
Meile *(= ca. 1,6 km)* mile [maɪl]
meilenweit for miles [maɪlz]
mein(e) ... my ... [maɪ] • **meine neuen** my new ones [wʌnz]
meinen *(glauben)* think [θɪŋk]; *(sagen wollen)* mean [miːn] **Meinst du wirklich?** Do you really think so?
meiner, meine, meins mine [maɪn]
Meinung: anderer Meinung sein (als) disagree (with) [ˌdɪsə'griː]
meist: (der/die/das) meiste ...; am meisten most [məʊst] • **die meisten Leute** most people
meistens usually ['juːʒuəli]
Meister/in *(Champion)* champion ['tʃæmpiən]
Meisterschaft championship ['tʃæmpiənʃɪp]
Melodie tune [tjuːn]
Menge: eine Menge *(viel, viele)* a lot (of) [lɒt]; lots (of) [lɒts]
Menschen people ['piːpl]
Menü 1. *(im Restaurant)* set meal [ˌset 'miːl] **2.** *(Computermenü)* menu ['menjuː]
merken: sich etwas merken remember sth. [rɪ'membə]
Messer knife [naɪf], *pl* knives [naɪvz]
Meter metre ['miːtə]
mich me [miː] • **mich (selbst)** myself [maɪ'self]
► S.167 Reflexive pronouns
Mikrofon microphone ['maɪkrəfəʊn]
Milch milk [mɪlk]
mild mild [maɪld]
Million million ['mɪljən]
Mindmap mind map ['maɪnd mæp]
Mini- mini- ['mɪni]
minus minus ['maɪnəs]
Minute minute ['mɪnɪt]
mir me [miː] • **mir (selbst)** myself [maɪ'self]
► S.167 Reflexive pronouns
mischen mix [mɪks]
Mischung mix [mɪks]; mixture ['mɪkstʃə]
mit with [wɪð] • **mit 16 (Jahren)** at 16 • **mit dem Auto/Zug/Rad/... fahren** go by car/train/bike/...
mitbringen bring [brɪŋ]
mitgenommen (wegen) *(aufgebracht, gekränkt)* upset (about) [ˌʌp'set]
mitmachen: bei etwas/jm. mitmachen join sth./sb. [dʒɔɪn]
Mitschüler/in classmate ['klɑːsmeɪt]
Mittagessen lunch [lʌntʃ] • **Was gibt es zum Mittagessen?** What's for lunch?
Mittagspause lunch break ['lʌntʃ breɪk]
Mitte centre ['sentə]; middle ['mɪdl]
Mitteilung *(Notiz)* note [nəʊt]
Mittel- *(Zentral-)* central ['sentrəl]
mittel(groß) medium ['miːdiəm]
Mittelteil middle ['mɪdl]
Mittwoch Wednesday ['wenzdeɪ, 'wenzdi] *(siehe auch unter „Freitag")*
Mix mix [mɪks]
mixen mix [mɪks]
Möbel furniture *(no pl)* ['fɜːnɪtʃə]
► S.162 Words without a plural
Möbelstück piece of furniture [ˌpiːs_əv 'fɜːnɪtʃə]
Mobiltelefon mobile (phone) [ˌməʊbaɪl 'fəʊn] *(BE)*; cellphone ['selfəʊn] *(AE)*
möchte: Ich möchte gern ... (haben) I'd like ... (= I would like ...) [laɪk] **Ich möchte gehen** I'd like to go **Ich möchte nicht gehen** I wouldn't like to go • **Möchtest du / Möchten Sie ...?** Would you like ...?
Mode fashion ['fæʃn]
Modell *(-auto, -schiff; Fotomodell)* model ['mɒdl]
Moderator/in presenter [prɪ'zentə]
modern modern ['mɒdən]
modisch *(schick, im Trend)* trendy ['trendi]
mögen like [laɪk]; *(sehr mögen)* love [lʌv] • **etwas lieber mögen** like sth. better • **etwas am liebsten mögen** like sth. best
möglich possible ['pɒsəbl]
Möglichkeit *(Gelegenheit, Chance)* chance [tʃɑːns]
Möhre carrot ['kærət]
Moment moment ['məʊmənt] • **im Moment** at the moment • **genau in dem Moment** just then • **Moment mal!** Wait a minute. ['mɪnɪt]
Monat month [mʌnθ]
Mond moon [muːn]
Monitor monitor ['mɒnɪtə]
Monster monster ['mɒnstə]
Montag Monday ['mʌndeɪ, 'mʌndi] *(siehe auch unter „Freitag")*
Mord murder ['mɜːdə]
morden murder ['mɜːdə]
Mörder/in murderer ['mɜːdərə]
morgen tomorrow [tə'mɒrəʊ] • **das Wetter von morgen** tomorrow's weather
Morgen morning ['mɔːnɪŋ] • **am Morgen, morgens** in the morning
Moschee mosque [mɒsk]
MP3-Spieler MP3 player [ˌempiː'θriː ˌpleɪə]
müde tired ['taɪəd]
Müll rubbish ['rʌbɪʃ]
Mülltonne bin [bɪn]; dustbin ['dʌstbɪn]
Multiple-Choice multiple choice [ˌmʌltɪpl 'tʃɔɪs]
Mund mouth [maʊθ] • **Halt den Mund!** Shut up. [ˌʃʌt_'ʌp]
murren grumble ['grʌmbl]
Museum museum [mju'ziːəm]
Musical musical ['mjuːzɪkl]
Musik music ['mjuːzɪk]
Musiker/in musician [mjuː'zɪʃn]
Musikinstrument musical instrument [ˌmjuːzɪkl_'ɪnstrəmənt]
müssen have to; must [mʌst] • **nicht müssen** needn't ['niːdnt]
Mutter mother ['mʌðə]
Mutti mum [mʌm] *(BE)*; mom [mɒm, *AE:* mɑːm] *(AE)*
Mütze cap [kæp]

N

Na ja ... / Na gut ... Oh well ... [əʊ 'wel]
Na und? So? [səʊ]
nach 1. *(örtlich)* to [tə, tu] • **nach draußen** outside • **nach drinnen** inside • **nach Hause gehen** go home • **nach Hause kommen** come home; get home • **nach oben** up; *(im Haus)* upstairs [ˌʌp'steəz] • **nach unten** down; *(im Haus)* downstairs [ˌdaʊn'steəz] **nach vorn** to the front [frʌnt] **2.** *(zeitlich)* after • **Viertel nach 11**

quarter past 11 [pɑ:st]
3. nach etwas fragen ask about sth. [ə'baʊt] • **jn. nach dem Weg fragen** ask sb. the way
Nachbar/in neighbour ['neɪbə]
nachdem after ['ɑ:ftə]
nachdenken über think about [θɪŋk]
Nachmittag afternoon [ˌɑ:ftə'nu:n]
am Nachmittag, nachmittags in the afternoon
Nachricht message ['mesɪdʒ]
Nachrichten *(im Fernsehen, Radio; Neuigkeiten)* news *(no pl)* [nju:z]
► S.162 Words without a plural
nachrufen: jm. Schimpfwörter nachrufen call sb. names
nachschlagen: etwas nachschlagen look sth. up [ˌlʊk_'ʌp]
nächste(r, s): am nächsten Tag the next day [nekst] • **der Nächste sein** be next • **Was haben wir als Nächstes?** What have we got next?
Nacht night [naɪt] • **heute Nacht** tonight [tə'naɪt] • **in der Nacht, nachts** at night
nahe (bei) near [nɪə]; close (to) [kləʊs]
Nähe: in der Nähe von near [nɪə]
Name name [neɪm]
Nase nose [nəʊz] • **die Nase voll haben (von etwas)** be fed up (with sth.) [ˌfed_'ʌp]
Nashorn rhino ['raɪnəʊ]
national national ['næʃnəl]
Naturkunde natural history [ˌnætʃrəl 'hɪstri]
natürlich of course [əv 'kɔ:s]
Naturwissenschaft science ['saɪəns]
Nebel fog [fɒg]
neben next to ['nekst tə]
nebenbei (bemerkt) by the way [ˌbaɪ ðə 'weɪ]
neblig foggy ['fɒgi]
nehmen take [teɪk] • **Ich nehme es.** *(beim Einkaufen)* I'll take it.
neidisch (auf) jealous (of) ['dʒeləs]
nein no [nəʊ]
nennen *(rufen, bezeichnen)* call [kɔ:l]; *(benennen)* name [neɪm]
nervös nervous ['nɜ:vəs]
nett nice [naɪs] • **Nett, dich kennenzulernen.** Nice to meet you.
neu new [nju:]
neueste(r, s) latest ['leɪtɪst]
nicht not [nɒt] • **nicht mehr** not (...) any more • **Das glaube ich nicht. / Ich glaube nicht.** I don't think so. **..., nicht wahr?** ..., right? • **Du machst Witze, nicht wahr? / Das ist nicht dein Ernst, oder?** You're joking, aren't you? • **nicht vor** *(erst um)* not ... until / not ... till • **noch nicht** not (...) yet [jet] • **(noch) nicht einmal** not even ['i:vn]
nichts nothing ['nʌθɪŋ]; not (...) anything ['eniθɪŋ] • **Nichts zu danken.** You're welcome. ['welkəm]
nicken (mit) nod [nɒd]
nie, niemals never ['nevə]
niemand nobody ['nəʊbədi]; not (...) anybody ['enibɒdi]
nirgendwo(hin) not (...) anywhere ['eniweə]
noch: noch ein(e) ... another ... [ə'nʌðə]; one more ... [mɔ:] • **noch 45 Pence** another 45 p • **noch einmal** again [ə'gen]; once more/once again • **noch nicht** not (...) yet [jet] **(immer) noch** still [stɪl]
Norden north [nɔ:θ] • **nach Norden** north • **Richtung Norden** *(Fahrtrichtung)* northbound ['nɔ:θbaʊnd]
nördlich north [nɔ:θ]
Nordosten north-east [ˌnɔ:θ'i:st]
nach Nordosten north-east
nordöstlich north-east [ˌnɔ:θ'i:st]
Nordwesten north-west [ˌnɔ:θ'west]
nach Nordwesten north-west
nordwestlich north-west [ˌnɔ:θ'west]
nörgeln grumble ['grʌmbl]
normalerweise usually ['ju:ʒuəli]
Notiz note [nəʊt] • **sich Notizen machen** take notes
November November [nəʊ'vembə]
null o [əʊ]; zero ['zɪərəʊ]; *(beim Sport)* nil [nɪl]
► S.162 A football match
Nummer number ['nʌmbə]
nun now [naʊ] • **Nun, ...** Well, ... [wel]
nur only ['əʊnli]; just [dʒʌst] • **nur zum Spaß** just for fun
Nuss nut [nʌt]
nützlich useful ['ju:sfl]

O

ob if [ɪf]
oben above [ə'bʌv]; *(an der Spitze)* at the top (of) [tɒp]; *(im Haus)* upstairs [ˌʌp'steəz] • **dort oben** up there
nach oben up; *(im Haus)* upstairs
Oberbegriff group word ['gru:p wɜ:d]
oberhalb von over ['əʊvə]; above [ə'bʌv]
Oberteil top [tɒp]
Obst fruit [fru:t]
Obstkuchen pie [paɪ]
Obstsalat fruit salad ['fru:t ˌsæləd]
obwohl although [ɔ:l'ðəʊ]
oder or [ɔ:] • **Das ist nicht dein Ernst, oder?** You're joking, aren't you?
offen open ['əʊpən] • **oben offener (Doppeldecker-)Bus** open-top bus
öffentliche(r, s) public ['pʌblɪk]
öffentliche Verkehrsmittel, öffentlicher Personennahverkehr public transport *(no pl)* [ˌpʌblɪk 'trænspɔ:t]
öffnen; sich öffnen open ['əʊpən]
oft often ['ɒfn]
ohne without [wɪ'ðaʊt]
Ohr ear [ɪə]
Ohrenschmerzen earache ['ɪəreɪk]
Ohrring earring ['ɪərɪŋ]
Oje! Oh dear! [əʊ 'dɪə]
okay OK [əʊ'keɪ]
Oktober October [ɒk'təʊbə]
Öl oil [ɔɪl]
Oma grandma ['grænmɑ:]; granny ['græni]
Onkel uncle ['ʌŋkl]
online, Online- online [ˌɒn'laɪn]
Opa grandpa ['grænpɑ:]
Oper opera ['ɒprə]
Operation (an) operation (on) [ˌɒpə'reɪʃn]
Opfer victim ['vɪktɪm]
Orange orange ['ɒrɪndʒ]
orange(farben) orange ['ɒrɪndʒ]
Orangenmarmelade marmalade ['mɑ:məleɪd]
Orangensaft orange juice ['ɒrɪndʒ dʒu:s]
ordentlich tidy ['taɪdi]
Ordnung: in Ordnung all right [ɔ:l 'raɪt]
Orgel organ ['ɔ:gən]
Ort place [pleɪs]; *(Einsatzort)* location [ləʊ'keɪʃn]
Osten east [i:st] • **nach Osten** east
Richtung Osten *(Fahrtrichtung)* eastbound ['i:stbaʊnd]
östlich east [i:st]
Outfit *(Kleidung; Ausrüstung)* outfit ['aʊtfɪt]

P

paar: ein paar some [səm, sʌm]; *(einige wenige)* a few [fju:]
Paar: ein Paar a pair (of) [peə]
Päckchen packet ['pækɪt] • **ein Päckchen Pfefferminzbonbons** a packet of mints
packen 1. *(Koffer, Auto)* pack [pæk]
2. *(greifen, schnappen)* grab [græb]
Packung packet ['pækɪt] • **eine Packung Pfefferminzbonbons** a packet of mints
Paddel paddle ['pædl]
Paddelboot canoe [kə'nu:]
paddeln paddle ['pædl]; *(Kanu fahren)* canoe [kə'nu:]

Paket parcel ['pɑ:sl]
Palast palace ['pæləs]
pantomimisch darstellen mime [maɪm]
Papa dad [dæd]
Papagei parrot ['pærət]
Papier paper ['peɪpə]
Park park [pɑ:k]
Parkplatz *(für viele Autos)* car park ['kɑ: pɑ:k]
Parlament parliament ['pɑ:ləmənt]
Partner/in partner ['pɑ:tnə]
Partnerstadt twin town [ˌtwɪn 'taʊn]
Party party ['pɑ:ti] • **eine Party feiern/veranstalten** have a party
passen fit [fɪt]
passieren (mit) happen (to) ['hæpən]
Pause break [breɪk] • **in der Pause** *(zwischen Schulstunden)* at break
Pence pence (p) [pens]
Person person ['pɜ:sn]
Personennahverkehr: öffentlicher Personennahverkehr public transport *(no pl)* [ˌpʌblɪk 'trænspɔ:t]
persönliche(r, s) personal ['pɜ:sənl]
Pfad path [pɑ:θ]
Pfeffer pepper ['pepə]
Pfefferminzbonbons mints [mɪnts]
Pfeife 1. *(zum Rauchen; Orgelpfeife)* pipe [paɪp]
2. *(Trillerpfeife)* whistle ['wɪsl]
pfeifen whistle ['wɪsl]
Pferd horse [hɔ:s]
Pferdeschwanz *(Frisur)* ponytail ['pəʊniteɪl]
Pfiff whistle ['wɪsl]
Pfund *(britische Währung)* pound (£) [paʊnd] • **Es kostet 1 Pfund.** It's £1.
Piano piano [pi'ænəʊ]
Picknick picnic ['pɪknɪk]
piepsen bleep [bli:p]
Piepton bleep [bli:p]
Pilz mushroom ['mʌʃrʊm, -ru:m]
pink(farben) pink [pɪŋk]
Pirat/in pirate ['paɪrət]
Pizza pizza ['pi:tsə]
Plan plan [plæn]
planen plan [plæn]
Planet planet ['plænɪt]
Platz *(Ort, Stelle)* place [pleɪs]; *(in der Stadt)* square [skweə]; *(runder Platz in der Stadt)* circus ['sɜ:kəs]; *(für Squash, Badminton)* court [kɔ:t]; *(Einsatzort)* location [ləʊ'keɪʃn]
Plätzchen biscuit ['bɪskɪt]
plaudern chat [tʃæt]
plötzlich suddenly ['sʌdnli]
plus plus [plʌs]
Pokal cup [kʌp]
Polizei police *(pl)* [pə'li:s]
Polizeiwache, Polizeirevier police station [pə'li:s steɪʃn]
Polizist/in policeman [pə'li:smən]/ policewoman [pə'li:swʊmən]
Poltergeist poltergeist ['pəʊltəgaɪst]
Pommes frites chips *(pl)* [tʃɪps]
Popcorn popcorn ['pɒpkɔ:n]
Pop(musik) pop (music) [pɒp]
Popsender *(Radio)* pop station ['steɪʃn]
Posaune trombone [trɒm'bəʊn]
Post *(Briefe, Päckchen, ...)* post [pəʊst]; *(Postamt)* post office ['pəʊst‿ɒfɪs]
Postamt post office ['pəʊst‿ɒfɪs]
Poster poster ['pəʊstə]
Postkarte postcard ['pəʊstkɑ:d]
prallen: gegen/auf die Windschutzscheibe prallen hit the windscreen ['wɪndskri:n]
Präsentation presentation [ˌprezn'teɪʃn]
präsentieren: (jm.) etwas präsentieren present sth. (to sb.) [prɪ'zent]
Preis 1. *(Kaufpreis)* price [praɪs]
2. *(Gewinn)* prize [praɪz]
pressen squeeze [skwi:z]
pro per [pɜ:, pə] • **einmal pro Woche** once a week / once per week
Probe *(am Theater)* rehearsal [rɪ'hɜ:sl]
proben *(am Theater)* rehearse [rɪ'hɜ:s]
probieren try [traɪ]
Problem problem ['prɒbləm]
produzieren produce [prə'dju:s]
Programm programme ['prəʊgræm]
Projekt (über, zu) project (on, about) ['prɒdʒekt] • **ein Projekt machen, durchführen** do a project
Provinz province ['prɒvɪns]
Prozent per cent (%) [pə'sent]
prüfen *(überprüfen)* check [tʃek]
PS *(Nachschrift unter Briefen)* PS [ˌpi:‿'es] (postscript ['pəʊstskrɪpt])
Publikum audience ['ɔ:diəns]
Pullover pullover ['pʊləʊvə]
Punk(rock) punk (rock) [pʌŋk]
Punkt *(bei Test, Quiz)* point [pɔɪnt]
Punktestand *(Spielstand)* score [skɔ:]
▸ S.162 A football match
Pute, Puter turkey ['tɜ:ki]
putzen clean [kli:n] • **Ich putze mir die Zähne.** I clean my teeth.
Putzfrau, -mann cleaner ['kli:nə]

Q

Quadratkilometer square km (sq km) [skweə]
quer über across [ə'krɒs]
Querflöte flute [flu:t]
Quiz quiz [kwɪz], *pl* quizzes ['kwɪzɪz]

R

Rad 1. wheel [wi:l]
2. *(Fahrrad)* bike [baɪk]
Rad fahren cycle ['saɪkl]; ride a bike [ˌraɪd‿ə 'baɪk]
Radfahrt bike ride ['baɪk raɪd]
Radiergummi rubber ['rʌbə]
Radio radio ['reɪdiəʊ] • **im Radio** on the radio
Radiosender radio station ['reɪdiəʊ ˌsteɪʃn]
Radweg cycle path ['saɪkl pɑ:θ]
Rap rap [ræp]
rappen rap [ræp]
Rapper/in rapper ['ræpə]
raten guess [ges]
Ratespiel quiz [kwɪz], *pl* quizzes ['kwɪzɪz]
Rätsel riddle ['rɪdl]; *(Geheimnis)* mystery ['mɪstri]
Rauch smoke [sməʊk]
rauchen smoke [sməʊk]
Raum room [ru:m]
realistisch realistic [ˌri:ə'lɪstɪk]
Recht haben be right [raɪt]
rechte(r, s) right [raɪt] • **rechts, auf der rechten Seite** on the right
(nach) rechts abbiegen turn right
nach rechts schauen look right
Rechtschreibung spelling ['spelɪŋ]
rechtzeitig in time [ɪn 'taɪm]
recycelt recycled [ˌri:'saɪkld]
Recycling recycling [ˌri:'saɪklɪŋ]
Redakteur/in editor ['edɪtə]
reden (mit, über) talk (to, about) [tɔ:k]; speak (to, about) [spi:k]
Wovon redest du? What are you talking about?
Refrain chorus ['kɔ:rəs]
Regal(brett) shelf [ʃelf], *pl* shelves [ʃelvz]
Regel *(Vorschrift)* rule [ru:l]
Regen rain [reɪn]
Reggae reggae ['regeɪ]
regnen rain [reɪn]
regnerisch rainy ['reɪni]
Reh deer, *pl* deer [dɪə]
reich rich [rɪtʃ]
reichen *(weitergeben)* pass [pɑ:s]
Reihe 1. Du bist an der Reihe. It's your turn. [tɜ:n] • **Wer ist an der Reihe?** Whose turn is it? [hu:z]
2. *(Sendereihe, Serie)* series, *pl* series ['sɪəri:z]
Reihenfolge order ['ɔ:də]
Reise trip [trɪp]; *(Fahrt)* journey ['dʒɜ:ni]
reisen travel ['trævl]
reiten ride [raɪd] • **reiten gehen** go riding
Reiterhelm riding hat ['raɪdɪŋ hæt]

Reitkappe riding hat ['raɪdɪŋ hæt]
Reitstiefel riding boots *(pl)* ['raɪdɪŋ buːts]
Reitweg bridle path ['braɪdl pɑːθ]
Religion *(Religionsunterricht)* RE [ˌɑːr‿'iː], Religious Education [rɪˌlɪdʒəs‿edʒu'keɪʃn]
rennen run [rʌn]
Reportage (über) report (on) [rɪ'pɔːt]
repräsentieren represent [ˌreprɪ'zent]
Rest rest [rest]
Restaurant restaurant ['restrɒnt]; *(Imbissstube, Café)* café ['kæfeɪ]
Resultat result [rɪ'zʌlt]
retten save [seɪv]
richtig right [raɪt]; *(korrekt)* correct [kə'rekt]
Richtung way [weɪ] • **in diese Richtung** this way • **in die falsche Richtung** the wrong way • **in welche Richtung?** which way? • **Richtung Norden** northbound ['nɔːθbaʊnd] • **Richtung Osten** eastbound ['iːstbaʊnd] **Richtung Süden** southbound ['saʊθbaʊnd] • **Richtung Westen** westbound ['westbaʊnd]
riechen smell [smel]
Riesenrad big wheel [wiːl]
riesig huge [hjuːdʒ]
► S.157 big – large – huge
Rindfleisch beef [biːf]
Ring ring [rɪŋ]
Rock skirt [skɜːt]
Rock(musik) rock (music) [rɒk]
Rolle role [rəʊl]
Rollenspiel role play ['rəʊl pleɪ]
Rollstuhl wheelchair ['wiːltʃeə]
römisch; Römer, Römerin Roman ['rəʊmən]
rosa pink [pɪŋk]
rot red [red]
Rückfahrkarte return ticket [rɪ'tɜːn ˌtɪkɪt]
Rucksack rucksack ['rʌksæk]
rufen call [kɔːl]; shout [ʃaʊt] • **die Polizei rufen** call the police
ruhig quiet ['kwaɪət]
rumhängen *(abhängen)* hang out [ˌhæŋ‿'aʊt] *(infml)*
rund round [raʊnd]
Rundgang (durch das Haus) tour (of the house) [tʊə]
runterladen download [ˌdaʊn'ləʊd]

S

Saal hall [hɔːl]
Sache thing [θɪŋ]
Saft juice [dʒuːs]
sagen say [seɪ] • **Sagt mir eure Namen.** Tell me your names. [tel] **jm. sagen, dass er/sie etwas tun soll** tell sb. to do sth.
Salat 1. *(Kopfsalat)* lettuce ['letɪs] **2.** *(Gericht, Beilage)* salad ['sæləd]
Salz salt [sɔːlt]
sammeln collect [kə'lekt]
Sammler/in collector [kə'lektə]
Samstag Saturday ['sætədeɪ, 'sætədi]
(siehe auch unter „Freitag")
Sandale sandal ['sændl]
Sandwich sandwich ['sænwɪtʃ]
Sänger/in singer ['sɪŋə]
Sanitäter/in paramedic [ˌpærə'medɪk]
Sattel saddle ['sædl]
Satz sentence ['sentəns]
sauber clean [kliːn] • **sauber machen** clean
Säule column ['kɒləm]
Sauna sauna ['sɔːnə] • **in die Sauna gehen** have a sauna
Saxophon saxophone ['sæksəfəʊn]
Schachtel packet ['pækɪt]
Schaf sheep, *pl* sheep [ʃiːp]
Schale bowl [bəʊl] • **eine Schale Cornflakes** a bowl of cornflakes
Schallplatte record ['rekɔːd]
scharf *(würzig)* spicy ['spaɪsi]
Schatten *(einer Person, eines Gegenstands)* shadow ['ʃædəʊ]
Schatz dear [dɪə]; sweetheart ['swiːthɑːt]
schätzen *(erraten)* guess [ges]
schauen look [lʊk] • **nach links/rechts schauen** look left/right
Schaufenster shop window [ˌʃɒp 'wɪndəʊ]
Schauspiel drama ['drɑːmə]
Schauspieler/in actor ['æktə]
scheinen *(Sonne)* shine [ʃaɪn]
scherzen joke [dʒəʊk]
scheu shy [ʃaɪ]
scheußlich horrible ['hɒrəbl]
schick *(modisch, im Trend)* trendy ['trendi]
schicken (an) *(Post, E-Mail)* send (to) [send]; mail (to) [meɪl] • **jm. eine SMS schicken** text sb. [tekst]
schieben push [pʊʃ]
schiefgehen go wrong
schießen: ein Tor schießen score (a goal) [skɔː], [gəʊl]
Schiff boat [bəʊt]; ship [ʃɪp]
Schild *(Zeichen)* sign [saɪn]
Schildkröte tortoise ['tɔːtəs]
Schimpfwort: jn. mit Schimpfwörtern hänseln, jm. Schimpfwörter nachrufen call sb. names
Schinkenspeck bacon ['beɪkən]
Schlaf sleep [sliːp]
Schlafanzug pyjamas *(pl)* [pə'dʒɑːməz]
schlafen sleep [sliːp]; *(nicht wach sein)* be asleep [ə'sliːp]
Schlafparty sleepover ['sliːpəʊvə]
Schlafzimmer bedroom ['bedruːm]
schlagen hit [hɪt]; *(besiegen)* beat [biːt] • **gegen/auf die Windschutzscheibe schlagen** hit the windscreen ['wɪndskriːn]
Schlagzeug spielen play the drums [drʌmz]
Schlange snake [sneɪk]
schlau clever ['klevə]
schlecht bad [bæd] • **schlechter** worse [wɜːs] • **am schlechtesten; der/die/das schlechteste** (the) worst [wɜːst] • **schlechtes Timing** bad timing • **schlecht in etwas sein; etwas schlecht können** be bad at sth.
Schleuse lock [lɒk]
schließen *(zumachen)* close [kləʊz]
schließlich at last [ət 'lɑːst]; *(zum Schluss)* in the end
schlimm bad [bæd] • **schlimmer** worse [wɜːs] • **am schlimmsten; der/die/das schlimmste** (the) worst [wɜːst]
Schlitten sledge [sledʒ]
Schlittschuh laufen skate [skeɪt]
Schlittschuhbahn ice rink ['aɪs rɪŋk]
Schloss castle ['kɑːsl]; *(Palast)* palace ['pæləs]
Schluss 1. end • **zum Schluss** in the end **2.** *(einer Geschichte, eines Films usw.)* ending ['endɪŋ]
Schlüssel key [kiː]
Schlüsselwort key word ['kiː wɜːd]
Schmuck jewellery ['dʒuːəlri]
schmutzig dirty ['dɜːti]
schnappen *(greifen, packen)* grab [græb]
Schnee snow [snəʊ]
Schneeschuh snowshoe ['snəʊʃuː]
Schneeschuhwandern snowshoeing ['snəʊʃuːɪŋ]
schneiden cut [kʌt]
schnell quick [kwɪk]; fast [fɑːst]
Schokolade chocolate ['tʃɒklət]
schon already [ɔːl'redi] • **schon?** yet? [jet] • **schon mal?** ever? ['evə] **(vorher) schon mal** before [bɪ'fɔː]
schön beautiful ['bjuːtɪfl]; *(nett)* nice [naɪs] • **schön ordentlich** neat and tidy
Schönheit beauty ['bjuːti]
Schrank cupboard ['kʌbəd]; *(Kleiderschrank)* wardrobe ['wɔːdrəʊb]
schrecklich terrible ['terəbl]; awful ['ɔːfl]
schreiben (an) write (to) [raɪt]
Schreiber/in writer ['raɪtə]

Schreibtisch desk [desk]
Schreibung *(Rechtschreibung, Schreibweise)* spelling ['spelɪŋ]
schreien shout [ʃaʊt]
Schriftsteller/in writer ['raɪtə]
Schritt step [step]
schüchtern shy [ʃaɪ]
Schuh shoe [ʃuː]
Schuld: jm. die Schuld geben (an) blame sb. (for) [bleɪm]
Schule school [skuːl] • **in der Schule** at school
Schüler/in student ['stjuːdənt]
Schulfach (school) subject ['sʌbdʒɪkt]
Schulheft exercise book ['eksəsaɪz bʊk]
Schulklasse class [klɑːs]; form [fɔːm]
Schulleiter/in head teacher [ˌhed 'tiːtʃə]
Schultasche school bag ['skuːl bæg]
Schulter shoulder ['ʃəʊldə]
Schulterpolster *(beim American Football)* pad [pæd]
Schuss shot [ʃɒt]
Schüssel bowl [bəʊl]
Schusswaffe gun [gʌn]
schützen: jn. schützen (vor) protect sb. (from) [prə'tekt]
Schützer *(Knieschützer usw. für Inlineskater)* pad [pæd]
schwach weak [wiːk]
schwarz black [blæk]
Schwarzbär black bear ['blæk beə]
Schweigen silence ['saɪləns]
Schwein pig [pɪg]
Schweinefleisch pork [pɔːk]
schwer *(schwierig)* difficult ['dɪfɪkəlt]; hard [hɑːd]
Schwester sister ['sɪstə]
schwierig difficult ['dɪfɪkəlt]; hard [hɑːd]
Schwierigkeiten trouble ['trʌbl] • **in Schwierigkeiten sein** be in trouble
Schwimmbad, -becken swimming pool ['swɪmɪŋ puːl]
schwimmen swim [swɪm]
schwimmen gehen go swimming
Schwimmer/in swimmer ['swɪmə]
See 1. *(Binnensee)* lake [leɪk]
2. *(die See, das Meer)* sea [siː]
segeln sail [seɪl]
sehen see [siː] • **Siehst du?** See?
Sehenswürdigkeiten sights *(pl)* [saɪts]
sehr very ['veri] • **Danke sehr!** Thanks very much! • **Er mag sie sehr.** He likes her a lot. [ə 'lɒt]
etwas sehr mögen/sehr lieben like/love sth. very much
Seife soap [səʊp]
sein *(Verb)* be [biː]
sein(e) ... *(besitzanzeigend)* *(zu „he")* his ...; *(zu „it")* its ...
seiner, seine, seins his [hɪz]
Seite 1. side [saɪd] • **auf der linken Seite** on the left • **auf der rechten Seite** on the right
2. *(Buch-, Heftseite)* page [peɪdʒ]
Auf welcher Seite sind wir? What page are we on?
selbst: über dich selbst about yourself [jə'self, jɔː'self]
▶ S.167 Reflexive pronouns
selbstverständlich of course [əv 'kɔːs]
seltsam strange [streɪndʒ]
senden (an) *(Post, E-Mail)* send (to) [send]; mail (to) [meɪl]
Sender *(Fernseh-, Radiokanal)* channel ['tʃænl]; *(Radio-, Popsender)* station ['steɪʃn]
Sendereihe series, *pl* series ['sɪəriːz]
September September [sep'tembə]
Serie *(Sendereihe)* series, *pl* series ['sɪəriːz]
Sessel armchair ['ɑːmtʃeə]
setzen: sich setzen sit [sɪt] • **Setz dich/Setzt euch zu mir.** Sit with me. • **sich mit jm. in Verbindung setzen** contact sb. ['kɒntækt]
Shorts shorts *(pl)* [ʃɔːts]
Show show [ʃəʊ]
sich (selbst) 1. *(zu „she")* herself [hə'self, hɜː'self]
2. *(zu „he")* himself [hɪm'self]
3. *(zu „it")* itself [ɪt'self]
4. *(zu „they")* themselves [ðəm'selvz]
5. sich (gegenseitig) *(einander)* each other [iːtʃ_'ʌðə]; one another [wʌn_ə'nʌðə]
▶ S.167 Reflexive pronouns
▶ S.168 Reflexiv im Deutschen – nicht reflexiv im Englischen
sicher 1. *(in Sicherheit)* safe (from) [seɪf] • **nicht sicher** *(gefährlich)* unsafe [ʌn'seɪf]
2. sicher sein *(nicht zweifeln)* be sure [ʃʊə, ʃɔː]
Sicherheit: in Sicherheit (vor) safe (from) [seɪf]
Sicht: aus meiner Sicht from my point of view [ˌpɔɪnt_əv 'vjuː]
sie 1. *(weibliche Person)* she [ʃiː]
Frag sie. Ask her. [hə, hɜː]
2. *(Ding, Tier)* it [ɪt]
3. *(Plural)* they [ðeɪ] • **Frag sie.** Ask them. [ðəm, ðem]
4. Sie *(höfliche Anrede)* you [juː]
Sieg win [wɪn]
Sieger/in winner ['wɪnə]
Siegesschuss winning shot [ˌwɪnɪŋ 'ʃɒt]
Siegtreffer winning shot [ˌwɪnɪŋ 'ʃɒt]
Silbe syllable ['sɪləbl]
singen sing [sɪŋ]
Single single ['sɪŋgl]
sitzen sit [sɪt]
Skateboard skateboard ['skeɪtbɔːd]
Skateboard fahren skate [skeɪt]
Sketch sketch [sketʃ]
Ski ski [skiː] • **Ski laufen/fahren** ski [skiː]
Skipiste ski slope ['skiː sləʊp]
Sklave, Sklavin slave [sleɪv]
SMS text message ['tekst ˌmesɪdʒ]
jm. eine SMS schicken text sb. [tekst]
Snack snack [snæk]
so 1. *(auf diese Weise)* this way; that way
2. so weit/gut/schlecht/... that far/good/bad/... • **So süß!** So sweet!
3. so groß/aufregend wie as big/exciting as
sobald as soon as [əz 'suːn_əz]
Socke sock [sɒk]
sodass so that
soeben just [dʒʌst]
Sofa sofa ['səʊfə]
Software software ['sɒftweə]
sogar even ['iːvn]
Sohn son [sʌn]
Sommer summer ['sʌmə]
sonderbar strange [streɪndʒ]
Song song [sɒŋ]
Songtext(e) lyrics *(pl)* ['lɪrɪks]
Sonnabend Saturday ['sætədeɪ, 'sætədi]
(siehe auch unter „Freitag")
Sonne sun [sʌn]
Sonnenbrille: (eine) Sonnenbrille sunglasses *(pl)* ['sʌnglɑːsɪz]
sonnig sunny ['sʌni]
Sonntag Sunday ['sʌndeɪ, 'sʌndi]
(siehe auch unter „Freitag")
sonst: Was weißt du sonst noch über ...? What else do you know about ...? [els]
Sorge worry ['wʌri] • **sich Sorgen machen (wegen, um)** worry (about) • **Mach dir keine Sorgen.** Don't worry.
sorgfältig careful ['keəfl]
sowie *(sobald)* as soon as [əz 'suːn_əz]
sowieso anyway ['eniweɪ]
Spaghetti spaghetti [spə'geti]
spannend exciting [ɪk'saɪtɪŋ]
sparen save [seɪv]
Spaß fun [fʌn] • **Spaß haben** have fun • **nur zum Spaß** just for fun
Reiten macht Spaß. Riding is fun.
Viel Spaß! Have fun! / Have a good time!
spät late [leɪt] • **Wie spät ist es?** What's the time? • **zu spät sein/kommen** be late

später later ['leɪtə]
spazieren gehen go for a walk [wɔ:k]
Spaziergang walk [wɔ:k] • **einen Spaziergang machen** go for a walk
Specht woodpecker ['wʊdpekə]
Speisekarte menu ['menju:]
Spiegel mirror ['mɪrə]
Spiel game [geɪm]; *(Wettkampf)* match [mætʃ]
spielen play [pleɪ]; *(Szene, Dialog)* act [ækt] • **Fußball spielen** play football • **Gitarre/Klavier/Schlagzeug spielen** play the guitar/the piano/the drums • **jm. einen Streich spielen** play a trick on sb.
Spieler/in player ['pleɪə]
Spielstand *(Punktestand)* score [skɔ:]
▸ S.162 A football match
Spielstein *(für Brettspiele)* counter ['kaʊntə]
Spion/in spy [spaɪ]
Spitze *(oberes Ende)* top [tɒp] • **an der Spitze (von)** at the top (of)
Sport; Sportart sport [spɔ:t] • **Sport treiben** do sport
Sportausrüstung, Sportsachen sports gear *(no pl)* ['spɔ:ts gɪə]
Sporthalle sports hall ['spɔ:ts hɔ:l]
Sportplatz *(Spielfeld)* field [fi:ld]
Sportsachen sports gear *(no pl)* ['spɔ:ts gɪə]
Sportunterricht PE [ˌpi:‿'i:], Physical Education [ˌfɪzɪkəl‿edʒu'keɪʃn]
Sprache language ['læŋgwɪdʒ]
Sprachmittlung *(Mediation)* mediation [ˌmi:di'eɪʃn]
sprechen (mit) speak (to) [spi:k]
Hier spricht Isabel. *(am Telefon)* This is Isabel.
springen jump [dʒʌmp]
Spülbecken, Spüle sink [sɪŋk]
Staat state [steɪt] • **die Vereinigten Staaten (von Amerika)** the United States (US) [juˌnaɪtɪd 'steɪts], [ˌju:‿'es]
Stadion stadium ['steɪdiəm]
Stadt *(Großstadt)* city ['sɪti]; *(Kleinstadt)* town [taʊn]
Stadtplan map [mæp]
Stadtzentrum city centre [ˌsɪti 'sentə]
Stahl steel [sti:l]
Stall *(für Kaninchen)* hutch [hʌtʃ]
Stammbaum family tree ['fæməli tri:]
Standpunkt point of view [ˌpɔɪnt‿əv 'vju:] • **von meinem Standpunkt aus gesehen** from my point of view
Star *(Film-, Popstar)* star [stɑ:]
stark strong [strɒŋ]
Start start [stɑ:t]
starten start [stɑ:t]
Statue statue ['stætʃu:]
Steak steak [steɪk]
Stecker plug [plʌg]
Steeldrum steel drum [ˌsti:l 'drʌm]
stehen stand [stænd] • **Hier steht: ...** *(im Text)* It says here: ... • **Wie steht es?** *(beim Sport)* What's the score?
▸ S.162 A football match
stehlen steal [sti:l]
Steigerung comparison [kəm'pærɪsn]
Stein stone [stəʊn]
stellen *(hin-, abstellen)* put [pʊt]
Fragen stellen ask questions
etwas auf die Beine stellen get sth. off the ground [graʊnd]
etwas lauter/leiser stellen turn sth. up/down [tɜ:n] • **(jm.) eine Falle stellen** set a trap (for sb.) [set] • **sich (hin)stellen** stand [stænd] • **Stell dir vor! / Stellt euch vor!** Guess what! [ˌges 'wɒt]
sterben (an) die (of) [daɪ]
Stern star [stɑ:]
Stichwort *(Schlüsselwort)* key word ['ki: wɜ:d]
Stiefel boot [bu:t]
still quiet ['kwaɪət]
Stille silence ['saɪləns]
Stimme voice [vɔɪs]
stimmen: Das stimmt. That's right. [raɪt] • **..., stimmt's?** ..., right?
stolz (auf jn./etwas) proud (of sb./sth.) [praʊd]
stoßen push [pʊʃ]
Strand beach [bi:tʃ] • **am Strand** on the beach
Straße road [rəʊd]; street [stri:t]
Straßenbahn tram [træm]
Streich trick [trɪk] • **jm. einen Streich spielen** play a trick on sb.
Streik strike [straɪk]
streiken 1. *(sich im Streik befinden)* be on strike [straɪk]
2. *(in den Streik treten)* go on strike
Streit argument ['ɑ:gjumənt]
streiten: sich streiten argue ['ɑ:gju:]
streng strict [strɪkt]
Stromschnellen rapids *(pl)* ['ræpɪdz]
Struktur structure ['strʌktʃə]
strukturieren structure ['strʌktʃə]
Strumpf sock [sɒk]
Strumpfhose tights *(pl)* [taɪts]
Stück 1. piece [pi:s] • **ein Stück Papier** a piece of paper
2. *(Titel auf CD)* track [træk]
Student/in student ['stju:dənt]
Studio studio ['stju:diəʊ]
Stuhl chair [tʃeə]
stumm: „stummer" Buchstabe *(nicht gesprochener Buchstabe)* silent letter [ˌsaɪlənt 'letə]
Stunde hour ['aʊə]; *(Schulstunde)* lesson ['lesn] • **eine halbe Stunde** half an hour [ˌhɑ:f‿ən‿'aʊə] • **ein 14-Stunden-Flug** a 14-hour flight **ein Supermarkt, der 24 Stunden geöffnet ist** a 24-hour supermarket
Stundenplan timetable ['taɪmteɪbl]
stündig: ein 14-stündiger Flug a 14-hour flight
Sturm storm [stɔ:m]
stürmisch stormy ['stɔ:mi]
stürzen *(hinfallen)* fall [fɔ:l]
suchen look for ['lʊk fɔ:]; search (for) [sɜ:tʃ]
Süden south [saʊθ] • **nach Süden** south • **Richtung Süden** *(Fahrtrichtung)* southbound ['saʊθbaʊnd]
südlich south [saʊθ]
Südosten south-east [ˌsaʊθ'i:st]
nach Südosten south-east
südöstlich south-east [ˌsaʊθ'i:st]
Südwesten south-west [ˌsaʊθ'west]
nach Südwesten south-west
südwestlich south-west [ˌsaʊθ'west]
Supermarkt supermarket ['su:pəmɑ:kɪt]
Suppe soup [su:p]
Surfbrett surfboard ['sɜ:fbɔ:d]
surfen gehen go surfing ['sɜ:fɪŋ]
im Internet surfen surf the internet [sɜ:f]
süß sweet [swi:t]
Süßigkeiten sweets *(pl)* [swi:ts]
Sweatshirt sweatshirt ['swetʃɜ:t]
Synagoge synagogue ['sɪnəgɒg]
Szene scene [si:n]

T

Tabak tobacco [tə'bækəʊ]
Tafel *(Wandtafel)* board [bɔ:d] • **an der/die Tafel** on the board
Tag day [deɪ] • **an jenem Tag** that day • **drei Tage (lang)** for three days • **eines Tages** one day
Guten Tag. Hello.; *(nachmittags)* Good afternoon. [gʊd‿ˌɑ:ftə'nu:n]
Tagebuch diary ['daɪəri]
Tagesdecke bedspread ['bedspred]
Tagesfahrkarte all-day ticket; *(der Londoner Verkehrsbetriebe)* Travelcard ['trævlkɑ:d]
Tal valley ['væli]
Talboden valley floor [ˌvæli 'flɔ:]
Talent talent ['tælənt]
Tank tank [tæŋk]
Tante aunt [ɑ:nt]; auntie ['ɑ:nti]

Tanz dance [dɑːns]
tanzen dance [dɑːns]
Tanzen dancing ['dɑːnsɪŋ]
Tänzer/in dancer ['dɑːnsə]
Tanzstunden, Tanzunterricht dancing lessons ['dɑːnsɪŋ ˌlesnz]
Tasche **1.** *(Tragetasche, Beutel)* bag [bæg] **2.** *(Hosentasche, Jackentasche)* pocket ['pɒkɪt]
Taschengeld pocket money ['pɒkɪt mʌni]
Tasse cup [kʌp] • **eine Tasse Tee** a cup of tea
Tätigkeit activity [æk'tɪvəti]
Tatsache fact [fækt]
tausend thousand ['θaʊznd]
Taxi taxi ['tæksi]
Team team [tiːm]
Teddybär teddy bear ['tedi beə]
Tee tea [tiː]
Teelöffel teaspoon ['tiːspuːn]
Teenager teenager ['tiːneɪdʒə]
Teenager- *(Jugend-)* teen [tiːn]
Teil part [pɑːt]; *(Abschnitt)* section ['sekʃn]
teilen: sich etwas teilen (mit jm.) share sth. (with sb.) [ʃeə]
Telefon (tele)phone ['telɪfəʊn] • **am Telefon** on the phone
Telefongespräch: ein Telefongespräch führen make a call [kɔːl]
Telefonnummer (tele)phone number ['telɪfəʊn ˌnʌmbə]
Teller plate [pleɪt] • **ein Teller Pommes frites** a plate of chips
Temperatur temperature ['temprətʃə]
Tempus *(grammatische Zeit)* tense [tens]
Tennis tennis ['tenɪs]
Termin appointment [ə'pɔɪntmənt]
Terminkalender diary ['daɪəri]
teuer expensive [ɪk'spensɪv]
Text text [tekst]
Theater theatre ['θɪətə]
Theaterstück play [pleɪ]
Thema, Themenbereich topic ['tɒpɪk]
Thermometer thermometer [θə'mɒmɪtə]
Tier animal ['ænɪml]; *(Haustier)* pet [pet]
Tierhandlung pet shop ['pet ʃɒp]
Tiger tiger ['taɪgə]
Timing: schlechtes Timing bad timing ['taɪmɪŋ]
Tipp tip [tɪp]
Tisch table ['teɪbl]
Tischtennis table tennis ['teɪbl tenɪs]
Tischtennisschläger table tennis bat [bæt]
Titel title ['taɪtl]; *(Musikstück auf CD)* track [træk]
Titelliste *(von zu spielenden Songs)* playlist ['pleɪlɪst]
Toast(brot) toast [təʊst]
Tochter daughter ['dɔːtə]
Toilette toilet ['tɔɪlət]
tolerant tolerant ['tɒlərənt]
toll fantastic [fæn'tæstɪk]; great [greɪt]
Tomate tomato [tə'mɑːtəʊ], *pl* tomatoes
Tondatei *(Soundfile)* sound file ['saʊnd faɪl]
Top *(Oberteil)* top [tɒp]
Tor *(im Sport)* goal [gəʊl] • **ein Tor schießen** score (a goal) [skɔː]
Torfrau, Torwart goalkeeper ['gəʊlkiːpə]
Tornado tornado [tɔː'neɪdəʊ]
Torte cake [keɪk]
Torwart goalkeeper ['gəʊlkiːpə]
tot dead [ded]
töten kill [kɪl]
Tour (durch das Haus) tour (of the house) [tʊə]
Tourist/in tourist ['tʊərɪst]
Track *(auf einer CD)* track [træk]
traditionell traditional [trə'dɪʃənl]
tragen *(Kleidung)* wear [weə]
Trainer/in coach [kəʊtʃ]
trainieren practise ['præktɪs]; train [treɪn]
Trainingsstunde, -einheit training session ['seʃn]
Traum dream [driːm]
träumen (von) dream (of, about) [driːm]
Traumhaus dream house
traurig sad [sæd]
treffen; sich treffen meet [miːt] **ein Abkommen/eine Abmachung treffen** make a deal [diːl] • **sich (regelmäßig) mit jm. treffen** *(mit jm. (aus)gehen)* date sb. [deɪt]
Treppe(nstufen) stairs *(pl)* [steəz]
Trick *(Zauberkunststück)* trick [trɪk]
Trikot: (Fußball-)Trikot football shirt
Trimester term [tɜːm]
trinken drink [drɪŋk] • **Milch zum Frühstück trinken** have milk for breakfast
Trommel drum [drʌm]
Trompete trumpet ['trʌmpɪt]
trotzdem anyway ['eniweɪ]
Truthahn turkey ['tɜːki]
Tschüs. Bye. [baɪ]; See you. ['siː juː]
T-Shirt T-shirt ['tiːʃɜːt]
tun do [duː] • **tun müssen** have to do • **tun wollen** want to do [wɒnt] **Tut mir leid.** I'm sorry. ['sɒri]
Tunnel tunnel ['tʌnl]
Tür door [dɔː]
Türklingel doorbell ['dɔːbel]
Turm tower ['taʊə]
Turnanzug leotard ['liːətɑːd]
Turnen *(Sportunterricht)* PE [ˌpiː‿'iː], Physical Education [ˌfɪzɪkəl‿edʒu'keɪʃn]
Turnschuhe trainers *(pl)* ['treɪnəz]
Tut mir leid. I'm sorry. ['sɒri]
Tüte bag [bæg]
Typ type [taɪp] *(infml)*
Tyrann *(Schultyrann)* bully ['bʊli]
tyrannisieren bully ['bʊli]

U

U-Bahn: die U-Bahn the underground ['ʌndəgraʊnd] *(BE)*; the subway ['sʌbweɪ] *(AE)*; *(in London)* the Tube *(no pl)* [tjuːb]
U-Bahn-Linie line [laɪn]
üben practise ['præktɪs]
über **1.** about [ə'baʊt] • **über dich selbst** about yourself **2.** *(räumlich)* over ['əʊvə]; *(quer über)* across [ə'krɒs]; *(oberhalb von)* above [ə'bʌv] **3.** *(mehr als)* over
überall everywhere ['evriweə]
überarbeiten: etwas überarbeiten revise sth. [rɪ'vaɪz]
übereinstimmen (mit) agree (with) [ə'griː] • **nicht übereinstimmen (mit)** disagree (with) [ˌdɪsə'griː]
überfliegen: einen Text überfliegen *(um den Inhalt grob zu erfassen)* skim a text [skɪm]
überleben survive [sə'vaɪv]
Überleben survival [sə'vaɪvl]
übernachten *(über Nacht bleiben)* stay [steɪ]
überprüfen check [tʃek]
überqueren cross [krɒs]
überraschen: jn. überraschen surprise sb. [sə'praɪz]
überraschend surprising [sə'praɪzɪŋ]
überrascht (über etwas) surprised (at sth.) [sə'praɪzd]
Überraschung surprise [sə'praɪz]
Überschrift title ['taɪtl]
übersetzen translate [træns'leɪt]
Übersetzung translation [træns'leɪʃn]
übrigens *(nebenbei bemerkt)* by the way [ˌbaɪ ðə 'weɪ]
Übung *(Schulbuch)* exercise ['eksəsaɪz] • **eine Übung machen** do an exercise
Übungsheft exercise book ['eksəsaɪz bʊk]
Uhr **1.** *(Armbanduhr)* watch [wɒtʃ]; *(Wand-, Stand-, Turmuhr)* clock [klɒk]

2. elf Uhr eleven o'clock • **7 Uhr morgens/vormittags** 7 am [ˌeɪ‿'em] **7 Uhr nachmittags/abends** 7 pm [ˌpiː‿'em] • **um 8 Uhr 45** at 8.45
Uhrzeit time [taɪm]
um 1. *(örtlich)* **um ... (herum)** round [raʊnd]; around [ə'raʊnd] • **um den See (herum)** around the lake **ganz um die Burg herum** all around the castle
► S.155 around
2. *(zeitlich)* **um 8.45** at 8.45 • **um sechs Uhr herum** *(gegen sechs)* around six
3. Es geht um Mr Green. This is about Mr Green.
4. um zu to
umdrehen: sich umdrehen turn [tɜːn]
Umfrage (über) survey (on) ['sɜːveɪ]
umher: in ... umher round [raʊnd]; around [ə'raʊnd] • **in der Stadt umher** around the town
► S.155 around
umher-: umhergehen walk around **umherrennen** run around **umherspringen** jump around
► S.155 around
umschreiben *(anders ausdrücken)* paraphrase ['pærəfreɪz]
umsehen: sich umsehen look round [ˌlʊk 'raʊnd]; look around [ˌlʊk‿ə'raʊnd]
umsteigen change [tʃeɪndʒ]
umziehen (nach, in) *(die Wohnung wechseln)* move (to) [muːv]
uncool uncool [ˌʌn'kuːl] *(infml)*
und and [ənd, ænd] • **Und? / Na und?** So? [səʊ]
unentschieden: 2:2 unentschieden 2 all
► S.162 A football match
Unentschieden draw [drɔː]
► S.162 A football match
unfair unfair [ˌʌn'feə]
Unfall accident ['æksɪdənt]
unfreundlich unfriendly [ʌn'frendli]
ungefähr about [ə'baʊt]
Ungeheuer monster ['mɒnstə]
ungerecht unfair [ˌʌn'feə]
ungesund unhealthy [ʌn'helθi]
unglaublich amazing [ə'meɪzɪŋ]
unglücklich unhappy [ʌn'hæpi]
unheimlich scary ['skeəri]
unhöflich rude [ruːd]
Uniform uniform ['juːnɪfɔːm]
unmöglich impossible [ɪm'pɒsəbl]
unordentlich untidy [ʌn'taɪdi] • **sehr unordentlich sein** *(Zimmer)* be a mess [mes]
Unordnung: alles in Unordnung bringen make a mess [ˌmeɪk‿ə 'mes]
Unrecht haben be wrong [rɒŋ]
uns us [əs, ʌs] • **uns (selbst)** ourselves [aʊə'selvz]
► S.167 Reflexive pronouns
unser(e) ... our ... ['aʊə] • **unser eigenes Schwimmbad** our own pool [əʊn]
unserer, unsere, unseres ours ['aʊəz]
unten below [bɪ'ləʊ]; *(im Haus)* downstairs [ˌdaʊn'steəz] • **am unteren Ende (von)** at the bottom (of) ['bɒtəm] • **dort unten** down there • **nach unten** down [daʊn]; *(im Haus)* downstairs
unter under ['ʌndə]; *(unterhalb von)* below [bɪ'ləʊ]
untere(r, s): am unteren Ende (von) at the bottom (of) ['bɒtəm]
unterhalb (von) below [bɪ'ləʊ]
unterhalten: sich unterhalten (mit, über) talk (to, about) [tɔːk]
Unterricht lessons *(pl)* ['lesnz]
unterrichten teach [tiːtʃ]
Unterschied difference ['dɪfrəns]
unterschiedlich different ['dɪfrənt]
unterstützen: eine Mannschaft unterstützen support a team [sə'pɔːt]
Untersuchung (über) *(Umfrage)* survey (on) ['sɜːveɪ]
unverschämt rude [ruːd]
Urgroßmutter great-grandmother [ˌgreɪt 'grænmʌðə]
Urgroßvater great-grandfather [ˌgreɪt 'grænfɑːðə]
Urlaub holiday ['hɒlədeɪ] *(BE)*; vacation [və'keɪʃn, *AE:* veɪ'keɪʃn] *(AE)* • **in Urlaub fahren** go on holiday • **in Urlaub sein** be on holiday

V

Vater father ['fɑːðə]
Vati dad [dæd]
Verabredung appointment [ə'pɔɪntmənt]; *(Date)* date [deɪt]
verabschieden: sich verabschieden say goodbye [ˌseɪ gʊd'baɪ]
verängstigt scared [skeəd]
verbinden *(einander zuordnen)* link [lɪŋk]
Verbindung *(Verknüpfung)* link [lɪŋk] • **in Verbindung bleiben** *(Kontakt halten)* keep in touch [tʌtʃ] • **sich mit jm. in Verbindung setzen** contact sb. ['kɒntækt]
verbringen: Zeit verbringen (mit etwas) spend time (on sth.) [spend]
Verein club [klʌb]
vereinigt: das Vereinigte Königreich *(Großbritannien und Nordirland)* the United Kingdom (UK) [juˌnaɪtɪd 'kɪŋdəm], [ˌjuː 'keɪ] • **die Vereinigten Staaten (von Amerika)** the United States (US) [juˌnaɪtɪd 'steɪts], [ˌjuː‿'es]
verfolgen follow ['fɒləʊ]
Vergangenheit past [pɑːst]
vergessen forget [fə'get]
vergeuden (für) waste (on) [weɪst]
Vergleich comparison [kəm'pærɪsn]
Vergnügen: Viel Vergnügen! Have a good time!
vergriffen sein *(ausverkauft sein)* be sold out [ˌsəʊld‿'aʊt]
verheiratet (mit) married (to) ['mærɪd]
verkaufen sell [sel]
Verkäufer/in shop assistant ['ʃɒp‿əˌsɪstənt]
Verkehr traffic ['træfɪk]
Verkehrsmittel transport *(no pl)* ['trænspɔːt] • **öffentliche Verkehrsmittel** *(öffentlicher Personennahverkehr)* public transport *(no pl)* [ˌpʌblɪk 'trænspɔːt]
verkehrsreich *(Straße)* busy ['bɪzi]
verkehrt *(falsch)* wrong [rɒŋ]
verknallt: in jn. verknallt sein have a crush on sb. [krʌʃ]
verknüpfen *(einander zuordnen)* link [lɪŋk]
Verknüpfung *(Verbindung)* link
verlassen leave [liːv]
verletzen hurt [hɜːt]
verletzt hurt [hɜːt]
verlieren lose [luːz]
vermissen miss [mɪs]
Vermittlung *(Sprachmittlung, Mediation)* mediation [ˌmiːdi'eɪʃn]
vermuten suppose [sə'pəʊz]
veröffentlichen publish ['pʌblɪʃ]
verpassen miss [mɪs]
verrückt mad [mæd]; crazy ['kreɪzi] **verrückt nach/auf etwas sein** be mad about sth.
Versammlung *(morgendliche Schulversammlung, oft mit Andacht)* Assembly [ə'sembli]
verschieden different ['dɪfrənt]
verschwenden (für) waste (on) [weɪst]
verschwinden disappear [ˌdɪsə'pɪə]
versprechen promise ['prɒmɪs]
verstecken; sich verstecken hide [haɪd]
verstehen understand [ˌʌndə'stænd]
versuchen try [traɪ]
vertreten *(repräsentieren)* represent [ˌreprɪ'zent]
verwenden use [juːz]
verwirrt puzzled ['pʌzld]
Video video ['vɪdiəʊ]
viel a lot (of) [lɒt]; lots (of) [lɒts]; much [mʌtʃ] • **viele** a lot (of); lots

(of); many ['meni] • **Viel Glück (bei/mit ...)!** Good luck (with ...)! **viel mehr** lots more • **Viel Spaß!** Have fun! / Have a good time! **wie viel?** how much? • **wie viele?** how many? • **Vielen Dank!** Thanks a lot!
vielleicht maybe ['meɪbi] • **du könntest vielleicht Hilfe brauchen** you might need help [maɪt]
Viertel: Viertel nach 11 quarter past 11 ['kwɔːtə] • **Viertel vor 12** quarter to 12
violett purple ['pɜːpl]
Virus virus ['vaɪrəs]
Vogel bird [bɜːd]
Vokabelverzeichnis vocabulary [və'kæbjələri]
Vokallaut vowel sound ['vaʊəl saʊnd]
voll full [fʊl] • **die Nase voll haben (von etwas)** be fed up (with sth.) [ˌfed_'ʌp]
Volleyball volleyball ['vɒlibɔːl]
von of [əv, ɒv]; from [frəm, frɒm] **ein Aufsatz von ...** an essay by ... [baɪ] • **von Montag bis Freitag** from Monday to Friday
► S.167 German „bis"
vor 1. *(räumlich)* in front of [ɪn 'frʌnt_əv]
2. *(zeitlich)* **vor dem Abendessen** before dinner [bɪ'fɔː] • **vor einer Minute** a minute ago [ə'gəʊ] **Viertel vor 12** quarter to 12 **nicht vor** *(erst um)* not ... until / not ... till
vorankommen: Wie komme ich voran? *(Wie sind meine Fortschritte?)* How am I doing?
vorbei (an) *(vorüber)* past [pɑːst]
vorbei sein be over ['əʊvə]
vorbereiten prepare [prɪ'peə] • **sich vorbereiten (auf)** prepare (for); get ready (for) ['redi] • **Dinge vorbereiten** get things ready
vorbringen: ein Argument vorbringen make a point [pɔɪnt]
Vordergrund foreground ['fɔːgraʊnd]
Vorhang curtain ['kɜːtn]
Vormittag morning ['mɔːnɪŋ]
Vorschrift rule [ruːl]
vorsichtig careful ['keəfl]
vorspielen *(pantomimisch darstellen)* mime [maɪm]
vorstellen 1. jm. etwas vorstellen *(präsentieren)* present sth. to sb. [prɪ'zent]
2. sich etwas vorstellen imagine sth. [ɪ'mædʒɪn] • **Stell dir vor! / Stellt euch vor!** Guess what! [ˌges 'wɒt]
Vorstellung *(Präsentation)* presentation [ˌprezn'teɪʃn]; *(Show)* show [ʃəʊ]
vorüber (an) *(vorbei)* past [pɑːst]
Vorwurf: jm. Vorwürfe machen (wegen) blame sb. (for) [bleɪm]

W

wachsen grow [grəʊ]
Waffe: (Schuss-)Waffe gun [gʌn]
wählen *(auswählen)* choose [tʃuːz]
wahr true [truː]
während *(als)* as [əz, æz]; while [waɪl]
wahrscheinlich probably ['prɒbəbli]
Wald forest ['fɒrɪst]; woods *(pl)* [wʊdz]
walisisch; Walisisch Welsh [welʃ]
Walross walrus ['wɔːlrəs]
Wand wall [wɔːl]
wann when [wen]
warm warm [wɔːm]
Wärmflasche hot-water bottle [ˌhɒt 'wɔːtə bɒtl]
warnen: jn. (vor etwas) warnen warn sb. (about sth.) [wɔːn]
warten (auf) wait (for) [weɪt] **Warte mal!** Wait a minute. ['mɪnɪt] **Wart's ab!** Wait and see!
warum why [waɪ]
was what [wɒt] • **Was fehlt dir?** *(bei Krankheit)* What's wrong with you? • **Was für ein Auto ...?** What kind of car ...? • **Was für ein interessantes Leben!** What an interesting life! • **Was gibt es zum Mittagessen?** What's for lunch? **Was haben wir als Hausaufgabe auf?** What's for homework? **Was hältst du von ...?** How do you feel about ...? • **Was ist los? / Was ist denn?** What's the matter? ['mætə] • **Was ist mit ...?** What about ...? • **Was kostet/kosten ...?** How much is/are ...? • **Was war das Beste an ...?** What was the best thing about ...? • **Was weißt du sonst noch über ...?** What else do you know about ...? [els] • **alles, was wir jetzt (noch) tun müssen, ...** all we have to do now ... • **wir wissen, was wir tun müssen / was zu tun ist** we know what to do
waschen wash [wɒʃ] • **Ich wasche mir das Gesicht.** I wash my face.
Wasser water ['wɔːtə]
Webcam webcam ['webkæm]
Website website ['websaɪt]
Wechselgeld change [tʃeɪndʒ]
wecken: jn. wecken wake sb. (up) [weɪk]
weg away [ə'weɪ] • **weg sein** *(nicht zu Hause sein)* be out [aʊt]
Weg way [weɪ]; *(Pfad)* path [pɑːθ]; *(Gasse)* lane [leɪn] • **auf dem Weg (zu/nach)** on the way (to) **etwas auf den Weg bringen** get sth. off the ground • **jm. den Weg beschreiben** tell sb. the way • **jn. nach dem Weg fragen** ask sb. the way
Wegbeschreibung(en) directions *(pl)* [də'rekʃnz]
wegbleiben *(draußen bleiben)* stay out [ˌsteɪ_'aʊt]
weggehen leave [liːv]; *(raus-, ausgehen)* go out
wehen blow [bləʊ]
wehtun hurt [hɜːt]; be sore [sɔː]
Weide field [fiːld]
weil because [bɪ'kɒz]
Weise *(Art und Weise)* way [weɪ] **auf diese Weise** this way/that way
weiß white [waɪt]
weit *(entfernt)* far [fɑː]
weiter: geradeaus weiter straight on [streɪt_'ɒn]
weitere(r, s): ein(e) weitere(r, s) one more [mɔː] • **weitere 45 Pence** another 45 p [ə'nʌðə]
weiter-: weitergeben pass [pɑːs] **weitergehen** walk on • **weiterlesen** read on • **weitermachen** go on • **weiterreden** go on • **weiterträumen** dream on
► S.152 on („weiter")
welche(r, s) which [wɪtʃ] • **Auf welcher Seite sind wir?** What page are we on? [wɒt] • **Welche Farbe hat ...?** What colour is ...?
wellenreiten gehen go surfing ['sɜːfɪŋ]
Wellensittich budgie ['bʌdʒi]
Welt world [wɜːld] • **auf der ganzen Welt** all over the world
wem? who? [huː] • **Wem gehören diese?** Whose are these? [huːz]
wen? who? [huː]
wenden: sich an jn. wenden turn to sb. [tɜːn]
wenig: am wenigsten least [liːst]
wenigstens at least [ət 'liːst]
wenn 1. *(zeitlich)* when [wen] **2.** *(falls)* if [ɪf]
wer? who? [huː] • **Wer ist dran / an der Reihe?** Whose turn is it? [huːz]
werden become [bɪ'kʌm] • **wütend/heiß/... werden** get angry/hot/... **du wirst frieren; ihr werdet frieren** you'll be cold (= you will be cold) [wɪl] • **du wirst nicht frieren; ihr**

werdet nicht frieren you won't be cold (= you will not be cold) [wəʊnt]
werfen throw [θrəʊ]
Werkstatt workshop ['wɜ:kʃɒp]
wessen? whose? [hu:z]
Westen west [west] • **nach Westen** west • **Richtung Westen** *(Fahrtrichtung)* westbound ['westbaʊnd]
westlich west [west]; western ['westən]
Wetter weather ['weðə]
Whisky whisky ['wɪski]
wichtig (für jn.) important (to sb.) [ɪm'pɔ:tnt]
wie 1. *(Fragewort)* how [haʊ] • **Wie bitte?** Sorry? ['sɒri] • **Wie geht es dir/Ihnen/euch?** How are you? [ˌhaʊ_'ɑ: jʊ] • **Wie heißt du?** What's your name? • **Wie komme ich voran?** *(Wie sind meine Fortschritte?)* How am I doing? • **Wie spät ist es?** What's the time? **Wie steht es?** *(beim Sport)* What's the score? • **wie viel?** how much? **wie viele?** how many? • **Wie war ...?** How was ...? • **Wie war das Wetter?** What was the weather like? • **Wie wär's mit ...?** What about ...? / How about ...?
2. so groß/aufregend wie as big/exciting as • **wie du sehen kannst** as you can see
3. wie ein Filmstar like a film star [laɪk] • **genau wie du** just like you
wieder again [ə'gen]
wiederholen *(Lernstoff)* revise [rɪ'vaɪz]
Wiederholung *(des Lernstoffs)* revision [rɪ'vɪʒn]
Wiedersehen: Auf Wiedersehen. Goodbye. [ˌgʊd'baɪ]
wiederverwendet/-verwertet recycled [ˌri:'saɪkld]
Wiederverwertung recycling [ˌri:'saɪklɪŋ]
wild wild [waɪld]
willkommen: Willkommen (in ...). Welcome (to ...). ['welkəm] • **Sie heißen dich in ... willkommen** They welcome you to ...
Wind wind [wɪnd]
windig windy ['wɪndi]
Windjacke anorak ['ænəræk]
Windschutzscheibe windscreen ['wɪndskri:n]
winken wave [weɪv]
Winter winter ['wɪntə]
wir we [wi:]
Wirbelsturm tornado [tɔ:'neɪdəʊ]
wirklich 1. *(tatsächlich)* really ['rɪəli] **Meinst du wirklich?/Glaubst du das wirklich?** Do you really think so?
2. *(echt)* real [rɪəl]
Wirklichkeit: in Wirklichkeit *(eigentlich)* actually ['æktʃuəli]
wirklichkeitsnah realistic [ˌri:ə'lɪstɪk]
wischen *(Fußboden)* wash [wɒʃ]
wissen know [nəʊ] • **Ich weiß es nicht.** I don't know. • **von etwas wissen; über etwas Bescheid wissen** know about sth. • **..., wissen Sie. / ..., weißt du.** ..., you know. **Weißt du was, Sophie?** You know what, Sophie? • **Woher weißt du ...?** How do you know ...?
wissen wollen wonder ['wʌndə]
Witz joke [dʒəʊk] • **Witze machen** joke
witzig funny ['fʌni]
wo where [weə] • **Wo kommst du her?** Where are you from?
Woche week [wi:k]
Wochenende weekend [ˌwi:k'end] **am Wochenende** at the weekend
Wochentage days of the week
Wofür? What for? [ˌwɒt 'fɔ:]
Woher weißt du ...? How do you know ...? [nəʊ]
wohin where [weə]; *(in welche Richtung)* which way
Wohlfahrtsorganisation charity ['tʃærəti]
Wohltätigkeitsbasar jumble sale ['dʒʌmbl seɪl]
wohnen live [lɪv]
Wohnheim *(Herberge)* hostel ['hɒstl]
Wohnung flat [flæt]
Wohnungstür front door [ˌfrʌnt 'dɔ:]
Wohnwagen caravan ['kærəvæn]
Wohnzimmer living room ['lɪvɪŋ ru:m]
Wolf wolf, *pl* wolves [wʊlf, wʊlvz]
Wolke cloud [klaʊd]
wollen *(haben wollen)* want [wɒnt] **tun wollen** want to do
Workshop workshop ['wɜ:kʃɒp]
Wort word [wɜ:d]
Wortbildung word building ['wɜ:d ˌbɪldɪŋ]
Wörterbuch dictionary ['dɪkʃənri]
Wörterverzeichnis vocabulary [və'kæbjələri]; *(alphabetisches)* dictionary ['dɪkʃənri]
Wortfeld word field ['wɜ:d fi:ld]
Wovon redest du? What are you talking about?
wund sein be sore [sɔ:]
würde: du würdest ... you would ... [wəd, wʊd]
Würfel dice, *pl* dice [daɪs]
Wurst, Würstchen sausage ['sɒsɪdʒ]
würzig *(scharf gewürzt)* spicy ['spaɪsi]
wütend sein (über etwas/auf jn.) be angry (about sth./with sb.) ['æŋgri]

Y

Yoga yoga ['jəʊgə]

Z

Zahl number ['nʌmbə]
zählen count [kaʊnt]
Zahn tooth [tu:θ], *pl* teeth [ti:θ] • **Ich putze mir die Zähne.** I clean my teeth.
Zahnschmerzen toothache ['tu:θeɪk]
zanken: sich zanken argue ['ɑ:gju:]
Zauberkunststück trick [trɪk] • **Zauberkunststücke machen** do tricks
Zebra zebra ['zebrə]
Zeh toe [təʊ]
Zeichen *(Schild)* sign [saɪn]
zeichnen draw [drɔ:]
Zeichnung drawing ['drɔ:ɪŋ]
zeigen show [ʃəʊ] • **auf etwas zeigen** point at/to sth. [pɔɪnt]
Zeile line [laɪn]
Zeit time [taɪm]; *(grammatische Zeit, Tempus)* tense [tens] • **Zeit verbringen (mit)** spend time (on) [spend]
Zeitschrift magazine [ˌmægə'zi:n]
Zeitstrahl timeline ['taɪmlaɪn]
Zeitung newspaper ['nju:speɪpə]; paper ['peɪpə]
zelten camp [kæmp]
Zentimeter centimetre (cm) ['sentɪmi:tə]
Zentral-, Mittel- central ['sentrəl]
Zentrum centre ['sentə]
zerbrochen broken ['brəʊkən]
Zeug *(Kram)* stuff [stʌf]
ziehen pull [pʊl]
ziemlich gut pretty good ['prɪti]; quite good [kwaɪt]
Ziffer number ['nʌmbə]
Zimmer room [ru:m]
Zirkus circus ['sɜ:kəs]
zittern shiver ['ʃɪvə]
Zone zone [zəʊn]
zu 1. *(örtlich)* to [tə, tu] • **zu Jenny** to Jenny's • **zu Hause** at home **zum Arzt** to the doctor's • **Setz dich zu mir.** Sit with me. • **auf jn./etwas zu** towards sb./sth. [tə'wɔ:dz]
2. zu Fuß on foot • **zum Beispiel** for example [ɪg'zɑ:mpl] • **zum**

Frühstück/Mittagessen/Abendbrot for breakfast/lunch/dinner **zum Schluss** *(schließlich)* in the end • **zu seinem Geburtstag** for his birthday
3. zu viel too much [tu:] • **zu spät sein/kommen** be late
4. versuchen zu tun try and do / try to do
5. um zu to
zubereiten *(kochen)* cook [kʊk]
Zucker sugar ['ʃʊgə]
zuerst first [fɜ:st]
Zug train [treɪn] • **im Zug** on the train
Zuhause home [həʊm]
zuhören listen (to) ['lɪsn]
Zuhörer/in listener ['lɪsnə] • **Zuhörer/innen** *(Publikum)* audience ['ɔ:diəns]
Zukunft future ['fju:tʃə]
zulassen, dass jd. etwas tut *(erlauben)* let sb. do sth. [let]
zum *siehe „zu"*
zumachen close [kləʊz]
zumindest at least [ət 'li:st]
zurück (nach) back (to) [bæk]
zurücklassen leave [li:v]
zusammen together [tə'geðə]
zusätzlich extra ['ekstrə]
Zuschauer/innen *(Publikum)* audience ['ɔ:diəns]
zusehen watch [wɒtʃ]
zustimmen: jm./etwas zustimmen agree with sb./sth. [ə'gri:]
zuvor: in der Nacht/Woche/... zuvor the night/week/... before [bɪ'fɔ:]
zuwenden: sich jm. zuwenden turn to sb. [tɜ:n]
zweimal twice [twaɪs]
zweite(r, s) second ['sekənd]
zweiwöchig: ein zweiwöchiger Urlaub a two-week holiday
Zwiebel onion ['ʌnjən]
Zwillinge twins *(pl)* [twɪnz]
Zwillingsbruder twin brother ['twɪn ˌbrʌðə]
zwischen between [bɪ'twi:n]

English sounds (Englische Laute)

Die Lautschrift in den eckigen Klammern zeigt dir, wie ein Wort ausgesprochen wird.
In der folgenden Übersicht findest du alle Lautzeichen.

Vokale (Selbstlaute)

[i:]	green	[eɪ]	skate
[i]	happy	[aɪ]	time
[ɪ]	in	[ɔɪ]	boy
[e]	yes	[əʊ]	old
[æ]	black	[aʊ]	now
[ɑ:]	park	[ɪə]	here
[ɒ]	song	[eə]	where
[ɔ:]	morning	[ʊə]	tour
[u:]	blue		
[ʊ]	book		
[ʌ]	mum		
[ɜ:]	T-shirt		
[ə]	a partner		

Konsonanten (Mitlaute)

[b]	box	[f]	full
[p]	play	[v]	very
[d]	dad	[s]	sister
[t]	ten	[z]	please
[g]	good	[ʃ]	shop
[k]	cat	[ʒ]	television
[m]	mum	[tʃ]	teacher
[n]	no	[dʒ]	Germany
[ŋ]	sing	[θ]	thanks
[l]	hello	[ð]	this
[r]	red	[h]	he
[w]	we		
[j]	you		

The English alphabet (Das englische Alphabet)

a	[eɪ]	**h**	[eɪtʃ]	**o**	[əʊ]	**v**	[vi:]
b	[bi:]	**i**	[aɪ]	**p**	[pi:]	**w**	['dʌblju:]
c	[si:]	**j**	[dʒeɪ]	**q**	[kju:]	**x**	[eks]
d	[di:]	**k**	[keɪ]	**r**	[ɑ:]	**y**	[waɪ]
e	[i:]	**l**	[el]	**s**	[es]	**z**	[zed]
f	[ef]	**m**	[em]	**t**	[ti:]		
g	[dʒi:]	**n**	[en]	**u**	[ju:]		

Illustrationen

Roland Beier, Berlin (S. 18; S. 20 (M); S. 24; S. 29; S. 41–42; S. 47; S. 50; S. 60; S. 64–65; S. 67; S. 77–78; S. 83; S. 95; S. 97; S. 101; S. 103; S. 118–119; S. 124–171); **Carlos Borrell**, Berlin (vordere u. hintere Umschlaginnenseite; S. 6 (u. 52); S. 17; S. 30; S. 74); **Graham-Cameron Illustrations**, UK: **Fliss Cary** (S. 23; S. 26–28; S. 34; S. 40; S. 44–46; S. 54; S. 61–62; S. 79–82; S. 102; S. 105); **John Rabou** (S. 48; S. 51); **Linda Rogers Associates**, London: **Gary Rees** (S. 108); **Michael Teßmer**, Hamburg (S. 111); **Korinna Wilkes**, Berlin (S. 91)

Bildquellen

action press, Hamburg (S. 53 re.: ALTERPHOTOS; S. 62 Bild 3: Everett Collection, Inc.; S. 92 Bild 1: Zuma Press Inc.; S. 94 oben: All Action, unten: Rex Features Ltd.; S. 96: 2Vista; S. 100: Wolfgang List; S. 131: ALL ACTION DIGITAL); **Alamy**, Abingdon (Inhaltsverz. (u. 117) bear: ImageState/Rosemary Calvert; S. 6 unten re. (u. 52): Paul Doyle, oben Mitte: The Photolibrary Wales, unten Mitte: Photofusion Picture Library/Vehbi Koca; S. 12 Bild 1: Peter Barritt, Bild 2: Ernst Wrba, Bild 3: Caroline Cortizo; S. 13 Bild 5: Peter Forsberg; S. 15 Bild B: Kevin Allen, Bild C: Richard Cooke; S. 18 Mitte: PCL/picturescolourlibrary; S. 19 oben li. (u. 132): The Print Collector, Mitte: Alex Beaton; S. 20 tire (M): Brand X Pictures/Burke/Triolo Productions; S. 25 oben: imagestopshop, Mitte: Stan Kujawa, unten: Trevor Smith; S. 30 Bild 1 u. 3: orkneypics; S. 31 Bild 6 (M): Doug Houghton, lamb and sheep: Suzy Bennett, sheep: orkneypics; S. 36 unten li.: Ingram Publishing (Superstock Limited); S. 37 Mitte: Malcolm Fife; S. 39 Mitte: Worldwide Picture Library/Hugh Webster, unten: Robert Harding Picture Library Ltd/Michael Jenner; S. 57 unten (u. 113 unten li.): artpartner-images.com; S. 62 Bild 2: UKraft; S. 68 icy bench (M): Reimar, skyline (M): Rohit Seth; S. 69 background: Douglas Peebles Photography; S. 70 oben li.: david sanger photography/davidsanger.com, Mitte li.: RubberBall, Mitte re.: Geoff du Feu; S. 72 li.: Alaska Stock LLC: C&C Bear Imagery; S. 74 Mitte: Robert McGouey; S. 79 re.: Elvele Images/Fritz Poelking; S. 81 li.: Helene Rogers, re.: Arco Images; S. 88 hat: Bill Brooks; S. 91 oben u. Mitte: Lebrecht Music and Arts Photo Library/Chris Stock/Lebrecht; S. 92 Bild 4: JUPITERIMAGES/Creatas; S. 104 unten (M): George S de Blonsky; S. 110 freak: JUPITERIMAGES/Creatas, loner: JUPITERIMAGES/Thinkstock; S. 112 Mitte re.: Lebrecht Music and Arts Photo Library; S. 117 oben: Wolfgang Kaehler, unten re.: david tipling; S. 120 unten: Hugh Threlfall; S. 122 video game character (M): JUPITERIMAGES/Brand X/Colin Anderson, unten: Andrew Woodley; **Peter Arnold**, New York: Steven Kazlowski (S. 79 li.); **Avenue Images**, Hamburg (S. 15 Bild A: Index Stock/David Ball); **A1PIX**, Taufkirchen (S. 63 unten li.); **Bildmaschine.de**, Berlin (S. 92 Bild 5: Peter Engelke); **Blickwinkel**, Witten: (S. 31 bird: H.J. Igelmund); **John Birdsall Social Issues Photolibrary**, Nottingham (Inhaltsverz. kids; S. 7–11; S. 15 Bild D (u. 128) foreground (M); S. 16 oben; S. 35; S. 52 Anna; S. 54–55; S. 68 re.; S. 70 unten re.; S. 73 oben; S. 88 li.; S. 89 re.; S. 90 Latisha); **Britain on View**, London (S. 15 Bild D (u. 128) background (M): Nigel Hicks; S. 18 unten re.: www.britainonview.com; S. 31 Bild 5: Joe Cornish; S. 39 oben: www.britainonview.com); **Cinetext Bildarchiv**, Frankfurt/Main (S. 62 Bild 4: Allstar; S. 123 (M)); **Corbis**, Düsseldorf (Inhaltsverz. (u. 15) Tower Bridge: Angelo Hornak; S. 6 oben li. (u. 52): Jeremy Horner; S. 13 Bild 4: Bill Varie; S. 18 oben: Toby Melville/Reuters; S. 37 oben: Roger Ressmeyer; S. 68 oben li.: RNT Productions; S. 69 oben: Dale C. Spartas, unten li.: Graham Bell; S. 70 unten li.: Ajax/zefa; S. 71 unten: Annie Griffiths Belt; S. 72 re.: Dale C. Spartas; S. 75 Mitte: Aristide Economopoulos/Star Ledger; S. 85: David Muench; S. 86: James Marshall); **Corel Library** (Inhaltsverz. Hoy; S. 69 unten re.); **defd Deutscher Fotodienst**, Hamburg (S. 99 Shrek); **Barbara Derkow Disselbeck**, Köln (S. 33); **Digitalstock**, Wangen/Markgröningen (S.63 unten re.); **Edinburgh Festival Fringe Society**, Edinburgh (S. 37 unten re.); **Erzgebirgische Volkskunst Richard Glässer GmbH**, Kurort Seiffen (S. 63 Mitte angel); **fabfoodpix.com**, London (S. 36 haggis); **FAN travelstock**, Hamburg (S. 22: Michael Schindel); **Fotosearch**, Waukesha (S. 66 boots: Brand X Pictures); **GB eye** Ltd, Sheffield (S. 55 poster: © 2006 MUML Crest & Imagery © MU Ltd.); **Getty Images**, München (S. 36 Mitte: Rubberball Productions, bagpipers: Tim Graham; S. 56 oben: AFP/Johannes Eisele; S. 58 oben li.: Man Utd via Getty Images/Matthew Peters, Mitte: Gary M. Prior; S. 59 oben li.: Michael Steele, oben re., unten re.: Bryn Lennon; S. 62 Bild 6: Evan Agostini; S. 75 unten: Medford Taylor; S. 76 unten: Josef Fankhauser; S. 91 unten: WireImage/John Stanton; S. 92 Bild 2: AFP/Tim Sloan; S. 99 Franz Ferdinand: Dave Hogan; S. 110 oben: Sabine Duerichen; S. 112 unten li.: altrendo images; S. 113 oben: Phil Cole; unten re.: Man Utd via Getty Images: John Peters); **Bonnie Glänzer**, Berlin (S. 21); **Randy Glasbergen**, Sherburne (S. 32); **Harbourfront Centre**, Toronto (S. 88 logo); **Dick Hemingway Photographs**, Toronto (S. 74 unten: Photographers Direct/Dick Hemingway); **Home Office**, London (S. 109: "ru alone when u meet online m8s in real life?" © Crown copyright material is reproduced with the permission of the Controller of HMSO and Queen's Printer for Scotland); **Ipon**, Berlin (S. 19 oben re.: Stefan Boness); **Keystone**, Hamburg (S. 36 oben li.: Topham Picturepoint); **laif**, Köln (S. 38 li.); **Louise Lazell**, UK (S. 107 oben); **LOOK**, München (S. 87: Thomas Peter Widmann; S. 112 unten re.: LOOK-foto/Ingolf Pompe); **The LS Lowry Collection**, Salford (S. 56 li.); **The Lowry**, Salford Quays (S. 56 re.); **OCS Group Marketing**, Lancashire (S. 66 oben); **mauritius images**, Mittenwald (S. 110 fat: Fancy); **PA Photos**, Nottingham (S. 59 Mitte; S. 104 oben); **Jacob Perlmutter**, UK (S. 106 u. 107 unten); **Photofusion**, London (S. 19 unten: Bipinchandra; S. 110 popular: Paul Baldesare); **Picture Alliance**, Frankfurt/Main (Inhaltsverz. (u. S. 58 oben re.) Old Trafford: dpa-Sportreport; S. 58 unten li.: dpa/dpaweb/epa Keystone Patrick B. Kraemer, unten re.: dpa-Report/Abaca Kempinaire-Gouhier; S. 59 unten li.: dpa-Sportreport; S. 62 Bild 1: dpa-Report/epa Lambert; S. 63 oben: Bildagentur Huber/R. Schmid, Chemnitz li.u. re. u. Mitte re.: ZB-Fotoreport/Wolfgang Thieme; S. 73 unten: dpa-Report/Keystone USA k03; S. 99 Rock am Ring: SCHROEWIG/Jens Koch; Alexander Kapranos: dpa/Harald Tittel; Nelly Furtado: dpa/Roland Weihrauch; **Picture Press**, Hamburg (S. 6 oben re. (u. 52): Maruan Bahrour; S. 89 oben li.: Frank P. Wartenberg); **Marion Schönenberger**, Berlin (S. 52–53; S. 98; S. 120 oben; S. 121); **Scottish Tartans World Register**, Crieff (S. 36 oben re.); **Nick Sharratt** (S. 114–116: illustrations taken from *Cliffhanger* by Jacqueline Wilson. Reprinted by permission of David Higham Associates Limited, London); **Shutterstock**, New York (S. 18 unten li.: Robyn Mackenzie; S. 52 screen image (M): Sean Nel; S. 68 Canadian flag: Sasha Davas, German flag: Kurt de Bruyn; S. 70 oben re. und S. 71 oben: Ronen; S. 76 oben li. u. re.: Tomasz Trojanowski; S. 79 Mitte: Ronnie Howard; S. 88 basketball: Vincent Giordano, (u. 90) CD: Andresr, film: Olga Langerova; S. 92 Bild 3 li.: Rafa Irusta, Bild 3 re.: Danny Smythe; S. 93: Edyta Pawlowska; S. 112 oben: Clarence s lewis, Mitte li.: David Romero Corral; S. 117 Mitte: Thomas O' Neil; S. 122 DVD cases (M): 3poD Animation); **Friedrich Stark**, Dortmund (S. 75 oben); **Stills-Online**, Hamburg (S. 66 helmet); **Stuck on Scotland Holidays**, Scotland (S. 38 re.); **Charles Tait Photographic Limited**, Orkney (S. 30 Bild 4 u. S. 43: www.charles-tait.co.uk); **Transport for London**, London (S. 14); **The Travel Library Ltd**, Fleet (S. 37 unten li.); **ullstein bild**, Berlin (S. 6 unten li. (u. 52): Wöstmann; S. 30 Bild 2: Still Pictures; S. 62 Bild 5: Imagno); **Webb Aviation**, Bramhall (S. 59 Velodrome exterior: webbaviation.co.uk); **WILDLIFE**, Hamburg (S. 30 salmon: J. Mallwitz)

Titelbild

Alamy, Abingdon (London Eye (M): Ian MacPherson); Corbis, Düsseldorf (bus (M): Royalty-Free); **IFA-Bilderteam**, Ottobrunn (Union Jack: Jon Arnold Images)

Textquellen

S. 34: *Billy doesn't like school really* by Paul Cookson taken from "The Works – Poems chosen by Paul Cookson". Macmillan Children's Books, London 2000. © Paul Cookson; S. 81: *Man kills bear* adapted from "Canoeist stabs bear", http://www.cbc.ca/canada/story/2006/07/22/bear.html (Stand: 22.04.2008); S. 106–107: *Pull in Emergency* adapted from "Night Haunts for Twilight Teens" by Sophie Heawood, taken from The Times, 12.08.2006. © NI Syndication Ltd. London; S. 111: *The lost girl* adapted from "The Mermaid Bride and other Orkney Folk Tales" told by Tom Muir. The Orcadian Limited (Kirkwall Press), Orkney. © 1998 Tom Muir and Bryce Wilson; S. 114–116: *Tim, a rock and a rope* adapted from "Cliffhanger" by Jacqueline Wilson, published by Corgi Yearling. Reprinted by permission of the Random House Group Ltd.; S. 117: *Safety in bear country* adapted from "The Mountain Guide – Safety in Bear Country" by Parks Canada, http://www.pc.gc.ca/docs/v-g/pm-mp/guidem-mguide/sec4/gm-mg4_e.asp (Stand: 22.04.2008); S. 119: *Snow storm* by Clare Bevan taken from "Read me and Laugh – A Funny Poem for Every Day of the Year" chosen by Gaby Morgan. © Macmillan Children's Books, London 2005; S. 120–123: *Fans* from "Forty Short Plays" by Ann Cartwright. Reprinted by permission of Harcourt Education, Oxford; S. 126–127: Auszüge von S. 311 and S. 725 aus "English G 2000 Wörterbuch – Das Wörterbuch zum Lehrwerk". Herausgegeben von der Langenscheidt-Redaktion Wörterbücher und der Cornelsen-Redaktion Englisch. © 2002 Cornelsen Verlag GmbH & Co. OHG, Berlin und Langenscheidt KG, Berlin und München

Liedquellen

S. 73: *Sk8er boi* by David Scott Alspach/Lauren Christy/Graham Edwards/Avril Ramona Lavigne. © Almo-Music Corp./Ferry Hills Songs/Mr. Spock Music/Rainbow Fish Publ./Warner-Tamerlane Publ. Co. Neue Welt Musikverlag GmbH, Hamburg. Rondor Musikverlag GmbH, Berlin; S. 107: *Backfoot*. © Pull in Emergency, UK; S. 113: *You'll never walk alone* by Oscar Hammerstein. © Williamson Music Inc. D/A/CH/osteuropäische Länder: EMI Music Publishing (Germany GmbH), Hamburg, *We are the champions* by Freddie Mercury. © by Queen Music Ltd. D/A/CH/Osteuropäische Länder: EMI Music Publishing Germany GmbH, Hamburg

First names (Vornamen)

Alexander [ˌælɪg'zɑːndə]
Alice ['ælɪs]
Alison ['ælɪsn]
Alistair ['ælɪstə]
Annabel ['ænəbel]
Arthur ['ɑːθə]
Ashley ['æʃli]
Asif [æ'siːf]
Avril ['ævrɪl]
Benjamin ['bendʒəmɪn]
Brandon ['brændən]
Charlene [ʃɑː'liːn]
Cindy ['sɪndi]
Clare [kleə]
Conan ['kəʊnən]
Craig [kreɪg]
Dean [diːn]
Deirdre ['dɪədri]
Dermot ['dɜːmət]
Dora ['dɔːrə]
Drugh [druː]
Eleanor ['elənə]
Elijah [ɪ'laɪdʒə]
Elizabeth [ɪ'lɪzəbəθ]
Faith [feɪθ]
Fiona [fi'əʊnə]
George [dʒɔːdʒ]
Graham ['greɪəm]
Hassan [hə'sɑːn]
Helen ['helən]
Jake [dʒeɪk]
Jamie ['dʒeɪmi]
Janet ['dʒænət]
Jenny ['dʒeni]
Jessica ['dʒesɪkə]
Jill [dʒɪl]
Jonathan ['dʒɒnəθən]
Jordan ['dʒɔːdn]
Julie ['dʒuːli]
Kahasi [kə'hɑːʃi]
Katie ['keɪti]
Katrina [kə'triːnə]
Keira ['kɪərə]
Ketevan [ˌketə'vɑːn]
Kirsty ['kɜːsti]
Latisha [lə'tɪʃə]
Mary ['meəri]
Michael ['maɪkəl]
Mika ['miːkə]
Mike [maɪk]
Mitsu ['mɪtsuː]
Natasha [nə'tæʃə]
Nathalie ['nætəli]
Nathan ['neɪθən]
Pamela ['pæmələ]
Patricia [pə'trɪʃə]
Paul [pɔːl]
Peter ['piːtə]
Petunia [pə'tjuːniə]
Robert ['rɒbət]
Sally-Ann [ˌsæli‿'æn]
Samantha [sə'mænθə]
Sandra ['sɑːndrə]
Sarah ['seərə]
Sean [ʃɔːn]
Shakira [ʃə'kɪərə]
Shania [ʃə'naɪə]
Sheena ['ʃiːnə]
Sherlock ['ʃɜːlɒk]
Solomon ['sɒləmən]
Vera ['vɪərə]
Walter ['wɔːltə]
Wayne [weɪn]
William ['wɪljəm]
Winston ['wɪnstən]
Yvonne [ɪ'vɒn]

Family names (Familiennamen)

Azad [ə'zɑːd]
Bailey ['beɪli]
Bale [beɪl]
Beckham ['bekəm]
Bennett ['benɪt]
Bevan ['bevn]
Burns [bɜːnz]
Byrd [bɜːd]
Cabot ['kæbət]
Cartwright ['kɑːtraɪt]
Collins ['kɒlɪnz]
Connery ['kɒnəri]
Cooper ['kuːpə]
Costelloe [kɒ'steləʊ]
Devlin ['devlɪn]
Doyle [dɔɪl]
Fagan ['feɪgən]
Farell ['færəl]
Farjeon ['fɑːdʒən]
Fleming ['flemɪŋ]
Gabriel ['geɪbriəl]
Garfunkel [gɑː'fʌŋkl]
Gordon ['gɔːdn]
Holmes [həʊmz]
Hooley ['huːli]
Jones ['dʒəʊnz]
Knightley ['naɪtli]
Kowalski [kə'wɒlski]
Lavigne [læ'viːn]
MacDard [mək'dɑːd]
MacLeod [mə'klaʊd]
McFadden [mək'fædn]
McKay [mə'kaɪ]
Melua ['meluə]
Merick ['merɪk]
Nagora ['nægərɑː]
O'Keefe [əʊ'kiːf]
Peterson ['piːtəsən]
Portman ['pɔːtmən]
Presley ['prezli]
Raleigh ['rɔːli]
Rooney ['ruːni]
Rowling ['rəʊlɪŋ]
Simon ['saɪmən]
Stephens ['stiːvnz]
Sutherland ['sʌðələnd]
Swann [swɒn]
Tilley ['tɪli]
Tonkins ['tɒŋkɪnz]
Twain [tweɪn]
Waites [weɪts]
Watt [wɒt]
Wilkes [wɪlks]
Williams ['wɪljəmz]

Place names (Ortsnamen)

Aberdeen [ˌæbə'diːn]
Albert Street ['ælbət striːt]
Aldgate East [ˌɔːldgeɪt‿'iːst]
Bakerloo [ˌbeɪkə'luː]
Batumi [bɑː'tuːmi]
Beirut [beɪ'ruːt]
Belfast [ˌbel'fɑːst]
Berlin [bɜː'lɪn]
Birmingham ['bɜːmɪŋəm]
Brick Lane [ˌbrɪk 'leɪn]
Burslem ['bɜːsləm]
Camden Lock [ˌkæmdən 'lɒk]
Chapleau ['ʃæpləʊ]
Charing Cross [ˌtʃærɪŋ 'krɒs]
Chelsea ['tʃelsi]
Cologne [kə'ləʊn] *Köln*
Covent Garden [ˌkɒvənt 'gɑːdn]
Ealing ['iːlɪŋ]
Earls Court [ˌɜːlz 'kɔːt]
Edinburgh ['edɪnbərə]
Flotta ['flɒtə]
Glasgow ['glæzgəʊ]
Globe Theatre [ˌgləʊb 'θɪətə]
Gretna Green [ˌgretnə 'griːn]
Helmsdale ['helmzdeɪl]
Houton ['huːtn]
Hoy [hɔɪ]
Hyde Park [ˌhaɪd 'pɑːk]
Inuvik [ɪ'nuːvɪk]
Kensington ['kenzɪŋtən]
Kirkwall ['kɜːkwɔːl]
Knightsbridge ['naɪtsbrɪdʒ]
Kutaisi [ˌkʊtə'iːsi]
Laventille [ˌlævən'tiːl]
Leicester Square [ˌlestə 'skweə]
Loch Ness [lɒx 'nes]
London ['lʌndən]
The **Lowry** ['laʊri]
Lyness ['laɪnes]
Majorca [mə'jɔːkə]
Manchester ['mæntʃestə]
Manchester Aquatics Centre [ˌmæntʃestər‿ə'kwætɪks ˌsentə]
Marble Arch [ˌmɑːbəl‿'ɑːtʃ]
Melbourne ['melbən]
Missinaibi Lake [ˌmɪsɪ'neɪbi 'leɪk]
Moaness ['məʊnes]
Montreal [ˌmɒntri'ɔːl]
Mount Everest [ˌmaʊnt‿'evərest]
Nelson's Column [ˌnelsnz 'kɒləm]
New York [ˌnjuː 'jɔːk]
Newcastle-under-Lyme [ˌnjuːkɑːsəl‿ˌʌndə 'laɪm]
Newfoundland ['njuːfəndlənd]
Nunavut ['nuːnəvuːt]
Old Trafford [əʊld 'træfəd]
Ontario [ɒn'teəriəʊ]
Orkney Islands ['ɔːkni‿ˌaɪləndz]
Ottawa ['ɒtəwə]
Oxford Circus [ˌɒksfəd 'sɜːkəs]
Paris ['pærɪs]
Piccadilly [ˌpɪkə'dɪli]
Piccadilly Circus [ˌpɪkədɪli 'sɜːkəs]
Port of Spain [ˌpɔːt‿əv 'speɪn]
Princes Street ['prɪnsəz striːt]
Quebec [kwɪ'bek]
Reading ['redɪŋ]
Redcliffe ['redklɪf]
Regent Street ['riːdʒənt striːt]
Richmond ['rɪtʃmənd]
The **River Clyde** [ˌrɪvə 'klaɪd]
The **River Thames** [ˌrɪvə 'temz]
Rochdale ['rɒtʃdeɪl]
Russell Square [ˌrʌsl 'skweə]
St Paul's Cathedral [sənt ˌpɔːlz kə'θiːdrəl]
San Francisco [ˌsæn frən'sɪskəʊ]
Staffordshire ['stæfədʃə]
Stirling ['stɜːlɪŋ]
Stoke-on-Trent [ˌstəʊk‿ɒn 'trent]
Stromness ['strɒmnes]
Tate Modern [teɪt 'mɒdən]
Tbilisi [tə'bliːsi]
Toronto [tə'rɒntəʊ]
Tower Hamlets [ˌtaʊə 'hæmləts]
Trafalgar Square [trəˌfælgə 'skweə]
Trinidad ['trɪnɪdæd]
Trocadero [ˌtrɒkə'dɪərəʊ]
Turin [ˌtjʊə'rɪn]
Vancouver [væn'kuːvə]
Victoria Station [vɪkˌtɔːriə 'steɪʃn]
Waterloo [ˌwɔːtə'luː]
Wawa ['wɑːwɑː]
Westminster ['westmɪnstə]
Whitechapel ['waɪtˌtʃæpl]
Wimbledon ['wɪmbldən]
Winnipeg ['wɪnɪpeg]

Other names (Andere Namen)

Celtic F. C. ['seltɪk]
Global Deejays [ˌgləʊbl 'diːdʒeɪz]
The **Jubilee Line** ['dʒuːbɪliː ˌlaɪn]
The **Lovin' Spoonful** [ˌlʌvɪn 'spuːnfʊl]
Maple Leafs [ˌmeɪpl 'liːfs]
Maroon 5 [məˌruːn 'faɪv]
Rangers ['reɪndʒəz]

Country/Continent	Adjective	Person	People
Africa ['æfrɪkə] *Afrika*	African ['æfrɪkən]	an African	the Africans
America [ə'merɪkə] *Amerika*	American [ə'merɪkən]	an American	the Americans
Asia ['eɪʃə, 'eɪʒə] *Asien*	Asian ['eɪʃn, 'eɪʒn]	an Asian	the Asians
Australia [ɒ'streɪliə] *Australien*	Australian [ɒ'streɪliən]	an Australian	the Australians
Austria ['ɒstriə] *Österreich*	Austrian ['ɒstriən]	an Austrian	the Austrians
Bangladesh [ˌbæŋglə'deʃ] *Bangladesch*	Bangladeshi [ˌbæŋglə'deʃi]	a Bangladeshi	the Bangladeshis
Belgium ['beldʒəm] *Belgien*	Belgian ['beldʒən]	a Belgian	the Belgians
Canada ['kænədə] *Kanada*	Canadian [kə'neɪdiən]	a Canadian	the Canadians
the Caribbean [ˌkærə'biːən] *die Karibik*	Caribbean [ˌkærə'biːən]	a Caribbean	the Caribbeans
China ['tʃaɪnə] *China*	Chinese [ˌtʃaɪ'niːz]	a Chinese	the Chinese
Colombia [kə'lɒmbiə] *Kolumbien*	Colombian [kə'lɒmbiən]	a Colombian	the Colombians
Croatia [krəʊ'eɪʃə] *Kroatien*	Croatian [krəʊ'eɪʃn]	a Croatian	the Croatians
the Czech Republic [ˌtʃek rɪ'pʌblɪk] *Tschechien, die Tschechische Republik*	Czech [tʃek]	a Czech	the Czechs
Denmark ['denmɑːk] *Dänemark*	Danish ['deɪnɪʃ]	a Dane [deɪn]	the Danes
England ['ɪŋglənd] *England*	English ['ɪŋglɪʃ]	an Englishman/-woman	the English
Europe ['jʊərəp] *Europa*	European [ˌjʊərə'piːən]	a European	the Europeans
Finland ['fɪnlənd] *Finnland*	Finnish ['fɪnɪʃ]	a Finn [fɪn]	the Finns
France [frɑːns] *Frankreich*	French [frentʃ]	a Frenchman/-woman	the French
Georgia ['dʒɔːdʒə] *Georgien*	Georgian ['dʒɔːdʒən]	a Georgian	the Georgians
Germany ['dʒɜːməni] *Deutschland*	German ['dʒɜːmən]	a German	the Germans
(Great) Britain ['brɪtn] *Großbritannien*	British ['brɪtɪʃ]	a Briton ['brɪtn]	the British
Greece [griːs] *Griechenland*	Greek [griːk]	a Greek	the Greeks
Holland ['hɒlənd] *Holland, die Niederlande*	Dutch [dʌtʃ]	a Dutchman/-woman	the Dutch
Hungary ['hʌŋgəri] *Ungarn*	Hungarian [hʌŋ'geəriən]	a Hungarian	the Hungarians
India ['ɪndiə] *Indien*	Indian ['ɪndiən]	an Indian	the Indians
Iran [ɪ'rɑːn, ɪ'ræn] *Iran*	Iranian [ɪ'reɪniən]	a Iranian	the Iranians
Ireland ['aɪələnd] *Irland*	Irish ['aɪrɪʃ]	an Irishman/-woman	the Irish
Italy ['ɪtəli] *Italien*	Italian [ɪ'tæliən]	an Italian	the Italians
Japan [dʒə'pæn] *Japan*	Japanese [ˌdʒæpə'niːz]	a Japanese	the Japanese
Lebanon ['lebənən] *Libanon*	Lebanese [ˌlebə'niːz]	a Lebanese	the Lebanese
the Netherlands ['neðələndz] *die Niederlande, Holland*	Dutch [dʌtʃ]	a Dutchman/-woman	the Dutch
New Zealand [ˌnjuː 'ziːlənd] *Neuseeland*	New Zealand [ˌnjuː 'ziːlənd]	a New Zealander	the New Zealanders
Norway ['nɔːweɪ] *Norwegen*	Norwegian [nɔː'wiːdʒən]	a Norwegian	the Norwegians
Pakistan [ˌpækɪ'stæn, ˌpɑːkɪ'stɑːn] *Pakistan*	Pakistani [ˌpækɪ'stæni, ˌpɑːkɪ'stɑːni]	a Pakistani	the Pakistanis
Poland ['pəʊlənd] *Polen*	Polish ['pəʊlɪʃ]	a Pole [pəʊl]	the Poles
Portugal ['pɔːtʃʊgl] *Portugal*	Portuguese [ˌpɔːtʃu'giːz]	a Portuguese	the Portuguese
Russia ['rʌʃə] *Russland*	Russian ['rʌʃn]	a Russian	the Russians
Scotland ['skɒtlənd] *Schottland*	Scottish ['skɒtɪʃ]	a Scotsman/-woman, a Scot [skɒt]	the Scots, the Scottish
Slovakia [sləʊ'vɑːkiə, sləʊ'vækiə] *die Slowakei*	Slovak ['sləʊvæk]	a Slovak	the Slovaks
Slovenia [sləʊ'viːniə] *Slowenien*	Slovenian [sləʊ'viːniən], Slovene ['sləʊviːn]	a Slovene, a Slovenian	the Slovenes, the Slovenians
Spain [speɪn] *Spanien*	Spanish ['spænɪʃ]	a Spaniard ['spænɪəd]	the Spaniards
Sweden ['swiːdn] *Schweden*	Swedish ['swiːdɪʃ]	a Swede [swiːd]	the Swedes
Switzerland ['swɪtsələnd] *die Schweiz*	Swiss [swɪs]	a Swiss	the Swiss
Turkey ['tɜːki] *die Türkei*	Turkish ['tɜːkɪʃ]	a Turk [tɜːk]	the Turks
the United Kingdom (the UK) [juˌnaɪtɪd 'kɪŋdəm, ˌjuː'keɪ] *das Vereinigte Königreich (Großbritannien und Nordirland)*	British ['brɪtɪʃ]	a Briton ['brɪtn]	the British
the United States of America (the USA) [juˌnaɪtɪd ˌsteɪts‿əv‿ə'merɪkə, ˌjuː‿es‿'eɪ] *die Vereinigten Staaten von Amerika*	American [ə'merɪkən]	an American	the Americans
Wales [weɪlz] *Wales*	Welsh [welʃ]	a Welshman/-woman	the Welsh

Infinitive	Simple past form	Past participle	
(to) **be**	**was/were**	**been**	sein
(to) **beat**	**beat**	**beaten**	schlagen; besiegen
(to) **become**	**became**	**become**	werden
(to) **begin**	**began**	**begun**	beginnen, anfangen (mit)
(to) **blow**	**blew**	**blown**	wehen, blasen
(to) **bring**	**brought**	**brought**	(mit-, her)bringen
(to) **build**	**built**	**built**	bauen
(to) **buy**	**bought**	**bought**	kaufen
(to) **catch**	**caught**	**caught**	fangen; erwischen
(to) **choose** [uː]	**chose** [əʊ]	**chosen** [əʊ]	(aus)wählen; (sich) aussuchen
(to) **come**	**came**	**come**	kommen
(to) **cut**	**cut**	**cut**	schneiden
(to) **do**	**did**	**done** [ʌ]	tun, machen
(to) **draw**	**drew**	**drawn**	zeichnen
(to) **drink**	**drank**	**drunk**	trinken
(to) **drive** [aɪ]	**drove**	**driven** [ɪ]	*(ein Auto)* fahren
(to) **eat**	**ate** [et, eɪt]	**eaten**	essen
(to) **fall**	**fell**	**fallen**	(hin)fallen, stürzen
(to) **feed**	**fed**	**fed**	füttern
(to) **feel**	**felt**	**felt**	(sich) fühlen; sich anfühlen
(to) **fight**	**fought**	**fought**	kämpfen
(to) **find**	**found**	**found**	finden
(to) **fly**	**flew**	**flown**	fliegen
(to) **forget**	**forgot**	**forgotten**	vergessen
(to) **get**	**got**	**got**	bekommen; holen; werden; (hin)kommen
(to) **give**	**gave**	**given**	geben
(to) **go**	**went**	**gone** [ɒ]	gehen, fahren
(to) **grow**	**grew**	**grown**	wachsen; anbauen, anpflanzen
(to) **hang out** *(infml)*	**hung out**	**hung out**	rumhängen, abhängen
(to) **have (have got)**	**had**	**had**	haben, besitzen
(to) **hear** [ɪə]	**heard** [ɜː]	**heard** [ɜː]	hören
(to) **hide** [aɪ]	**hid** [ɪ]	**hidden** [ɪ]	(sich) verstecken
(to) **hit**	**hit**	**hit**	schlagen
(to) **hold**	**held**	**held**	halten
(to) **hurt**	**hurt**	**hurt**	wehtun; verletzen
(to) **keep**	**kept**	**kept**	(be)halten
(to) **know** [nəʊ]	**knew** [njuː]	**known** [nəʊn]	wissen; kennen
(to) **lay** the table	**laid**	**laid**	den Tisch decken
(to) **leave**	**left**	**left**	(weg)gehen; abfahren; verlassen; zurücklassen

Infinitive	Simple past form	Past participle	
(to) **let**	**let**	**let**	lassen
(to) **lose** [uː]	**lost** [ɒ]	**lost** [ɒ]	verlieren
(to) **make**	**made**	**made**	machen; bauen; bilden
(to) **mean** [iː]	**meant** [e]	**meant** [e]	bedeuten; meinen
(to) **meet**	**met**	**met**	(sich) treffen
(to) **pay**	**paid**	**paid**	bezahlen
(to) **put**	**put**	**put**	legen, stellen, *(wohin)* tun
(to) **read** [iː]	**read** [e]	**read** [e]	lesen
(to) **ride** [aɪ]	**rode**	**ridden** [ɪ]	reiten; *(Rad)* fahren
(to) **ring**	**rang**	**rung**	klingeln, läuten
(to) **run**	**ran**	**run**	rennen, laufen
(to) **say** [eɪ]	**said** [e]	**said** [e]	sagen
(to) **see**	**saw**	**seen**	sehen; besuchen, aufsuchen
(to) **sell**	**sold**	**sold**	verkaufen
(to) **send**	**sent**	**sent**	schicken, senden
(to) **set** a trap	**set**	**set**	eine Falle stellen
(to) **shine**	**shone** [ɒ]	**shone** [ɒ]	scheinen *(Sonne)*
(to) **show**	**showed**	**shown**	zeigen
(to) **shut up**	**shut**	**shut**	den Mund halten
(to) **sing**	**sang**	**sung**	singen
(to) **sit**	**sat**	**sat**	sitzen; sich setzen
(to) **sleep**	**slept**	**slept**	schlafen
(to) **speak**	**spoke**	**spoken**	sprechen
(to) **spend**	**spent**	**spent**	*(Zeit)* verbringen; *(Geld)* ausgeben
(to) **stand**	**stood**	**stood**	stehen; sich (hin)stellen
(to) **steal**	**stole**	**stolen**	stehlen
(to) **stick**	**stuck**	**stuck**	herausragen, herausstehen
(to) **swim**	**swam**	**swum**	schwimmen
(to) **take**	**took**	**taken**	nehmen; (weg-, hin)bringen; dauern, *(Zeit)* brauchen
(to) **teach**	**taught**	**taught**	unterrichten, lehren
(to) **tell**	**told**	**told**	erzählen, berichten
(to) **think**	**thought**	**thought**	denken, glauben, meinen
(to) **throw**	**threw**	**thrown**	werfen
(to) **understand**	**understood**	**understood**	verstehen
(to) **upset**	**upset**	**upset**	ärgern, kränken, aus der Fassung bringen
(to) **wake** up	**woke**	**woken**	aufwachen; wecken
(to) **wear** [eə]	**wore** [ɔː]	**worn** [ɔː]	tragen *(Kleidung)*
(to) **win**	**won** [ʌ]	**won** [ʌ]	gewinnen
(to) **write**	**wrote**	**written**	schreiben

Key to the self-assessment tests

Unit 1 ▸ p. 29

1 Thames
2 Tube
3 Tower Bridge
4 Piccadilly Circus
5 Buckingham Palace
6 Houses of Parliament
7 C get
8 A change
9 C platform
10 A ticket
11 B meat
12 C bacon
13 B so
14 A After I spoke to the teacher, I tried to work harder.
15 A I don't usually like trying foods from different countries, but I liked the food at the Bangladeshi café.
16 C Dear Dora
17 B went, was
18 C took
19 B hasn't been
20 C Yes, I have.
21 B haven't done

Unit 2 ▸ p. 47

1 Orkney
2 capital
3 salmon
4 dance/play the fiddle
5 rock
6 loch
7 C car park
8 A coast
9 B text message
10 C turn
11 D great
12 D Perspektive
13 B funktionieren
14 A Look up all three in an English–German dictionary.
15 C If Tom goes to the party, I will stay at home.
16 A If kids in my class were horrible to me, I would tell my teacher.
17 B If I was in his class, I would be happy.

Unit 3 ▸ p. 67

1 drums
2 Trinidad
3 the Lowry
4 Old Trafford
5 Nathan Stephens
6 C dinner
7 D something skaters wear on their heads
8 B Berlin.
9 D Talk about yourself all the time.
10 B racket
11 C fan
12 D sports hall
13 1 skiing – B slope
2 ice hockey – C ice rink
3 football – A pitch
4 badminton – D court
14 1 living room – B armchair
2 bathroom – C shower
3 kitchen – A sink
15 D lift
16 A who
17 that I want to visit
18 B Most students like Frau Marx.

Key to the self-assessment tests

Unit 4 ▸ p. 83

1 Canada is much bigger/larger than Germany, but it doesn't have as many people.
2 snowshoeing, canoeing, hunting, ice hockey 1 point for each answer
3 Toronto, Ottawa, Vancouver, Winnipeg, Montreal 1 point for each answer
4 province
5 C per cent
6 B easy-going
7 B relaxed
8 C point
9 D blame
10 A from
11 B lyrics.
12 brainstorm/collect ideas, write the text and finally check and revise/correct it.
13 in a list or a mind map.
14 adjectives and adverbs / linking words
15 D am not allowed to
16 C be able to
17 B have to
18 John was talking to himself but ...
19 A Robert felt proud when people liked his DJing.
20 Sam and Robert took photos of each other.

Unit 1–5 ▸ p. 101

1 Scotland, Wales 2 points
2 London, Thames 2 points
3 underground/Tube 1 point
4 Orkney Islands 1 point
5 Manchester 1 point
6 word field: transport ▸ P 2 (p. 20)
1 point for three or more words,
1 point for the name of the word field
7 word field: electronic media ▸ P 2 (p. 38)
1 point for three or more words,
1 point for the name of the word field
8 word field: town/city ▸ P 1 (p. 38)
1 point for three or more words,
1 point for the name of the word field
9 word field: sport ▸ P 2 (p. 60)
1 point for three or more words,
1 point for the name of the word field
10 word field: music ▸ p. 11 • P 1 (p. 93)
1 point for three or more words,
1 point for the name of the word field
11 word field: country
1 point for three or more words,
1 point for the name of the word field
12 scan 1 point
13 skim 1 point
14 paraphrasing 1 point
15 brainstorming 1 point
16 topic sentence/first sentence 1 point
17 linking words 1 point
18 **who**, **what**, **when**, **where**, **why** (and **how**); you can use them to write a report
1 point for all five Ws,
1 point for saying what you can use them for
19 Make a personal checklist of mistakes that you often make. 1 point
20 Robert hasn't been to New York yet, but he went to London last summer. 1 point
21 If you were in London now, what would you want to do? 1 point
22 Do you know the girl who has just fallen off her bike? 1 point
Mum likes the book (that) I gave her as a birthday present. 1 point
23 I wasn't hungry because I had already eaten. 1 point
24 The film was very exciting. It was about two spies who were trying to kill each other. 1 point
My sister and I aren't allowed to ride our bikes when it's raining – my mum is afraid we'll hurt ourselves. 1 point
In three years I will be able to speak English better. 1 point
I felt ill and stayed at home. 1 point

Classroom English

Was *du* im Klassenzimmer sagen kannst	What *you* can say in the classroom
Du brauchst Hilfe	**You need help**
Können Sie mir bitte helfen?	**Can you help me, please?**
Auf welcher Seite sind wir, bitte?	**What page are we on, please?**
Was heißt ... auf Englisch/Deutsch?	**What's ... in English/German?**
Wie spricht man das erste Wort in Zeile 2 aus?	**How do you say the first word in line 2?**
Können Sie bitte ... buchstabieren?	**Can you spell ..., please?**
Können Sie es bitte an die Tafel schreiben?	**Can you write it on the board, please?**
Kann ich es auf Deutsch sagen?	**Can I say it in German?**
Können Sie/Kannst du bitte lauter sprechen?	**Can you speak louder, please?**
Können Sie/Kannst du das bitte noch mal sagen?	**Can you say that again, please?**
Über Texte und Themen sprechen	**Talking about texts and topics**
Ich finde die Geschichte ...	**I think the story is ...**
schön/interessant/langweilig/schrecklich/....	**nice/interesting/boring/terrible/...**
Es war lustig/gruselig/langweilig/..., als ...	**It was funny/scary/boring/... when ...**
Ich fand es gut/nicht gut, als ...	**I liked it/didn't like it when ...**
Ich finde, Tom hat recht/nicht recht, weil ...	**I think Tom is right/wrong because ...**
Ich bin mir nicht sicher. Vielleicht ...	**I'm not sure. Maybe ...**
Was meinst du?	**What do you think?**
Ich stimme ... zu/nicht zu, weil ...	**I agree/disagree (with ...) because ...**
Hausaufgaben und Übungen	**Homework and exercises**
Tut mir leid, ich habe mein Schulheft nicht dabei, Herr ...	**Sorry, I haven't got my exercise book, Mr ...**
Ich habe meine Hausaufgaben vergessen, Frau ...	**I've forgotten my homework, Mrs/Ms/Miss ...**
Ich kann Nummer 3 nicht lösen.	**I can't do number 3.**
Entschuldigung, ich bin noch nicht fertig.	**Sorry, I haven't finished yet.**
Ich habe ... Ist das auch richtig?	**I've got ... Is that right too?**
Tut mir leid, das weiß ich nicht.	**Sorry, I don't know.**
Was haben wir (als Hausaufgabe) auf?	**What's for homework?**
Bei der Partnerarbeit	**Work with a partner**
Kann ich mit Julian arbeiten?	**Can I work with Julian?**
Wer ist dran? - Du bist dran.	**Whose turn is it? - It's your turn.**
Ich finde, wir sollten/könnten ...	**I think we should/could ...**
Was machen wir zuerst?	**What are we going to do first?**
What your teacher says	**Was dein/e Lehrer/in sagt**
Open your books at page 24, please.	Schlagt bitte Seite 24 auf.
Look at the picture/line 8/... on page 24.	Seht euch das Bild/Zeile 8/... auf Seite 24 an.
Copy/Complete the chart/network/...	Übertragt/Vervollständigt die Tabelle/das Wörternetz/...
Correct the mistakes.	Verbessert die Fehler.
Take notes.	Macht euch Notizen.
Do exercise 3 for homework, please.	Macht bitte Übung 3 als Hausaufgabe.
Have you finished?	Seid ihr fertig? / Bist du fertig?
Switch off your mobile phones.	Schaltet eure Handys aus.
Walk around the class and ask other students.	Geht durch die Klasse und fragt andere Schüler/innen.
Discuss ... with ...	Diskutiere/Diskutiert ... mit ...
Give a presentation about ...	Halte/Haltet einen Vortrag über ...
Report to the class.	Berichte/Berichtet der Klasse.